PLACES WITH A HEART

THAILAND

TRAVELERS' SELECTION OF 100 HOTELS, RESORTS
AND DESTINATIONS THAT WILL ALSO CHARM YOU

PLACES WITH A HEART

THAILAND

PUBLISHER
Encyclea

An Imprint of Asiatype, Inc.
11/F, Columbia Tower
Greenhills, Mandaluyong City
1550, Philippines
Tel. No.: 63 (0) 2 725-6262
Fax No.: 63 (0) 2 727-6053
E-mail : info@encyclea.com
Web : www.encyclea.com

COLOR SEPARATION
Asiatype Incorporated
PRINTED IN HONGKONG
Paramount Printing Company Limited

FIRST EDITION
October 2003

On the cover: Anantara Resort and Spa (Hua Hin), Golden Buddha Beach Resort
(Kuraburi), The Regent Chiang Mai Resort and Spa (Around Chiang Mai), and
The Thai House (Bangkok).

Photo credits on page 327.

Phanom Rung Temple, Isaan Region

PLACES WITH A HEART

Which of us has not been faced with the dilemma of choosing a hotel when planning a holiday to an unknown destination whether it is for a weekend break from the capital city or an extended stay? This choice can be the determining factor on which depends the success of the vacation. It can be quite a disaster for those seeking solitude and nature to find their hotel is located in an urban jungle! On the other hand, those who cannot do without excitement, animation and a large choice of activities, would be disappointed to find themselves on a deserted island in a small resort conceived for disciples of Robinson Crusoe!

Information in this respect given by classic guidebooks—some excellent but general by nature—the hotels themselves, travel agents and Internet sites, are generally of little help.

The objective of this guide is to help travelers in the choice of a hotel by sharing with them our most pleasant experiences, while giving them all the indications necessary to make up their minds.

To us, the best places are not necessarily the most expensive nor the most plush: the beauty of the site where the hotel is located, its history, the harmony or originality of its architecture, the attention given to the interior decoration, the warmth of the welcome, the service, the value for money, possible excursions in the area, are the essential ingredients that make a place appealing.

Sometimes, we decided to mention places of particularly striking natural or historical interest, though only simple hotels can be found in the vicinity. Yet, all our selected resorts and hotels comply with a standard of minimum comfort.

"Places With a Heart, Thailand" is therefore a very subjective book. Even the places that we deem charming may have certain aspects less appealing to others. Charm, above all the standards and norms, is mostly a love-story between a person and a place. By preference, our *coups de coeur* are given to places of exception.

This guidebook is by no means exhaustive, as that was not our goal. We have certainly, by ignorance, lack of time or difficulty of gaining access, missed some places that may have deserved mention. For this we apologize.

Each one, whether alone or with company, full of energy and thirsting for adventure or merely needing a moment to unwind and relax, with a substantial budget or with less limited means, fond of secret hideaways or lively resorts, should be able to find a good match with his own expectations.

THAILAND

Thailand has a reputation of being a country very popular with tourists, and it is true of certain places such as Hua Hin, Phuket or Samui. Nevertheless, even here, it is possible to find a quiet, peaceful hotel. Moreover, it is an undeniable fact that certain seaside locations conceal extremely refined resorts that are unfortunately quite costly.

It would be diminishing Thailand to limit it to its most well known seaside resorts. It is in fact a very diverse country where numerous regions are scarcely visited and remain to be discovered.

If you move away only about a hundred kilometers to the north of Phuket, the region of Khao Lak will astonish you with its rainforest cascading down the mountain slopes to the shore fringed with long golden deserted beaches. Cheow Lake, surrounded by limestone peaks, in the Khao Sok National Park, in the heart of the mountainous massif situated between Khao Lak and Surat Thani, is of a timeless beauty. The island of Koh Chang, off the East coast, is still draped in primary jungle whereas its archipelago of virgin islands rests in pure aquamarine waters.

The Central Plains, often overlooked by travelers, offer fantastic journeys into Thailand's ancient capitals where art, history and architecture unveil with silent parks protected by revered Buddha images. The road along these royal cities starts right off Bangkok with the ruins of Ayutthaya, through Lopburi, Kamphaeng Phet, Phitsanulok, Si Satchanalai, to the magnificent city of old Sukhothai, an exquisite UNESCO world culture and heritage site.

The Northern region could perfectly be the one and only focus destination of a trip to Thailand. This land has kept a very unique and soul-touching personality with breathtaking mountainous landscapes, bucolic valleys and teak-forested hills, singular art and culture, and a large number of charming hotels and resorts. The city of Chiang Mai is an amazingly inviting city with a village-like atmosphere, and fabulous ancient Lanna and Burmese temples. Close encounters with Akha, Hmong, Karen, Lahu, Lisu and Yao hilltribes scattered around the region build up unforgettable memories.

The East is unknown—and according to our standards comprises few charming hotels—but the region has conserved extremely beautiful Khmer temples. The monsoon adorns the landscape with rice fields of emerald hues, while revealing all its secret beauty.

Our wish is that through this guide, readers will be able to discover and appreciate the beauty and hospitality of Thailand.

Whatever accommodation you choose, luxury hotel or simple family resort, you will be welcomed with the traditional "Sawasdee Ka," accompanied by the same smile, warmth and natural elegance.

We wish you bon voyage!

Lily Yousry-Jouve   Anne-Marie Zicavo-Detay

ABOUT THE AUTHORS

Lily Yousry-Jouve

Born in Cairo to a French mother and an Egyptian father, a well-known artist, she grew up, though, in Paris. She learned to paint while she was a child, but she studied law, specializing in city planning, at the Sorbonne.

She dedicated her time to painting when she settled with her husband Marcel Jouve in Nairobi, Kenya in 1992. Then they moved to Manila, Philippines, where they lived from 1996 to 2000, before going back to France where she went back to law, for a while, in the Environment Ministry.

When she lived in Manila, visiting and painting "Philippines' hidden landscapes," the theme of one of her exhibits, gave her the idea to give information in a guidebook, "100 Resorts in the Philippines — Places with a Heart," about the best places she had seen in the Philippines.

Then, she decided to apply the same concept to another guidebook about Thailand. She had many opportunities to visit Thailand, particularly the national parks. From her visits, she also brought back paintings, some of which are reproduced in this guidebook.

PHOTOGRAPHY

*A*nne-Marie Zicavo-Detay

Anne-Marie Zicavo-Detay has become a hungry traveler, particularly since her first encounter with Asia in 1996, when she relocated with her husband to the Philippines. A French citizen born in Germany and educated in Barcelona, Spain, she worked for 20 years with high-tech American companies conducting Human Resource programs. Based on her own traveling experience, she published a successful children's book in 1999. Back in France for a few years, she enjoyed her trips to Thailand to co-write this guidebook and to discover the beauties of this amazing land. The areas she covered are the Central Plains, the Golden Triangle, Mae Hong Son, and together with Lily Yousry-Jouve, the cities of Bangkok and Chiang Mai and its surroundings. Back to Asia, Anne-Marie spent a year in Shanghai and now lives in Hong Kong, China.

*M*arcel Jouve

Born in Nimes, France, Marcel Jouve graduated as an agricultural engineer in Grignon, near Paris. Himself an environment enthusiast, he worked for several years in the French Ministry of Environment, before joining the Ministry of Foreign Affairs. He was posted as cooperation and cultural councilor in Kenya from 1992 to 1996, then in the Philippines until the year 2000.

Ever since he was a child, Marcel Jouve has been partial to nature and photography. These two passions, later on, led him to discover other countries.

The following chapters have been written respectively by:

Bangkok and around Bangkok: *Lily Yousry-Jouve and Anne-Marie Detay*
Kanchanaburi, Hua Hin, Pattaya and Koh Samet: *Lily Yousry-Jouve*
The Center Plains: *Anne-Marie Detay*
The East: *Lily Yousry-Jouve*
The North, Chiang Mai and around: *Lily Yousry-Jouve and Anne-Marie Detay*
The Golden Triangle and Mae Hong Son: *Anne-Marie Detay*
The Southwest Peninsula: *Lily Yousry-Jouve*
The Southeast Peninsula: *Lily Yousry-Jouve*

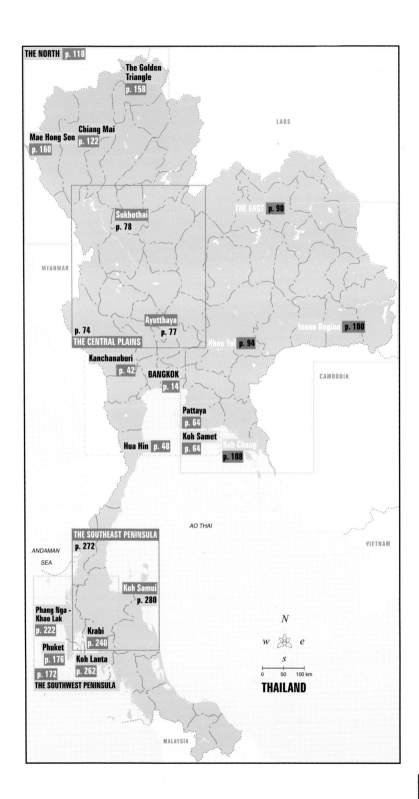

THE NORTH p. 118

The Golden Triangle p. 158

LAOS

Chiang Mai p. 122

Mae Hong Son p. 160

MYANMAR

Sukhothai p. 78

THE EAST p. 90

Ayutthaya p. 77

p. 74
THE CENTRAL PLAINS

Isaan Region p. 100

Khao Yai p. 94

Kanchanaburi p. 42

CAMBODIA

BANGKOK p. 14

Pattaya p. 64

Koh Samet p. 64

Hua Hin p. 48

Koh Chang p. 108

AO THAI

VIETNAM

THE SOUTHEAST PENINSULA p. 272

ANDAMAN SEA

Koh Samui p. 280

Phang Nga - Khao Lak p. 222

Krabi p. 240

Phuket p. 176

Koh Lanta p. 262

THE SOUTHWEST PENINSULA

N
W e
S
0 50 100 km

THAILAND

MALAYSIA

CONTENTS

GENERAL INFORMATION AND HOW TO USE THE PRACTICAL DATA SHEET

For each resort a practical data sheet can be found at the end of each review. It begins with the Contact Section and is followed by the How to get there Section, the Accommodation Section, the Food and Beverage and Other Services Section, the Sports and Activities Section and the Price Section. Each section has its own icon.

THE CONTACT SECTION

Under this section you will find all the necessary information so as to make the booking by yourself. The information is this section is arranged in the following order:

1. The resort's name, address, telephone, fax, e-mail details and the contact person's name (if useful).
2. The resort's booking office's address, telephone, fax, e-mail details.
3. The resort's website, if any.

BOOKING OFFICE

In most cases the resorts have their own booking office on the spot and another one in Bangkok. For the most well known resorts, they generally prefer direct booking, while for the smaller ones booking through the Bangkok office may be more effective.
In Thailand bookings made via e-mail usually result in a quick response.

PEAK SEASON

Plan your trips well ahead if you intend to travel during peak seasons such as Christmas, New Year's eve, Chinese New Year, as resorts are often fully booked months in advance. Some hotels require a minimum stay of several days during peak season.

PHONE NUMBERS

Phone numbers may change. If a phone number is no longer accessible, you are advised to contact the Directory Assistance at the following number: 13 for numbers in Bangkok metropolitan area and 183 for the provinces.
You can also contact the Bangkok office of the Tourism Authority of Thailand or the one covering the relevant region. A listing of TAT offices is also provided in the annex of the guidebook.
Phone numbers indicated in the guide are the numbers to dial from abroad to Thailand: 66 (dialing code of Thailand) + regional dialing code (without 0) + number of the hotel.
To dial a number from Thailand: dial 0 + the regional dialing code + the number of your correspondent.
To dial a number from Thailand to a mobile phone: dial 01 or 09 (depending on the mobile phone number) + the number of your correspondent.
To dial a number from Thailand to abroad: dial 001 + the country dialing code + the regional dialing code + the number of your correspondent .

THE HOW-TO-GET-THERE SECTION

Under this section you will find all the necessary information so as to make the transportation arrangements by yourself out of Bangkok, in the following order:

1. A brief description of the different modes of transportation to be used followed by an estimate of the total travel time needed. For places around Bangkok accessible by land, the distance from Bangkok is usually indicated.

Ex.: By air, land and sea (6 hours)

2. A step by step access guide detailing: the type of transport used (plane, train, car, bus, ferry, boat, etc.); the time needed; the name of the transportation company; the starting point and the arrival point; the frequency of service.

frequency of service. It would be better to check schedules each time you make travel plans.

TRANSFER ARRANGED BY THE RESORT
Special mention is made of those resorts arranging for transfer of their guests from the nearest airport or train/bus terminal or ferry, or directly from Bangkok.

THE ACCOMMODATION SECTION

UNITS
A mention of the number of rooms and a brief description of the resort's room categories including a list of facilities available, such as a private terrace, a bathroom (private or common, with shower or bathtub, with cold or hot water, hairdryer), air-conditioning or fan, a telephone, a TV set, minibar, a coffee/tea maker, a safe box.

THE FOOD AND BEVERAGE SECTION

FOOD AND BEVERAGE
A brief description of the resort's restaurant(s) and bar(s) facilities.

TYPE OF CUISINE
A list of the different cuisines offered by the restaurant(s).

QUALITY
Assessment of the quality of food if tested. It can be:

Average The food is of average quality and/or the selection of dishes is limited.

Familial The food is not sophisticated but is home-cooked, family style and good.

Good There is a wide selection of dishes and the food is rather sophisticated.

Excellent Everything is perfect!

Note: Thai cuisine is usually very good, even in small restaurants or stalls.

OTHER SERVICES SECTION

A list of services and facilities offered by the resort other than those mentioned in the sports and activities section, such as

Travelers departing from cities other than Bangkok should refer to the transportation list where connections with some other cities are indicated.
Only the most convenient and speedy means of transportation have been generally described in detail.

SEVERAL ACCESS OPTIONS
Where several access options of equal interest exist, these will be indicated in similar manner.

INDICATIVE TOTAL TRAVEL TIME
Travel times are given from the departure time of the plane, train, or bus. It is assumed that travelers depart from Bangkok's domestic airport or bus/train terminal, or from Bangkok's center if access is by land.

SCHEDULES OF TRANSPORTATION COMPANIES
Schedules and routes serviced by domestic airlines, bus/train and shipping companies frequently change. For this reason, the airlines transportation list found at the end of this book does not indicate precise schedules but instead only indicates the

business center, internet services, gift shop, babysitting, children's playground/ kid's club, doctor on call, safety deposit box at reception, tour desk, car rental.

WATER SPORTS AND ACTIVITIES

 Pool(s) (with a mention of a kiddie pool), Beach (with a mention of the quality or suitability for swimming), Snorkeling, Diving (with a mention of the diving sites and of the availability of a diving center on the spot), Island hopping, Tours to and/or around island(s), Kayaking, Other boats for rent...

OTHER SPORTS AND ACTIVITIES

Spa, Fitness center, Tennis, Table tennis, Golf, Billiards, Trekking, Mountain biking, Horseback riding, Game room, TV-video room, Library...

THE PRICE SECTION

 THE PRICE ICON
The icon represents an elephant that was inspired by the representation of a royal elephant found on an old Thai manuscript.

HOW TO DETERMINE THE PRICE CHARGED BY THE RESORT
It can be determined as follows:

 One elephant means that the price is below 1,000 bahts;

Two elephants means that the price is between 1,000 and 1,999 bahts;

Three elephants means that the price is between 2,000 and 2,999 bahts;

Four elephants means that the price is between 3,000 and 4,999 bahts;

Five elephants means that the price is between 5,000 and 9,999 bahts;

Six elephants means that the price is above 10,000 bahts.

PRICING POLICY
The Price indicated under each resort is the price per room, for 2 people, unless otherwise indicated. There is not usually a big difference of rate between single and double room occupancy.

PUBLISHED RATES VERSUS ACTUAL RATES

The rates given in this book are published rates applicable during the high season, to the cheapest room category.

In Thailand, prices vary according to three seasons: low season (usually from April to October, corresponding to rainy season), high season (usually from January to April) and peak season (Christmas, New Year's Eve).

During low season, rates could be discounted by 50 %. Likewise during peak season a surcharge of 20 % to 50 % may be added and a minimum stay period is sometimes requested.

For some regions, such as Koh Samui, the rainy season is different, so check the climate section indicated for each region.

Promotional packages are often extended at the resort's sole discretion. You may also get a better tariff by consulting the resort's internet web site.

Credit cards are widely accepted. Major currency bills and travelers checks are cashed easily at hotels. When it is not the case, it is mentioned.

OTHER DISCOUNTS
To get a better rate in Thailand it is advisable to book through a travel agency or through the Internet. A listing of some travel agencies and sites is provided in the appendix of the guidebook.

As far as lodging is concerned, children sharing the parent's room are normally free of charge under the condition that no additional bed is requested. Additional beds are charged usually about 500 bahts. Children below 12 are given a 50% discount. Discounts for long stays are common practice. Special rates are sometimes offered on weekdays.

DEPOSIT

For your booking to be confirmed many resorts require a deposit to be made which can be anything between 30 % to 100 % of the price. Make sure that you are given a receipt for your payment and that you are aware of the cancellation policy of the resort or the travel agency. Sometimes it is very strict and you can easily lose 100 % of your deposit.

 ### HEART ICON
All the resorts selected in this guidebook are attractive either on their own right or because they are gateways to places well worth a visit.

However, some of them stood out for us because of a particular charm: these are our "*coups de cœur*" and we have identified them with a curiously heart-shaped seashell of the *cardium* family. You may be surprised to observe that some small resorts with simple amenities but full of atmosphere and in remarkable sites, were awarded a heart while more classical five stars hotels were not. That's our deliberate choice. The very few hotels we have judged outstanding in all respects were awarded two hearts.

THE SPECIAL ICONS

 ### CLIMATE ICON
In Thailand it is possible to distinguish three seasons:
• The hot-dry season—February to May, average day temperature 34°C;
• The wet (monsoon) season—June to October, average day temperature 29°C;
• The cool season—November to January, average day temperature 20°C.
Much lower temperature are experienced in the north and northeast. The south and southeast regions have little variation in temperature, averaging 28°C.
There is a variety of climates, the rainy season being completely different in Koh Samui and in the east coast of the southern peninsula. In the mountainous regions, rains are heavier.
The monsoon season in Thailand does not involve months of continual rain, but is best described as being unpredictable, with heavy showers and frequent thunderstorms, generally with sunny mornings.
No season is to be avoided to plan a visit to Thailand, all the more so as prices decrease considerably during the rainy season.

 ### FESTIVAL ICON
The main festivals are mentioned on a regional basis.

LEGEND TO MAPS

——— Major Road

——— Secondary Road

——— Rough Road

🏠 Resort / Hotel

✴ Place of Interest

◎ City

⊙ Town

○ Village

✈ Airport

Bangkok and around Bangkok

River Kwai

Painting by Lily Yousry-Jouve

Bangkok

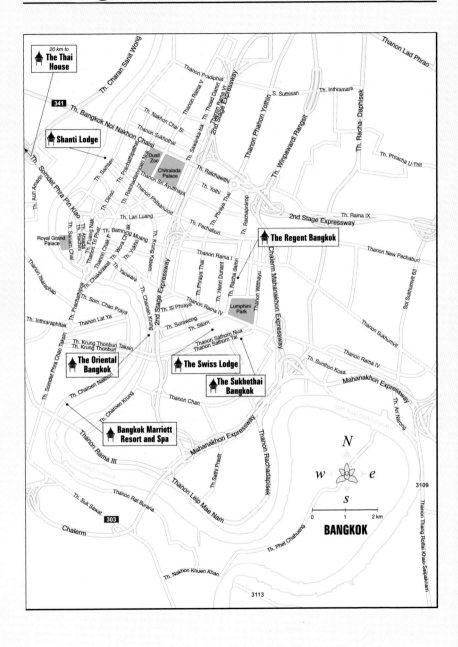

20 km to
The Thai House

341

Th. Charan Sanit Wong

Thanon Pradiphat

Thanon Lad Phrao

Th. Bangkok Noi Nakhon Chaisi

Th. Nakhon Chai Si

Thanon Rama V

Th. Thoet Damri

Thanon Rama VI

2nd Stage Expressway

S. Suthisan

Th. Inthramara

Th. Somdet Phra Pin Klao

Thanon Sukhothai

Sawankalok

Thanon Phahon Yothin

Th. Winpawardi Rangsit

Th. Racha-Daphisek

Shanti Lodge

Th. Samsen

Th. Prachathipatai Nai

Dusit Zoo

Chitralada Palace

Thanon Sri Ayuthaya

Th. Ratchawithi

Th. Yothi

Th. Ratchaprarop

Th. Phracha U-Thit

Th. Aun Amarin

Th. Dinso

Th. Fuang Nak

Thanon Phitsanulod

Th. Lan Luang

Th. Phraya Thai

2nd Stage Expressway

Th. Rama IX

Thanon New Pechaburi

Royal Grand Palace

Th. Sanam Chai

Th. Ratchini

Th. Atsada

Thanon Tri Phet

Th. Chakrawat

Th. Wora Chak

Th. Yukhon

Th. Chalak P.

Th. Bamrung Muang

Th. Krung Kasem

Th. Pechaburi

The Regent Bangkok

Th. Racha damri

Chalerm Mahanakhon Expressway

Thanon Itsaraphap

Th. Prachathipok

Th. Som. Chao Praya

Thanon Lat Ya

Yaowara

2nd Stage Expressway

Th. Charoen Krung

Thanon Rama I

Th. Phraya Thai

Th. Henri Dunant

Th. Si Phraya

Thanon Rama IV

Lumphini Park

Th. Witthu

Th. Inthraraphitak

Th. Surawong

Th. Silom

Thanon Sukhumvit

Soi Sukhumvit 63

Th. Krung Thonburi Taksin

Th. Krung Thonburi

Thanon Sathon Nua

Thanon Sathorn Tai

Thanon Rama IV

The Oriental Bangkok

The Swiss Lodge

Th. Sunthon Kosa

Mahanakhon Expressway

Th. Charoen Nakhon

Th. Charoen Krung

The Sukhothai Bangkok

Th. Ari Narong

Thanon Chan

Bangkok Marriott Resort and Spa

Thanon Rama III

Mahanakhon Expressway

Th. Sath Pradit

Thanon Rachadapisek

N

W — e

S

3109

Th. Suk Sawat

Thanon Rat Burana

Thanon Leip Mae Nam

0   1   2 km

BANGKOK

Thanon Thang Rotfai Khao-Saijaknam

Chalerm

303

Th. Phet Chahueng

3113

Th. Nakhon Khuen Khan

Bangkok

Foreword: Bangkok— Krungthepmahanakorn —deserves an entire guidebook for itself. Consequently, there is no question of trying to describe it in its entirety here but merely to share our preferred places.

Opinions on the capital are very wide-ranging— some justifiably criticize its traffic jams, pollution and sprawling developments but despite this, Bangkok remains an enthralling city of magnetic charm because of its intense verve, colorful effervescence and striking contrasts: the temple with polished tiled roofs scintillating under the sun flanked by two contemporary towers, stalls of scented jasmine garlands on sidewalks near the shopping malls, the peaceful *soi* concealing ancient houses amidst exuberant gardens only a few minutes away from a noisy, congested street...

The Chao Phraya River is the soul of the city, along which the historic center and, more recently, a few striking luxury hotels such as the legendary **The Oriental, Bangkok** and, slightly isolated, **Bangkok Marriot Resort and Spa** were built. Twenty-two kilometers north from the center of old Bangkok, is **The Thai House,** where you can stay in a traditional Thai house and take cooking classes.

THE PRECINCTS OF THE GRAND PALACE *(Na Phra Lan Road)* City within a city, the grounds of the Grand Palace extend over 21 hectares enclosed by high walls. Besides the Grand Palace (abandoned by the King), it shelters numerous outbuildings and the religious complex of Wat Phra Kaeo, built at the end of the 18th century.

Catching your eye at the entrance of Wat Phra Kaeo are the towering golden spires of its *chedi*s, beyond a vast expanse of lawns; numerous temples with facades inlaid with mirrors and multicolored

The Grand Palace – Wat Phra Kaeo

ceramics and polished green and orange tiled roofs sparkle under the sun. The décor is somewhat extravagant where statues of mythical animals and demons observe the faithful laying down their offerings. The royal chapel shelters the Emerald Buddha, discovered in the 15th century at Chiang Rai. The paintings in the galleries of the cloister are particularly beautiful.

The Grand Palace, accessible through a door situated at the southwest, is composed of several edifices of which the Dusit Maha Prasad, a white pavilion surmounted by a multi-tiered roof and a nine-story spire, is the most harmonious.

Note: Open from 8:30 a.m. to 3:30 p.m. You must be dressed properly.

The Temples

From among the 400 temples, or *wat*, that Bangkok possesses, our favorites are:

WAT PO *(Thai Wang, 10 minutes' walk from the Grand Palace)* Wat Po or "Temple of the Sleeping Buddha", founded

Bangkok Buddha

in the 16th century, is the most ancient sanctuary in Thailand and one of the most venerated. It is particularly animated because monks live here and it houses a traditional massage center where you can have a massage at a very reasonable rate. Wat Po comprises a number of temples, the main one containing the Sleeping Buddha, entirely covered in gold and occupying a building 46-meter long and 15-meter high whose walls are decorated with attractive bas-reliefs. This temple is surrounded by galleries sheltering 394 sitting buddhas.
Note: Open from 8 a.m. to 6 p.m.

WAT ARUN OR THE TEMPLE OF DAWN *(Arun Amarin Road or access by boat at the Tha Tien Pier near Wat Po)* From the Tha Tien jetty there is a good view of the sanctuary whose silhouette is mirrored in the Chao Phraya. The architecture of the temple, erected in the 19th century, is influenced by Khmer art, with a spectacu-

lar 79-meter high central pagoda inlaid with colored cut-glass and porcelain.
Note: Open from 8:30 a.m. to 5:30 p.m.

WAT BENJAMABOPITR OR THE MARBLE TEMPLE *(Sri Ayutthaya Road)* This temple dating back to 1899, in white Carrare marble, rests in the middle of gardens. The cloister contains 52 buddhas illustrating the different periods of Buddhist art.
Note: Open from 7 a.m. to 6 p.m.

THE GOLDEN MOUNTAIN AND WAT SAKHET *(Rajdamnern avenue)* Beautiful ancient trees surround the small man-made hill where the temple is perched. From the terrace at the summit, you enjoy a wonderful view of the city.

The Museums

THE HOUSE OF JIM THOMSON *(Soi Kasemsan 2, Rama I Road)* The house is famous, as much for its architecture and the beautiful Asian works of art that it contains, as for the person to whom it belonged and whose presence is felt around. Jim Thomson, an American architect, ex-officer of the Intelligence Services during the Second World War, with a fabulous and mysterious destiny — he disappeared in the jungles of the Cameron Highlands of Malaysia — revealed the splendor of Thai silks to the western world. In a luxuriant garden on the

Jim Thomson house

banks of a *klong*, he had assembled several teak houses originating from different regions of Thailand thus forming a wonderful dwelling place. It has an agreeable terrace café in the garden and a little boutique but the main boutique is on Surawong Road.
Note: Open from 9 a.m. to 4:30 p.m.

SUAN PAKKAD PALACE *(353 Sri Ayutthaya Road)* Transported into the heart of a beautiful garden are six traditional wooden houses on stilts dating back to the 19th century. They have numerous Thai works of art. At the far end of the garden is a precious lacquered wooden pavilion, a masterpiece of Siamese art. Very beautiful decorations and interior lacquered panels describe episodes from the life of Buddha and scenes from the Ramayana.
Note: Open from 9 a.m. to 4 p.m.

VIMANMEK PALACE *(Ratchawithi Road)* In the midst of a verdant lawn stands an elegant pale wood palace, the largest teak palace in the world. Dating back to the 19th century, it served as the residence of King Rama IV. Its 81 rooms have furniture and objects belonging to the Royal Family and numerous ancient photos evoking their lives.
Note: Open daily from 9:30 a.m. to 3:15 p.m.

THE ROYAL BARGES MUSEUM *(Klong Bangkok Noi, not far from the Phra Pinklao bridge)* The barges, with painted and finely sculpted long streamlined prows, are kept on the waters, under shelter of a large shed. Originally used as war ships, now they ply the Chao Phraya River: the spectacle for processions must be a treat for the eye.
Note: Open daily from 8:30 a.m. to 4:30 p.m.

THE NATIONAL MUSEUM *(Na Phra That Road)* The National Museum is one of the largest in Southeast Asia. It contains an invaluable and interesting collection of Asian works of art. The most remarkable rooms are those featuring the Sukhothai and Ayutthaya periods. The Museum also comprises objects

Ayutthaya

relating to the life of the Royal Court (jewelry, palanquins, traditional dance masks, costumes, musical instruments, furniture).
Note: Open from Wednesday to Sunday from 9 a.m. to 12 noon and from 1 p.m. to 4 p.m. Guided tours in several languages.

Discovering the *klongs* of Bangkok

A boat trip is a marvelous means of discovering another more secret facet of Bangkok. You penetrate into narrow *klongs*, come across ancient wooden houses on stilts, neglected gardens, modest temples and small shopping stalls on the water. The ideal method is to group-rent a long-tail boat and thus move away from the canals more frequented by the ferries and stop at your own leisure.

There are several main canals in Bangkok: Bangkok Noi and Bangkok Yai (Tha Chang pier) and Bangkok Mon (Tha Tien pier) and the Om Klong that goes up to Nonthaburi.

The Markets

CHATUCHAK MARKET *(at the intersection of Paholyothin and Kamphaeng roads)* A fabulous ambiance reigns in this market covering several hectares. In the maze of specialized alleys, you will find nearly everything from Thai blue and white dinnerware to clothing, flowers, animals, handicrafts, basketwork and furniture, all at a much lower price than those of

The Summer Palace—Bang Pa-In

uptown boutiques. There are cafés to stop by and have a drink or a meal.

Note: Open on weekends from 8 a.m. to 5 p.m. —accessible by skytrain (Mo Chit station).

THE FRUIT AND FLOWER MARKET OF PAK KLONG TALAT *(Maharat Road)* This is a spectacular market on the banks of the river where a variety of tropical plants and cut flowers such as orchids, lilies and roses as well as fruits are on sale at prices that withstand all competition. The market is particularly lively in the evenings. The **Thewet Market**, along Phadung Krung Kasem *klong* is also reputed for its orchids (Samsen road). At the back of the flower market and a stone's throw away from the Chao Phraya river is the friendly and inexpensive **Shanti Lodge.**

Shopping

It is obviously impossible to describe everything here! There are three large shopping areas, each bursting with shopping centers and boutiques: the Silom area, Patpong, Suriwong—where the very beautiful **Sukhothai Hotel** and the small **Swiss Lodge** are situated; the area of Sukhumvit, New Phetchaburi; and that of Siam (Rama 1, Rajdamri, Pratunam, Ploenchit) where the elegant **Regent Hotel** is located.

JIM THOMSON'S THAI SILK *(9 Surawong Road)* The store is located in a pretty building, several stories' high. Silk is available in all its forms and colors—furnishing materials, much cheaper than in Europe, clothes, ties, shirts, purses in all sizes, and even toys. The boutique also proposes the services of a tailor. You can have a drink or lunch on an agreeable restaurant paneled in teak.

Note: Open from 9 a.m. to 9 p.m.

ASIA BOOKS This bookstore chain proposes very beautiful photo books on architecture, decoration and gardens, and many English-language titles, on other Asian countries as well. It has several branches in town; the one at 221 Sukhumvit, between Sois 15 and 17, is open until 9 p.m. and is the best stocked *(www.asiabook.com).*

RIVER CITY SHOPPING COMPLEX *(23, Yota Road, Sampanthawong; facing the Sheraton Hotel, along the Chao Phraya)* This fabulous shopping complex is dedicated to Asian antiques, furniture and works of art. You can visit it just to feast your eyes on the boutiques that really look like small muse-

ums. Don't miss also "Jaana" shop (number 246) for creative beads and necklaces, and "The Golden Triangle" shop (number 301) for inventive Hilltribe garments.
Note: Open from 11 a.m. to 6 p.m.

SILOM VILLAGE *(Silom Road)* This center is very agreeable, situated off the road in a peaceful patio surrounded by small shops specialized principally in leather. There are also garments, handicrafts and a boutique of Chinese antiques. You can have a meal notably at "Ruen Thep" restaurant (open 'til late at night).

The Restaurants

Thai cuisine being one of the world's best, we would like to mention a few restaurants, while noting that street stalls can offer excellent meals.
— *Baan Chiang* – 14 Soi Sriviang, Silom Road (Tel.: 66 (0) 2 236-7045). Warm décor in a beautiful old house surrounded by a garden, specialized in the cuisine of Isan.
— *Le Café Siam* – 4 Soi Sri Akson, Chua Ploeng, Sathorn (Tel.: 66 (0) 2 671-0030 to 31; e-mail: *lecafsiam@gymmi.com*) Pretty house in colonial style constructed in 1921 in the middle of a tranquil garden, furnished with antiques for sale. Proposes good Thai and French cuisine.
— *Bussaracum* – Sethiwan Building, Pan Road, North Sathorn Road (Tel.: 66 (0) 2 266-6312 to 18). Royal Thai cuisine in an elegant décor.
— *Celadon* – Sukhothai Hotel, 13/3 South Sathorn Road (Tel.: 66 (0) 2 287-0222; e-mail: *reservations@sukhothai.com*). One of the best Thai restaurants in Bangkok, in two glass pavilions resting in the middle of a lotus-filled pond or on a terrace.
— *Mango Tree* – 37 Soi Anumarn Rachthon, Surawongse Road (Tel.: 66 (0) 2 236-2820). In this ancient 80-year old Thai house, the restaurant proposes quality Thai cuisine to the accompaniment of classical music.

— *Sala Rim Naam* – Oriental Hotel, 48 Oriental Avenue (Tel.: 66 (0) 2 437-6211, 437-3080). The Thai restaurant of **The Oriental, Bangkok** is situated on the opposite riverbank of the Chao Phraya, accessible by shuttle. Dine on the terrace on the edge of the river or in the traditionally-styled pavilion accompanied by a classical Thai show. Good Thai cuisine.
— *Tongue Thai Restaurant* – 18-20 Charoen Krung Soi 38 (Tel.: 66 (0) 2 630-9918 to 19). Around the corner from **The Oriental**, this restaurant is in an ancient boutique-house and specializes in vegetarian food.
— *Supatra River House* – 266 Soi Wat Rakhang, Arun Amarin Road (Tel.: 66 (0) 2 411-0305) On the banks of the Chao Phraya, this private house was converted into a restaurant by its owner in 1999. It enjoys a good view of the Grand Palace that it faces.
— *River Cruise Dinners* aboard rice barges (*Manohra* with the **Bangkok Marriot Resort and Spa**; *Oriental Queen* with **The Oriental, Bangkok**.)
— *Harmonique* – 22 Charoen Krung Soi 34 (Tel.: 66 (0) 3 237-8175). Restaurant in an ancient boutique-house filled with antiques.
— *Spice Market* – **The Regent, Bangkok**, 155 Ratchadamri Road (Tel.: 66 (0) 2 251-6127). Excellent food in a traditional market-like atmosphere.
— *Baan Khanitha* – Sukhumvit Road, Soi 23 (Tel.: 66 (0) 2 258-4181). Situated in a pretty wooden house in a calm garden, it specializes in royal Thai cuisine.
— *Cabbages and Condoms* – 10 Sukhumvit Road, Soi 12 (Tel.: 66 (0) 2 229-4610 to 29) Dine in the garden or in one of the air-conditioned rooms. Good Thai cuisine at reasonable prices. The profits go to the Family Planning and the fight against AIDS.
— *Lemongrass* – 5/1 Sukhumvit, Soi 24 (Tel.: 66 (0) 2 258-8637). Refined settings and delicious Thai cuisine.

The Sukhothai Bangkok 💚

The Sukhothai, a haven of serenity in the heart of Bangkok, is, without doubt, by virtue of its interior architecture, the most beautiful of the city's hotels. Right from the entrance hall, framed by pools of water, which reflect a temple and bells of the Sukhothai kingdom, you enter a world apart, far from the sounds of the city, which is nonetheless close by, with the Silom commercial center only a 15-minute drive away.

At the end of a long path bordered by trees, two pavilions of traditional architecture stand before the low, sober, white silhouette of the hotel.

The interior designer, Edward Tuttle, also responsible for the décor of the Amanpuri in Phuket, was inspired by the 13th-century Sukhothai city, as well as other Asian architectures, which he reinterpreted in a very individual way, using a rather minimalist style wherein each detail becomes symbolic.

The designer played with the theme of reflections through his use of water and mirrors. The volumes wind around patios, inside which pools of water are the central elements, reflecting upon their perpetually rippled surfaces superb *chedis* of red brick or bronze with elongated spires. Mirrored walls and ceilings reflect stone *apsaras* into infinity and give the place a magical touch. The two Thai pavilions, which make up the hotel's Celadon Restaurant, have transparent glass walls crowned by pagoda-shaped roofs and float like bubbles over the rectangular pools filled with water lilies. The Thai cuisine there is excellent and you can dine either upon an open breezy terrace in winter, or in the air-conditioned dining rooms. The atmosphere is spellbinding in the evenings, when the illuminated pavilions are reflected upon the surface of the pools and the warm glow of candlelight makes the dark wooden floorboards gleam, casting long shadows upon the black granite of the tables, each adorned with a single, white lotus flower.

The Sukhothai's reception and adjoining rooms have immense ceilings and are decorated with simple sophistication. The black granite at the foot of the walls is finished with silks of muted shades of green and tan, and upon certain mirrored panels hang sculpted terracotta door shutters. Statues of Buddha and abstract floral compositions punctuate the space with their presence and their ephemeral beauty.

The pure perspective of the long corridor leading to the hotel's interior is decorated with simple metal torches and the play of light and texture has a surreal effect.

The rooms in the building behind the reception are the most pleasant as they look out over the beautiful interior gardens and pools. The rooms situated in a second building facing the reception have pleasant, though less unusual, views of the swimming pool.

The rooms are all elegantly decorated in a style that spurns unnecessary detail, and wherein traditional Thai elements are particularly well accentuated. The Superior Rooms, carpeted in gray and tan silk, are handsomely furnished in wood and black granite. The bathrooms, tastefully arrayed with mirrors, black granite and wood, are sublime, their bathtubs set into alcoves. The Deluxe rooms are much larger, and the Deluxe suites boast a fine entrance, paneled in teak, and a lounge decorated with ancient blue and white Thai pottery. The Executive Garden Suite, with its large bay windows overlooking the gardens, is princely, its alcoves filled with precious celadons, its great, teak

four-poster bed and sofas upholstered in silk.

So, this is a distinctly elegant address and if you cannot afford the luxury of staying there, you can always console yourself by having a sumptuous dinner at the Celadon, hailed as one of the city's best Thai restaurants.

THE SUKHOTHAI BANGKOK

13/3 South Sathorn Road
Bangkok 10120
Tel   66 (0) 2 287-0222
Fax   66 (0) 2 287-4980
           285-0133
E-mail   *info@sukhothai.com*
reservations@sukhothai.com
Web   *www.sukhothai.com*

By land
Car 30- to 45-minute drive from Bangkok International Airport via the expressway (airport is 25 kilometers north of the city).
Note: *Transfer from airport can be arranged by the resort.*

224 Units
110 Superior rooms • 36 Deluxe rooms • 38 Executive suites • 25 Deluxe suites • 12 Garden suites • 2 Terrace suites • 1 Sukhothai suite
All rooms have private bathroom (separate bathtub and shower, hot water, hairdryer, air-conditioning, telephone, cable TV (and pay movies), Internet access, room fax machine (on request in Superior rooms), minibar, safety box. Executive suite, Garden suite, Deluxe suite have an open plan bedroom/living room or separate bedroom and living room and 2 TV (in Deluxe suite only), CD player, tea/coffee maker.

Food and Beverage Outlets
Restaurants: Celadon (one of the best in Bangkok) • Colonnade • Terrazo
Cuisine Offered: Thai • International • Italian
Quality: Excellent cuisine and service

Bar: The Bar

Other services: Business center • Shopping arcade • Babysitting • Medical services
Note: *24-hour room service.*

Water sports and Other Activities
Swimming pool • Spa • Holistic methods • Fully-equipped and supervised gym • Tennis • Squash • Golf courses outside Bangkok center

 Per room
per night

The Oriental, Bangkok

L egendary hotel on the banks of the Chao Phraya River, The Oriental lives up to its reputation as one of the world's most renowned for the excellence of its service. It is an authentic claim as the service is unbelievably efficient and attentive with no less than 1000 employees at your service! It begins with a graceful hostess bearing jasmine and orchid bracelets who greets you on arrival, then continues with another one who escorts you to your room, appearing like magic whenever you need her, with the ultimate being the Desk Manager who addresses you by name, being able to personally identify each of the hundreds of hotel residents! And, yes, there is the river, magnificent and lively, pulsating with the colorful pageant of the long-tail boats—a feast for the eyes!

The Oriental was Bangkok's first hotel, founded in the 19th century. The most ancient part of the hotel still exists, concealed in a small garden facing the river with a beautiful neo-classical façade. Its ground floor shelters the Author's Lounge where you can enjoy a cup of tea in what used to be the original hotel, since covered by a glass roof. Also in this house are the four Author Suites, refined and full of a charm akin to the olden day palaces.

The reception evokes a baroque palace, with its white marble floor reflecting enormous wooden bells suspended from the high ceiling. A vast glass wall looks onto the garden and the swimming pool surrounded by frangipanis and bougainvillea. An arcade leads to the river after running alongside the Bamboo Café where the upholstery of the bamboo furniture in motifs of African animals provides a muffled "safari" ambiance.

Indulging in a drink at the terrace facing the Chao Phraya River towards the end of the afternoon, when the sun's warm golden glow takes on a dreamy haze is a must. Then embark on the Oriental's rice barge for a dinner at the Tim Naan Restaurant across the river, where the luxurious Spa is also located.

The hotel, completely renovated in 2001 for its 125th anniversary, comprises two wings in which the very comfortable rooms are situated, all enjoying river views via large bay windows.

The majority are Superior rooms situated in the River Wing are decorated in a style that blends modernism with Thai elements such as the astute lacquered black and gold cabinet concealing the television set and the luxurious wooden minibar. The walls are lined with raw silk in beige and gold tones and orchids adorn the furniture. The superb bathrooms, in the spirit of the 1920s, have teak flooring and wall lamps in molten glass. Sliding paneled doors separate the different areas. The Deluxe rooms, in the Garden Wing, are cozy and cheerful in a harmony of vivid colors. They are generally on split-levels, comprising a lounge area corner and, in some of them, a small greenhouse.

The various suites have been named after the celebrities who have resided there and inspired the décor.

As such, the Graham Greene suite is in a harmony of lime green, with a living room embellished with celadons and an angled terrace facing the river, while the rather extravagantly stylish Barbara Cartland suite is in shades of pink. Several crowned heads and famous actors have stayed in the fabulous 300-square-meter Oriental suite.

Antiques aficionados will be in their element: the Oriental Place is across the road and River City's fabulous antique center is a few minutes' drive away by the hotel's complimentary shuttle service, bus or boat. The river journey is already a pleasure on its own. You can embark at the private jetty of the Oriental for a river cruise by long-tail boats, along the canals of Bangkok or to the ancient city of Ayutthaya (one of the journeys will be then by air-conditioned bus).

THE ORIENTAL, BANGKOK

48 Oriental Avenue,
Bangkok 10500
Tel　66 (0) 2 659-9000
Fax　66 (0) 2 659-0000
E-mail
orbkk-reservations@mohg.com
Web　*www.mandarin-oriental.com*

 By land
Car 30- to 45-minute drive from Bangkok International Airport via the expressway (airport is 25 kilometers north of the city).
Note: *Transfer from airport can be arranged by the resort.*

 374 Units
Rooms (in River Wing or Garden Wing): 264 Superior rooms • 14 Deluxe rooms • 22 Deluxe Corners in River Wing • 35 Garden Wing rooms (small living room, some with small conservatory)
All rooms and suites have private bathroom (separate bathtub and shower), air-conditioning, 2 lines IDD phone, Internet access, voicemail, fax machine/printer on request (complimentary), cable TV, CD, minibar, coffee/tea maker, safety box.
Suites (in River Wing): 5 Deluxe two-bedrooms suites • 13 Executive suites • 10 Deluxe suites (balcony and sitting room) • 7 Deluxe Top on top floor • Selandia suite (2 bedrooms and sitting room) • Siam suite (2 bedrooms, sitting room, living room) • The Oriental suite (2 bedrooms, sitting room, dining room, service pantry, 300 m^2) • 4 Author's suites in Author's house

 Food and Beverage Outlets
Restaurants: Sala Rim Naam (terrace or air-conditioned sala, classical Thai dances) • Le Normandie (on the top floor) • The China House (in a colonial residence next to the hotel main entrance) • Lord Jim's (on first floor facing the Chao Phraya) • Ciao • The Verandah breakfast • Riverside Terrace (breakfast, barbecue, buffet)
Cuisine Offered: Thai • French • Chinese • Seafood • Italian • Continental • Asian
Bars: Author's Lounge • The Bamboo Bar
Quality: Excellent cuisine and service

Other services: Business center • Shops • Child care center • Free shuttle boat to Taksin Bridge sky train station and to River city shopping center from 6 am to midnight (15 minutes) • Free shuttle bus to River city • Limousine or taxi service • Helicopter service
Note: *Personal butler service for each guest.*

 Water sports and Other Activities
2 Swimming pools • Spa • Complimentary yoga classes • Fully-equipped sports center • Tennis and squash courts • Thai cooking school • Long-tail boat and motor launches river tours • Day trip to Ayutthaya on Oriental Queen cruiser (1 way by air-conditioned coach, the boat leaves at 8 a.m. and return at 5 p.m.) • Golf courses outside Bangkok center

 Per room
per night

Bangkok Marriott Resort and Spa

The Bangkok Marriott Resort, slightly on the outskirts of the city center, has the agreeable atmosphere of a holiday resort. Its 4.5-hectare park along the Chao Phraya was designed by Bill Bensley, who has endowed some areas with an unexpected wild look. Ferns, philodendrons and orchids cling onto the trunks of tutelary trees, banyan trees with aerial root weave a curtain through which the river shimmers and the joyous birdsongs are heard at dawn and dusk.

A footbridge spans an astonishing leafy river: a *klong* traversing the park before emptying into the Chao Phraya is covered the whole length by an entanglement of climbing plants, so dense that they totally camouflage the water. From here the view onto the Chao Phraya, framed by ficus trees and creepers, through which you will discern the silhouette of ancient rice barges, is quite disconcerting.

Large white multistory buildings that house the rooms, whose balconies overflow with bougainvillea, frame this profusely verdant space in the heart of which the rectangular swimming pool embedded in a teak terrace is the main attraction. Recessed ponds and more private terraces have been laid out, dominated by a superb Jacuzzi. The place becomes particularly lively in the middle of the day.

Traditionally tiled roofed passageways delimit the swimming pool, surrounded by groves and coconut trees. A portico gives access to the large terrace that runs along the Chao Phraya and the place is shaded by banyan trees and decorated by stone elephants and jars festooned with bougainvillea. At the close of day, it is enjoyable to have a drink at the bar, in a small traditional pavilion, and gaze at the pageant that unfolds on the river where barges and slender boats parade incessantly. The Terrace restaurant is situated at one extremity of the terrace with tables slightly close to each other. The jetty for the hotel's complimentary rice barges going to the metro station or to the River City's antique shopping center is also here.

The Bangkok Marriott Resort and Spa comprises several restaurants. For a romantic dinner, you should reserve a dinner cruise aboard its rice barge or at Trader Vic's with subtle Polynesian décor in a harmony of tobacco-brown and black colors.

The large reception with a marble floor, arcaded walkways, white balustrades and antique wooden furniture in certain common areas, gives the hotel an undeniably agreeable colonial aspect.

All rooms benefit from direct or oblique views of the river. The Deluxe rooms and Junior suites are very comfortable, spacious and sober with beautiful wooden floorings, but are somewhat lacking in originality.

The spa, romantically isolated at the rear of the garden, surrounded by palm trees and cannas, is very attractive.

Note that you can sleep overnight in one of the four luxurious cabins of the **"Manohra Song,"** a magnificent ancient rice barge and so visit Ayutthaya—a genuine splurge but absolutely fabulous.

BANGKOK MARRIOTT RESORT AND SPA

On the Chao Phraya River,
257 Charoen Nakorn Road,
Bangkok
Tel   66 (0) 2 476-0022
Fax   66 (0) 2 476-1120
E-mail
bangkokmarriott@minornet.com
Web   *www.marriotthotels.com*

By land
Car 30- to 45-minute drive from Bangkok International Airport via the expressway (airport is 25 kilometers north of the city)
Note: *Transfer from airport can be arranged by the resort. The resort is only 3.5 kilometers away from the city center.*

413 Units
344 Deluxe rooms • 54 Junior suites • 14 Deluxe suites • 1 Presidential suite (with river and garden view)
All rooms have tiny balcony, private bathroom (separate bathtub and shower only in the suites, hairdryer), air-conditioning, IDD 2-line phone with voice mail, cable TV (in-room movies), minibar, safety box, coffee/tea maker.

Food and Beverage Outlets
Restaurants: Riverside Terrace (BBQ buffet—Thai show) • Trader Vic's • Benihana • Kabuki • The Rice Mill • The Market (breakfast, international buffet—on the riverside) • The Manohra Dining (dinner cruises on rice barge boat)
Cuisine Offered: International • Thai • Polynesian style • Japanese (Teppanyaki style) • Cantonese
Quality: Very good

Bars: Elephant Bar (jazz) • Loy Nam Bar (pool side) • Long Tail Bar (by the river)

Other services: Business center • Boutiques • Child care services • Small kid 's club • Tour desk and car rental • Complimentary river shuttle to sky train and River city • Beauty parlor • 24-hour room service

Water sports and Other Activities
Swimming pool with Jacuzzi • Mandara spa • Health club • Tennis • Manohra luxury cruises on the Chao Phraya river (*www.manohracruises.com*) • Golf course (90-minute drive)

 Per room per night

The Regent Bangkok

If you think that picking up any luxury five-star hotel in the middle of the business and shopping district of Bangkok will offer the same experience, the Regent will prove you wrong. A feeling of lightness suddenly fills the air as one reaches the low-rise building of this recently and completely renovated city palace. Is it the symbolic welcome of the two royal white stone elephants? Or the beaming smiles of the staff, gently helping you out of your taxi car? Or is it the peacefulness of the twin pools under the large entrance portico? At this point in time, one knows that whatever comes next is just going to be p.e.r.f.e.c.t. Or just about.

What makes the immense lobby such a stunning one? Probably the subtle mix of classical magnificence, Thai art at its best, and ageless comfort. Grand columns, silk hand-painted ceiling and wall murals representing the Thai cosmos as well as a fabulous procession to a royal coronation, together with wood furniture, soft colors, and sophisticated zen-styled flower arrangements spray out a serene atmosphere inside this *elegantissimo* lounge, suffused with afternoon sunlight and tuberose sweet smell. A perfect place for a drink served by the most graceful waitresses in town, wearing gold-veil-like outfits whose elegance is only rivaled by sandstone *apsaras* on Angkor's carved murals.

Superior rooms offer extremely spacious and elegant accommodation with silks from Jim Thompson, teak wood furniture and artifacts, Thai antiques, and tremendously luxurious marble bathrooms; Deluxe rooms grant panoramic views on the Royal Bangkok Sports Club, or overlook the pool side. But there is another accommodation alternative at the Regent, which can be resisted only by budget consciousness: the Cabana rooms. Located by the pool terrace area, these few rooms are a pure dream of privacy and create a genuine 'resort-in-the-city' feel. In this hiding-place, one just forgets the frantic city as one's gaze rolls off the Cabana's charming room into the quiet private patio, the lush landscaped garden, the lotus pond, the light-footed Thai statues, …

Fine cuisine at the Regent is a scrumptious culinary journey between continents. Here, palate delight mixes with what calls for state-of-the-art creative contemporary dining venues' design. Created by inspired architect Tony Chi, a family of four very special restaurants makes a choice almost impossible. Peppy and casual Italian *Biscotti* — also serving enticing breakfasts for both mouth and eye — is praised by Condé Nast Traveler as 'one of the world's most exciting restaurants.' *Shintaro* creates revolutionary styles of sushi in a minimalist decor diffusing the very essence of Japanese aesthetics. *Aqua* is a refreshing spot to have a relaxed meal or drink, right in the middle of an open-air tropical courtyard, cross-cut by babbling-water ponds where spoiled ducks bathe joyfully. Scenic and chic *Madison* grill sets new rules for modern refinement, featuring an innovative open-kitchen. Not part of the Chi-family settings, the *Spice Market* offers some of the very best Thai cuisine in the country, within a charming traditional market-like yet delightful atmosphere.

The Health Club and Spa, another Tony Chi's perfect world, completes this idyllic set up.

The Regent Bangkok has undoubtedly signed a new and unprecedented definition of urban luxury and hospitality.

THE REGENT BANGKOK

155 Rajadamri Road,
Bangkok 10330
Tel 66 (0) 2 251-6127
66 (0) 2 254-9999
Guest Fax 66 (0) 2 253-9195
Reservation
Fax 66 (0) 2 254-5391
E-mail *rcm.reservations@fourseasons.com*
Web *www.fourseasons.com*
www.regenthotels.com

By land
Car 30- to 45-minute drive from Bangkok International Airport. Centrally located on one of Bangkok's most famous boulevards, facing the Royal Bangkok Sports Club.
Note: *Private fleet of chauffeured Mercedes limousine service available for airport transfers.*

356 Units
313 Superior and Deluxe rooms (42 m²) • 7 rooms (52 m²) • 1 suite 'Cabana'-type (77 m², with private entrance and open on a tropical garden) • 16 Junior (72 m²) • 10 Superior (84 m²) • 8 Deluxe suites (126 m²) • 1 luxurious homelike Rajadamri suite (600 m²)
Note: *5-star service by a staff of more than 600 employees, fully dedicated to hospitality.*

Food and Beverage Outlets
Restaurants: Extremely varied and superbly decorated dining outlets: Shintaro (sushi counter) • The Spice Market (terrace by poolside) • Biscotti • The Terrace (by pool-side) Aqua (stylish garden bar and snack) • Madison (beef and seafood grill)
Cuisine Offered: Thai • Japanese • Italian • Western
Quality: Outstanding food and service

Other services: Business center • High-tech 'on-wheel' mobile office • Parichart shopping garden

Water sports and Other Activities
Swimming pool • Luxurious health club with squash court • Yoga lessons • Massage

Per room per night not inclusive of breakfast

The Swiss Lodge

The Swiss Lodge offers careful services in an intimate environment, making it good value for money. The fact of having just about fifty rooms sets it apart from the plethora of middle-class hotels offering similar services in Bangkok.

The white sober building slightly off the tranquil shady Convent road, not far from Silom, is barely noticeable. Everything inside is well maintained in accordance with good old Swiss tradition. The small bay-window lobby with white marble floors is invitingly bright, with two lounge areas laid out on both sides of the entrance. It is attractively decorated with eye-catching wooden armchairs in Chinese design, a red lacquered screen and a beautiful floral composition.

The welcome is cheery and professional with transport reservations, organization of excursions through a travel agency, a business center, a library, and a small swimming pool on the fifth floor being some of the services and amenities available.

Immaculate rooms possess all the elements of comfort with functional furniture in white-leaded wood, a minibar at an angle lined with mirrors to give the impression of space, and bathrooms in marble. A bay window looks onto a building that is unfortunately quite close by.

A few extra touches come in the form of the morning newspaper placed in front of your door and the name and contact details of your housekeeper.

The "Swiss Lodge Restaurant," on the ground floor, is cozy with lace curtains and wooden tables covered in spruce red tablecloths. The walls are decorated in a funny manner with cuisine-related collages from Swiss and

French newspapers and magazines made to look like wallpaper. As its name suggests, the restaurant serves Swiss cuisine, notably delicious cheese fondues that can be quite disconcerting in Bangkok.

There is ample opportunity to taste Thai cuisine in the vicinity. Among others, at walking distance, is a very good Thai restaurant, "Ban Chiang" (14 Soi Srivieng Silom Road), in a beautiful traditional teak house in the middle of a garden. A bit further on, the renowned "Bussaracum" (Sethiwab Building, 139 Pan Road, North Sathon Road) serves Royal Thai cuisine in an elegant décor. The Chinese restaurant on the top floor of the Silom Sofitel offers original cuisine in a rather spectacular setting towering above the city with a panoramic view through a glass wall.

THE SWISS LODGE

3 Convent Road, Silom,
Bangkok 10500
Tel   66 (0) 2 233-5345
Fax   66 (0) 2 236-9425
E-mail *info@swisslodge.com*
Web   *www.swisslodge.com*

By land
Car 30- to 45-minute drive from Bangkok International Airport (airport is 25 kilometers north of the city) to The Swiss Lodge.
Note: *Transfer can be arranged by the resort.*

57 Units
24 Standard rooms • 30 Superior rooms • 3 Deluxe rooms
All rooms have private bathroom (bathtub, hot water), air-conditioning, IDD phone, Internet access, cable TV, minibar, safety box. Deluxe rooms have coffee/tea maker and CD player.

Food and Beverage Outlets
Restaurant: The Swiss Restaurant
Cuisine Offered: Swiss • International
Quality: Good

Other services: Business center with Internet • Limousine service • Tours and excursions (ask reception)
Note: *24-hour room service.*

Water sports and Other Activities
Small swimming pool with sun terrace • Fitness center nearby • Massage (contact reception) • Library

 Per room per night

Mekhala

Languidly installed on the rear deck of an ancient rice barge, you can delight in gazing the spectacle of life along the Chao Phraya between Bangkok and Ayutthaya.

And what a spectacle it is! The animation on the river is in full swing at Bangkok. Around the Grand Palace you are witness to an unbelievable to and fro of boats of every size—speedboats with streamlined prows, rice barges, tourist launches, tugboats…

Beyond the suburbs, the tugboats remain numerous, a multitude of factories having been implanted along the Chao Phraya River. It is only near Ayutthaya that you begin to perceive peaceful countryside. All along the river, you can see numerous small temples and houses on stilts where folk get on with the tasks of daily living. Further on, the river is swathed in water hyacinths and some winters, thousands of migrating egrets come here to rest on the trees bordering the river, forming a strange blossoming of white flowers on the bare branches.

In the evening, the barge moors at the jetty in front of a small temple, serene except for the barking of the numerous dogs, joyful on the occasion, and the quacking of the ducks! You can witness the first ceremony in the temple at six in the morning. Sunrises and sunsets on the river are frequently magical, the sky and water aflame with the same orange and delicate mauve hues.

The rice barge in red wood with a heavy bulbous hull, comprises a spacious deck that practically nothing separates from the river, equipped with deck chairs, armchairs and small cane colonial-styled tables. Inside, shaded from the sun by a pagoda-styled roof, is a second resting area furnished with soft sofas to lie down on. There is also a small bar from where drinks can be ordered.

In the evenings, tables are set on the deck, prettily decorated with flowers and excellent Thai cuisine is served in attractive blue and white porcelain plates. Tables are generally grouped together but can be separated on request.

The rice barges possess only either six or nine cabins thus assuring a certain privacy. The cabins are well designed and cozy, paneled in wood and well lit by semi-circular glass bowls. They have elevated beds and smaller ones lower down more suited for a child, as well as bathrooms equipped with a shower.

The cruise spans two days and one night between Bangkok and Ayutthaya or the other way round, according to your desire. One of the journeys takes place in an individual minibus with a driver and a private guide.

In one half-day, the Summer Palace of Bang Pa In and the more renowned temples of Ayutthaya are visited, with the rest of the time being spent on the boat. After lunch in a restaurant in Ayutthaya, an hour's river cruise by long-tail boat is on offer.

Departure from Bangkok by boat takes place in the afternoon with a return by minibus also in the afternoon, whereas departures from Bangkok by minibus are in the morning with a return by boat in the morning. If you have the choice, opt for the departure by boat, which is more picturesque as the boat passes in front of the Ayutthaya temples.

MEKHALA

East West Siam Co. Ltd.,
183 Regent House,
15/F, Rajdamri Road, Lumpini,
Patumwan Bangkok 10330
Tel   66 (0) 2 651-9101
Fax   66 (0) 2 651-9766
E-mail
mekhalacruise@east-west-siam.com
eastwestsiam@east-west-siam.com
Web   *www.east-west-siam.com*

1. Program down (bus+boat)
Day 1: Depart from your hotel around 8 a.m. and travel by minibus to Ayutthaya. Visit of Ayutthaya. Lunch at a local restaurant and then travel to Bang-Pa-In by long-tail boat to visit the Summer Palace. Board the Mekhala and cruise down the Chao Phraya River to Wat Kai Tia. Dinner and overnight on board.
Day 2: After breakfast, cruise down the river to Bangkok. Arrive there in the late morning.
2. Program up (boat +bus) (best option)
Day 1: Start cruising up the Chao Phraya River around 3 p.m. After sunset, the boat docks at Wat Kai Tia. Dinner and overnight on board.
Day 2: After breakfast, depart for Bang-Pa-In to visit the Summer Palace. Continue by long-tail boat to Ayutthaya. After lunch at a local restaurant, visit of Ayutthaya. Late in the afternoon transfer by minibus to your hotel in Bangkok.

6 or 9 Cabins
Mekhala fleet consists of 3 boats with a total capacity of 21 cabins housing 42 passengers. The boats have 6 or 9 double berth cabins. All cabins have private bathroom (shower, hot water), air-conditioning.

Food and Beverage Outlets
Candlelit dinner of Thai cuisine is served on the deck. There is a covered corner bar on the deck.
Quality: Good food and friendly service

Other services and facilities: Telephone • Sunbathing deck • Magazines • Indoor games

Per person per night. Transfer from Bangkok, full board and excursion in Ayutthaya and Bang Pa included.

Note: *Package per person for 2 days and one night, price includes double bed cabin, meals, tea and coffee during the cruise, entrance fees and guide in Ayutthaya and Bang-Pa-In, one transfer only in Bangkok from your hotel to Mekhala pier or vice-versa.*

The Thai House

Close your eyes and imagine that you are hopping on to a long-tail boat at a Chao Phraya's pier and then, taken along the river and the *klongs* all the way up to the private pier of a stunning traditional Thai house. Now imagine this house will be your home for as long as your stay. If you think this is all too good to be true, plan a stay at The Thai House for a few days, only 22 kilometers away from the old city of Bangkok, and experience for yourself the genuine traditional Thai life style within a graciously hospitable family.

There is no check-in at The Thai House, but instead, a cordial welcome from Pip, soul of the place, and her fluent English-speaker daughter Pang. There are no keys to the rooms either, as there is no reason to lock up the doors. Antique clocks hanging on the veranda's walls are stopped, as time does not really mean much inside this house reviving ancestral days. All these signs tell just one simple thing: here is a place for sheer relaxation and certainly not for those in need of action.

Pip was born on this land belonging to her parents and grew a true passion for rural Thai way of life. A few decades of professional life in tourism with her husband made them both realize that foreign visitors were long-ing to experience the genuine taste of the country. In 1990, they made their dream come true. Twenty-five crafts-men from Ayutthaya province custom-built this cluster house made of three separate pavilions set on a raised ter-race amidst a lush mango orchard. The love and care put into this house is extreme: some intricate wood carvings actually took more than a year to per-form. The result is a perfectly harmo-nious and elegant teak house. The ground floor of the Thai House is used as a lobby, dining room, and sitting area under the sheltered patio. Two flights of external stairs lead to the second floor tiled terrace, which flows into three separate wing-roofed pavilions, each housing two vast bedrooms. A huge col-lection of potted palms and tropical plants decorate the terrace, perpetrating a centuries-old Thai tradition and creat-ing a flighty green screen against the dark wood of the encircling walls.

A double wooden door opens onto the serene beauty of the teak nest room, which displays the essence of the whole house. Glossy teak floors reflect green palm leaves dancing out-side the numerous glass-free windows. A cool breeze blows in the light-laced cotton curtains. Following tradition, the beds and seating triangular pillows are simply placed on the floor. Very high ceilings provide the necessary space for air circulation, making for cool nights even in the hottest months of the year. As sleep closes one's eyes, it is a wonderful moment to only hear the barking of a dog in the neighbor-hood, the croaking of a frog or two, and a gecko's sounds in the distance. This is indeed an Asian night in pure traditional Thailand. In the morning, a shower inside the scrubbed communal bathroom pavilion offers an unex-pected view through the window onto the top of the trees, where blue-winged birds come in softly for landing.

In 1992, Pip transformed her family kitchen and herb garden into a Thai cooking school which became quite popular with overseas visitors booking for one to three days' classes. Life at the Thai house very much resembles life of a rural family: shopping adventure at the local market in the morning, cooking, taking a nap during the hottest hours of the afternoon, and enjoying a tour along the close by *klongs* aboard Pip's neighbor's long-tail boat, at sunset. Dinnertime is gathering time in family atmosphere for all the guests around the one or two communal tables, for savoring Pip and her students' cuisine and making new friends among this small home-stay community.

THE THAI HOUSE

32/4 Moo 8, Tambol Bang Maung, Amphoe Bangyai, Nonthaburi 11140

Tel   66 (0) 2 997-5161
                 903-9611
Fax   66 (0) 2 903-9354
E-mail
pip_thaihouse@hotmail.com
Web   *www.thaihouse.co.th*

1. By land (about 45 minutes)
The Thai house is located approximately 22 kilometers from the center of old Bangkok. It takes a 30- to 45-minute drive depending on traffic over the Phra Pinklao Bridge, then onto the Bangbuathong-Suphan Road for 20 kilometers.

Note: *If specifically requested, Thai House's family can pick up guests at Bangkok airport or anywhere in the city. For those wishing to arrive by taxi, it is recommended to phone the Thai House's family and have the taxi driver explained how to get there.*

2. By boat (1 hour)
Jump on long-tail boat at Tha Chang boat pier on the Chao Phraya River (close to Grand Palace) to Bangyai boat station. At Bangyai boat station, take a taxi boat to the Thai House.

Note: *The Thai House also charters direct boat transfer to pick-up guests along the Chao Phraya's boat piers.*

9 Units
6 Twin rooms and 1 single room on the second floor and 2 extra twin rooms on the ground floor.
All rooms are equipped with thick mattresses on the floor, fan and mosquito screens on windows. Spotless communal showers and toilets in pavilion adjacent to the rooms' pavilions.

Food and Beverage Outlets
1 Family-type dining room (on the ground floor)
Cuisine Offered: Exclusively homemade Thai. Also, cooking class students' own-made dishes. Very limited choice of drinks.
Quality: Good family-type cuisine, cooked with much love and care.

Water sports and Other Activities
Fun and friendly Thai cooking classes taught by Pip, the Thai House owner • Morning fresh market tour • Long-tail boat tour around the klongs • Bicycle rides and many encounters with local life

Per room per night inclusive of breakfast

Shanti Lodge Bangkok

Northof Bangkok, at the back of the flower market and a stone-throw from the Chao Phraya river, a street busy with food vendors, tuk-tuks, and world-wide travelers leads to Thewet temple. A few guest houses align along the street. Yet, one and only one stands out as the beating heart of this lively neighborhood: the Shanti Lodge. With superlative sense of hospitality, inventive and cosy decor, flowers and greenery everywhere, this family-owned inexpensive guest house is a friendly and precious oasis inside smoky Bangkok. An indulging port for back-packers, families, young and older travelers coming from all over the world.

A wonderful couple created the Shanti Lodge 20 years ago: South-African Kim and her Thai husband "Happy," Step by step, they not only expanded this early tiny guest house—recently adding a fetching dining-drinking room with a romantic verandah—but certainly made it flourish as an inspiring and funky place where guests keep coming year after year or use it as a home-platform while traveling around Asia.

A powerful atmosphere blooms all over Shanti Lodge, from early morning till late at night, sparkled by the energy of ever present Mr. Happy. A fragrant pink honeysuckle winds along the wood *trellis* outside wall of the dining and bar area,

where glasses and bottles are aligned against a striking turquoise wall. On the bar counter, yellow-ripe bananas and passion fruits await orders for instant-made fruit shakes. Small tables skirted with acidulous colored cotton cloths bring a zest of Italian touch to this exotic room, cooled off by the swirl of a ceiling fan.

Rooms at Shanti are set in two distinct houses: the original one and its next-door-neighbor house. In both buildings, accommodation shows the same addiction from Kim to create a fresh and smiling world. Cooling greens and blues adjacent to energizing pinks and oranges run along the corridor walls where framed photographs show treasure moments of the big Shanti-family, i.e. the owners, staff members, and guests altogether. The labyrinth-type stairs running up and down the floors of each of the two old houses add to the charm of the place — except for carrying up luggage. Rooms are an inviting place with walls painted in vibrant colors and naive hand-painted friezes. With very simple amenities — no bedside table and lamp, but some rooms displaying a fish tank! — they are all surgically clean. Tiles on the floor are colorful and fancy miniature porcelain fauna decorate the wall of the shower area; shells ornate mirrors topping the mini-sized basin, making the whole room a fresh and pleasant place to rest.

Another well-achieved 'feel-good' atmosphere may be found around the communal showers' area suffused with natural sunlight and with fresh orchids hanging in every shower. It is preceded by a cute terracotta jars, ferns and orchids mini-garden carefully looked after by Yuan, the ever-smiling and efficient reception manager.

One of the many sources of joy at Shanti is the wonderful vegetarian and Thai food — using organic vegetables as much as possible — prepared by an old-timer talented cook. Every dish coming out of this female-run kitchen is fresh, crunchy, and tasty. Homemade muesli served with homemade yogurt and a fruit galore has been a favorite with every one at breakfast for years.

As the night comes in, dimmed lights and candles turn the ground-floor dining room into a warm enticing cocoon attracting all passers-by in for a drink or a meal. Now comes the best time of the day for Mr. Happy to freely express his tremendous talent for hospitality. With superbly D-J'ed blends of R&B and World music, friendly chats with everyone, 'Thai-tanic' cocktails blended by lovely PanKaew behind the bar, Happy welcomes his guests into the sensual Shanti-night...

SHANTI LODGE BANGKOK

37 Sri Ayutthaya Road, Soi 16, Si Sou Thewet, Bangkok
Tel   66 (0) 2 281-2497
            628-7626
Note: *To secure your booking, it is highly recommended to reserve with 1 week notice (not earlier) and confirm your stay one day before arrival.*

By land
Car 30- to 45-minute drive from Bangkok International Airport. Located Northwest of central Bangkok, right behind the National Library. Easy access to central Bangkok by Chao Phraya River Express Boat from Tha Thewet pier.

33 Units
32 Rooms and 1 10-bed dormitory set within 2 buildings:
5 Large-sized double rooms (with private bathroom—shower—and air-conditioning) • 12 Medium-sized double rooms (with private bathroom—shower; 9 with fan, 3 with air-conditioning) • 3 Twin rooms (with private shower, communal toilet and air-conditioning) • 12 Double rooms (with communal shower and toilet; 9 with fan, 3 with air-conditioning)
Note: *Cold shower only. No telephone in rooms. Rooms on the Soi are quieter than rooms on the main street.*

Food and Beverage Outlets
1 Restaurant and bar
Cuisine Offered: Vegetarian • Western • Thai
Quality: Very good and healthy food using non-organic vegetables. Very simple and friendly service.

Other services: Public telephone available at the reception • Internet corner • Small shop selling traditional Thai sarongs and clothes to help sustaining a village community • On-site travel agency

Water sports and Other Activities
Massage on request

Per room per night, not inclusive of breakfast
Note: *Payment in cash and Baht only.*

Kanchanaburi

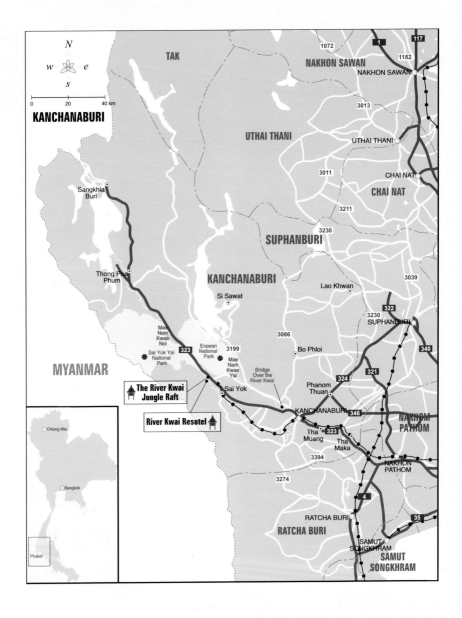

Many visitors come to Kanchanaburi to see the railway bridge over the River Kwai and the War Memorials. But the region also deserves to be visited for its magnificent natural surroundings, made of hillsides, jungles, waterfalls, limestone caves, with an abundance of national parks, which are more our focus. Two hotels, situated in the heart of nature, along the River Kwai Noi, have been selected: the **River Kwai Resotel** and **The River Kwai Jungle Rafts**.

KANCHANABURI *(130 kilometers from Bangkok and one hour from the River Kwai Resotel)* Two rivers, Kwai Noi River and Kwai Yai River, encompass the town. If you are interested only by war souvenirs (Museum of the Second World War, military cemeteries, Bridge on the River Kwai— 4.5 kilometers from town) it is better to stay in town at the pretty floating hotel, pleasingly set at a distance on an islet, the **Kasem Island Resort**: 27 Chaichumphon Road, Meuang, Kanchanaburi 71000 (Tel.: 66 (0) 3 451-3359 or 66 (0) 2 255-3603). Fax: 66 (0) 2 255-3604. (Note: this hotel is only accessible by boat). There is a nice outing by train from Kanchanaburi to Nam Tok (70 kilometers). The rail track runs along the River Kwai and in some areas the view plunges down into spellbinding precipices.

SAI YOK NATIONAL PARK *(1 hour from the River Kwai Resotel)* The park is accessible either by car (route no. 323) or by boat. From the River Kwai Resotel or The River Kwai Jungle Rafts, it is about an hour by boat along the limestone gorges draped in the jungles of the Kwai Noi River. In the park's interior itself, there are few hiking trails. Beautiful waterfalls cascade down the cliffs into the river. Among the cave, the most famous is the Tham Dao Wadung to the north of the park, which comprises eight underground chambers containing stalactites and stalagmites.

Further on, along route no. 323, are the distant Songkhla Buri and its superb mountainous scenery, but an overnight stay is unavoidable given the length of the journey.

ERAWAN NATIONAL PARK *(1 hour from the River Kwai Resotel)* Erawan National Park is undeniably the most beautiful of the parks in the region. Its petrifying seven-tiered waterfall is absolutely extraordinary, due to the colors of the rocks polished by the waters that accumulated limestone deposits. This phenomenon explains the surprising light pink color of the stone and the turquoise of the freshwater pools formed at the hollows of the different waterfalls. The most picturesque is the third one, about 20 meters in height, easily accessible by foot and where you can swim. It forms a natural basin of a fantastic opalescent turquoise, surrounded by ancient trees with battered trunks whose multiple roots interlock entangle just beneath the surface on the edge of the riverbanks.

There are few paths in the park, only an educational track, 1 kilometer long, that traverses a bamboo forest and another 2.2-kilometer long track, steep and slippery towards the end, leading to the waterfall's different levels. There are also several caves within the park: Tham Phra That (12 kilometers to the northwest of the visitors' center) and Thung Wang Badan.

Access: Nineteen kilometers away from the River Kwai Resotel parking lot, take a left turn in the direction of "Sisawat" along route no. 3457 and continue in this direction on route no. 319 until you see "Erawan Waterfall" indicated on the left. It is here that the visitors' center is situated.

SRI NAKHARIN NATIONAL PARK This park extends *Erawan National Park (route no. 3497)* near a dam having created a vast lake surrounded by forested hills.

River Kwai Resotel

You reach the River Kwai Resotel after a short trip up the river through limestone gorges swathed in jungle. A vast park filled with trees, plants and flowers where butterflies and multicolored birds flit will appeal to lovers of nature and peaceful surroundings.

Quite different from the numerous hotels in the region that have an impersonal and disproportionate appearance, River Kwai Resotel possesses a pleasant warm family atmosphere.

Its rustic architecture, with the exception of an appalling dyke, blends in well with the natural environment. The octagonal cottages with white half-timbered walls crowned with thatched roofs are concealed in the midst of the vegetation. Some, under renovation during our visit, have a nice view onto the river, along a pretty wooden promenade, whereas those behind look onto an expanse of water. There are also three beautiful two-story cottages, enclosed in a little private garden, ideal for one family.

The rather subdued interior of the paneled rooms and the exposed beams of the ceiling in the form of a dome give the cottages the congenial atmosphere of a mountain refuge. Besides, spacious rooms have functional bamboo furniture and subtle, although somewhat dim, lighting. The attached bathrooms covered with beautiful handcrafted tiles are well conceived.

A large wooden three-story pavilion shelters a hall containing antique table-football games on the ground floor, a restaurant on the first floor and a massage parlor on the top floor. The large hall of the particularly attractive restaurant is the place to meet after a day of exploration in the neighboring national parks. It is exposed on both sides to the forest and, at its entrance, thin philodendron roots cascade down from the roof forming a sort of delicate veil.

Overlooking the river, from the terrace, it offers a scenic view onto the abrupt cliffs on the opposite bank. The interior décor is very original, composed of a multitude of everyday antique objects and borrowings from nature hung on the exposed beams of the high ceiling such as superb twisted creepers, wooden elephant bells, horse halters and saddles, agricultural tools, copper vine dusters, wooden pitchers, large grains in the form of giant beans and old black and white photos. The showcases contain a collection of tools, pottery and wickerwork.

In the evening, the multiple oriental light suspensions in the form of teardrops give a magical aspect to the site, whereas the strident whirring of the cicadas and a cool nocturnal breeze waft in from the forest.

The fact that you can easily get away for an outing without having to take a car or boat is an added advantage. Just behind the resort is a small road, tarred over 4 kilometers, that ultimately transforms into a dirt track, on which you can go by foot or bicycle to discover a pleasing countryside in the midst of forest-covered hills.

The resort can organize numerous excursions to the nearby national parks or the Bridge on the River Kwai. If you stay for several days, it is interesting to spend overnight at the River Kwai Jungle Rafts—the latter belongs to the same owner and is situated 15 minutes from there by boat.

RIVER KWAI RESOTEL

 River Kwai Noi, Saiyoke District, Kanchanaburi
Tel   66 (0) 1 809-0623
           1 745-4158
Booking Office in Bangkok
River Kwai Resotel Ltd.,
133/14 Ratchaprarop Road,
Makkasan, Rajthevee,
Bangkok 10400
Tel   66 (0) 2 642-6361 to 2
           642-5497
           475-373
           453-069
Fax   66 (0) 2 246-5679
E-mail *flortel@samart.co.th*
           info@riverkwaifloatel.com
Web   *www.riverkwaifloatel.com*

 By land and boat (4 hours)
Car 4 hours from Bangkok (190 kilometers from Bangkok; 69 kilometers from Kanchanaburi). Drive along road 323 (Bangkok/Thong Pha Phum/Kanchanaburi. Turn left at Km 56; for another 2 kilometers drive to the river and Resotel parking lot. The resort is signaled by a signboard only 16 kilometers before arrival. The way is not always clear, as sometimes road 323 is indicated as A 2. *Boat* 10 minutes (there is another access by land only but it is more difficult to find).
Note: *Transfer can be arranged by the resort. You also have an access to Kanchanaburi by train from Bangkok Thonburi railway station (2 ½ hours only, but few trains).*

 77 Units
74 Cottages • 3 Family cottages (with 2 or 3 bedrooms)
All rooms have private balcony, private bathroom (shower, hot water), air-conditioning, small TV.

 Food and Beverage Outlets
1 Restaurant and 1 bar
Cuisine Offered: Thai cuisine (quite spicy) • International buffet
Quality: Familial

Other services: Fax and telephone at the information center

Water sports and Other Activities
Swimming pool • Massages • Table football • Canoeing • Rafting • Fishing • Mountain biking (22 kilometers of trails behind the resort) • Trekking • Birdwatching • Elephant riding • Walking to Lawa cave • Excursions to the nationals parks, Mon Tribal Village, Hell Fire Pass Museum

 Per room per night

The River Kwai Jungle Rafts

E choes and cries from the jungle, the rustling of the wind through the trees and the swift whispering of the river are what prevail here. The absence of electricity, telephone and television that enchants all the visitors to the River Kwai Jungle Rafts.

The 25-minute boat journey from the pier of the River Kwai Resotel situated lower down on the river is part of the adventure, along narrow gorges where a profusion of plants and creepers cascade down abrupt rocks walls.

The arrival at the River Kwai Jungle Rafts, after a meander of the river, allows you to discover a long stretch of wooden floating houses reflected in the water, almost hidden under their thick thatched roofs. What is most striking is the multitude of crotons, orchids, begonias, caladiums, ferns, commelines, sage, rubber and ficus trees gaily hung from the ceilings of the terraces in all sort of containers— coconut shells, earthen pots, split bamboo poles, and plants in their trays on the pontoons.

The natural setting is fantastic, with the houses facing the ochre limestone cliffs from which twisted trees and slender bamboo cling. A small wooden bridge gives access from the restaurant to the sandy bank where domesticated elephants, belonging to an inland Mon Village that can be visited, come to take a dip.

Linked by footbridges, each house has three rooms with a bamboo pontoon and a common covered terrace, equipped with tables, chairs and a hammock on the edge of the water that is quite in demand! There is a nice floating house exposed to the river that shelters the restaurant and the log bar. Large rustic wooden tables and others, more intimate, are disposed here. Set menus meals are served at fixed times in buffet style and you can have a peek at the kitchen where the cooks are busy in the shadowy light.

The rooms are small and dim because of the low roof of the common terrace at the entrance. They are very simple but clean with a large bed and a little washroom. A private balcony with a hammock is situated at the back. The wooden partitions being rather thin, the rooms can be quite resounding if the neighbors are noisy, which was not the case during our visit.

Service, though with a smile, is more nonchalant than at the River Kwai Resotel, hotel belonging to the same chain and situated 15 minutes from here by boat and to which you can be taken if you wish. Far from civilization, time is of no consequence here.

In the evenings when the cicadas begin to buzz, oil lamps are arranged in front of your door. After dinner, the inhabitants of the Mon village close by put on a traditional show in a "*theater*" house. This show is not very professional but the dancers and spectators seem to enjoy themselves.

Erawan National Park

THE RIVER KWAI JUNGLE RAFTS

River Kwai Noi, Saiyoke District, Kanchanaburi

Booking Office in Bangkok
River Kwai Floatel Co. Ltd.,
133/14 Ratchaprarop Road,
Makkasan, Rajthevee,
Bangkok 10400

Tel	66 (0) 2 642-6361 to 2
	642-5497
	2 475-373
	2 453-069
Fax	66 (0) 2 246-5679
E-mail	*info@riverkwaifloatel.com*
	flortel@samart.co.th
Web	*www.riverkwaifloatel.com*

By land and boat (4 ½ hours)
Car 4 hours from Bangkok (190 kilometers from Bangkok; 69 kilometers from Kanchanaburi). Drive along road 323 Bangkok/Thong Pha Phum/Kanchanaburi. Turn left at Km 56 for another 2 kilometers drive to the river and Resotel parking lot.
The resort is signaled by a signboard only 16 kilometers before arrival. The way is not always clear, as sometimes road 323 is indicated as A 2. *Boat* 15 minutes from Resotel parking lot

Note: *Transfer can be arranged by the resort. The resort is accessible only by boat. You also have an access to Kanchanaburi by train from Bangkok Thonburi railway station (2 ½ hours only, but few trains).*

98 Units
All rooms in two floating wings have tiny private bathroom (shower with cold water).
No electricity, oil lantern.

Food and Beverage Outlets
1 Restaurant and 1 bar
Cuisine Offered: Thai • Western
Quality: Familial

Water sports and Other Activities
Swimming (in the river) • Fishing • Canoeing • Bamboo rafting • Elephant riding • Trekking • Birdwatching • Mountain biking • Theater raft for Mon folk dance during evenings • Excursions to the national parks and caves, Mon tribal village, Hell Fire pass memorial

Per person per night on full board basis

Hua Hin

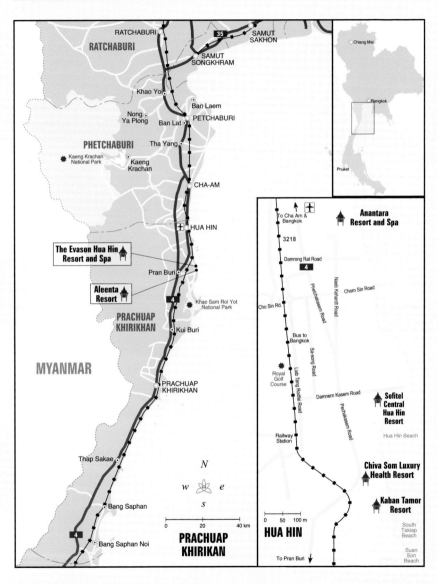

Climate	Two pronounced seasons: hot-dry from March to May; rainy from June to October; rain is not daily and is in short spells. Cool season from November to February

Hua Hin

The red and yellow chocolate box station and the extensive Railway Hotel since renamed **Sofitel Central Hua Hin Resort** are the only remnants of Hua Hin's history as the first seaside resort of Thailand in the 1920s.

Towers and luxury hotels now border the coastline, attracting a clientele composed primarily of European and Thai families.

Those who dream of white sandy deserted beaches will be disappointed — the narrow beach is crammed with deck chairs and parasols — but at only two and a half hours from Bangkok, Hua Hin nevertheless remains an enjoyable getaway destination.

A light-hearted carefree atmosphere reigns on the beach where swimmers, vendors, masseurs and even trotting horses come together in bonhomie. The finest part of the beach is that between the Sofitel Central Hua Hin Resort and the Marriott.

Hua Hin abounds in luxury hotels but on the 5-kilometer long Hua Hin beach, only the **Sofitel Central Hua Hin Resort** built within a 14-hectare park and imbued with a certain colonial charm, the beautiful **Anantara Resort and Spa Hua Hin** and the exclusive **Chiva-Som Luxury Health Resort** with its ultra sophisticated spa have been selected.

To the south, **Kaban Tamor Resort** is a reasonably-priced small hotel on Takiab beach. Further south stands **The Evason Hua Hin** and its appealing minimalist architecture, while the intimate **Aleenta Resort** is located on a beautiful isolated beach.

Besides proposing numerous nautical activities and several golf courses, Hua Hin presents the advantage of being well situated for visiting the blond-teak palace of **Marukathayawan** (15 kilometers) and the **Phetchaburi temples** (60 kilometers). Of

Banpu Beach, Khao Sam Roi Yot

Khao Sam Roi Yot National Park

particular interest to nature lovers, Hua Hin is the point of access to the superb national parks of **Khao Sam Roi Yot** and **Kaeng Krachan:**

KHAO SAM ROI YOT NATIONAL PARK *(65 kilometers south of Hua Hin)* The high,

sharp, gray limestone cliffs of the "park of the 300 peaks" rise up dramatically in the midst of flatlands devoted to aquaculture and marshes.

It is possible to penetrate by boat on four kilometers, through Khao Daeng's freshwater marshland and observe the numerous bird species — more than 300 listed in the park. The ideal time to visit is during the migration period between September and November.

From the visitors' center, two hiking trails have been developed: the "Horseshoe Trail," where you have a good chance of spotting macaque monkeys or langur monkeys whose beautiful eyes are circled

Hua Hin railway station

in white, and the "Mangrove Trail" inhabited by monitor lizards, crabs and birds. The adventurous can relish a firstclass view by climbing to the top of Khao Daeng (30 minutes from the visitors' center).

The beaches have retained their untamed beauty, such as the Laem Sala beach surrounded by huge cliffs. To get there from Ban Pu Beach, one must take a boat or climb an abrupt trail.

The park also comprises several caves, the most interesting of which is Tham Phraya Nakhon accessible from Laem Sala beach. A little temple bathed in a halo of light nestles romantically in the cliff's hollow.

KAENG KRACHAN NATIONAL PARK *(100 kilometers, north of Hua Hin, west of Phetchaburi)* Kaeng Krachan is an immense mountainous park, 2920 square kilometers wide, reaching 1200 meters at its highest point. To the west, it extends to the Burmese border that runs along the Tenasserim range. Strangely enough, this park, endowed with a very rich flora and fauna, does not receive many visitors, even though it has several roads suitable for vehicles and many good trails.

You can spend days discovering wonderful landscapes of high limestone cliffs encircling a dense damp jungle, waterfalls and a grassy savannah. The park has a profuse birdlife and is home

Elephant training center

to big mammals such as tigers, leopards, elephants and bears. If you want to fully enjoy the park, you should stay in one of the park's rustic bungalows, built along the artificial lake. There is a small restaurant on the spot.

Khao Sam Roi Yot Temple

Sofitel Central Hua Hin Resort

The Railways Hotel was built in 1923 on the completion of the Railway track linking Bangkok and Hua Hin. The National Railway Company, owner of an immense piece of land on the shoreline, awarded the construction to Italian architect A Rigazai. Since 1986, the French hotel group Accor runs the hotel.

The initial hotel had only 14 rooms in 1922, and over the years the "Colonial" and "Garden" wings were added to the original "Railway Wing" which itself has been expanded. The entire construction has recently been refurbished.

The expansion project was undertaken with absolute regard for the original colonial architecture and the ensemble is so harmonious that only the professional eye can distinguish between the initial, scrupulously conserved building and the recent additions.

The two- or three-story low buildings are crowned with red-tiled roofs. Their immaculate white walls, columns and exterior corridors comprising finely carved balustrades that connect the rooms, thrust you back into the 1920s. The vast and luxurious reception opens onto the gardens and is a dazzling white symphony of shining marble floors, walls and columns contrasting sharply with the dark wood of the double scrolled central staircase. The terrace area is an inviting place to unwind with an evening cocktail.

Ever since its inauguration, the hotel has basked in the renown of its spectacular fifteen-hectare garden, the most beautiful of Hua Hin, particularly the extraordinary and extravagant giant topiary gardens. Generations of gardeners have sculpted bushes in the form of birds in flight, larger-than-life elephants, rabbits and deers, in the midst of a green lawn bordered by bushes of bougainvillea and flower beds of colorful cannas. Near the original area, the garden has preserved its centennial banyan trees, its frangipanis, and flame trees.

The colonial style is featured in all the rooms, with slight variations. As such, the Garden wing is a harmony of green and white with floral fabrics accentuating a pastoral aspect, whereas the

Colonial wing is more classical, while the Railway wing's loftier ceilings and preserved antique furniture has much of the atmosphere of the bygone days.

On the ground floor of this wing is the "Museum"—a captivating circular area opening on one side onto the distant sea and onto the topiary garden on the other. On the terrace, shielded by a glass canopy, you can indulge in a cup of coffee, and soak up the atmosphere while listening to retro music. The place displays numerous pieces of antiques.

The choice of restaurants at the Sofitel Central is particularly varied, but should you be compelled to try only one, opt for the "Palm Seafood Terrace," near the sea, in a charming greenhouse that shines like a precious stone in the evenings. It is elongated by a terrace where it is nice to dine on the delectable seafood cuisine accompanied by one of the good wines featured on the menu in the gentle breezes of a winter evening.

The beach in front of the hotel is a genuine golden-sanded shore. Hawkers of deck chairs, sometimes so crammed together at Hua Hin that it is impossible to move, have been ousted to the sides, much to their chagrin but to the entire satisfaction of the clientele. Besides, each wing of the hotel has its own big swimming pool nearby.

SOFITEL CENTRAL HUA HIN RESORT

1 Damnernkasem Road,
Prachuab Khirikhan, Hua Hin, 77110
Tel 66 (0) 32 512-021 to 38
Fax 66 (0) 32 511-014
E-mail *reservation@sofitel.co.th*
sofitel@sofitel.co.th
Web *www.accorhotels.com/asia*

 1. By air and land (55 minutes)
Plane 40 minutes daily flight on Bangkok Airways to Hua Hin. *Car* 15 minutes from airport (7 kilometers).
2. By car (2 ½ hours) from Bangkok (210 km). Take the Thonburi-Paktho Road, pass Samut Songkhram, turn left onto Petchkasem highway and follow the direction of Prachuab Khirikhan.
3. By train (4 hours)
Train 4 hours from Bangkok Hua Lamphong railway station to Hua Hin railway station (10 daily departures). *Car* 5 minutes (0.5 kilometer) from railway station.
Note: *Transfer can be arranged by the resort. Many travel agencies can organize your transfer by minibus from any hotel in Bangkok to your hotel in Hua Hin.*

 207 Units
177 Superior and Deluxe rooms and 30 Suites distributed in 3 wings: 60 units in Garden Wing • 47 units in Railway Wing (the oldest) • 100 units in Colonial Wing
All rooms have private balcony, private bathroom (shower, hot water, hairdryer), air-conditioning, IDD phone, satellite TV, minibar, safety box. Only Deluxe rooms and Suites have separate bathtub and shower.

 Food and Beverage Outlets
Restaurants: Railway • Palm Seafood Pavilion (seafood fine dining) • Salathai (at the Central Hua Hin Village)
Cuisine Offered: Thai • International
Quality: Excellent cuisine and service
6 Bars
Other services: Internet • Shops • Babysitting • Kid's Club • Guest relations desk • Medical service • Car rental • 24 hours room service

 Water sports and Other Activities
3 Swimming pools with kiddie pools • Beach • Beach and water volleyball • Sea canoeing • Yacht charter
Other sports and activities
Spa • Fitness center • Tennis • Croquet • Badminton • Volleyball • Billiards • Snooker and game room • Library • Table tennis • Petanque • Darts • VTT • Putting greens • 6 Golf courses nearby (the closest one being only 500 meters away) • Elephant riding • Night market (500 meters) • Khao Sam Roi Yot (45 minutes) • Pala-U waterfall (60 kilometers)

 Per room per night

Chiva-Som Luxury Health Resort

Chiva-Som Luxury Health Resort is renowned for its gigantic, ultra-modern and sophisticated medicinal therapy and Spa center, famous as much for its architecture as for the innumerable healing therapies on offer, administered by a team of thirty therapists. It is open to non residents.

The Spa is permeated with an aura of mystery; its labyrinthic corridors made of precious materials, white and green marble and wood, lead to the different treatment rooms, and occasionally emerge, rather unpredictably, onto open-air patios and basins filled with rose petals. The hydrotherapy center in emerald tones conjures up scenes of a cavern while, adding to the strangeness of the setting, is the water source gushing from a stone globe laid down on the floor. A narrow vent leads to the circular, and surreal "floating tank" where patients float in the salt waters, conducive to absolute relaxation and rejuvenation.

Chiva-Som is also equipped with a colossal interior swimming pool for aquatic gym exercises, a fitness center in individual pavilions, a whirlpool bath designed for underwater massages, yoga and Thai massage rooms as well as beauty saloons. In order to complement your treatment with a balanced diet, a low-calorie spa cuisine is served in the green "Emerald" dining room where calories are indicated on the menu.

In addition to all this pampering, the accommodation, be it in the traditional Thai pavilions, grouped in threes along the lagoon, and sharing a relaxation sala, or in the rooms situated in the three-story buildings facing the sea, in a more classical western décor, is luxurious and well appointed. The swimming pool is located near the sea, fringed by an attractive and peaceful sandy beach.

The hallmark of the common areas at Chiva-Som is a blend of sophistication and rigor. The entrance courtyard, protected by high walls and devoid of any vegetation is virtually austere.

Note the amazing perspective of the Orchid Lounge whose vanishing point is a statue of a Hindu god nestling in a stone alcove: the entrance to the high pavilion is initially marked by a Hindu statue resting in the midst of a lotus pond, whereas behind, large jars set on invisible Plexiglas sockets float unrealistically on a second pond of turquoise waters.

In contrast with this stony rigor, mundane banyan trees, palm trees, bougainvillea and trimmed bushes intermingle in an interior garden traversed by a meandering stream spanned by small bridges.

CHIVA-SOM LUXURY HEALTH RESORT

73/4 Petchkasem Road, Hua Hin, Prachuab Khirikham 77110
Tel 66 (0) 32 536-536
Fax 66 (0) 32 511-154
E-mail *reservation@chivasom.com*
Web *www.chivasom.com*

By air and land (1 hour)
Plane 40 minutes daily flight on Bangkok Airways to Hua Hin. *Car* 20 minutes from airport.
2) By car (2 ½ hours) from Bangkok (215 kilometers). Take the Thonburi-Paktho Road, pass Samut Songkhram, turn left onto Petchkasem Highway and follow the direction of Prachuab Khirikhan.
3) By train (4 hours)
Train 4 hours from Bangkok Hua Lamphong railway station to Hua Hin railway station (10 daily departures). *Car* 10 minutes (7 kilometers) from railway station.
Note: *Transfer can be arranged by the resort. Many travel agencies can organize your transfer by minibus from any hotel in Bangkok to your hotel in Hua Hin.*

57 Units
33 Ocean View rooms
7 Suites in 3-story buildings (there is an elevator) • 17 Thai Pavilions
All rooms have private terrace or balcony, private bathroom (separate bathtub and shower, hot water, hairdryer), air-conditioning, IDD phone, satellite TV, DVD player, minibar, kettle with limes, safety box. All suites at Chiva-Som come with a private butler who offers 24-hour service to guests.

Food and Beverage Outlets
Restaurants: The Emerald room (fine dining restaurant with spa cuisine) • The Taste of Siam (seaside restaurant with vegetarian cuisine for lunch, snacks)
Bar: Piano lounge
Other services: Internet • Boutique • Limousine service • Shuttle service to Hua Hin

Water sports and Other Activities
Swimming pool • Beach • Kayaking • Pool volleyball

Other sports and activities
Spa • Holistic medical programs • Yoga and Tai Chi Pavilion • Bathing Pavilion with ozonated indoor pool • Huge indoor for aqua aerobics • Outdoor massage pavilions • Fitness services • Board games • Library • Cooking classes • Arts and crafts room • Golf can be arranged at nearby facilities
Note: *Chiva-Som provides a huge choice of consultations, heath treatments and fitness classes (consult the web site)*

No children under age 16; smoking and use of mobile phones prohibited; alcohol available after 6 p.m. only.

🐘🐘🐘🐘🐘🐘 Per room per night. 3 Spa cuisine meals, individual health consultation, one daily massage, daily fitness activity program, steam, sauna and Jacuzzi.

Anantara Resort and Spa

Standing at the end of a long tree-lined avenue, the ochre-red walls adorned with elephant frescos encircling Anantara endow it with the appearance of an ancient Thai city.

An impression of luxury and refinement exudes from the onset at the magnificent reception area open onto the gardens. The handsome ancient Thai furniture and antique objects give it an atmosphere of yesteryear. In its continuation, linked by a vast terrace that overhangs the extensive free-form swimming pool, a pavilion shelters the bar decorated with country artifacts.

The resort is composed of several clusters of pavilions in traditional architecture amidst 5.7 hectares of a remarkable landscape garden designed by Mr. Bensley.

The single-story buildings sheltering several rooms are grouped together in two distinct areas of the resort near the shore, around a lagoon.

The "Lagoon" is the more recent and original part of the hotel: the pavilions are set along a romantic lagoon meandering like a river teeming with pink and white lotus and water lilies that burst into bloom only in the mornings.

In this part of the garden, the landscape artist has paid special attention to detail: sofas make the small *salas* standing along red-graveled alleys comfortable, attractively varnished jars beautify the flower beds, stone statues adorned with hibiscus flowers materialize in unexpected places.

Distinctive Thai-styled rooms are each decorated in a different manner and the extremely lofty ceilings of the "Deluxe Lagoon villas" give them a very spacious aspect. They have wonderful terraces dominating the lagoon that you can picture while taking your breakfast, which is served there.

The other pavilions are located in a garden dotted with beautiful banyan trees. The rooms, while less spacious, are nevertheless pleasant, and decorated in traditional style. Some rooms look out onto the sea. Deck chairs are disposed on the lawn slightly overhanging the beach, but the guests apparently prefer the large swimming pool.

The Anantara Spa is extraordinary and surrealistic, evoking a painting of the Italian artist Chirico! In a world apart, at the end of the garden, it lies in a circular enclosure surrounded by high walls in red laterite or painted in ochre orange. An exterior wooden footbridge looking onto the lagoon encircles it whereas a second interior circular alley links the spa rooms. These are concealed in secret patios accessible through monumental double shuttered doors surmounted by an imposing portico framed by tall palm trees. Each room in the spa is composed of a black gravel floored patio with a shower and an air-conditioned room. Here you enter into a haven of absolute refinement and relaxation.

ANANTARA RESORT AND SPA

43/1 Phetkasem Beach Road, Prachuab Khirikhan, Hua Hin 77110
Tel 66 (0) 32 520-250
Fax 66 (0) 32 520-259
E-mail *info@anantara.com*
Web *www.anantara.com*

1. By air and land (45 minutes)
Plane 40 minutes daily flight on Bangkok Airways to Hua Hin. *Car* 5 minutes from airport (7 kilometers).
2. By car (2 ½ hours) from Bangkok (210 kilometers). Take the Thonburi-Paktho Road, pass Samut Songkhram, turn left onto Petchkasem Highway and follow the direction of Prachuab Khirikhan.
3. By train (4 hours)
Train 4 hours from Bangkok Hua Lamphong railway station to Hua Hin railway station (10 daily departures). *Car* 5 minutes (0.5 kilometer) from railway station.
Note: *Transfer can be arranged by the resort. Many travel agencies can organize your transfer by minibus from any hotel in Bangkok to your hotel in Hua Hin.*

197 Units
159 Village rooms (Deluxe Garden • Garden terrace • Sea view)
38 Lagoon rooms (Superior and Deluxe) in two-story clusters.
All rooms have private balcony or terrace, private bathroom (bathtub, hot water, hairdryer), air-conditioning, IDD phone, satellite TV, minibar, coffee/tea maker, safety box. Lagoon rooms have private terrace with private dining capacity, CD player, bathroom with separate bathtub and shower.

Food and Beverage Outlets
Restaurants: Baan Thalia • Isara café (breakfast) • Rim Nam • Sai Tong (on the beach —seafood and grill)
Cuisine Offered: Italian • Thai • International
Quality: Very good

2 Bars

Other services: Internet • Shop • Babysitting • Kid's club • Tour desk • Hotel limousine service • Shuttle bus to Hua Hin

Water sports and Other Activities
2 Swimming pools • Beach • Sailing • Canoeing • Windsurfing

Others sports and Activities
Mandara spa • Fitness center • Tennis • Table tennis • Croquet • Petanque • Darts • Board volleyball • Library • Thai cooking classes • Fruit carving • Mountain biking • Golf can be arranged at nearby facilities • Excursions to Pala-U waterfall, Sam Roi Yot (58 kilometers), Kaen Krachan, Phetchaburi.

 Per room per night

The Evason Hua Hin

Exuding character and refined beauty, Evason's originality inspires and thrills the senses. With creative flair the owners, Sonu Shivdasani and his wife, Eva, have imagined a new concept, favoring a minimalist, sometimes surreal architecture that draws attention to the innovative details. In Thailand the group also owns Evason Phuket.

The resort lies in a pleasant, peaceful countryside, with the pointed silhouettes of Khao Sam Roi Yot National Park outlined in the distance.

The ambiance is set on arrival at the unobtrusive open-air reception looking onto a large floral and wooded park. A play of shallow ponds, thoughtfully designed on various levels, evokes rice field terraces.

A long alley covered with a marquee leads to the restaurants and the sea. In the evening musicians perform on a platform in the middle of the water. The décor is ideal for intimate dining soothed by the melancholy sounds of the traditional instruments.

Accommodation ranges from standard rooms to sublime private villas. Located in single-story buildings behind the reception, the standard rooms already capture the essence of Evason, with a uniquely alluring décor in a gentle harmony of ecru and white and rustic-styled furniture in white-leaded wood. Suspended from the ceiling by a bamboo framework, the mosquito netting veils the large romantic bed swathed in white blankets. Similarly designed, though more spacious, the "Studios" are rooms located in one-story buildings on tall wooden stilts. They benefit from vast terraces equipped with comfortable deck chairs.

Special mention must be made of the very secluded and private villas. Served by a play of bridges, they are enclosed in private patios, and grouped together on an elevated wooded platform. Some have a view of the swimming pool and the ocean. The patios are their biggest attraction, boasting a swimming pool, a sala, and a sunk exterior bathtub. The bathrooms are full of nooks and corners, and include open-air showers.

In the evenings, magical abstract designs are formed along the alleys by a myriad of small metal lamps hanging from each villa's entrance.

The resort is separated from the sea by a sandy driveway that is fortunately not often used. The beach being reduced to a narrow stretch of sand, the majority of the guests prefer lolling around the immense, spectacular swimming pool facing the ocean, designed according to the same pattern of ponds cascading one into the other, with small islets arranged for the deck chairs.

In a separate pavilion, the Evason spa in tastefully elegant décor is a haven of relaxation. At the end of the park, a little world apart for "Just Kids" is endowed with a huge swimming pool, a batik workshop and a large game room. Do not miss taking a glimpse of the common restrooms where taps looking like dragonflies and toilets resting in the midst of a water-lily pond are evidence that there is decidedly nothing banal or predictable about Evason!

THE EVASON HUA HIN

9 Parknampran Beach,
Prachuab Khirikhan, 77220
Tel 66 (0) 32 632-111
Fax 66 (0) 32 632-112
E-mail rsvn@evasonhuahin.com
Web www.sixsenses.com

1. By air and land (1 ½ hours)
Plane 40 minutes daily flight on Bangkok Airways to Hua Hin. *Car* 45 minutes to Evason (37 kilometers).
2. By car (3 hours) from Bangkok to Evason (237 kilometers). After Hua Hin keep on road no. 4 direction to Pranburi, then you will see the Evason sign board. Evason is 10 kilometers away.
3. By train (4 ½ hours)
Train 4 hours from Bangkok Hua Lamphong railway station to Hua Hin railway station (10 daily departures). *Car* 30 minutes from Hua Hin to Evason (30 km).
Note: *Transfer can be arranged by the resort. Many travel agencies can organize your transfer by minibus from any hotel in Bangkok to your hotel in Hua Hin.*

185 Units
63 Evason rooms · 74 Studios · 8 Beach Front Studios in low-rise buildings · 40 Pool Villas
All rooms have private balcony or terrace, private bathroom (bathtub, hot water, hairdryer), air-conditioning, IDD phone, satellite TV, DVD player (on request in Evason rooms and Studio), minibar, coffee/tea maker, and safety box
The Beach Front Studios have separate bathtub and shower and huge terrace. Pool Villas include outdoor garden area, sala, private pool and outdoor bathtub.

Food and Beverage Outlets
Restaurants: The restaurant (breakfast, western and Thai for dinner) · The Beach restaurant · The Other restaurant (Asian fusion, only for dinner)
In room-dining available 24 hours a day.
Cuisine Offered: Western · Thai · Asian · International
Quality: Very good
Bars: The bar (snacks) · The wine cellar (wine tasting)
Other services: Internet · Shops · Babysitting · Kid's club · Shuttle service to Hua Hin · Guest relations · Medical services (resident nurse)

Water sports and Other Activities
Swimming pool · Beach · Kiddie pool · Windsurfing · Water skiing · Canoeing · Sailing · Snorkeling · Diving (available at Bangsapan about 2–3 hours drive) · Fishing
Other sports and activities
Six Sense Spa · Fitness center · Tennis court · Volleyball · Basket ball · Badminton · Golf courses (Hua Hin) · Games · Snooker · Library (CD and movies) · Cycling · Mountain biking · Evason activity program, trekking, elephant riding, Pala-U waterfall (½ day excursion), rock climbing, Khao Sam Roi Yot (25 minutes, day excursion), Kaeng Krachan (day excursion), Phetchaburi (1 ½ hour drive).

 Per room per night

Kaban Tamor Resort

Situated on the edge of the Takiab Beach, an extension of Hua Hin, this recent small resort is a good option for travelers seeking a more family atmosphere than the one usually offered by this category of hotel in Hua Hin.

Due to the narrow shape of the land, the single-story villas are aligned, side-by-side, along a winding alley, trimmed with plants and bushes, leading to the sea.

Round and white, crowned by stucco, conical-shaped roofs, the color of straw, with exterior spiral staircases, they have a pleasant look of huge seashells,

but it is in fact a Mediterranean style that inspired the Thai architect.

Numerous bay windows all around the room, the use of light colors such as white on the walls and high conical ceilings and amber for the wooden flooring render the very spacious interiors bright and cheerful. A section of wall against which the large white bed stands, delimits the space between the bedroom and the entrance. A small alcove has been created for the bureau with a television set perched precariously above, but this design mistake is in the process of being rectified.

The semi-circular bathrooms decorated with attractive, shining, turquoise blue handcrafted tiles are sizable and pleasant with interesting curved showers lit by a round window opened in the roof. Attractive petal arrangements that decorate the beds in the evenings convey a touch of thoughtfulness and attention to detail.

A new "Spa Wing," as well as a spa, were under construction when we visited. Similarly styled, but more independent, some of the villas in this new wing have a Jacuzzi fitted in the terrace. The architect's creativity has resulted in an original underground spa that evokes a cave with its stone-covered floor, irregular curved walls, a plant-filled pond and a large Jacuzzi at the foot of a waterfall.

The small restaurant located in a circular low villa, extended by a terrace sheltered by a bamboo pergola, is open onto the sea with a few tables disposed on the sea wall. A few stairs lead to the water, but the absence of an authentic beach and the close proximity to the town doesn't make the area very attractive for swimming. There is a miniature but refreshing swimming pool surrounded by a few deck chairs facing the ocean but the site is more suitable as a center from which to visit the region.

KABAN TAMOR RESORT

122/ 43-57 Takiab Road,
Prachuab Khirikhan,
Hua Hin 77310
Tel 66 (0) 32 521-011 to 3
Fax 66 (0) 32 521-014
E-mail *info@kabantamor.com*
Web *www.kabantamor.com*

1. By air and land (1 ½ hours)
Plane 40 minutes daily flight on Bangkok Airways to Hua Hin. *Car* 25 minutes from airport.
2. By car (2 ½ hours) from Bangkok (216 kilometers). Take the Thonburi-Paktho Road, pass Samut Songkhram, turn left onto Petchkasem Highway and follow the direction of Prachuab Khirikhan.
3. By train (4 hours)
Train 4 hours from Bangkok Hua Lamphong railway station to Hua Hin railway station (10 daily departures). *Car* 15 minutes from railway station.
Note: *Transfer can be arranged by the resort from Hua Hin. Many travel agencies can organize your transfer by minibus from any hotel in Bangkok to your hotel in Hua Hin.*

29 Units
Rooms are in single-story or two-story chalets (garden or sea view). There are 6 new single-story chalets in Spa wing. All rooms have private tiny balcony, private bathroom (shower, hot water), air-conditioning, IDD phone, satellite TV, minibar.

Food and Beverage Outlets
1 Restaurant and 1 bar
Quality: Average

Other services: Internet • Babysitting (on request only) • Free transfer service to Hua Hin center • Taxi rental (ask reception)

Water sports and Other Activities
Swimming pool • Beach (unattractive for swimming) • Canoeing • Water skiing • Banana boats • Speedboat

Other sports and activities
Spa with Jacuzzi

 Per room per night

Aleenta Resort

leenta is an appealing small resort facing a long stretch of sandy shore, fringed at one extreme by a steep bank. This newly opened resort is constructed in the heart of a peaceful countryside along a path where only a few houses have been built with a backdrop of forested hills. The Khao Sam Roi Yot National Park is not very far.

Brimming with ideas, the tasteful and creative owners, Anchalika Kijkanakorn and her brother, conferred the realization of their dreams with an architect, enthusiastically combining various styles. The Mediterranean facet is dominant with shining white, sometimes circular, sometimes cubic constructions, sharply contrasting with the crystal-clear blue seawaters.

In order to make optimal use of a narrow piece of land, while endowing every construction with a sea-view, the architect designed buildings on varied levels, the common areas being on the heights, accessible by stairways.

From the entrance, a staircase leads to an indoor restaurant, largely exposed to the sea breezes by generous openings, and to a large curved open-air bar. A few steps away lies a miniature semi-circular Jacuzzi swimming pool with water flowing over the edges, overhanging a drop. The panoramic view of the ocean from the deck chairs riveted in the teak terrace is breathtaking and gives you the impression of being at the helm of a boat departing for a distant shore…

The tiny spa is perched even higher up, in a turret wide-open onto the sea, with an original conical ceiling sheathed by concentric vegetal plaits.

The "Pool suites" are circular cottages with conical thatched roofs, aligned along the beach of golden sand. The spectacle of the ocean can be relished from the bedroom through a semi-circular bay window. The terrace fitted with a Jacuzzi, deck chairs and hammock temptingly invites one to blissful farniente!

The "Beach house" is an interesting cubic two-story construction culminating in a Greek-looking roof terrace. Partially shaded by a pergola, it is equipped with comfortable sofas and a refreshing outdoor shower. A great deal of time is spent here and it is an ideal place from where to watch the sunrise.

Several rooms are accommodated in a white two-story turret including a superb circular penthouse with bay windows that occupies the entire top floor.

The sober, tasteful interior décor is the result of much thought and consideration. Interiors portray walls, curtains and ecru floors in a harmony of light colors, in sharp contrast with the more somber-colored, stylish wooden Chinese furniture. The bathrooms blend white roughcast walls, wood and stone with shower cubicles covered with black stones, their large pommel knobs providing very relaxing showers. In the cottages these are in the open air.

Aleenta also proposes an independent villa, further away along the beach.

The charmingly peaceful beach along the tranquil coastline, pleasing accommodation and a nice national park at half an hour's distance that offers a break from days of gentle relaxation between the sea and the terrace, are a successful synthesis of some of the attractions effectively proposed by Aleenta.

ALEENTA RESORT

183 Moo 4, Paknampran, Pranburi, Prachuab Khirikhan 77220
Tel 66 (0) 32 570-194
Fax 66 (0) 32 570-220

Booking Office in Bangkok
Aleenta Resort, 3 Ladpraow Soi 95
Bangkok 10310
Tel/Fax 66 (0) 2 539-6761
Fax 66 (0) 2 539-6760
E-mail gm@aleenta.com
Reservations
reservations@aleenta.com
Web www.aleenta.com

 1. By air and land (1 ½ hour)
Plane 40 minutes daily flight on Bangkok Airways to Hua Hin. *Car* 50 minutes to Aleenta.
2. By car (3 ½ hours) from Bangkok (about 300 kilometers). From Hua Hin drive south towards Pranburi. In the center of Pranburi, turn left onto Ratbamrong Road (large intersection). After about 3 kilometers bear right at the fork and go straight about another 3 kilometers. You will pass a large temple, Wat Na Huai. After the temple wall ends turn right. There are signs here for Aleenta (about 7 kilometers away).
3. By train (4 ½ hours)
Train 4 hours from Bangkok Hua Lamphong railway station to Hua Hin railway station (10 daily departures). *Car* 40 minutes from Hua Hin (about 37 km).
Note: *Transfer can be arranged by the resort from Bangkok. Many travel agencies can organize your transfer by minibus from any hotel in Bangkok to your hotel in Hua Hin.*

 11 Units
3 Pool suites (on the beach) • 1 Two-story beach house (2 bedrooms) • 4 Garden suites • 1 Penthouse (in a 1 three-story pavilion) • 1 Grand villa (on the beach further on; living room, kitchen, 3 bedrooms)
All rooms have private balcony or terrace, private bathroom (shower, hot water), air-conditioning, safety box. The Pool suites have small Jacuzzi; 2 Garden suites have sunken bathtub.

 Food and Beverage Outlets
1 Restaurant and 1 bar
Cuisine Offered: Thai • International Private dining on the beach (on request)
Other services: Telephone (at restaurant) • Car rental • Scooter rental • Excursions can be organized

Water sports and Activities
Plunge pool • Beach

Other sports and activities
Spa • Excursions to Khao Som Roi Yot National Park or the Pala-U Waterfalls, golf (30 minutes)

 Per room per night

Pattaya and Koh Samet

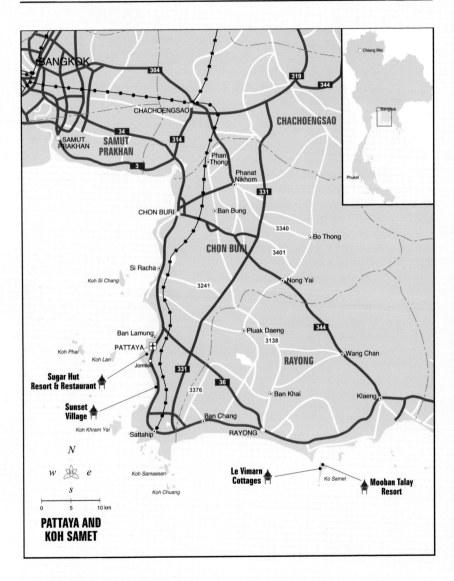

Chiang Mai

BANGKOK
304
319
344
CHACHOENGSAO
CHACHOENGSAO
Bangkok
SAMUT PRAKHAN
34
SAMUT PRAKHAN
314
3
Phan Thong
Phanat Nikhom
Phuket
331
CHON BURI
Ban Bung
3340
Bo Thong
CHON BURI
3401
Si Racha
Koh Si Chang
3241
Nong Yai
Ban Lamung
Pluak Daeng
3138
344
Koh Phai
PATTAYA
Wang Chan
Koh Lan
Jomtien
RAYONG
Sugar Hut Resort & Restaurant
331
36
Sunset Village
3376
Ban Khai
Klaeng
Koh Khram Yai
Ban Chang
Sattahip
RAYONG

N
w *e*
s
0   5   10 km

Koh Samaesan
Koh Chuang
Le Vimarn Cottages
Ko Samet
Mooban Talay Resort

PATTAYA AND KOH SAMET

Climate   Rainy season from May to October
Best season to visit the islands is between November and April

Pattaya

The seaside resort of Pattaya extends the length of three bays: the Bays of Pattaya in the center, Jomtien to the south, and Hat Nakhua to the north, the latter two being less developed.

Pattaya is a bustling, noisy and polluted city. Large contemporary buildings, towers, hotels, tourist agencies, restaurants, souvenir shops and nightclubs are aligned in an uninterrupted manner along the road and the sea shore—few hotels in fact have direct access to the beach. The Pattaya beach, jam-packed with parasols and deck chairs, is quite unattractive in its concrete environment. The thud and swish of jet skis swerving on the waves vie with the cacophony of hooting horns and screeching brakes made by passing automobiles.

Notorious for its nightlife, Pattaya nevertheless attracts millions of tourists due its proximity to Bangkok and the variety of activities it proposes: water skiing, sailing, surfboarding, parachute gliding, golf, tennis and go-karting.

To escape the madding crowd, you can take a fast-boat to the coral islets nearby: Koh Larn, Koh Sak, Koh Krok (about an hour's journey) where, however, marine traffic and pollution have taken their toll on the coral. Koh Rin, Koh Phi, Koh Man Wichai, Koh Keung Baddan and Koh Leaum have been better protected by the Royal Thai Navy and are more suitable for diving (about 1- to 2-hour journey).

All the same, even Pattaya has its "charming hotel," **Sugar Hut Resort and Restaurant,** a gem of traditional architecture secluded in a wooded park behind the Jomtien Beach. Further on, basking in a tranquil environment, is the unassuming **Sunset Village** lying directly on the edge of the shore.

Koh Samet

Half an hour away from the coast off Ban Phe, Koh Samet is a pretty little undulating forested island, 7 by 3 kilometers, that is part of the National Marine Park named after it.

The development of the tourist industry has remained limited to the East Coast, the West Coast being too rugged, with only a bumpy dirt track serving the beaches. Numerous basic, low-priced bungalows have sprung up here heedless of the surrounding environment. With the beaches and nearby constructions often strewn with litter it is better to avoid staying on the east coast.

Isolated at Noina Cape, the northern tip of the island, **Mooban Talay Resort** is the epitome of charm and serenity. In addition, the west coast harbors a golden sandy beach, facing the setting sun in the sheltered Ao Phrao Bay, or "Bay of Paradise." The most striking of the three hotels occupying the beach is **Le Vimarn Cottages.** Nearby, in a lower price range, is the **Ao Praho Resort**. From Mooban Talay, a visit to the **Khao Chamao National Park** on the mainland, or, 20 km from the latter, to the **Khao Wong National Park** can be arranged. These mountainous and wooded parks are home to elephants, gaurs and bears. The Khao Chamao Park is known for its eight-tiered waterfall, accessible by a track that runs through a magnificent forest (5 km from the park office).

To the east of Koh Samet, a dozen islets surrounded by coral reefs are suitable for diving: Koh Talu fringed by a sandy beach and the Koh Man group of islets where marine turtles can be observed.

Koh Samet

Sugar Hut Resort & Restaurant

Not far from the commotion and turmoil of Pattaya, Sugar Hut is an astounding gem not to be overlooked. The contrast with the town is striking as, once you enter the grand tree-lined alley leading to the lobby, the exterior din and clamor fade, giving way to the wind's rustling in the trees, raucous peacock calls and cicadas whirring and chirping at eventide.

In 1984, Doctor Sunya personally designed the twenty teak Ayutthaya-styled houses which he then had constructed in a large wooded park.

From the midst of a profusion of trees, only the weathered tiled stream-lined roofs of the villas on high stilts are visible. Squirrels frisk in the alleys fringed by strelitzias and cannas among which iridescent blue butterflies dance and flit.

Villas are distributed in three clusters, each of which possesses its own swimming pool and, despite their proximity to each other, intimacy is preserved thanks to the surrounding vegetation. Consequently, the vista from the spacious and delightful terraces, well equipped with teak furniture, is solely of the trees and the bluish glare of the swimming pool.

Superbly conceived, the architecture of the villas retains a spirit of days gone by, while assuring maximum comfort. Two pavilions on stilts are inter-linked by a terrace: one shelters the bedroom and the bathroom, the other somewhat smaller and accessible by a footbridge, houses a snug living room furnished with a cozy couch where you can curl up and read, watch television, or simply admire the garden through the large bay windows.

A splendid wholly-red teak room boasts floors with large boards, coffered panels, trapezoidal window-shutters and entrance doors, and a large low platform in which a soft mattress is embedded. The platform occupies nearly all the space, but the high ceiling, the beautiful terrace and the garden extension create an impression of space. It is astutely designed so as to fit in three drawers and chests on the sides.

In the evening, two bedside lamps decorated with birds and spotlights diffuse a perfect reading light. In accordance with tradition there are no panes on the windows but these are, together with the bed and the door, fitted with mosquito netting.

The spacious bathrooms have a lot of character: entirely in teak, they are lit by a small glass roof under which plants thrive. There is a large open terracotta-tiled area for the shower, and, as in days of old, a big varnished jar filled with water.

Two aquariums in the bathroom, each one home to a little warrior fish, fragrant camphor sachets, a flower placed on the pillow in the evenings, the jar at the foot of the villa to rinse down after a day on the beach are some of the little details that add a personal touch.

The Thai restaurant in a traditional pavilion is renowned for its excellent cuisine and it is advisable to book in advance. The tables are disposed either on the terrace, from the midst of which emerges a beautiful tree, or in one of the rooms on the side open onto the garden. Dine at leisure in western style or on cushions at traditional low Thai tables.

 SUGAR HUT RESORT & RESTAURANT
391/18 Moo 10, Tabphya Road, Pattaya City, Chonburi 20260
Tel 66 (0) 38 364-186
    38 251-686
Fax 66 (0) 38 251-689
E-mail sugarhut@cnet.net.th
Web www.sugar-hut.com
    www.sugarhut.co.th

 By land (2 hours)
136 kilometers from Bangkok on Highway no. 3. Sugar Hut is on the way to Jomtien Beach.

Note: *Transfer can be arranged by the resort from Bangkok. Many travel agencies can organize your transfer by minibus from any hotel in Bangkok to your hotel in Pattaya. There is another access option by train but it is not very convenient.*

 28 Units
5 Two-bedroom villas • 22 One-bedroom villas • 1 Thai House
All rooms have living room, private terrace, private bathroom (shower, hot water, hairdryer), air-conditioning, IDD phone, satellite TV, minibar, safety box.

 Food and Beverage Outlets
1 Restaurant and bar
Cuisine Offered: Thai • International
Quality: Very good Thai cuisine

Other services: Internet • Babysitting (on request)

 Water sports and Activities
3 Swimming pools with 1 sauna

Other sports and activities
Spa • Fitness center • Tennis • Golf • Excursions to the islands can be organized (ask reception)

 Per room per night

Sunset Village

Sixteen kilometers from Pattaya, the peaceful setting of the Sunset Village, a resort of simple comforts, is reassuring.

Set apart on an extensive plantation, it lies along a golden sandy beach fringed by clear blue seawaters in which swimming is sheer pleasure. Thanks to its setting in a creek, the beach is virtually exclusive. Urbanization here is less conspicuous. Coming from Jomtien, the main Sukhumvit road linking Pattaya to Rayong runs alongside a few more modern high-rise towers surrounded by farmland on hold, then a small deserted road, fringed with multi-colored bougainvillea, leads to the seashore where the hotel is situated.

A familial, carefree and unpretentious atmosphere pervades the Sunset Village resort. The owners have favored the use of natural materials such as bamboo and straw for the construction. As a result, you can feel really far from the hectic agitation of Pattaya, even if the city's high towers, looming in the distance, are perceptible from the beach.

The individual or duplex cottages are located either along the beach with the sea a stone's throw away, or grouped in the heart of the garden on a large wooden platform on stilts. With the exception of the three most pleasant "Sunrise cottages" built right against the vegetation at the back of the garden, facing a vast sprawling lawn open onto the sea, the bungalows are generally quite close to one another. The simple rooms lined with plaited bamboo possess the essential modern comforts and amenities such as air conditioning, hot water and a minibar.

The common areas are welcoming, whether at the reception or the vast rustic pavilion of the restaurant dominating the sea. It must be said that some renovations would be appreciated.

A small swimming pool has been constructed on a wooden terrace along the beach under the shade of the trees.

SUNSET VILLAGE

89/5 Soi Sunset 4, Sukhumvit Road, Najomtien, Sattahip Chonburi
Tel   66 (0) 38 237-940
                  235-377 to 9
Fax   66 (0) 38 237-941
E-mail   *cs@sunsetvillage.co.th*

Booking Office in Bangkok
61/58-59 Taweemitr Soi 8,
Rama 9 Road, Bangkok
Tel   66 (0) 2 247-6700 to 1
Fax   66 (0) 2 246-6766
Web   *www.sunsetvillage.co.th*

By land (2 hours) 162 kilometers from Bangkok on Highway no. 3 (Sukhumvit road), 16 kilometers from Pattaya, you will see on the right the signboard of Sunset Village. The resort is on Sunset Beach.

Note: *Transfer can be arranged by the resort from Bangkok. Many travel agencies can organize your transfer by minibus from any hotel in Bangkok to your hotel in Pattaya. There is another access option by train but it is not very convenient.*

50 Units
16 Rooms in 8 Duplex sunset cottages • 11 Sunset cottages Superior • 15 Sunrise cottages • 1 Twin cottage (2 bedrooms) • 7 Honeymoon suites
All rooms have private balcony, private bathroom (shower, hot water), air-conditioning, satellite TV, minibar, Honeymoon suites have bathroom with bathtub, outdoor shower and hairdryer.

Food and Beverage Outlets
1 Restaurant and bar
Cuisine Offered: Seafood • Thai • Continental

Other services: Internet • Tour desk • Limousine service

Water sports and Activities
Swimming pool • Beach • Catamaran windsurfing

Other sports and activities
Tennis • Darts • Snooker • Sauna • Golf chipping and putting green

Per room per night

Le Vimarn Cottages

usk looms over the Bay of Ao Prao and the wooded hills assume ardent bronze hues that, when mirrored in the ocean, give the swimmer the intoxicating sensation of penetrating in molten gold. While the last stragglers leave their footprints in the smooth sand, the meditative linger on, reclining in deck chairs arranged on the original individual wooden platforms in the shade of the tortuous trees aligned along the shore. Moored in the bay are boats returned from the day's diving awaiting the dawning of another day.

The serene creek is occupied by merely three hotels that take good care to maintain the area, whereas most of the beaches of the east coast, on the other side of the island, are unfortunately quite polluted and dirty.

A delightful swimming pool, surrounded by a teak terrace, slightly overhangs the seashore. It is tastefully decorated with bronze Sukhothai bells and fish sculptures. The silhouette of the encircling frangipanis is mirrored on its ceramic blue bottom while their pink and white flowers exhale a sweet fragrance at twilight.

Behind the expanse of a well-maintained lawn, small white cubic cottages on stilts lie tiered on the hill, shaded under a colorful vegetation. From their trellis-topped terraces, they enjoy views of the nearby sea or the garden. Linked by an intriguing geometrical network of wooden bridges and stairways, their painted white interiors with furniture and flooring in dark wood are soothingly sober. In contrast, the vast lobby is sophisticated: a high and long marquee supported by coconut trees with a swollen base leads from the beach to a discreet reception office. A superb floral composition and elegantly designed light rattan designer sofas adorn the area, bathed in the sunlight that streams in towards the end of the afternoon.

The restaurant, decorated in the same refined style, is separated from the reception by a pond. Dining on the teak terrace, a few steps down below, listening to the waves breaking on the sand, is a pleasant way to end the day.

A sandy trail links the three hotels that occupy the beach. On the other side of the bay, the lower priced "Ao Prao Resort" belongs to the same owner, but its architecture is somewhat heteroclite.

LE VIMARN COTTAGES

Ao Prao Beach, Koh Samet

Booking Office in Bangkok
361 Krungthonburi Road,
Klong Sarn, Bangkok 10600
Tel   66 (0) 2 438-9771 to 2
Fax   66 (0) 2 439-0352
E-mail *rsv@aopraoresort.com*
            adm@aopraoresort.com
Web   *www.aopraoresort.com*

By land and sea (3 ½ hours)
Car 3 hours from Bangkok to Ban Phe pier, opposite to Koh Samet (200 kilometers).
Boat 40 minutes from Ban Phe.

Note: *The resort organizes either the transfer by van from Bangkok or from Ban Phe to their private pier on Koh Samet. Many travel agencies can organize your transfer by minibus to the pier or you can take the public bus at Ekkamai bus station.*

18 Units
All rooms have private balcony, private bathroom (shower, hot water, hairdryer), air-conditioning, IDD telephone, TV, minibar.

Food and Beverage Outlets
1 Restaurant and bar
Cuisine Offered: Thai • International

Other services: Internet • Babysitting • Safety box at front desk • Parking in Seree Ban Phe

Water sports and Other Activities
Swimming pool • Beach • Snorkeling • Diving (in Koh Kudi, Koh Talu, Hin Khao islands with Ao Prao diving center, Tel: 66 (0) 3 864-4100 to 3; e-mail: *aopraodivers@hotmail.com*) • Canoeing • Sailing • Windsurfing • Catamaran fishing

Other sports and activities
Beach volleyball • Football • Mountain biking • Massages

 Per room per night

Mooban Talay Resort

"I dreamt about a place
The wind for sensation
The sea for passion
So I made it my refuge…"

Mooban Talay, or literally, "the Village of the Sea," is the realization of a dream sprung from the association between an architect and a sea lover. It is one of those places where a special atmosphere of serenity reigns beyond the beauty of the architecture and the environment. It is an unexpected, secluded place, at the northern tip of the island at one extremity of a pretty golden sandy beach surrounded by rocks.

Mooban Talay also tells the legend of "Pra Apai Manee," a tale of love between a prince and a mermaid, written by the poet Sunthorn Poo at the end of the 19th century. This story is depicted in a variety of details in all the rooms by way of the décor, sculptures and more abstract paintings.

The little silhouette of a statue sculpted in a tree-trunk emerges in shadow play at the entrance of the large shaded stone-paved alley, along which the low-roofed villas are raised. With a desire to evoke the impression of a traditional village, the architect accentuated geometric alignment in the design of the villas and the passages. The purity of the lines is in harmony with the elements, epitomized here by the water and the trees.

The first villas, painted in warm shades of ochre yellow, face the shore and the azure waters. Extended by beautiful terraces, they look onto a verdant lawn surrounded by frangipanis in the midst of which two massage salas lie, adding a romantic touch. Afterwards, at the foot of a forested hill behind, a second series of villas were constructed on both sides of a pond filled with water lily and papyrus. The villas are endowed with delightful terraces furnished with a collection of Thai cushions, but you can also unwind in one of the common sala pavilions built in the midst of the ponds.

Identical in dimension and design with a minimalist décor, the villas are very soothing to the eye and spirit. Minor details here and there differentiate them, such as a wooden sculpted panel or an abstract fresco above the bed sunk in a vast wooden platform. The soft lighting diffused by two wicker lamps creates a certain ambiance, but is insufficient for reading in the evening.

The bathrooms are innovative with an outdoor shower in a black-stoned patio opening onto the foliage. They are decorated with large terracotta jars filled with water in accordance with the tradition of bygone days.

Small deck chairs shaded by straw parasols lie invitingly on the sand. For exclusive use by the residents of Mooban Talay, the area is exceptionally peaceful. An enjoyable swimming pool hemmed in by a low stonewall faces the sea.

The restaurant is a tasteful, very spacious and airy pavilion, with a high structure of exposed crossbeams, open onto the ocean where an excellent Thai cuisine is served.

The resort has its own private jetty from where you can set off to explore the neighboring isles or go scuba diving (the resort possesses its own diving center). The resort also organizes excursions to the coast or to the national parks at an hour's distance away.

MOOBAN TALAY RESORT

Far end of Noina Bay,
at the top north side of Koh Samet
1/8 Moo 4 Ban Phe
Muang, Rayong 21160

Tel	66 (0) 1 838-8682
	1 923-3610
	9 896-7170
Fax	66 (0) 38 616-788
E-mail	*info@moobantalay.com*
Web	*www.moobantalay.com*

By land and sea (3 ½ hours)
Car 3 hours from Bangkok to Ban Phe pier, opposite to Koh Samet (200 kilometers)
Boat 30 minutes from Ban Phe.

Note: *The resort organizes the transfer from Ban Phe to their private pier on Koh Samet. Many travel agencies can organize your transfer by minibus or you can take the public bus at Ekkamai bus station.*

24 Units
5 Beach front villas • 8 Sea view villas • 11 Pond Garden villas
All rooms have private balcony, private bathroom (shower, hot water, hairdryer), air-conditioning, and minibar.

Food and Beverage Outlets
1 Restaurant and 1 bar
Cuisine Offered: Asian • Western
Quality: Good

Other services: Telephone (reception) • Small gift shop • Island taxi service • Motorcycle rental

Water sports and Other Activities
Swimming pool • Beach • Snorkeling and diving (in Koh Kudi, Koh Talu, Hin Khao islands with Ocean Plus Sports Diving Center) • Sea canoeing • Jet skiing • Water skiing • Wakeboarding

Other sports and activities
Massages • Excursions to Khao Chamao and Khao Wong national parks (on the mainland)

 Per room per night

The Central Plains

Sukhothai Temple   *Painting by Lily Yousry-Jouve*

The Central Plains

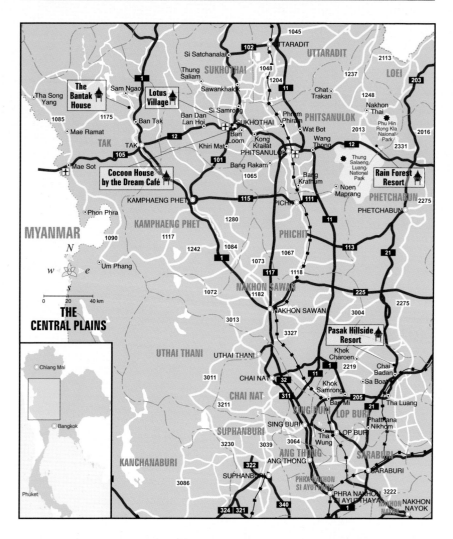

    Climate   Two pronounced seasons: hot-dry from March to May; rainy from June to October; rain is not daily and is in short spells; cool season from November to February

Loy Krathong and Candle Festival: On the full moon day of the 12th lunar month (usually in November)—In Sukhothai, this celebration takes place in the famous historical park. There are a Krathong competition, a beauty contest in Thai traditional costumes, and a Thai carnival.

The Central Plains

The Central Plains host some of the country's most precious treasures: rice fields and fabulous archaeological sites along this 'Ancient Cities Road' to the North.

AYUTTHAYA *(1½ hour; 85 kilometers from Bangkok)* If your visit to Thailand is limited to a few days in Bangkok, the ancient capital city of Ayutthaya is a major "must-see" archaeological site. Laying in the middle of large parks, it is criss-crossed by canals—some may be visited by boat. The site is on the UNESCO World Heritage List. Although the site is reachable by train or by bus, there is a much more adventurous and romantic alternative journey: by boat up the Chao Phraya River, possibly aboard the **Mekhala** for an overnight stay.

A visit to Ayutthaya is not only the discovery of what used to be one of the most magnificent capitals of Siam but also a powerful teaching about impermanence. What used to be a huge and majestic city for four centuries, encircled by 12 kilometers of fortified walls, with many palaces and more than 400 splendid temples admired by all western visitors, was savagely destroyed by the Burmese in 1767.

Only ruins and headless Buddha images remain of the shining glory of a kingdom. A touching representation of this gone-by time is an ever-smiling Buddha head woven into the roots of a tree, near a complex of souvenirs' and cold drinks' vendors!

Although many *wats* have been restored with an extensive use of concrete, a day spent around Ayutthaya's relics feels very much like a walk along the quiet alleys of a gone earthly paradise.

The complete list of temples would be too long to go through and besides, the spell of Ayutthaya is not dependent on the visit of one specific temple. The archeological site should rather be explored and felt as a whole, each ruin or Buddha image relic bringing one element to the

Sukhothai Historical Park

Sukhothai Historical Park

bigger picture of this tragic ancient city. **Wat Yai Chai Mongkol** is one of the most interesting temples, with one of the highest *chedis* in Ayutthaya. It is surrounded by a series of Buddha stone statues, puzzlingly smiling at eternity. **Wat Phra Ram** is a fine example of the Ayutthaya style. A stone *prang* on an elevated base flanked by four smaller *chedis* topped by high spires. **Wat Sri Samphet** was the most imposing architectural grouping of Ayutthaya with the alignment of its three tall well-preserved *chedis* giving some idea of its proportions. **Wat Raj Burana** is dominated by a well conserved *prang*. Lion statues surrounded by overgrowing vegetation grant **Wat Thammikarat** a charming atmosphere.

LOPBURI *(80 kilometers north of Ayutthaya)* The city of Lopburi, where both Khmer and later King Narai's buildings remains can be seen. Although the modern city not only lacks pleasant accommodation options but also mere interest, except for the huge population of wild monkeys to be found literally everywhere, the ancient city is nevertheless worth a day or two-visit.

Although the Khmer relics scattered around Lopburi cannot stand the comparison with the Khmer archaeological sites in Isaan, their location in the middle of a busy small city makes them an unusual setting. The most attractive spot in Lopburi,

though, is **King Narai's palace**, influenced by both Khmer and European architectural standards. The palace sits inside the old city, protected by a massive surrounding wall. Within a magnificent and charming park, the ancient palace's ruins unfold in a very romantic manner. The **Lopburi National Museum** is also located here and displays, in a simple way, an amazingly rich collection of Khmer, Lopburi and Dvaravati statues.

Staying at the **Pasak Hillside Resort**, outside the city, is an option for enjoying the comfort of homey bungalows within a nature retreat, in the vicinity of some interesting historical spots.

PHITSANULOK *(377 kilometers north of Bangkok)* The city of Phitsanulok stands halfway between Bangkok and Chiang Mai. Although it was a capital city as well and despite its lovely floating houses on the Nan River, the city is not particularly attractive today.

A huge fire burned most of the city in 1959 and the atmosphere is rather busy and noisy. Phitsanulok is nevertheless home to one of the most revered temples of Thailand: **Wat Phra Si Ratana Mahathat** (or Wat Yai). Its Buddha image's standards, with flame-shaped *mandorla*, are a model for contemporary representations of the Buddha.

Phitsanulok is located in the vicinity of two beautiful national parks: **Thung Salaeng Luang** and **Phu Hin Rong Kla**, where trekking adventures are very attractive and, as far as Phu Hin Rong Kla is concerned, offer historical interest.

This mountainous region, close to the Lao border and China, was used in the 1970s as the strategic base-camp for the People's Liberation Army of Thailand. The **Rain Forest Resort** is located right at the junction of these two parks, along the river.

SUKHOTHAI *(470 kilometers North of Bangkok)* The gem of the kingdom shines

Sukhothai Historical Park

in Sukhothai. The city, named 'Dawn of Happiness' in Pali, symbolizes the birth of Thailand as a unified kingdom. It also radiates as the cultural center of the country.

As such, the Sukhothai Historical Park is an absolute must-see archaeological site which certainly requires more than a day-visit, especially for those who want to explore areas outside the official boundaries of the historical park.

The park can be explored by different means: on foot, by bike, or by *samlors* (motorcycle with front-seating benches). Early morning, when sunrise lights on the Buddha statues' smiling faces and late afternoon are the best times of the day to appreciate the breathtaking beauty of the temples, palaces and the Buddha images.

The best time of the year to witness the full splendor of Sukhothai is at the time of Loy Krathong festival, when people come around the temples' ponds to float their offerings—made of banana-leaf woven baskets holding a flower, a coin, incense and a small lit candle—to the water goddess.

A number of monuments should absolutely not be missed when visiting the historical park. Among them are the majestic and vast **Wat Mahathat** complex with its center *chedi* surrounded by an incredible number of smaller *chedis* and two huge standing Buddha statues encapsulated inside high walls; the lovely **Wat Sra Si** hosting a seated Buddha image in the middle of a quiet pond. Outside the Park, **Wat Si Chum** hosts a famous and gigantic seated Buddha. This is one of the most impressive monuments of Sukhothai. Accommodation at the **Lotus Village** or at the new-arriving **Cocoon by the Dream Café** is located in the new city of Sukhothai, only 12 kilometers from Sukhothai Historical Park. Both are very helpful in arranging visits to the parks.

SI SATCHANALAI *(524 kilometers from Bangkok; 1 hour drive away from Sukhothai)* The more isolated site of Si Satchanalai is set amidst tobacco fields. Many transport options are available in Sukhothai to visit Si Satchanalai: taxi, guided tours. The simplest way is to ask your hotel or guest house to arrange it for you.

Although this site undoubtedly offers relics of lesser importance than the wonders of Sukhothai, it is worth a visit for strolling about the *chedis* scattered along the Yom river, all the way up to the hills covered with wild vegetation.

Sukhothai Historical Park

Pasak Hillside Resort

The land around Lopburi is very flat, and so for many miles. Yet, an unexpected rock mass comes into view about five kilometers after the Lumnarai junction: two spectacular high peaks linked by a smooth U-shaped curve, like on a child's drawing. They are named the Lom Fung. At the foot of this double-headed hill, rather unexpectedly too, a peaceful small-sized resort welcomes nature friends for a quiet weekend retreat only a few hours' drive from Bangkok.

The Pasak Hillside Resort is an unusual resort. It belongs to the Betagro Group, an agriculture and industrial firm. Amongst its numerous activities, Betagro undertook in 1996 a reforestation development in the area located above the Pasak River basin in Lopburi province. To help this land become in 15

years' time a vast green and fertile teak forest, specific technology was imported from Israel. Within this 2,300-rai property, Betagro has set aside an area for the development of a 'natural' resort aimed primarily at accommodating the owners of the reforested land visiting their growing forest, but also nature lovers coming from the big city of Bangkok, to breath some fresh air under a clean and clear sky.

The setting of the Pasak Hillside Resort is unpretentious, but yet nicely designed and equipped. A large lobby and dining area welcome guests under a lofty ceiling, widely open onto the entrance garden and, on the opposite side, onto the flowering garden gently flowing towards the bungalows facing the vast artificial lake. The main building is topped with a high wooden tower.

This is the shelter of the observatory from where guests enjoy star-gazing when darkness closes in upon the resort.

The wooden bungalows, although quite close to each other, provide a homey environment for resting amidst wonderfully maintained and trimmed garden alleys. They are all elegantly decorated, in western mountain style: a small verandah overlooking the nature, and, inside, walls with wood panels painted with warm colors, rustic and cozy furniture, nice cotton fabrics for bed covers and curtains. Bathrooms are quite attractive with some beautiful stone paneling on the walls. They are also well equipped with hot shower and natural light diffused by ceiling light wells.

Four forest villas are located right in the middle of the teak forest, in total isolation. Guests going for this very close-to-nature option can be driven back and forth by the resort's van anytime.

The Pasak Hillside Resort is a fair accommodation to use as a base from where to visit Lopburi, accessible by a 15 minute-drive only, as well as other natural attractions like the Srithep historical park and the Wang Kan Lueng waterfall. Be aware, though, that before the karaoke room is built to entertain guests in the evening, this place is only good for nature lovers looking for silence and peace!

PASAK HILLSIDE RESORT

11, Moo 1, Nikom Lumnarai, Chaibadarn, Lopburi 15130
Tel 66 (0) 1 946-4756
854-6346
947-7500

Booking Office in Bangkok
Pasak Hillside Co. Ltd.,
Betagro Tower (North Park),
323 Vibhavadi, Rangsit Road,
Laksi, Bangkok 10210
Tel 66 (0) 2 955-0555 ext. 2511
Fax 66 (0) 2 955-0303
E-mail phlb@betagro.com
ruethaiv@betagro.com
Web www.betagro.com

 By land
1. By car (2 hours) The resort is located 190 kilometers from Bangkok. Drive on the Bangkok–Saraburi Highway all the way up to Saraburi. Then take the Saraburi-Petchaboon to Chaibadan District. After Lumnarai junction, the resort is situated 5 kilometers after passing Chaibadan.
2. By train (3 hours) From Hualamphong railway station in Bangkok, trains cover the 150 kilometers to Lopburi in approximately 2 hours 40 minutes. Also available, 1 hour-journey trains coming from Ayutthaya. *Car* 15-minute drive to the resort

Note: *If requested in advance, the resort will arrange for pick-up at Lopburi railway station or bus station (free of charge). The journey by bus from North and Northeastern bus terminals in Bangkok, to Lopburi takes 3 hours.*

 20 Units
4 Forest homes (located in the middle of the teak forest) •
4 Lakeside villas (with largest sized rooms) •
12 Bungalows (in the garden)
All units have private small terrace, bathroom (hot shower), air-conditioning, cable TV, and minibar.

 Food and Beverage Outlets
One large sheltered terrace restaurant
Cuisine Offered: Thai
Quality: Good

Water sports and Activities
Mountain biking • Canoeing on the artificial lake • Birdwatching
More unusual activities are camping near the lake, very popular with the young ones, and stargazing from the observatory.

 Per room per night inclusive of breakfast

Rain Forest Resort

Nature lovers will be totally taken in by the tranquil atmosphere of this remote and folk resort, located a 45-minute drive away from the city of Phitsanulok, right on the border of the two national parks of Thung Salaeng Nuang and Phu Hin Rong Kla. From the roadside, one can hardly imagine what hides behind the sheltered entrance hall that welcomes guests with a stunningly huge earthenware jar displaying an armful of tropical flowers. In fact, every step forward will take you deeper and deeper into another world, where nature is the main guest.

The resort's site unfolds in rather steep manner from the road level down to a bubbling river dotted with massive polished rocks. Yet the downhill slope is virtually unseen, as an incredibly wild and dense rain forest invades the hilly ground. Fluorescent leaves, striped palms, thick bushes, exotic flowers, clusters of bamboo, tufts of grass, fine lianas weeping from rain trees, and so much more foliage literally fill in the whole space with every existing shade of green color, transforming the way to your cottage into quite an amusing jungle expedition, among giant butterflies. Down by the river, in a refreshing and totally unwinding atmosphere, a set of Robinson Crusoe-type bamboo platforms under plain dry palm leaves' roofs make a wonderful observation deck for discovering local life on the river. They can also become a very special and wild dining room for those who want to savor a private meal served on the low tables, while reclining on throw cushions.

The cottages, built on piles with local material exclusively, to harmoniously blend into the environment, are indeed screened with lush vegetation. As one walks down the narrow serpentine path to reach them, they seem to spring from the jungle only when being closely approached.

Depending on their target capacity—up to seven people!— they offer vast to extremely commodious living area as well as individually arranged settings.

Still, all of them exude the same authentic yet tasteful, homelike yet original atmosphere. A pleasant small veranda with rustic wood furniture invites guests into their own room. Inside, both the architecture and decoration use very simple and natural elements, as if the inside world was to reflect the outside one. White walls are partially covered with dark and shiny stones also used for tiling the floors, solid wooden beams support high ceilings, and thick natural cottons cover the large beds. A vase displaying wild flowers stands on the crude dressing table and some framed unassuming watercolors hang on the wall. Bathrooms are particularly attractive, with light wells open through the roof that suffuse sun beams onto the dark and polished stones of the open shower and the wild palm growing at its side. Some bathrooms are a strong manifest of the commitment to respect the environment which characterizes the Rain Forest Resort, as they sometime include a massive rock out of the ground, which has remained untouched to become part of this ecology-type decoration.

The restaurant is located on the upper part of the resort, beside the entrance hall, the tiny gift shop, and small reception desk. Set on a number of different and uneven wooden platforms, if offers a friendly and casual ambiance, folk decoration with wooden chairs and heavy stone table tops, a veranda overlooking the luxurious garden, delicious homemade Thai, Chinese and Western food, and excellent locally-grown coffee. It is indeed an inviting spot to enjoy simple but savory meals during your stay in this peaceful resort celebrating the charms of nature, in a very friendly manner.

RAIN FOREST RESORT

42 M.9 Kangsopa, Wangthong, Phitsanulok 65220
Tel   66 (0) 55 293-085 to 6
Fax   66 (0) 55 293-086
E-mail   rnforest@loxinfo.co.th
Web   www.rainforestthailand.com

1. By air and land (2 ½ hours)
Plane 45 minutes flight from Bangkok to Phitsanulok airport (3 daily flights) with Thai Airways. The airport is 15 minutes by car from city center. ***Car*** (1 hour) See ahead.
2. By land (about 8 hours) ***Train*** (5 to 6 hours) over 489 kilometers from Bangkok Hua Lamphong railway station to Phitsanulok. ***Car*** (1 hour) The resort is located 45 kilometers East of Phitsanulok, toward Lom Sak and Petchaboon, 29 kilometers ahead of Wangthong, and 300 meters before the Kangsong waterfall.
Note: *Transfer by Rainforest private van can be arranged with pick-up at airport, bus or railway station.*

16 Units
10 Standard cottages (for 2 people) • 2 Cottages (for 4 people) • 1 Cottage (for accommodating a group or family up to 7 people) • 2 VIP cottages (for 2 people) • 1 VIP cottage (with 2 bedrooms, for 4 to 6 people; it is larger, better decorated, and equipped with minibar).
All units have a small private veranda, private bathroom (hot shower), air-conditioning, and TV.

Food and Beverage Outlets
1 Restaurant
Cuisine Offered: Thai • Chinese • Western
Quality: Very good

Other services: Organization of excursions on request.

Water sports and Activities
Trekking can be arranged within the two nearing national parks of Thung Salaeng Nuang and Phu Hin Rong Kla • Rafting at Kangsong and Kangsopa waterfalls (between June and November) • Biking • Visit of historical parks

Per room per night

Lotus Village

A visit to Sukhothai may be pretty exhausting, as the discovery and contemplation of the extraordinary monuments scattered inside the historic park and its surroundings require hours of cycling, walking and even hiking. Most of the time in tropical temperatures. Hence, a relaxing place to sit back is key to a beneficial stay in this UNESCO world culture and heritage city. The Lotus Village, a charming family guest house surrounded by a refreshing garden is a recommended choice to take advantage of the two Sukhothai's: the new town and the archaeological one, only 12 kilometers apart.

Sukhothai native Tan and her French husband Michel Hermann opened a pleasant and unpretentious guest house back in 1996, in Tan's old family house facing the tranquil waters of the Mae Nam Yom. Along the vast garden adorned with lawn, flowery bushes and an old mango tree shadow-ing the fish and lotus pond, they first built small bungalows in the very traditional way: teak structures built on piles with a verandah. Although the bungalows are quite close to each other, the rattan armchair and reading table on each house's roofed terrace create this relaxing and homey feeling which makes travellers cheerful and fit for ongoing adventures. Bedrooms are cozy and easy, decorated in full countryside Thai style: hand-sewn colorful bed covers, Thai triangular cushions, wood and bamboo furniture on polished teak floors...

Two new two-story mansions have recently been added, facing the fish and lotus pond. Rooms are much more spacious here and offer quite a different atmosphere depending on their location. Rooms on the second floor are the most pleasant ones, with large bamboo beds on varnished teak floors, whereas rooms with direct access to the garden are more common, with tiled floors and functional furniture to resist potential water damage during the rainy season. Bathrooms are only functional, with no specific attention to decor.

A set of larger traditional houses, at the other end of the garden with direct access to the street, can welcome lower budget families or groups of friends, up to six per house.

The warm-hearted and friendly ambiance of the Lotus Village thrives around the 'lobby' and the covered terrace where Tan and Michel have created a really cozy environment to treat their guests. Decorated with unassuming Thai and Burmese antique furniture, the lobby-reception-and-sitting room area is an inviting spot to relax while browsing the fine collection of books on Asian art and culture, magazines and newspapers on display. Nothing has been forgotten, even a windowed-cabinet serving as a pocket-size gift shop for a selection of ceramic items and daily board-posting of local air temperature and humidity!

Breakfasts are served on the adjoining covered terrace with a sense of refinement rarely to be seen in any guest house, anywhere. The tropical garden around this area has been totally redesigned and cooled off with a few tiny pools of running water. Teak cutlery and lotus-shape-folded linen napkins are the everyday setting for serving freshly squeezed orange juice, the best coffee in the whole region—made with an imported Italian coffee maker—a tasteful homemade mango marmalade; and, as an auspicious sign for welcoming the day, a thousand smiles from the friendly and caring staff.

To complete the guest-devoted attraction of the Lotus Village, Michel is a talkative and knowledgeable host who will try his best to help you by organizing a customized tour around Sukhothai aboard the guest house's minivan.

LOTUS VILLAGE

170, Ratchathanee Street, Sukhothai 6400
Tel   66 (0) 55 621-484
Fax   66 (0) 55 621-463
E-mail   mail@lotus-village.com
Web   www.lotus-village.com

 1. By air and land (1 hour and 45 minutes) *Plane* 50 minutes flight from Bangkok to Sukhothai by Bangkok Airways (1 daily flight). *Car* 31 kilometers from the airport to Lotus Village. Transfer by Bangkok Airways shuttle bus-to-bus station (27 kilometers). Shuttle or tuk-tuk from bus station (4 kilometers).

2. By car (about 6 hours) Sukhothai is located 440 kilometers from Bangkok. Take the superhighway no. 1, then Kamphaeng Phet, and turn to 101 to Sukhothai. Lotus Village is at the new town.

Note: *You may also travel by train to Phitsanulok and then take a local bus to Sukhothai, some 50 kilometers away. Transfer can be arranged by the resort from airport or railway station.*

 29 Units
5 Standard *old bungalow* rooms (with fan, private bathroom and veranda—good for 2) • 10 Superior *new mansion* rooms (with fan or air-conditioning, and private bathroom—good for 3) • 13 Rooms (with double bed, fan, and 1 bathroom shared between 4 people) • 1 Family house (with 5 beds)

 Food and Beverage Outlets
Breakfasts and drinks only
Quality: Very good

Other services: Telephone and Internet access available at reception.

 Water sports and Activities
A vast choice of excursions to close by cultural sites and museums can be arranged with the help of Michel and Tan.

 Per room per night inclusive of breakfast

Cocoon House by the Dream Café

Cocoon House is the name given by enchantress Chaba Suwatmaykin to a handful of charming yet rather monastic small rooms. They have been in use for quite some time in the shadow of Chaba's terribly charming Dream Café. But our attention was caught by the raising of a few amazing new bungalows, still in development at the time of writing. Considering the magic and perfect talent of Chaba in creating feel-good atmospheres, the future Cocoon House will, no doubt, be one of the best places to stay in Sukhothai, very soon.

The Dream Café, located right in the center of the new city of Sukhothai, is a restaurant widely recommended to visitors. Within a homely interior atmosphere enhanced by a mesmerizing exhibition of curios mixed with some really precious antiques—fabulous owner's private collection of ancient ethnic fabrics—it is an unequalled place in town to savor a meal after a day amidst the old temples of the historic park. From home-owned Thai recipes, or Chinese and European delicacies, every dish is exquisitely cooked by a talented Burmese cook and served by a caring staff. Unusual herbal 'energy' cocktails—for stimulating male and female sensuality—should not be missed here as they perfectly match this captivating, quaint, and easy place filled with softly diffused opera and jazz tunes.

In the backyard, a narrow garden alley leads to a small wooden house. This offers a very rustic but wonderfully charming shelter to five small and simple rooms. Although the owner's intention is no other than to simply accommodate a few low to mid-budget travelers, the rooms provide more than basic lodging. All equipped with electric fans and hot showers, the five rooms have an appeal which comes from the ambiance rather than the bare comfort of the extremely simple amenities. Thanks to an attention to detail and the perfect style of the owner, each room is decorated with tastefully selected native handicraft and antiques. This makes the difference. At night, the soft lighting of this quite rough house and the incense-scented silence of the untamed backyard makes this place an intimate and peaceful—as well indeed as good value-for-money—place to sojourn.

Soon the backyard will host a totally different world. We were lucky enough to see art lover and Sangkhalok Museum curator Chaba at architectural work during our last stay in Sukhothai. Although it is too early to assess any achievement yet, we bet the new Cocoon House will come out of the ground as a blooming serene haven, fully inspired by Sukhothai culture: A hidden nature kernel at the heart of the city with herb garden and running water arranged in the authentic traditional Thai way — or better said in the authentic creative Chaba' way—six uniquely designed bungalows, maybe an unostentatious spa, and other discoveries for some voluptuous relaxation environment invented and designed by this Lady of grace and hospitality. So, watch out for new Cocoon House, soon!

COCOON HOUSE BY THE DREAM CAFÉ

86/1 Singhawat Road,
Sukhothai 64000
Tel   66 (0) 55 612-081
Mobile 66 (0) 1 532-3998
Fax   66 (0) 55 622-157
E-mail *chaba_s@hotmail.com*

1.By air and land (1 hour and 45 minutes) *Plane* 50 minutes flight from Bangkok to Sukhothai by Bangkok Airways (1 daily flight). *Car* 27 kilometers from the airport to Sukhothai.
2. By Car (about 6 hours) Sukhothai is located 440 kilometers from Bangkok. Take highway number 1 through Nakhon Sawan and Kamphaeng Phet.

Note: *You may also travel by train to Phitsanulok and then take a local bus to Sukhothai, some 50 kilometers away. Transfer from and to the airport by Bangkok Airways shuttle bus or tuk-tuk from bus station (4 kilometers).*

5 Units
5 Rooms (private bathroom—hot shower—fan, and mosquito net on windows)
Soon available: 6 Thai-style cottages (with private bathroom—hot shower—fan or air-conditioning).

Note: *No telephone in the rooms but available through the Dream Café.*

Food and Beverage Outlets
Meals at neighboring Dream Café, under same management
Cuisine Offered: Thai • Chinese • European
Quality: Excellent food and friendly service

Water sports and Activities
Sukhothai Archaeological Park or Sawankhalok Museum visits can be arranged by Chaba on individual request. Thai cooking school can also be arranged on request.

Per room per night not inclusive of breakfast

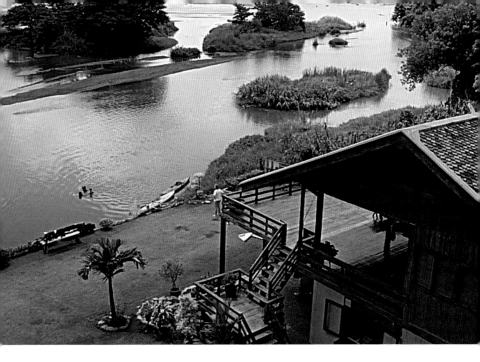

The Bantak House

The Bantak House stands out as a uniquely small, secluded, private and charmingly local place to enjoy the serenity and natural beauty of northwestern Thailand's Tak province.

Owned and operated by dynamic Danish husband-and-Thai wife team of Nong and Michael Schulz, this two-story teak wood home-cum-hotel is a labor of love that rapidly became a favorite getaway destination for their Bangkok-bound expatriate friends. They only threw the heavy teak wood gates of this spectacular Riverfront property open to the outside world three years ago, after much prompting from overseas associates looking to book private vacations off the over-beaten tourist track.

The traditional Thai-style house is not the victim of an over-indulgent interior designer, but is rather a living space that is instantly comfortable and familiar. Located on the wide and rather shallow Ping River, The Bantak House is located 25 kilometers downstream from the Bhumibol Dam, ensuring a steadily regulated flow of clean water. The dam and the surrounding mountains offer spectacular views, manicured parkland, and one of the most naturally scenic golf courses in Thailand (*www.tga.or.th*).

Despite being located on the water, there are no mosquito problems, and many guests are quite content to sleep out on the giant deck under the stars in the cool night air.

Tak can be fairly cool during the winter season, so the day usually begins with a hearty breakfast being served in the small, cozy dining room. As an option, there is nothing quite like enjoying a hot mug of fresh brewed Danish coffee as you sit by the river watching the rising sun cut through the morning mist as it rises off the water.

During the day, there are numerous opportunities for outdoor activity, such as cycling, kayaking or golfing. The

Burmese border is a two-hour drive away through the spectacular hills that provide excellent white water rafting opportunities, and a number of adventure tours or day trips can be arranged, for instance to the old capital of Sukhothai, easily done in an afternoon from the house.

The views over the steadily-moving water are spectacular and extremely soothing, particularly in the evening from the enormous outdoor balcony located on the upper deck. The friendly staff are as adept at mixing a superb gin and tonic as they are at preparing a wonderful range of grilled steaks, fish, or traditional Thai dishes in the kitchen and barbecue area below the deck. Service, like the overall ambiance, is informal but efficient and you are made to feel more like a long-lost member of the family than an out-of-towner.

After dinner, you can relax in the comfort of the upstairs living room, listen to music or relax in front of the television, where cable service brings in news, movies, music and sports from around the world. Another option may be to make the 20-minute drive into the city of Tak, where there is a vibrant, but limited nightlife.

If you are a 5-star junkie, this is not the place for you. However, if you want to enjoy a quiet, relaxing, laid back vacation where you can enjoy the rustic charms and spectacular setting of rural Thailand, there is probably no better place to be.

(With the kind contribution of Leslie Walsh)

THE BANTAK HOUSE

128 Moo 9, Tambon Koh Tapau,
Amphoe Bantak 63120

Booking Office in Bangkok
The Arrivals Company 6, Soi 6,
Laemthong 2, Pattanakarn Road,
Pravet, Bangkok 10250
Tel   66 (0) 2 319-0396 to 7
Fax   66 (0) 2 719-4173 to 4
E-mail *michaels@kscl5th.com*
Web   *www.bantakhouse.com*
Owner Michel Schultz or
            contact Asian Sky:
E-mail *msbkk@ksc.th.com*
Web
www.britishacorn.com/tourism

 1. By air and land (2 ½ hours)
Plane 45 minutes flight on Thai Airways to Phitsanulok (3 daily flights). **Car** 1 hour (100 kilometers) from Sukhothai airport; 1 ½ hours (150 kilometers) from Phitsanulok airport to Bantak House.
2. By land (6 hours)   **Car** About 6 hours (450 kilometers) drive north of Bangkok.
Note: *Transfer from airport can be arranged by the resort.*

 Private house
Lower level (living room area, dining room, kitchen, 2 bedrooms, 2 bathrooms, an office/guestroom, covered patio) • Upper level (1 master bedroom with private bathroom, satellite TV and stereo room, and huge deck partly covered)
The 3 bedrooms are with air-conditioning and all bathrooms have hot water.

 Food and Beverage Outlets
Cuisine Offered: Thai • Western
Quality: Familial
Other services: Babysitting (on request) • Tours • Small library

Water sports and Activities
2 Kayaks (free) • Mountain bikes and kids bikes (free) • 18-hole golf course (25 km, sets of golf clubs are provided) • Visit to Sukhothai (day trip), visit to Bhummiphol dam (25 km), visit to Maesot and Burmese border (day trip); Umphang (Thee Lor Sue falls) (5 to 6 hours to reach Umphang)
Note: *Tours with 4-wheel drive vehicle and English-speaking escort.*

 Per room per night on full board basis; minimum of 3 nights—cash only.

The East

Phimai Temple

Painting by Lily Yousry-Jouve

The East

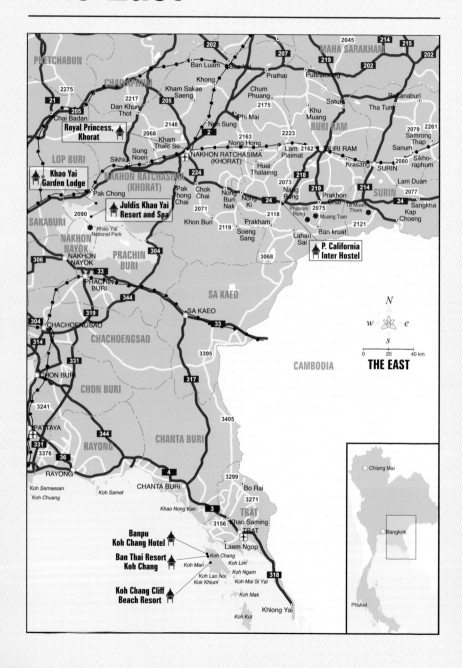

Ta Muan Thom

Khao Yai

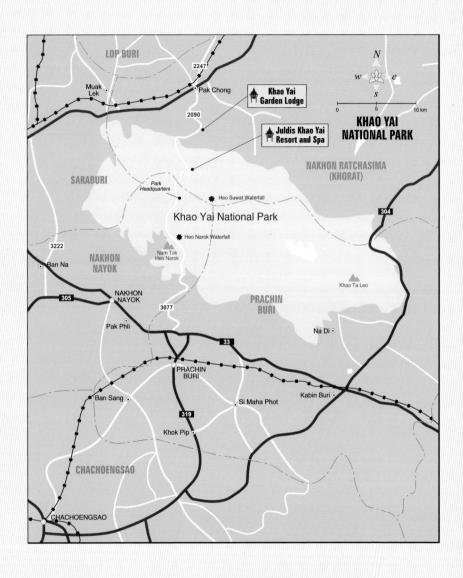

Map labels:

LOP BURI

2247

Muak Lek

Pak Chong

2090

Khao Yai Garden Lodge

Juldis Khao Yai Resort and Spa

KHAO YAI NATIONAL PARK

N / W — E / S

0   5   10 km

SARABURI

NAKHON RATCHASIMA (KHORAT)

Park Headquarters

Heo Suwat Waterfall

Khao Yai National Park

304

Heo Narok Waterfall

3222

Ban Na

NAKHON NAYOK

Nam Tok Heo Narok

Khao Ta Leo

NAKHON NAYOK

3077

PRACHIN BURI

305

Pak Phli

Na Di

33

PRACHIN BURI

Ban Sang

Si Maha Phot

Kabin Buri

319

Khok Pip

CHACHOENGSAO

CHACHOENGSAO

Climate **Khao Yai:** Rainy season from May to October, heavy rains and leeches on the hiking trails;
Cold season from November to February (night temperatures fall to 10° C.); hot season from March to April.

Khao Yai National Park

Khao Yai National Park has an area of 2,168 square kilometers and is listed as a UNESCO World Heritage Site. This mountainous region, culminating at 1,400 meters, comprises several different types of forests and is one of the largest Asian tropical rainforests at this altitude. You are plunged into a world of leaping waterfalls and forests bursting with macaques, gibbons, sambar deers, elephants, bears, gaurs, panthers and tigers. There are great numbers of birds and more than five species of hornbills.

The visitors' center, about 20 kilometers from the entrance to the park, will give you a very schematic map of the 50 kilometers of existing trails. If you wish to hike into the interior of the park, either for a few hours or for a few days, a guide is very strongly recommended because the paths frequently disappear. **Khao Yai Garden Lodge** can organize treks around your particular centers of interest—flora, fauna, birds, butterflies…and the resort can provide you with an English-speaking guide.

In the interior of the park are several beautiful waterfalls and observation towers, where you can watch the sambar deers, accessible without a guide. The **Hew Na Rok Waterfall** is the most spectacular, about 20 kilometers by car to the south of the visitors' center. From the parking lot, you have to walk about 1 kilometer and go

Hew Na Rock waterfall, Khao Yai

down some rather steep wooden steps to reach a platform beneath the first level of the waterfall. Here, the water sheet tumbling down through jungle clad gorges is superb! A second waterfall, the **Hew Su Wat Waterfall**, about 10 kilometers east of the visitors' center, is equally popular.

You can stay at the pleasant **Juldis Khao Yai Resort and Spa**, 5 kilometers from the park entrance, or at the lively **Khao Yai Garden Lodge**, 15 kilometers from the entrance. The two hotels are located on the access road to the park.

Khao Yai National Park

Juldis Khao Yai Resort and Spa

The Juldis Resort and Spa is situated between two jungle-covered hills, five kilometers from the Khao Yai National Park and in beautiful gardens which make it quite attractive. The hotel is popular for Thai weekend seminars and is the best choice amongst the enormous and currently deserted hotels, which were built all along the road leading to the national park, at the time of Asian economic expansion about 10 years ago.

The park is very romantic with its fine old trees in the middle of perfectly groomed green lawns and its lake filled with large pink lotus flowers. The paths wind between banks of colorful Busy Lizzies and under arching convolvulus, climbing vines and pergolas of vivid hibiscus. Roses are cut from the rose garden each morning for the floral arrangements, which grace the common areas of the hotel.

The two charming "Suite Houses," near the rose garden, have an air of English cottages with their white half-timbered walls. They can be separated into two, each with its own main room at the first floor, and lounge below. The interior design incorporates some attractive personal touches, such as the wooden sideboard at the entrance and some watercolors. From the balcony, you have an attractive view across the meandering river with its carpet of green duckweed.

Lower down, along a small stream near the forest, bungalows have been constructed on a large wooden platform on stilts, with a series of gangways connecting them, each quite independent of the others. Large bay windows allow for excellent observation of the natural surroundings. The bungalows are spacious, each comprising a lounge and two rooms. The floors are tiled with shining black stones. The bungalows are closed during the rainy season, due to the possible flooding of the river.

The other rooms are located in several long classical buildings near the reception, the balconies offering a clear view over the pool surrounded by flamboyant and ficus trees or over the lake. The rooms are of a good size, bright and comfortable, but furnished in a rather functional manner.

Apart from the resort are the "Mansions," large deserted buildings constructed rather close to each other. Although the rooms, which are for sale or for rent, are comfortable, it is much more pleasant to stay in the resort itself.

The bar, with its leather and wooden furniture, has an understated elegance, whereas the outside restaurant is a little depressing. The air-conditioned windowed area is brighter, especially in the morning. There is a second, cozier restaurant with a paneled interior, which is more pleasant, but the cuisine here is limited to the grill. Furthermore, it is difficult to make conversation when the orchestra begins to play in the evenings.

The resorts doesn't organize excursions to Khao Yai National Park itself, but will contact agencies or hotels for you, such as Khao Yai Garden Lodge.

At the back of the park, a small quiet road leads into a secondary forest for about one kilometer, where it is extremely pleasant to walk.

JULDIS KHAO YAI RESORT AND SPA

54 Moo 4, Thanarat Road,
Thumbol Moo-sri, Pak Chong,
Nakhon Ratchasima 30130

Tel	66 (0) 44 297-272 to 76
Tel/Fax	66 (0) 44 297-297
E-mail	*juldis@khaoyai.com*
Web	*www.khaoyai.com*

Booking Office in Bangkok
9/66 Buxted House Building,
Ratchadapisek Road, Ladyao,
Jatujak, Bangkok 10900

Tel	66 (0) 2 556-0251 to 56
Fax	66 (0) 2 556-0258

By land
1. By car (2 hours) 185 kilometers from Bangkok. Take highway no. 1 direction Saraburi, just before Saraburi take road no. 2, on the left direction Nakhon Ratchasima, in Pak Chong take road no. 2090 (Thanarat road) direction Khao Yai national park. The resort is on the left side of the road.
2. By train and car (4 hours)
Train 3 ½ hours from Bangkok Hua Lamphong railway station to Pak Chong.   *Car* ½ hour, 17 kilometers from Pak Chong to the resort.
Other access options: By bus from northeastern bus terminal to Pak Chong; by plane from Bangkok to Nakhon Ratchasima airport (about 100 kilometers from Pak Chong).
Note: *The resort can pick you up in Pak Chong or in Nakhon Ratchasima (ask in advance as the resort has only one van).*

97 Units
88 Rooms • 7 Bungalows • 2 Suites Houses
All rooms have private balcony, private bathroom (hot water, bathtub), air-conditioning, IDD telephone, TV, minibar. The Suite Houses have 2 bedrooms, 2 bathrooms (separate shower and bathtub), 2 living rooms (you can rent only half of the Suite House), and coffee/tea maker. The bungalows have 2 bedrooms, 2 bathrooms (shower), and 1 living room.

Food and Beverage Outlets
2 Restaurants and 1 bar
1 Steak House
Cuisine Offered: Thai
Quality: Good

Other services: Internet • Shop • Safety box (at reception)

Water sports and Activities
Swimming pool • Small spa • Biking • Golf (Khao Yai Country golf at 10 kilometers) • Excursions in Khao Yai national park (ask reception in advance)

Per room per night

Khao Yai Garden Lodge

Khao Yai Garden Lodge is a lively hotel, managed by the dynamic Klaus Derwantz. He offers a wide range of accommodation, suitable for every budget, which guarantees the hotel is always busy, and he specializes in the organization of excursions into the Khao Yai National Park. These excursions can range from a few hours to treks lasting several days, with experienced English-speaking guides. Juldis Resort, our second resort selected for this region, regularly calls on Klaus' services for their clients.

If you ask well enough in advance, Klaus can arrange an exploration of the park with your specific interests in mind, whether these be flora or fauna. At the time of our visit, he was expecting a group of scientists interested in lepidoptera. Klaus is completely familiar with the area and is himself an ardent butterfly and orchid enthusiast, with an orchid collection in his garden. He is working on a book about the natural history of Khao Yai, which will be published in German. You will see beautiful photographs of butterflies and beetles in the resort, which he has spent months to collect.

The resort is situated beside the small road that accesses the park, on a long one-hectare piece of land. The large restaurant with its eclectic decor directly overlooks the road. It has become the great meeting place for travelers.

A path, planted with orchids, serves the different buildings, which house the rooms and the bungalows. The whole is a mixture of styles, created by Klaus, as the fancy took him. The first buildings have very simple rooms with shared bathroom facilities. The "Suites," situated in a two-story building facing a patio filled with bamboo, are spacious and comfortable, with pleasant décor, although rather crowded. Each is furnished differently, whether in a traditional style, with wooden furniture inlaid with mirrors or lacquered, or in a more modern style with bamboo furniture. They have a large lounge area and lovely marble bathrooms. Khmer bas-reliefs, statuettes, Thai dolls and masks complete the décor. The most pleasant rooms are those in the corner of the building as they are lighter than the others, with a lounge set in a glass alcove.

At the bottom of the garden, there is an attractive small swimming pool surrounded by greenery with a waterfall falling from a stonewall.

Further on, the brick-walled bungalows covered with climbing plants offer pleasant accommodation. A new building, under construction at the time of our visit, will offer spacious, bright rooms with large bay windows and terraces.

KHAO YAI GARDEN LODGE

135 Thanon Thanarat Road, 30130 Pak Chong, Nakhon Ratchasima 30130
Tel 66 (0) 44 365-178
365-167
Mobile 66 (0) 1 876-9450
Fax 66 (0) 44 365-179
E-mail
khaoyaigarden@hotmail.com
Web
www.khaoyai-garden-lodge.com
Contact Klaus Derwantz

 By land
1. By car (2 hours) 175 kilometers, take highway no. 1 direction Saraburi, just before Saraburi take road no. 2 on the left direction Nakhon Ratchasima, in Pak Chong take road no. 2090 (Thanarat road) direction Khao Yai. The resort is on the left side of the road, 7 kilometers from Pak Chong.
2. By train and car (4 hours)
Train 3½ hours from Bangkok Hua Lamphong railway station to Pak Chong railway station.
Car 15 minutes, 7 kilometers from Pak Chong to the resort.
Other access options: By bus from northeastern bus terminal to Pak Chong; by plane from Bangkok to Nakhon Ratchasima airport (about 100 kilometers from Pak Chong).
Note: *Transfer can be arranged by the resort.*

 43 Units
12 rooms with shared bathroom (6 with hot water only) · 8 rooms with private bathroom (hot shower) and fan · 6 rooms with private bathroom (hot shower) and air-conditioning, cable TV, minibar, safe box

Food and Beverage Outlets
1 Restaurant and bar
Cuisine Offered: Thai · Isaan · European · Chinese
Quality: Familial

Other services: Overseas calls and faxes · car rental · Travel confirmation and booking · foreign exchange · Excursions

Water sports and Activities
Table tennis · Darts · Bikes · Massages · Herbal sauna · Excursions and trekking in Khao Yai national park with guides

 Per room per night

Isaan Region (Khmer Temples)

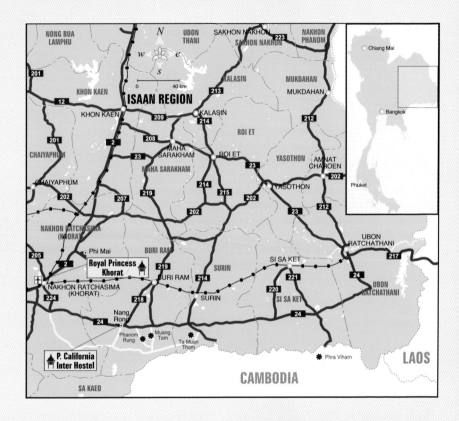

Climate **Khorat region:** Rainy season from May to October (heavier rains in September, but, as this is a comparatively dry area, the rains don't have as much impact and the rice paddies are more beautiful during this season).

Prasat Hin Phimai Festival: Late October/early November. This festival, which coincides with Loy Krathong, draws thousands of people. There are exhibitions of traditional music, dance and theatre, as well as a laser light and fireworks show at the ruins.

The Surin Elephant Round-up: Around mid-November. Surin has been an elephant habitat from ancient times and the local people of Surin are skilled in rounding up, training and controling elephants. Planned activities during the festival include a parade of elephants.

The Khmer Temples of the Khorat Plateau

The Khorat Plateau, on Thailand's border with Cambodia, conceals some wonderful temples, legacies of the Khmer kingdom, which dominated a large part of Southeast Asia between the 7th and 14th centuries. The best season to visit this extremely flat region, with wide expanses of rice terraces, is the rainy season. The monsoons transform this arid area into a gentle and pleasant landscape, brimming with all the tones of green, gold and silver, the rice paddies dotted with majestic trees, under whose abundant foliage, farmers and buffaloes take shelter during the oppressive heat of the day.

Tree trunks emerge from pyramid-shaped termite mounds, giving them a strange aspect. Very few tourists venture to this region, and the lack of public transport means it is preferable to come here with a rented car, unless you are willing to spend a great deal of time traveling. There really is no hotel in the area that one could describe as 'charming,' only the large hotels in the provincial capitals, comfortable but impersonal. **The Khorat Princess** is the best choice amongst this category, and there are small guest houses. In this respect, **P. California Inter Hostel** at Nang Rong is good value for money and is located close to the temples.

PHIMAI *(60 kilometers from Khorat and 90 kilometers from Nang Rong).* The town of Phimai was formerly connected to Angkor by a 250-kilometer-long laterite road. The temple is situated in the center of the town but, having entered it, you discover a lovely park with fine old trees where only the vibrant cooing of the turtle doves can be heard. Dating back to the 11th and 12th centuries, this harmonious and well-proportioned temple has been carefully restored. An alley with nagas leads to the white sandstone sanctuary tower which stands apart from the rest of the temple of

Phanom Rung Temple

Phimai Temple

pink sandstone and red laterite. The conical pyramid-shaped tower is set in the middle of a courtyard in the form of a cross, whose corridors mark the four cardinal points. In the shadowy light, a Buddha is silhouetted in the archway of a door. The original stone sanctuary roof and some finely sculpted bas-reliefs have been maintained.

There is also a museum in the town. If you wish to visit the temple at dawn, the simple **Phimai Old Guest House** is just a few meters away on foot. There are a few rooms, of which some are air-conditioned, with communal bathrooms, but some renovation would be a good idea.

PHANOM RUNG *(28 kilometers from Nang Rong and 126 kilometers from Khorat).* Phanom Rung, built at the summit of an ancient, wooded volcano, used to be a stop between Phimai and Angkor. The temple, dedicated to Shiva, symbolizes Mount Kailasa. It was constructed between the 10th and 12th centuries. The temple has been similarly restored.

The site attracts numerous visitors, especially groups of Thai school pupils, so, if you wish to contemplate it peacefully, you should come here very early in the morning, or at the end of the afternoon, when the setting sun casts a shimmering amber light on the stone.

A road leads to the volcano's summit, but it is more spectacular to see the temple from the plateau down below; the main tower is superbly outlined here, dominating a long and majestic avenue of stone lotus flowers, which leads to the steps guarded by Nagas. The temple has retained some of its lintels and finely carved bas-reliefs.

MUANG TAM *(18 kilometers to the southeast of Phanom Rung).* There is a peaceful atmosphere in this small temple, whose four cardinal points are marked with pools filled with lotus blossoms. The temple, dating from the 11th century, is in the process of restoration.

Not far from the temple and close to the parking area, there is a large rectangular reservoir around which you can walk and observe the scenes from rural life. There is a small restaurant near the parking area, well known for its delicious soups.

TA MUAN THOM *(112 kilometers from Nang Rong and 200 kilometers from Khorat).* This site comprises three structures, situated along the same road, at a distance of a few hundred meters from each other. **Bai Khlim** was a resting place for the pilgrims, but nothing remains now apart from the ruins of the main building. **Prasat Ta Muan Tod**, 300 meters further on, was a hospital; it is in a better condition, and, in particular, has retained its stone roof. Another 700 meters further on, **Ta Muan,** close to the Cambodian border, is engulfed by extremely dense jungle. The ruins are tinged with tragic nostalgia; fallen and scat-

Phanom Rung Temple

tered sandstone blocks make a chaotic scene, invaded by wild plants and creepers. The temple has not yet been restored but it is nonetheless captivating for this. You should not stray from the footpaths, which would be rather difficult in fact as the jungle is particularly dense, because there are still landmines buried here.

Access: The temple is 58 kilometers south of Prasat Muang Tam on a well-maintained and little frequented road. Twenty-five kilometers after Ban Kruat, turn to the right to the village of Ta Muan; the temple is well-signposted and you continue on the road leading to the Cambodian border for about 13 kilometers.

PHRA VIHARN *(240 kilometers from Nang Rong and 340 kilometers from Khorat).* Phra Viharn, or "the mountain of the sacred monastery" was constructed on a spectacular site, on a 547-meter high promontory, dominating the Cambodian plain. This setting and the early morning mists, which occasionally swirl through, add to its mystery. In fact, the temple is situated on Cambodian territory, but, because of its configuration, it can only be visited from Thailand. A visit here is always uncertain as the access can be denied for various reasons, notably the disagreements between the two countries concerning the entrance fees.

The temple was constructed between the 10th and 12th centuries and has not yet been restored after its long abandonment. Monumental staircases take you to several stone causeways and *gopuras* through which you reach the principal sanctuary, overlooking the precipice. Several exquisite bas-reliefs have been preserved.

Note: As the temple is a three-hour journey from Nang Rong, and four and a half hours from Khorat, you need to find accommodation in the area. Two small hotels, in the Kantharalak district, in the Si Sa Ket province and approximately 30 kilometers from the temple, offer accommodation: **M.K. Hotel**, *Tel.: 66 (0) 45 661-171 and* **Kantharalak Palace Hotel**, *Tel.: 66 (0) 45 661-085. Both these hotels have air-conditioned rooms with bathrooms attached.*

Ta Muan Temple

Royal Princess, Khorat

Part of the Thai Dusit hotel chain, the comfortable Royal Princess is located two kilometers from the center of Khorat, a town with no real touristic interest, but which makes a good stepping-stone for the Khmer temples.

The large nine-story rectangular building is surrounded by a strip of tree-planted land, which is already quite welcome in such a concrete town. The spacious and luminous white reception area with its extremely high ceilings has huge bay windows opening to the trees on both sides. There is elegance in the brightly colored chequered floor, the columns, the panels of openwork wood and the magnificent floral compositions.

Gracious and smiling hostesses wait for you at the reception counter, discreetly installed on one of the sides.

It is pleasant to have a drink at the bar, situated on a dais in the middle of the reception area, decorated with green plants and miniature aquariums. In the evening, comfortably ensconced in an armchair, you can listen to the musicians, pianists and double-bass players, who perform there.

A wide granite staircase leads below to an huge room where buffet meals are served. The more intimate Chinese restaurant just beside is well known in town for its cuisine, excellent, by the way. The bay window on this side opens onto a pool, surrounded by bougainvillea and pot plants.

An effort has been made to decorate the corridors serving the rooms, which are often dreary places in these large provincial hotels. The rooms are pleasant, although furnished in a very functional way, and have rather small bathrooms. The large bay windows in the form of arches give the rooms their attractive air. The Standard and Deluxe rooms are of identical size and only differ slightly in furnishings, with the Deluxe having an extra corner lounge.

The other large hotel in the town is the **Sima Thani**, with 265 rooms, situated on the main road at the entrance to the town. It is also very comfortable, with rather more luxurious bathrooms, but the whole is colder and more impersonal, especially the dark and enormous reception area.

The Sima Thani Hotel, Mittraphap Road, Tel: 66 (0) 44 213-100; Fax: 66 (0) 44 233-121; e-mail: *sales@simathani.co.th*; web: *www.simathani.co.th*

Phanom Rung Temple

ROYAL PRINCESS, KHORAT

 1137 Suranarai Road, Naimuang District, Amphur Muang, Nakhon Ratchasima 30000
Tel 66 (0) 44 256-629 to 35
Fax 66 (0) 44 256-601
E-mail *pkk@dusit.com*
Web *http://korat.royalprincess.com*
Central reservations
Tel 66 (0) 2 636-3333
Fax 66 (0) 2 636-3562

 1. By plane and land (1½ hour)
Plane 50 minutes on Thai Airways from Bangkok to Nakhon Ratchasima (6 weekly flights). ***Car*** 35 minutes (36 kilometers) from airport.

Note: *Transfer can be arranged by the resort.*

2. By land (2 ½ hours)
Car 264 kilometers from Bangkok. Take highway no. 1 direction Saraburi, just before Saraburi take road no. 2 direction Nakhon Ratchasima on the right. The road between Saraburi and Nakhon Ratchasima is in poor condition.

Other access options: By bus from northeastern bus terminal; by train from Hua Lamphong railway station to Nakhon Ratchasima railway station.

 186 Units
134 Standard rooms • 42 Deluxe rooms • 10 Suites

All rooms have private bathroom (with bathtub, hot water, hairdryer), air-conditioning, IDD telephone, TV, minibar, safety box. Deluxe rooms have tea/coffee maker.

 Food and Beverage Outlets
Restaurants: The Empress • Princess Café
Cuisine Offered: Chinese • Thai • Continental
Quality: Good Chinese cuisine

1 bar at Lobby Lounge

Other services: Business center • Foreign exchange • Souvenir shop • Babysitting • Barber shop and beauty saloon • Car parking • Tour desk

 Water sports and Activities
Swimming pool • Fitness center • Children playground • Golf driving range • Massage

 Per room per night

P. California Inter Hostel

Wicha Littidej, a former guide who specialized in the Isaan temples, will be your host in his small house, which is well situated for visits to the temples of Phanom Rung and of Muang Tam. From there, it is an equally easy day excursion to visit the temple of Ta Muan Thom, near the Cambodian border.

At the time of his retirement, Mr. Wicha Littidej had the extremely good idea of moving to Isaan with his family and of making his home into a guest house.

The fact that the project was originally set up around an idea he shared with a Californian friend explains the name given to the house.

Mr. Wicha Littidej is a charming man, with whom you can take pleasure in conversing in English or even a little in French. He will give you all the information necessary to explore the area, which, of course, he knows perfectly. If you wish, he will meet you at Khorat or Buriram airport, or he can help you hire a car, motorbike or bicycle.

His simple double-story white house is new and spruce, having just opened in 2002. It has the advantage of being surrounded by a small garden, set slightly away from the center of the town, facing the rice fields.

Its 12 rooms are impeccably clean, with tiled floors, functional wrought-iron furniture and minuscule bathrooms. The rooms are all identical in size and differ only in their level of comfort and their situation on the ground or second floor. The latter have a more pleasant view, but do not have air conditioning. There is also an individual bungalow, which comprises two rooms, facing the rice paddies. There is only one reproach for the hotel and that is the quite hard mattresses!

Breakfast is the only meal prepared by the hotel, but, for the other ones, you can ask your host to order them from a neighboring restaurant. They will be served to you on the terrace of the second floor of the house, which is the most pleasant place to relax and look over the rice fields strewn with trees. It is also an excellent point for observing the numerous birds that inhabit the surrounding groves.

At a modest price, the P. California Inter Hostel is a good alternative to the large, impersonal hotels of Khorat, too far from the temple sites to really make the most of them. In addition, you will be better advised in your visits in the region.

Ta Muan Thom Temple

P. CALIFORNIA INTER HOSTEL

59/9 Sangkhakrit Road,
Nang Rong,
Buriram, 31110
Tel/Fax   66 (0) 4 462-2214
Mobile   66 (0) 1 808-3347
           (0) 9 947-5449
E-mail   *califomia8gh@yahoo.com*
Web
www.geocities.com/california8gh
Contact   Mr. Wicha Littidej

 1. By plane and land (2 ½ hours)
Plane 50 minutes on Thai Airways from Bangkok to Nakhon Ratchasima (6 weekly flights). *Car* 1 ½ hour (98 kilometers) to Nang Rong.
2. By land (4 hours) 320 kilometers, from Bangkok take highway no. 1 direction Saraburi, turn to road no. 2 at Saraburi to Si Kiew intersection, connecting to highway no. 24 for Chokechai district and further to Nang Rong.
Other access options: By bus from north-eastern bus terminal to Rang Rong; by train from Hua Lamphong railway station to Lam Plaimat station (100 km after Nakhon Ratchasima and 40 km north of Nang Rong) in about 5 hours.
Note: *Transfer can be arranged by the resort.*

 12 Units
2 Standard rooms (with fan and cold water) · 4 Deluxe rooms (with fan and hot water) · 2 Standard rooms (with air-conditioning and cold water) · 2 Deluxe rooms (with air-conditioning and hot water) · 1 Private bungalow (with 2 bedrooms and hot water)
All rooms have private bathroom (shower), cable TV.

 Food and Beverage Outlets
Only breakfast is served. Dinner and lunch can be ordered from a nearby restaurant.
Cuisine Offered: Isaan · Western
Quality: Familial

Other services: Internet and fax · Bike · Motorbike and car for rent

 Activities
Excursions to: Phimai (90 kilometers); Phanom Rung (28 kilometers); Muang Tam (8 kilometers from Phanom Rung); Ta Muan Tom, Prasat Bai Khlim and Prasat Ta Muan Tod (112 kilometers).

 Per room per night

Koh Chang

TRAT

3156

3148

Koh Pui

⊙ Laem Ngop

Koh Chang Noi

Ao Khlong Son

Passenger ferry

Passenger ferry

**Banpu
Koh Chang Hotel**

White Sand Beach

**Ban Thai Resort
Koh Chang**

Than Mayon
Waterfalls

Klong Prao Beach

Khlong Plu
Waterfalls

Koh Selak

Kai Bae Beach

Koh Lim

Koh Chang

Koh Suwan

**Koh Chang Cliff
Beach Resort**

Koh Yuak

N

w $\quad$ e

s

0 $\quad$ 2.5 $\quad$ 5 km

KOH CHANG

Koh Man

Koh Prao Noi

Koh Prao Nok

Koh Mo Noi

Ao Bang Bao

Koh Mai Si Lek

Koh Ngam

Koh Mai Si Yai

Koh Lao Noi

Koh Laoya

Koh Khlum

Koh Chan

Chiang Mai

Koh Wai

Koh Bai Tang

Bangkok

Koh Nok Nok

Koh Nok Noi

Koh Kradat

Koh Kham

Koh Mak

Phuket

Koh Rang

Koh Ra Yang

Koh Tun

Climate $\quad$ Two pronounced seasons: hot-dry from March to May; rainy
from June to October

The amazing sight of the island's lofty silhouette swathed in dense vegetation greets the sea-borne traveler arriving at Koh Chang. Here the humid tropical primary forest is still intact and cascades down the mountains right to the shore.

Koh Chang is the largest island in an archipelago composed of 50 islands incorporated in the Koh Chang National Marine Park. With an area of about 500 square kilometers it is the second largest island in Thailand after Phuket.

The population is sparse and tourism is little developed, but some of the first projects are a matter of concern, particularly to the south in the superb Ao Bang Bao Bay where a hotel complex, comprising a gigantic concrete seven-floor liner, is already underway, completely disfiguring the site. Two tarred roads do not allow for a complete tour of the island: one goes down to the east to the Sa Lak Pet village, the other one runs the length of the west coast up to Bang Bao.

Most of the bungalows are located along the west coast where the best beaches are found.

The Beaches:

—*Ao Klong Son*: it is the first beach you will come across upon arrival from the pier, concealed at the foot of a wooded hill, in the hollow of a virtually sheltered pretty bay with mangrove-trimmed shores. The immense, recently inaugurated **Aiyapura Resort and Spa** is located here. It is very comfortable but devoid of charm.

—*Hat Sai Khao* (White Sand Beach): it is the longest and most frequented of the beaches, and retains a pleasing ambiance despite the many bungalows that line its shore. Nevertheless, the beach is reduced to a thin strip of sand. The **Banpu Koh Chang Hotel** with a family oriented informal atmosphere is a very good choice.

—*Hat Klong Phrao Beach*: it is quite a pleasant beach, with several bungalows and a small fishing village; it includes an area named "Chaiyachet" to the north, with superb rock formations emerging from the turquoise waters. It can be reached by entering the premises of the resort which occupies this place.

—*Kai Bae Beach*: a pretty tranquil beach of golden sand lies opposite the three

Hat Klong Phrao Beach

Chaiyachet, Hat Klong Phrao Beach

deserted islets of Koh Yuak and its tiny sandy beach, Koh Mon Nok, and Koh Mon Nai. Crystal-clear depths permit delightful snorkeling. **Koh Chang Cliff Beach Resort** is located along this beach.

— *Ao Bang Bao*: this sumptuous bay with a particularly stunning beach fringed by forest at the extreme southern tip of the island is in the process of being spoiled by the construction of a gigantic hotel complex.

The Waterfalls

Among the numerous waterfalls of the island, the most renowned are:

— *Klong Plu waterfalls*: the waterfalls are located on the west coast of Koh Chang, accessible from Ao Klong Prao by a small track that goes through the forest (20 minutes' walk from the park entrance). You can dive into the freshwater pool in its hollow…but it is evidently teeming with people!

— *Than Mayom waterfalls*: on the east coast, this three-tiered waterfall is more spectacular after the rainy season than the former and offers a scenic view of the island.

It must be noted that the very beautiful forest of Koh Chang is difficult to explore, due to the lack of hiking trails and the absolute necessity of having a guide.

center) and "Koh Chang Divers," both on White Sand Beach; "Sea Horse Dive Centre" at Koh Chang Cliff Beach resort on the Kai Bae Beach and "Paradise" at Klong Prao Resort.

Among the islands to explore, the most renowned are:

HIN LUKBATH near the west coast of Koh Chang, off Bang Bao, is a good diving site for beginners.

KOH KHLUM offers a good site for diving at Larn Hin.

KOH NGAM at the extreme end of Koh Chang, near the coast, where a narrow isthmus separates two symmetrical crescent-shaped sandy bays. The lagoons are favorable to swimming, snorkeling, and diving.

KOH LAOYA is a group of three heavily forested islands renowned for their beaches of white sand and their rather shallow coral reefs, notably at Laoya Klang. A footbridge links the islands of Laoya Klang and Laoya Nai.

KOH WAI is a beautiful rocky islet where several bays of red sand lie huddled. Some of the coral reefs are accessible from the beach.

KOH RANG, further off *(1 ½ hours from Koh Chang)* is a group of 12 islands. The largest, Koh Rang Yai, is cloaked in forest. The San Chao Beach of powdery sand is one of the most attractive with coral reefs rich in marine life. Turtles come to lay their eggs in the neighboring islets. Koh Kra, Koh Thong Lang and Koh Thian to the northeast of Koh Rang Yai are also good diving sites.

KOH MAK *(between Koh Chang and Koh Kood, 40 kilometers from the mainland)* is a group of nine islands, the biggest of which is flat, carpeted with coconut trees and rubber plantations, but shelters an isolated beach and coral reefs in its bay. Large rocks fringe the Koh Kham Beach a kilometer to the north.

The Islands surrounding Koh Chang

The large number of islands situated at the southern tip of Koh Chang can be visited by speedboat during the day, from October to May. Some of these comprise modest small bungalows suitable for an overnight stay.

As yet quite unexplored, the Marine Park has diving sites still quite intact and fairly shallow, rich in marine fauna. Only a handful of scuba diving centers are located on the island: "Eco-Divers" at Banpu Koh Chang Hotel (*charny@hotmail.com*, PADI

Koh Chang Cliff Beach Resort

The tranquil beauty of Kai Bae Beach, surrounded by mountains clad in a dense mantle of rainforest, makes you wish to sojourn here for many days and clear your mind of everything but the sweet things of life.

The golden sand and limpid turquoise waters promise sun-soaked days devoted to swimming and relaxation on the deck chairs placed along the shore. A speedboat transports you, if desired, to the three small wooded islets lying opposite the resort for snorkeling. On one of them, a small deserted sandy creek is coiled. A few meters from the shore, a floating pontoon has been built for swimmers.

Numerous activities proposed by the resort include diving (there is a diving center on site), jaunts through the forest on elephant back, visits to the waterfalls or excursions by speed-boat to the superb isles further on at the southern tip of Koh Chang.

The architecture of the resort is rather heteroclite but the whole place, devoid of ostentation, is nevertheless pleasing, in a large wooded land that has been left in its natural state, cut across by a small river teeming with water lilies.

From the reception, at the entrance of the resort, several long gangways overhang stretches of wild grass and tiny bridges span the water.

The footbridges lead to the low-lying concrete duplex "Garden View Suites" constructed with no particular pattern. Very large, with a living room and bedroom, they are unusually bare and decorated in a rather prosaic style: white tiled floors, walls in the same tone, pinewood furniture and comfortable but very standard bathrooms. The rooms open via a French window onto a large wooden terrace equipped with plastic chairs.

On the other hand, the view of the river, the pastoral garden, and the blue band of sea is quite delightful.

The "Sea View Pool" rooms in the new single-story building facing the swimming pool and the sea are cozier, with beautiful marble floors, furniture in ceruse wood, and paneling and tapestries for decoration. They have agreeable private balconies equipped with wooden furniture and adorned with stone bas-reliefs. The bathrooms are well conceived, covered with handcrafted tiles in pretty pastel shades and partitions for the different sections.

The attractive swimming pool is surrounded by a low red brick wall whose entrance is marked by statues and sculptures of elephants. The "Coco Pub" nearby looks directly onto the sea.

Isolated at one end of the land, an older building, perched on the rocks, shelters the "Cliffs View" rooms.

From the bedroom terrace you have a superb panoramic view onto the sea and the forested mountains.

The planked terraces, however, need some renovation. The interior is furnished in a simple manner and the bathrooms are minuscule. At the peak of the hill are individual Thai villas with a more traditional Thai interior decor.

KOH CHANG CLIFF BEACH RESORT

Kai Bae Beach, Koh Chang, Trat
Tel/Fax   66 (0) 1 945-5827
E-mail   *cliffbeach@hotmail.com*

Booking Office in Bangkok
118 Vibhavadi, Rangsit Road
(Soi 2), Dindang, Bangkok 10400
Tel   66 (0) 2 692-0122
       692-0314
Fax   66 (0) 2 276-9629
Web
www.kohchangcliffbeach.com

1. By land and sea (7 hours)
Car 5 hours (317 kilometers) from Bangkok to Trat or directly to Laem Ngop pier, the main pier of embarkation for Koh Chang, 16 kilometers from Trat. The most preferred road is Bangna/Chonburi/Ban Bung-Klaeng/Chanthaburi/Trat or Laem Ngop. *Boat* 1 hour from Laem Ngop to Dan Khao on northeast coast of Koh Chang (during high season hourly ferry). There are some vehicle-carrying ferries. *Car* 40 minutes from Dan Khao.

Note: *Transfer from Bangkok could be organized by the resort. There are many vans plying between Bangkok and Laem Ngob or you can take an air-conditioned bus from Ekkamai bus station or the northern bus terminal.*

2. By air, land and sea (3 hours)
Plane 50 minutes flight from Bangkok to Trat by Bangkok Airways (1 daily morning flight, 3 afternoon weekly flights). *Car* 20 minutes transfer from Trat Airport to Laem Ngop. *Boat* 1 hour from Laem Ngop to Dan Khao on northeast coast of Koh Chang (during high season hourly ferry). *Car* 40 minutes from Dan Khao.

43 Units
16 Garden View suites • 12 Pool Side suites • 8 Cliff View suites • 2 Cliff View suites • 5 Thai houses
All rooms have private balcony or terrace, private bathroom (shower, hot water), air-conditioning, cable TV, minibar, safety box in Cliff View suites only and at reception.

Food and Beverage Outlets
Restaurants: The Cliff restaurant • Coco bar
Cuisine Offered: Thai • Western

Other services: Babysitting (on request)

Water sports and Activities
Swimming pool with Jacuzzi • Beach • Snorkeling and diving in islands close by with Sea Horse Diving Center • Speedboat • Banana boat • Kayaking • Fishing

Other sports and activities
Mini golf course, elephant riding in jungle.

 Per room per night

Banpu Koh Chang Hotel

Banpu Koh Chang, with a relaxed family atmosphere, is one of the most pleasant resorts in the island of Koh Chang. Privileging the use of natural materials, as did till recently the hotels of Koh Chang, the modestly-sized Banpu respects the beauty of this mountainous untamed island, draped in a superb rainforest cascading down to the coastal road.

"White Beach," along which the resort is built, is in fact reduced to a narrow strip of golden sand, but the lounge chairs disposed around the nearby swimming pool compensate for this inconvenience. At low tide, a waiter on standby at the swimming pool will go to the trouble of installing chairs on the wet sand from where you can contemplate the spectacle of the setting sun with your feet in the water, if the tide coincides. As some hotel residents spend a large part of the day lounging and lazing here, there is a real competition for the lounge chairs and some clients reserve them in the morning!

The narrow piece of land on which the wooden, stone, and straw constructions have been raised was planted with an exuberance of coconut palm and other trees, bougainvillea, and flower massifs.

The main single-story building sheltering some of the rooms, situated at the rear of the land, is evocative of a comfortable mountain chalet with walls in wooden logs and balustrades carved out of tree trunks, an impression confirmed when you enter the room. Cozy interiors are paneled from ceiling to floor. Well-conceived, cheerful bathrooms are covered in turquoise ceramic handcrafted tiles. Each room has a small terrace equipped with armchairs, with an agreeable view of the ocean from the second floor.

The individual wooden bungalows on stilts, with thatched roofs that almost touch the ground, are more spacious, built slightly close to each other, with an identical décor. Those that face the swimming pool are fine for plunging into the water from the bed, but during the day there is a distinct lack of peace and quiet.

The large pavilion that shelters the restaurant becomes an animated spot in the evenings. You can dine indoors or on the terrace. In the evenings, a barbecue is installed on the sand and there is a wide choice of fish, shellfish and crab that you can have grilled in front of your eyes.

The seashore, the swimming pool a hop skip and a jump away, the small stalls and the cyber café, just opposite on the other side of the road, are all easily accessible from the resort.

There is no dearth of activities: you can rent a canoe, go by fast boat from the hotel towards one of the beautiful virgin islands of the south, equipped with a picnic and snorkeling equipment, explore one of the waterfalls in the forest, or simply abandon yourself to sweet reverie, between the sea and the swimming pool, as many families do.

BANPU KOH CHANG HOTEL

9/11 Moo 4, White Sand Beach, Koh Chang, Trat 23120
Tel 66 (0) 1 863-7314
935-6953

E-mail *kohchang@banpuresort.com*
Web *www.banpuresort.com*
Booking Office in Bangkok
45/9 Soi Rawadee 5, Tiwanon Road, Muang, Nonthaburi 11000
Tel 66 (0) 2 580-3596
589-1177
(0) 1 304-4321
Fax 66 (0) 2 588-4887
E-mail *sales@banpuresort.com*

 1. By land and sea (6 ½ hours)
Car 5 hours (317 kilometers) from Bangkok to Trat or directly to Laem Ngop pier, the main pier of embarkation for Koh Chang, 16 kilometers from Trat. The most preferred road is Bangna/Chonburi/Ban Bung-Klaeng/Chanthaburi/Trat or Laem Ngop. *Boat* 1 hour from Laem Ngop to Dan Khao on northeast coast of Koh Chang (during high season hourly ferry). There are some vehicle-carrying ferries. *Car* 20 minutes from Dan Khao.

Note: *There are many vans plying the route between Bangkok and Laem Ngob or you can take an air-conditioned bus from Ekkamai bus station or the northern bus terminal. Transfer could be organized by the resort.*

2. By air, land and sea (2 ½ hours)
Plane 50 minutes flight from Bangkok to Trat by Bangkok Airways (1 daily morning flight, 3 afternoon weekly flights). *Car* 20 minutes transfer from Trat Airport to Laem Ngop. *Boat* 1 hour from Laem Ngop to Dan Khao on northeast coast of Koh Chang (during high season hourly ferry). *Car* 20 minutes from Dan Khao.

 38 Units
28 Rooms in two-story building •
10 Bungalows
All rooms have private balcony, private bathroom (shower, hot water), air-conditioning, TV, minibar, safety box.

 Food and Beverage Outlets
1 Restaurant and bar
Cuisine Offered: Thai • Seafood, BBQ
Quality: Good family-type food

Other services: Shop • Babysitting (on request) • Taxi rental

 Water sports and Activities
Swimming pool • Beach • Kayaking • Snorkeling (20 min. away by hotel speedboat) • Diving in the islands (the reception will put you in contact with a dive center) • Island hopping in the southern islands (day excursion) • Excursions around the island (with the minibus of the hotel or taxi) • Mountain biking

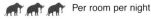 Per room per night

Ban Thai Resort Koh Chang

Mr. Tukta Prit put his heart and soul into the design and conception of his little resort that opened at the start of 2003. With relatively modest means and the drawback of a tiny plot, he nevertheless managed to create a pleasant atmosphere.

The traditional architecture, the thought and attention given to the various elements of decoration, deserve specific mention, all the more so as most of the other Koh Chang hotels, with greater potential at the outset, did not have this approach.

There is an attractive perspective from the entrance, through an arched porch flanked by dragons, onto a luminous view of sea and sky. Three pavilions with white walls adorned by terracotta bas-reliefs and roofs in green tiles lie aligned along a narrow stone-paved alley. Large jars filled with green plants decorate the doorways at the entrances.

The more agreeable rooms are the "Sea View" rooms housed in a fourth pavilion facing the sea. They have a large common terrace on the upper floor. Though the interiors are a bit dim with light filtering in through minute windows, they denote a certain studied elegance. The rooms have a living room area on a split level with a few steps separating it from the bedroom whose ceiling is in the form of a ship's prow. Painted entirely in white, they also include terracotta lamps and a bed draped in green damask. A writing table is installed in a separate corner near the entrance to the bathroom. These bathrooms are interesting, plastered with stones, with a sculpted elephant head by way of a showerhead and a round terracotta basin resting on a stone column.

The traditional interior decoration of the sea view restaurant is innovative and well-designed, with oriental brick windows, statues, large terracotta jars and colorful Thai cushions around the low Thai tables. The restaurant is extended by a terrace that runs along White Beach, rocky at this location.

BAN THAI RESORT KOH CHANG

 6/7 Moo 4, White Sand Beach, Koh Chang, Trat 2310
Owner Mr. Tukta Prit

 1. By land and sea (6 ½ hours)
Car 5 hours (317 kilometers) from Bangkok to Trat or directly to Laem Ngop pier, the main pier of embarkation for Koh Chang, 16 kilometers from Trat. The most preferred road is Bangna/Chonburi/BanBung-Klaeng/Chanthaburi/Trat or Laem Ngop. *Boat* 1 hour from Laem Ngop to Dan Khao on north east coast of Koh Chang (during high season hourly ferry). There are some vehicle-carrying ferries. *Car* 20 minutes from Dan Khao.

Note: *There are many vans plying the route between Bangkok and Laem Ngob or you can take an air-conditioned bus from Ekkamai bus station or the northern bus terminal.*

2. By air, land and sea (2 ½ hours)
Plane 50 minutes flight from Bangkok to Trat by Bangkok Airways (1 daily morning flight, 3 afternoon weekly flights). *Car* 20 minutes transfer from Trat Airport to Laem Ngop. *Boat* 1 hour from Laem Ngop to Dan Khao on northeast coast of Koh Chang (during high season hourly ferry). *Car* 20 minutes from Dan Khao.

 18 Units
9 Rooms • 2 Sea View rooms • 1 Superior room (on 2nd floor) • 6 Standard rooms (in 3 pavilions at ground level)
All rooms have private bathroom (shower, hot water), air-conditioning, TV. Sea View rooms have minibar.

 Food and Beverage Outlets
1 Restaurant and bar
Cuisine Offered: Thai
Quality: Familial

 Water sports and Activities
Beach

 Per room per night

The North

Chiang Mai Valley

Painting by Lily Yousry-Jouve

The North

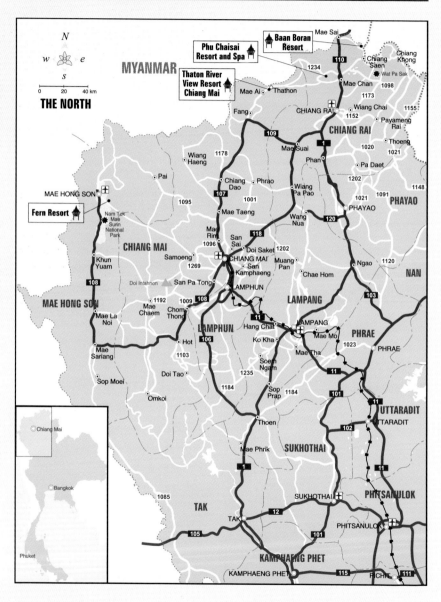

Climate   Two pronounced seasons: hot-dry from March to May; rainy from June to October; cool season from November to February—night temperatures can drop to zero in the mountains

The North

The North of Thailand is an extremely vast mountainous region comprising 17 provinces. It is home to approximately 500,000 hilltribe people originating from the nearby countries of Myanmar, Lao, and China. They all have retained their ethnic and cultural identity, therefore maintaining an authentic and distinct way of life. Very hospitable and open, the people of Northern Thailand have certainly contributed in making this region one of the most attractive in the country, especially for visitors looking for a genuine traveling experience. The Northern region is also famous for its Kingdom of Lanna (one million rice fields) filled with historic yet active temples to be seen within and around the gorgeous city of Chiang Mai, once Lanna capital for as long as five centuries.

Wat Phra That Hariphunchai, Lamphun

Chiang Mai and around Chiang Mai

LAMPHUN (*26 kilometers south of Chiang Mai*) and **LAMPANG** (*about 100 kilometers southeast of Chiang Mai*) South of the city of Chiang Mai, the small city of **Lamphun** hosts the **Wat Phra That Hariphunchai**, the largest *wat* and one of the most important in

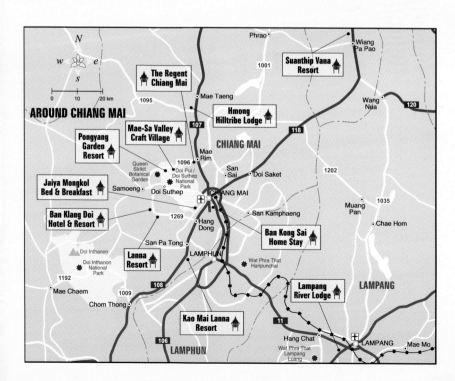

Wat Phra Kaeo Don Tao, Lampang

Lanna. The *Ho Trai,* an elegant wooden triple-roofed building, and the bronze gong, in its open pavilion, are particularly striking.

On the Chiang-Mai-Lamphun Road is the untouched and simple old Lanna cluster of houses, **Ban Kong Sai Home Stay.**

Lampang has long been known for its old-fashioned horse-drawn carriages transportation, although its use now seems to be limited to tourists. The modern city offers little interest and its streets are packed with cars and *tuk-tuk* traffic jams. Yet, its many teak Burmese temples—such as **Wat Phra Kaeo** and **Wat Suchadaram**—surrounded by peaceful gardens and an amazing house supported by 116 teak pillars (Baan Sao Nak) make it a charming stop on the road to Chiang Mai.

Lampang is also a short drive away from one of the most beautiful and traditional of all Lanna *wats,* **Wat Phra That Lampang Luang** (20 kilometers south).

Near the Mae Wang River, set in a lush garden, is the **Lampang River Lodge.**

Chiang Mai

Chiang Mai, the Rose of the North, was founded more than 700 years ago as capital of the Kingdom of Lanna and was only integrated in 1939 into the Kingdom of Thailand.

With a fast growing population of approximately 1.8 million people today, with 400,000 in the city itself, Chiang Mai is ranked second biggest city after Bangkok. But it has, surprisingly enough, been able to keep its original charm untouched and its atmosphere has remained very friendly and village-like.

The attraction of the city comes from a crucible of different interests, smoothly blending together: the most hospitable people, a strong cultural heritage, a lively old city, a vast and excellent value for money choice of accommodation and entertainment venues, a traditional as well as creatively redesigned handicraft, a distinctive cuisine, wonderfully cool nights, and a pivotal location to reach many other interesting spots. This may explain why Chiang Mai is the sort of place where visitors keep extending their stay day after day, sometimes week after week.

The city of Chiang Mai has two beating hearts:

THE OLD CITY   The old city, surrounded by a moat, is home to some of the region's most interesting *wats*; three of them should not be missed when touring the ancient city: **Wat Chiang Man**, the most ancient one, **Wat Chedi Luang** near the Tha Pae Gate, and **Wat Phra Singh**, the most venerated and biggest *wat* of all.

A pleasant village atmosphere prevails within the old city. A perfect place to savor this traditional ambiance of Chiang Mai is the **Tamarind Village,** the village-designed hotel located right in the heart of the old city.

Wat Thon Kwain, Hang Dong

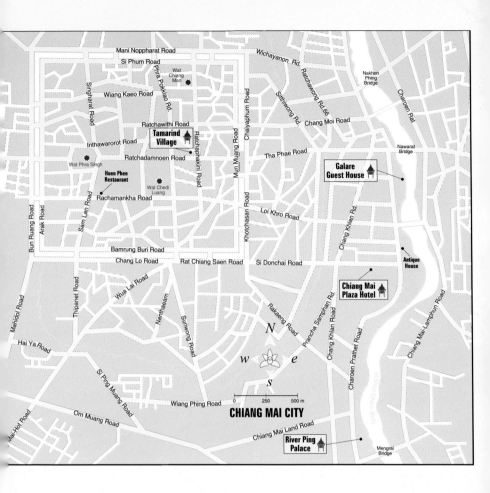

CHIANG MAI CITY

Chiang Mai Festivals

Umbrella Festival: 3rd weekend of January. Held in the village of Bo Sang (8 kilometers from Chiang Mai) where hundreds of young girls hold umbrellas in a very colorful parade.

Flower Festival: 1st weekend of February—held when flowers are at their best (colorful parade).

Songkran Festival: Around April 13—Celebrated throughout Thailand but the wettest and wildest celebrations are at Chiang Mai.

Inthakhin Festival: During the 8th lunar month (can be either May or June). This festival, peculiar to Chiang Mai, is held for six days to celebrate and pay respect to the city pillar.

Loy Krathong Festival: On the night of the full moon of the 12th lunar month (usually November) The Ping River becomes a sea of glittering floating lights, fireworks are let off everywhere, particularly along the river banks and there are parades in the streets.

THE NIGHT MARKET The second beating heart is the world-famous Night Market, where shopping becomes an ethnic and cultural experience.

Nowhere else in Thailand can one find such a wide range of high quality handicrafts sold at such reasonable prices. The choice is just unbelievably huge, ranging from tribal woven and embroidered textiles, Thai silk and cotton, jewelry and gems, celadon pottery, wood carving, bronze, Burmese lacquerware, authentic and less authentic antiques, to mass-manufactured counterfeits of international luxury name brands.

Both **Galare Guest House** and **Chiang Mai Plaza** are located in the vicinity of the Night Market. Further south, along the Ping River, the **River Ping Palace** offers nice rooms in an ancient teak house. Local villagers around Chiang Mai craft most of the handicrafts sold locally. City's guided tour agencies offer half and full day journeys to take visitors to witness the traditional crafting techniques used by these talented workers.

Dining in Chiang Mai is another enchanting cultural experience. Inexpensive and enticing restaurants abound everywhere. **Huen Phen**, a favorite with local people, offers fabulous Northern Thai food within an ancient teak house beautifully decorated with the owner's personal memorabilia (112 Rachamongka Road Phrasing, A. Muang, Chiang Mai; Tel.: 66 (0) 53 277-103). The **Antique House**, also located in an ancient teak house, surrounded by a small garden, is another nice place to have dinner (71 Charoen Prathet Road, A. Muang, Chiang Mai; Tel.: 66 (0) 53 276-810 Fax: 66 (0) 53 213-058). Four and a half kilometers from the city center, **Baan Suan restaurant**, designed by the architect of the Regent Hotel, is the ultimate restaurant for elegance and great cuisine, at an exceptionally reasonable price (51/4 Moo 1, Chiangmai-Sankanpaeng Road, Tasala,

Doi Suthep

Chiang Mai; Tel/Fax: 66 (0) 53 262-568). In Chiang Mai, new hotels and guest houses pop up every year, adapting to the growing number of both Thai and foreign visitors. Just outside the city, a handful of lovely hotels and one fabulous resort offer tempting accommodations options.

THE MAE SA VALLEY *(20 kilometers Northwest of Chiang Mai)* The lush Mae Sa Valley is a lovely area. Although many tourist activities are being developed in this enchanting nature area together with a growing number of hotels, it still offers a peaceful countryside atmosphere. The charming **Pong Yang Garden Resort** and **Mae-Sa Valley Craft Village** are located right along the main road, up to the top of a hill. On the way, don't miss to visit the **Queen Sirikit Botanical Garden.**

Off the Maerim-Samoeng Road, **Hmong Hilltribe,** encircled with wooded hills, is a simple, yet deliciously bucolic resort.

The famous **Regent Chiang Mai Hotel**, a tremendously luxurious resort and spa is also located in the Mae-Sa Valley. Its unique setting in a traditional Lanna-style village amidst rice terraces make it a genuinely original location to enjoy the many charms of Chiang Mai and its surroundings.

The Hang Dong-Samoeng Road This scenic road, starting Southwest of Chiang Mai, meets up the Mae-Sa Valley Road and allows you to circuit around the Doi Suthep

Washiratharn Falls, Doi Inthanon National Park

and Doi Pui massifs. Along the road, set in beautiful gardens, are two charming and affordable resorts, **Lanna Resort** and **Ban Klang Doi Hotel and Resort.**

DOI SUTHEP *(16 kilometers West of Chiang mai)* The 1601-meter Doi Suthep and its neighboring peak Doi Pui are considered the home of the Chiang Mai's guardian spirits.

Surrounded by the forest, halfway up to Doi Suthep, on a spur overlooking the city, is the highly venerated Wat Phra Boromathat Doi Suthep. The 24-meter *chedi* is covered entirely in gilded copper plates; at the corners are massive Burmese-style filigreed sacred parasols, glittering in the sun. The serenity of the place is somewhat disturbed by the numerous food and souvenir stalls at the foot of the *wat* and by the funicular that has been built…

Doi Suthep National Park can be explored through a network of trails. One of them, four-kilometer long, leads to the beautiful Sai Yai waterfall.

SOUTH OF CHIANG MAI AND DOI INTHANON NATIONAL PARK *(60 kilometers from Chiang Mai)* Seven kilometers only from Chiang Mai, in a peaceful, residential area at the foot of Doi Kham and Doi Kaew, is the exclusive **Jaiya Mongkol Bed and Breakfast.** Further south, 30 kilometers from Chiang Mai, on the way to Doi Inthanon, on the Hang Dong–San Patong Road, is the original **Khao Mai Lanna Resort Hotel,** where you will sleep in ancient tobacco barns converted into a resort.

Doi Inthanon, Thailand's highest mountain (2,565 meters) offers a fabulous encounter with an altitude forest unveiling chestnut trees' gold and green moss-grown branches and lichened high oaks.

This exceptional relic of the Himalayas nestles a unique type of vegetation and animal life. Miniature orchid gardens and ferns unveil around the peak. During the month of February, magnolias and rhododendrons are in full bloom.

At Km 48, an easy pathway, 360 meters long, climbs to the summit and offers a breathtaking view onto this verdant and rich vegetation. The most interesting pathway—Kew Mae Pan (3 kilometers, 2 hours)—starts from the pass located at Km 42. A guide will be waiting for you near the small hut next to the cold drinks and food stands. Do not miss the chance to savor in the crispy cool air some tasty grilled herb-sausages.

The park is also filled with waterfalls. On sunny days, the Washiratharn waterfall (Km 20) is crowned by an everlasting rainbow; the multi-level Pha Dok Siew (Km 26) is another gorgeous one. The peaceful Ma Ya waterfall, one of the widest in Thailand, can be reached by the road located outside the park (get out of the Jomthong-Doi Inthanon Road at Km 1, then drive on for 14 kilometers and walk for 400 meters).

Doi Inthanon Rainforest

Lampang River Lodge

In staying at the Lampang River Lodge you have the advantage of being near the town of Lampang — away from the tourist crowds, but with many interesting temples — and basking in an exquisite natural environment. Leaving behind the noise of the main road, which leads from Tak to Lampang, you enter a vast park that stretches along the Wang River. It is bristling with philodendrons, bamboo groves, palm, araucaria, erythrinas, ficus and albisia trees.

At the entrance, you will discover a lagoon, its banks bordered with flower beds. The seven "Superior" cottages were built, raised on stilts, in the center, and are accessed by a tiny wooden bridge. Their terraces, furnished with comfortable chairs, offer a pleasant view of the lake where ducks swim and several boats are moored.

Further away, in a small area surrounded by trees, a stunning sacred ficus tree marks the entrance to a large and tall wooden Lanna pavilion, open to the park, which houses the reception area, as well as one of the restaurants.

Most of the "Standard" semi-detached cottages are situated at the back, separated by several sinuous paths leading through lovely vegetation that occasionally takes on a very jungle-like aspect.

All the cottages, whatever their category, are very similar; entirely made of wood, they are architecturally simple buildings, with attractive triangular pediments, carved with a fan shape and with the traditional *kalae* at the peaks of the roofs. The interiors are pleasant and comfortable, with plaited bamboo covering the walls. Bay windows open out over either the lagoon or the garden.

The rustic furniture is of good taste, with beds covered with bright fabrics, wicker chairs, a Thai sofa and an amusing wooden dressing table. A carved triangular panel above the bed, lamps shaped like ducks and Thai paintings combine to give the room a warm atmosphere. The bathrooms are cheerful and functional.

The Wang River marks the boundary of the grounds. It is here, clasped between the two arms of the river, that the Sala Sunset Restaurant was built; you reach it by a long suspended wooden walkway that sways gently above the void.

Tables are arranged under the shade of a pergola overgrown with climbing vines on a lovely terrace overhanging the Wang River. The restaurant is decorated with drums, agrarian objects, and fishing traps.

Near the Sala Sunset, a large children's playground has been built, and a brand new swimming pool by the lagoon awaits you, offering a refreshing swim after touring the temples.

The Lampang River Lodge, like the "Hmong Hilltribe," the "River Kwai Resotel" and the "River Kwai Jungle Rafts," both in Kanchanaburi, favor rustic architecture and are set harmoniously within their natural surroundings, while offering guests a good level of comfort.

LAMPANG RIVER LODGE

330 Moo 11 Tambol Champoo, Amphur Muang, Lampang 52000
Tel/Fax 66 (0) 5 422-6922
(0) 1 224-1173
Booking Office in Chiang Mai
Lampang River Lodge Co., Ltd., Rincome Hotel, Apartment F, Huey Kaew Road, Chiang Mai 50000
Tel/Fax 66 (0) 5 321-5072
Booking Office in Bangkok
133/14 Ratchaprarop Road, Makkasan, Rajthevee, Bangkok 10400
Tel (66) 02 642-6361 to 2
(66) 02 642-5497
Fax (66) 02 246-5679
E-mail flortel@samart.co.th
info@riverkwaifloatel.com
Web www.riverkwaifloatel.com

1. By air and land via Chiang Mai (3 hours) **Plane** 1 hour and 10 minutes flight from Bangkok to Chiang Mai on Thai Airways (11 daily flights) or on Bangkok Airways. **Car** 2 hours from Chiang Mai airport (114 kilometers).
2. By air and land via Lampang (1 ½ hour). **Plane** 65 minutes from Bangkok to Lampang on Thai Airways (2 daily flights). **Car** 15 minutes, 6 km south of Lampang, on highway no. 1, on the right (you have to make a U-turn slightly further on, and retrace your steps for a few hundred meters to turn left at the sign board).
3. By land (10 hours)
Train 10 hours by Special Express train leaving from Hua Lamphong railway station every evening to Lampang station (air-conditioned cabins with sleeping berths). **Car** 15 minutes
Note: *Transfer from can be arranged by the resort.*

68 Units
61 Standard cottages • 7 Superior cottages
All rooms have private terrace, private bathroom (shower, hot water), and air-conditioning, telephone. Superior cottages have bathtub, TV and minibar.

Food and Beverage
2 Restaurants
Cuisine Offered: Thai • Western
Bar: Sala Sunset
Other services: Taxi rental (ask at reception)

Water sports and Activities
Swimming pool • Kids' playground • Thai massages and many temples in Lampang to discover, Doi Khun Tan national park between Lamphun and Lampang.

Per room per night

Tamarind Village 💕

At the heart of the northern region, reigns the ancient city of Chiang Mai. In its center, protected by high city walls, lies the old town with its many revered temples. Right in the middle of it, reached by two different and neatly designed entrance paths, you will find the Tamarind Village Hotel. Recently built around a magnificent 200-year-old tamarind tree and neighboring the spire of an old *chedi*, it is an impeccable spot for a fulfilling stay.

Mr. Amaradist Smuthkochorn, along with three partners, is the owner of this newborn hotel. An accomplished master of hospitality, Mr. Amaradist has spent 16 years at the legendary Oriental Hotel in Bangkok. For the Tamarind Village, he has deliberately chosen understatement and simplicity to bring out the power of the traditional environment in this singularly set and extremely chic hotel. This is the very striking impression that fills your eyes as you step into this fabulous place.

The hotel structure is inspired by ancient local villages, facing inward. Nestled within a white-walled enclosure, it is divided into three private courtyards, where only the sky, the spire of the nearby *chedi* and the gigantic tamarind tree break into the tranquil atmosphere.

The first courtyard sets a superb dark blue pool; a large swimming pool indeed, but such a picturesque one too, as its dark and clear surface reflects the whole courtyard's architectural lines; and the silent bare-footed steps of the sarong-dressed female staff. A few elegant sunbathing chairs lie on the plain tiled deck surrounding the pool, in quiet and friendly manner. In this same courtyard, stands the restaurant in a two-story traditionally-designed house, with open sides facing the pool. This is a very welcoming and casual place to eat meals—

tastefully decorated three-sided open lobby. Sets of two-story traditionally-designed houses, with tiled plunging roofs, separate the two garden-like courtyards, but also nicely connect to each other by roof-sheltered outside galleries.

especially an excellent and hearty buffet breakfast — or to sip a drink. As the night comes in with its gentle breeze, soft lighting sets a totally different scenery for romantic candle-lit dinners with tasty homemade Thai dishes, delicately spiced by a gifted young Thai-American lady cook.

The two other courtyards provide home for the guest room, which are reached through a rustic as well as

No lush tropical greenery in this finely designed architecture. In return, trees and palms have been rather scarcely displayed around the yards as natural sculptures standing out against the sky and white walls.

Rooms on the ground floor open directly onto the lawn, providing a pleasant feeling of homeliness.

The essence of Tamarind Village is yet again fully revealed within the warm feel of intimacy created inside the

rooms. Resolutely simple and with few pieces of furniture, the atmosphere blooms with a cozy and elegant interior design. The balcony's coffee-table and cushioned teak wood sofa, the simple and inviting writing table, the artistic black and white collection of photographs, the softness of the polished bamboo rug, the warmth of the soft lighting at night, the soothing of all the natural materials and fabrics in muted colors, the bareness and perfect layout of the bathroom, e.v.e.r.y.t.h.i.n.g here has been carefully selected and arranged to produce a delightful yet uncomplicated harmony and an overall sense of extreme elegance, to enchant guests with a taste for beauty and simplicity.

TAMARIND VILLAGE

50/1 Rajdamnoen Road, Sri Phom Muang, Chiang Mai 50200
Tel   (053) 418-898
             418-899
Fax   (053) 418-900
E-mail
sales@tamarindvillage.com
Web *www.tamarindvillage.com*

1. By air and land (1 ½ hour)
Plane 1 hour and 10 minutes flight from Bangkok to Chiang Mai on Thai Airways (11 daily flights) or on Bangkok Airways. *Car* 15 minutes from airport (5 kilometers).
2. By land (11 ½ hours) *Train* 11 to 12 hours (about 700 kilometers) by Special Express train leaving from Hua Lamphong railway station every evening (air-conditioned cabins with sleeping berths). *Car* 15 minutes from railway station.

Note: Limousine service can be arranged for pick-up from and transfer to airport, railway station or bus terminal.

40 Units
30 Superior rooms • 6 Deluxe rooms • 4 Standard rooms
All Superior and Deluxe rooms have private bathroom (shower, hot/cold water), air-conditioning, IDD phone and computer hook-up for Internet dial, cable TV and minibar. The Deluxe Rooms open to their private balcony, whereas the 30 Superior rooms do not. Only Standard rooms located at the back are slightly smaller and do not provide TV and minibar.

Food and Beverage Outlets
One restaurant
Cuisine Offered: Homestyle Thai • Vegetarian and light upon request
Quality: Excellent food and service

Water sports and Activities
The hotel organizes a wonderful city sightseeing tour aboard a local tricycle.

Other activities
The hotel also organizes a packaged four-day tour from Chiang Mai to Luang Prabang, Laos, by boat along the Khong River, a few nights in Luang Prabang and direct flight back to Chiang Mai.

Per room per night not inclusive of breakfast

Galare Guest House

Is this really a guest house? Or better yet a small hotel? Whichever the category, Galare Guest House is one of the best value-for-money, friendly and perfectly located places to stay in Chiang Mai… when you want to save some money for shopping at the night bazaar!

The Galare is not a major discovery for this guidebook, as its rooms have been in good service for 20 years. Thus, like a generation of visitors before us, we couldn't but appreciate the calm and relaxing atmosphere of this unassuming place, hidden at the back of a quiet *soi* near the Narawat bridge. Mr. Poonsak Suvannoparat erected the building on a family-owned piece of land by the Ping River. As a university professor of mathematics, the least one can say is that he was neither trained to architecture nor to hotel management. But he achieved both with quite some talent: the guest house's final plans came out of his own

sketches, and since his retirement from university, he has been running his hospitality business with much success.

Within walking distance of Charcon Prethet and Tha Pae roads, the Galare is found at the far end of Soi 2. The building is a L-shaped three-story, brick and wood structure, edging a pleasant garden protected from the *soi* by a fence wall. *Galare*—or *kalae*—top the tiled roof; these are the cross-shaped wood carving pieces symbolizing buffalo horns in Lanna architecture. A covered gallery, overlooking the garden's lawn, runs along the three levels of the building, giving access to the rooms. With its dark wood exterior staircases and balconies' white balusters, the Thai character of Galare seems to flirt with some Mexican style. At the opposite end of the property, the few tables and chairs of a cozy restaurant are laid out on a covered terrace overlooking the yellowish waters of the Ping River.

The rooms, much more spacious than one would normally expect for a guest house, are very simply but pleasantly furnished with rattan bedside tables and armchairs, or sofas in the larger rooms. In fact, comfort has been given the priority over any fancy interior decoration: king-size beds, satellite TVs, telephones, fans, solar-powered air-conditioning, and refrigerators in all rooms. Bathrooms are spotless.

A family atmosphere is in the air, everywhere. An ever-smiling, considerate, and helpful staff welcome you at all times—in perfect English—by the small reception desk. Just around the corner is a small but well thought-out computer area for Internet access reserved for the guests. A very serious and customer-friendly on-site travel agent provides reliable sightseeing tours and treks around the region. Other guests would simply recline in the peaceful center garden or by the pocketsize lawn terrace overlooking the river.

The open-air restaurant is another unwinding and friendly venue where guests gather for breakfasts. At this early time of the day, the sun pours like honey into the covered terrace where tables are nicely laid. Attentive staff serve a delicious 'à la carte' breakfast menu cooked in the family-size adjoining kitchen.

With a staff of 20 to serve 35 rooms' guests, Galare is certainly not a common guest house!

GALARE GUEST HOUSE

7, Chareon Prathet Road, Soi 2, Chiang Mai 50100

Tel (053) 818-887
821-011
Fax (053) 279-088
E-mail galare_gh@hotmail.com
Web www.galare.com

1. By air and land (1 ½ hour) **Plane** 1 hour and 10 minutes flight from Bangkok to Chiang Mai on Thai Airways (11 daily flights) or on Bangkok Airways **Car** 25 minutes from airport.

2. By land (11 ½ hours) **Train** 11 to 12 hours (about 700 kilometers) by Special Express train leaving from Hua Lamphong railway station every evening (air-conditioned cabins with sleeping berths) **Car** 15 minutes from railway station.

Units

35 rooms equipped with individually controlled air-conditioning and fan, refrigerator, telephone, satellite TV, private bathroom with hot shower.

Food and Beverage Outlets

Restaurant by the river serving breakfasts and simple meals. Room service also available.
Cuisine Offered: Thai • Western
Quality: Good food and friendly service

Other services Internet access through self-service computer by the front desk.

Water sports and Activities

Treks • Tours and any travel arrangements through Lanna Travel Service, based at the guest house (lanna_travel@hotmail.com)

Per room per night not inclusive of breakfast

River Ping Palace 💙

The River Ping Palace was taken over in June 2002 by Esther, a young Chinese woman from Singapore, who has restored the hotel to its former beauty.

A vast and beautiful 130-year-old teak house in the traditional Lanna style, the River Ping Palace is brimming with character. Set on the banks of the Ping River, it is surrounded by a small luxuriant garden, bursting with ficus and giant pandanus trees, cannas, strelitzias, and red poinsettias.

The rooms are in the house and those most sought-after are located on the second floor, in the original part, accessible by an outside staircase. They are distributed on both sides of a large communal area, paneled in teak and illuminated by small red lanterns—Esther's favorite color—and closed by red-and-gold-colored folding doors.

Each of the rooms is furnished in a slightly different way with antique wooden furniture. All in teak, they are not very spacious, but they retain the subtle atmosphere of days long gone. Each is dominated by a large, teak four-poster bed draped with a mosquito net and has an ancient chest of drawers. White opaline lamps are suspended from the high ceilings.

The larger "Suite" enjoys a charming view over the Ping River. There is no real view from the other rooms and it is better to keep the colored, frosted-glass windows closed.

The recently renovated rooms offer all modern conveniences: air-conditioning, refrigerator and modern bathroom.

There is a small communal lounge upstairs, overlooking the river on one side and furnished with antiques. On the ground floor, a more recent extension houses three other, more expensive rooms. They enjoy a terrace leading out over the river, which you can admire from a comfortable sofa. The rooms are pleasant inside, their red coffered ceilings making a striking contrast with the white walls and the lovely antique furniture.

The many paintings adorning the walls are the work of young, contemporary Thai artists.

The restaurant, in a traditional Lanna-style wooden pavilion, opens onto the garden and is further extended by a terrace overlooking the river. An especially lovely place, the restaurant is beginning to attract customers from outside. There is a wooded park on the opposite bank of the river and, in these verdant surroundings, you will finally feel far enough from Chiang Mai. In the evening, the lights of the small red lanterns strung along the bank accentuate the exotic aspect of the place.

The hotel has the slight drawback of being beside a fairly busy small road, but, at the same time, it is convenient as you can find a taxi easily.

Dynamic and welcoming, Esther will be pleased to help you call a taxi or rent a car, if you wish. From her small office, she will organize a reasonably-priced excursion or trek and she has a list of suggested itineraries, which she would be delighted to share with you.

RIVER PING PALACE

385/2 Charoen Prathet Road, Changklan Muang, Chiang Mai 50100
Tel/Fax 66 (0) 53 274-932
E-mail
thingesther@netscape.net
riverpingpalace@netscape.net
Contact Esther Ting, General Manager

1. By air and land (1 ½ hour)
Plane 1 hour and 10 minutes flight from Bangkok to Chiang Mai on Thai Airways (11 daily flights) or on Bangkok Airways. *Car* 10 minutes from airport (7 kilometers).
2. By land (11 hours)
Train 11 to 12 hours (about 700 kilometers) by Special Express train leaving from Hua Lamphong railway station every evening (air-conditioned cabins with sleeping berths). *Car* 20 minutes from railway station.
Note: *Transfer from Chiang Mai airport or railway station by the resort's mini-bus can be arranged free-of-charged.*

8 Units
3 Rooms on the ground floor with private terrace • 5 Rooms on the second floor including one suite
All rooms have private bathroom (shower, hot water, hairdryer), air-conditioning. The suite on the second floor has bathtub and minibar.

Food and Beverage Outlets
1 Restaurant
Cuisine Offered: Thai
Quality: Good

Other services: Internet • Car rental

Water sports and Activities
Massages (ask in advance), excursions could be organized (ask reception)

Per room per night

Chiang Mai Plaza Hotel

If you went by their looks only, these two high and modern buildings with assertive international style would not match the selection criteria for a guidebook such as this one. Yet, because of a wide range of qualities, the Chiang Mai Plaza Hotel happens to be a pleasant and very reasonably-priced luxury hotel.

The city of Chiang Mai has two beating hearts: the old city surrounded by a moat and the area extending between Tha Pae Road and the river, with the attractive night bazaar in the middle. Perfectly located, the Plaza stands within a 5 minutes' walking distance from the bazaar, away from the noisy and crowded main street. With its double 12-story white façade preceded by an immense parking area, the Plaza discloses one characteristic of glamour: SPACE! Rarely—or never—is such a grandiose example of lobby to be found in any other hotel of the same cate-

gory. Opulent and conventional luxury is the decorative theme of this huge lounge, in which clusters of upholstered armchairs are geometrically displayed over thick carpets. Opposite the lobby-bar area, a miniature Thai house welcomes everyday, from 6:00 p.m. to 8:00 p.m., a family of musicians playing Northern Thai music, thus bringing genuine vernacular spirit into this tremendous space, filled with guests at this time of the day. At the far end of the lobby, a crew of extremely dedicated and professional staff welcome guests with legendary northern warmth, behind a reception desk matching the size of the room! A replica of an ancient Thai city, with brick walls and hieratic Sukhothai Buddha statues lit by votive candles, sets an unexpected décor along the large corridor leading to the mountain view wing.

Accommodation at the Plaza is characterized by generous space, even for standard rooms, city or mountain view alike. Through an entrance hall, one walks into an extremely commodious living area. Polished dark wood frames the large windows opening onto the gorgeous mountain backdrop of Chiang Mai, or onto the city roofs extending along the river. Room furniture is generously available, with very large beds, an inviting coffee table with a pair of armchairs. Rich fabrics, although slightly outdated, along with some Lanna artifacts, diffuse an altogether pleasant atmosphere. Bathrooms, recently renovated, provide the very best amenities within a sober and rich setting making use of marble and dark wood.

During the hottest months, guests thoroughly enjoy the large and mineral water-clean swimming pool located on the second floor of the building. Thanks to the hotel's location aside the busy area of Tha Pae that is becoming highly polluted, this open-air pool provides the pleasure of breathing a seemingly better and cleaner air while exercising in the middle of the city. A few Thai-style-roofed sun-shelters and a bar around the pool add some character to this otherwise unadorned area.

Although the restaurant's indoor area is not of particular interest and lacks intimacy, its garden-like terrace where buffet breakfasts are served is a peaceful haven surrounded by huge trees. A perfect fresh and shady spot for planning your day in Chiang Mai.

CHIANG MAI PLAZA HOTEL

92 Sridonchai Road,
Chiang Mai 50100
Tel 66 (0) 53 270-036 to 50
Fax 66 (0) 53 279-457

Booking Office in Bangkok
99/99 Rungroj Building
2/F, Vipavadee Rangsit Road,
Ladyao, Bangkok 10900
Tel 66 (0) 2 276-2622 to 27
Fax 66 (0) 2 276-2628 to 29

 1. By air and land (1 ½ hour)
Plane 1 hour and 10 minutes flight from Bangkok to Chiang Mai on Thai Airways (11 daily flights) or on Bangkok Airways **Car** 15 minutes from airport (7 kilometers).
2. By land (11 ½ hours) **Train** 11 to 12 hours (about 700 kilometers) by Special Express train leaving from Hua Lamphong railway station every evening (air-conditioned cabins with sleeping berths). **Car** 5 minutes from railway station (2 kilometers).

Note: Limousine service can be arranged for pick-up from and transfer to airport, railway station or bus terminal.

 445 Units
225 Standard rooms • 214 Deluxe rooms • 3 Junior suites • 1 Executive suite • 2 President suites
All rooms have private bathroom (hot water, hairdryer), air-conditioning, IDD phone, TV, minibar, coffee/tea maker.

 Food and Beverage Outlets
1 Restaurant, 1 lobby bar and 1 poolside bar
Cuisine Offered: Thai • Western
Quality: Good

Other services: Internet access at the business center • Shopping Arcade • Babysitting • Efficient travel desk

 Water sports and Activities
Swimming pool • Fitness room • Sauna • Snooker

 Per room per night not inclusive of breakfast

Jaiya Mongkol
Bed & Breakfast ♥

When he was feeling a little bored after his retirement from the Bangkok Post, Norachai Prasertmanukitch decided to settle in Chiang Mai and open his superb house to guests. Chiang Mai is a region he knows extremely well, his father having been governor here. Mr. Prasertmanukitch knows everyone in the town and is able to assist you with your every request: a private excursion with a driver and guide who speaks your language, a traditional dinner on the terrace of his house followed by a classic show, a dinner in town or a course in Thai cuisine.

Jaiya Mongkol Bed and Breakfast will thus enchant those who appreciate staying in a fine, traditional Lanna house and letting themselves be guided by a knowledgeable host. Clearly, although the price of the guest house is reasonable with regards to the quality of the lodging, the individual excursions will add to your expenses. Alternatively, you can go there with your own car and organize your stay yourself with Prasertmanukitch's helpful advice.

The guest house is located in a peaceful, residential area at the foot of Doi Kham and Doi Kaew. Ajarn Chunlathat Kittibutra, the famous architect of the Regent Hotel in Chiang Mai, designed the house, which comprises several teak Lanna pavilions on stilts, connected to each other by a whole play of footpaths, and exterior terraces with elaborate railings, through which the sun casts abstract designs on the floors. It is full of delightful corners in which to enjoy moments of solitude, while contemplating the beauty of the garden, filled with longane trees and flowers.

The interior of the house is paneled in teak, including the bathrooms, with coffered ceilings and beautiful wooden floors. No less than 100 teak pillars support the framework of the house! The windows are attractively hung with curtains of traditional designs, there are comfortable benches and armchairs, displays of shell or porcelain collections, even silver toilet articles arranged in your bathroom.

Two rooms are especially intended for guests. They are independent, accessible by a footbridge to the second floor or by a private staircase. Each has its own terrace and private bathroom. They are decorated sparingly with lovely Burmese furniture. On the ground floor, there is a fully equipped kitchen for the use of the guests, where you prepare tea or coffee, or even your meals if you wish.

During the high season, the more heavily decorated rooms of Mr. Prasertmanukitch's two children, which share a bathroom, can be made available to guests.

The copious breakfasts with a different variety of fruits each day are prepared by your host and served on the wide covered terrace on the ground floor facing the mountains, graced by a beautiful flowering tree whose blossoms give out an exquisite scent in the evening. Dinner can also be arranged, on request, and is served on the terrace. For a change of scenery you can dine nearby, in the unusual 'Rainforest' restaurant or in town.

JAIYA MONGKOL BED AND BREAKFAST

320 Moo 1, Baan Tong Gai, Chiang Mai Hangdong Road, Tumbon Nong Kwai, Amphur. Hang Dong, Chiang Mai 50230
Tel 66 (0) 53 430-665
431-219
(0) 9 851-6732
Fax 66 (0) 53 234-576
E-mail
jaiya_mongkol@hotmail.com
Web *www.infothai.com/jaiya*
Owners and Operators:
Khun Norachai and Naruemol Prasertmanukitch

1. By air and land (1 ½ hour)
Plane 1 hour and 10 minutes flight from Bangkok to Chiang Mai on Thai Airways (11 daily flights) or on Bangkok Airways. *Car* 10 minutes from airport (5 kilometers).
2. By land (11 ½ hours)
Train 11 to 12 hours (about 700 kilometers) by Special Express train leaving from Hua Lamphong railway station every evening (air-conditioned cabins with sleeping berths). *Car* 20 minutes from railway station (12 kilometers).
Note: *Transfer from Chiang Mai can be arranged by the resort (free pickup).*

4 Units
2 Rooms with private terrace and private bathroom; 2 rooms sharing a bathroom (shower, hot water, hairdryer)
All rooms have air-conditioning, minibar, guest veranda and common sitting room with cable TV, VCR and stereo.

Food and Beverage Outlets
Breakfast is served on the terrace. For lunch and dinner, you can have it at home on request, or in a nearby restaurant. Self service western pantry for making snacks, coffee, and tea. Lunch box on request.

Other services: Free Transportation to the Night Bazaar in Chiang Mai • Reservations for outside meals • 4-seater saloon car rental with or without driver

Water sports and Activities
Thai culinary art school nearby • Massages (on request) • All local tours can be organized with English-speaking guide (Doi Inthanon, Doi Suthep, Elephant Safari, Temples, visit to Laos and Burma, etc.)

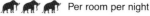 Per room per night

Ban Kong Sai Home Stay

If you love Thailand, you may not have resisted the temptation of browsing the superb 'Thai Style' book by Luca Tettoni and William Warren. If you have, you must have fallen in love with the old northern house featured under the 'Chiang Mai Rustic' heading, on pages 134 to 137. What the book does not say is that you can actually jump into the glossy pages and make yourself at home in this very same house for a few days. Because the lovely Ban Kong Sai is now open to guests again.

The guest house is located in the peaceful village of Kong Sai, seven kilometers away from Chiang Mai on the ancient Yang Na tree-lined elephant route to Lamphun. Although the two locations are only separated by a mere 15-minute drive, you will need your own car to freely drive back and forth and to fully enjoy your stay. Also, be prepared to ask your way a number of times inside the village as directions to the guest house are not yet adequately sign-posted. Having complied with these two requirements you can dip into the totally unspoilt and easy atmosphere of this ancient Northern Thai house.

Ban Kong Sai is set in the middle of a vast homey garden planted with old trees. Its structure consists of three traditional teak wood houses; all three are built to the original architectural scheme of the region: a set of teak posts supporting a platform arranged with separate rooms.

On the ground floor of the main house, open and airy, a collection of cushions thrown on a large polished teak wood stage sets the tune of this uncommonly genuine place. Here is the focal point of the peaceful and totally relaxed life enjoyed at Ban Kong Sai, where the few guests meet for a chat on the swinging wooden sofa, or quietly read lying on Thai cushions behind the fresh shade of a bamboo curtain. It is here too, on the old dining table laid with faded embroidered tablecloth, that homemade breakfasts are served with the kindness of true hospitality.

The ambiance within the four large rooms on the second floor is bewitching. Floors, walls, and high-vaulted ceilings all made of teak perform to make you feel encased in warmth. They display the simplest but most pleasant setting for experiencing the simplicity of real life. No exotic ostentation here. Just a genuine and family taste of Northern Thailand. Except for surprising high-tech remote controls for operating electrical fans and light switches (!) and fresh flowers arrangements everywhere, the rooms are only decorated with timeworn furniture and curios: old rustic cabinets, unpretentious canopy beds with romantic mosquito nets swinging in the afternoon breeze, and a display of hand-woven fabrics. Bathroom amenities are just very simple, but the room becomes an unusual morning concert hall for free bird-singing in the mango tree outside by the window.

A second and smaller house in the garden—called the family house—is an idyllic haven for one or two people looking for total privacy, with its large room, bathroom and charming terrace hidden in full greenery. No wonder this house is a favorite of artists, like this British writer who rented the house for three months recently for isolated work on her new novel.

A stay at Ban Kong Sai can produce this extraordinary memory of having gazed on a fragment of a fading world, and having genuinely experienced a parcel of Thai life. Thanks to its owners, this world is still alive.

BAN KONG SAI HOME STAY

232 Moo 6, Kong Sai Soi 5,
Chiang Mai–Lamphun Road,
Nong Phung, Sarapee,
Chiang Mai 50140
Tel/Fax 66 (053) 321-439
Mobile 66 (09) 554-6679

Booking Office in Bangkok
Mobile 66 (01) 628-3605
E-mail
ban_kong_sai@hotmail.com
Web www.bankongsai.com

1. By air and land (1 ½ hour) **Plane** 1 hour and 10 minutes flight from Bangkok to Chiang Mai on Thai Airways (11 daily flights) or on Bangkok Airways. **Car** 25 minutes drive from airport to the resort.
2. By land (11 ½ hours) **Train** 11 to 12 hours (about 700 kilometers) by Special Express train leaving from Hua Lamphong railway station every evening (air-conditioned cabins with sleeping berths). **Car** 25 minutes from railway station.

Note: Free transfer from and to airport can be arranged if requested in advance. Phone available 24 hours for direction. Free shuttle to Night Bazaar in Chiang Mai.

3 Houses
Main house: 4 bedrooms (2 double and 2 twins) located on the second floor, with fan. 3 Separate bathrooms: 1 large bathroom on the second floor and 2 smaller ones on the ground floor (hot shower).
Family house: 1 bedroom (double bed + small bed) with private balcony, private bathroom (hot shower), air-conditioning.
Small house: 1 bedroom (single) with private balcony, private bathroom (hot shower) and fan.

Food and Beverage Outlets
Cuisine Offered: Thai homemade cuisine. Limited choice of drinks.
Quality: Family type

Other services: Telephone and e-mail at reception

Water sports and Activities
Many activities can be arranged with the help of Ban Kong Sai's owner, Pakawan. Among them: Home Thai cooking lessons with Pakawan • Badminton in the garden • Tricycle riding through the village and close by cultural sites • Rice growing with local farmers from May to July • Visits to Chiang Mai

Per room per night inclusive of breakfast

The Regent Chiang Mai 💕 Resort and Spa

The Regent Chiang Mai Resort and Spa is a star sparkling with unique bloom not only in Northern Thailand, but also amidst the very exclusive list of world-famous Asian luxury resorts.

The contrast with bustling Chiang Mai is striking as one walks into the fabulous open-sided lobby dominating the resort like a temple in traditional Thai villages. Stress-inducing urban surroundings totally evaporate here, replaced by an alluring invitation to some exotic adventure. Even signing in at reception becomes a very special moment of welcome, as a cool towel,

ters of two-story wooden Pavilion Suites are set in a horseshoe shape encircling emerald terraces of lush rice paddies, with the misty blue horizon line of Doi Suthep and Doi Pui background of mountains.

The splendor of the resort becomes charmingly homelike as one climbs the dark wooden stairs into the Pavilion Suite. A feeling of comfort and ease fills the spacious and elegantly furnished living space where Northern Thailand interior design elements are unostentatiously displayed. The large dressing/bathroom is gorgeously designed and equipped with more than what is usually expected in such a luxurious environment. Around the bathtub, a sober-lined picture window overlooks a secluded tropical garden in full bloom.

One of the gems of private comfort revealed at the Regent appears behind a set of double wooden doors: the *sala*, an open-sided verandah connected to the Suite by a wooden footbridge. This is the most enchanting cocoon for relaxing on the huge elephant bed covered with Thai triangular pillows, overlooking the garden as the sun sets down in golden beams.

Trying to fully enjoy Regent Chiang Mai's wonders will take you more than one stay. Endless walks through the 20 acres of landscaped gardens give a sense of a rare and exotic nature; they also provide unusual encounters like

jasmine garland, and a chilled spicy lemon grass drink are handed by friendly hotel staff, under the gentle flight of calico lanterns hanging from a stunning high-vaulted ceiling.

A few steps forward from this central point, on a sun-shimmering water garden terrace, the eye plunges into the magic of this Lanna-styled paradise. The resort, nestled in the Mae Rim valley, has been designed with much talent by both famous Thai architect Ajarn Chulathat Kitibutr and American 'Asiaphile' landscape architect Bill Bensley. Here, clus-

the Regent's pet water buffalo family wandering through the alleys.

An early morning swim in the spectacular no-limit swimming pool, set right above the misty rice paddies, builds a long-lasting memory of what perfect well-being means.

Another jewel of the resort hides nestled in lush tropical vegetation: the Lanna Spa. This temple of harmony seems to have been designed as the embarking point to a tri-dimensional heaven aimed at mind, body, and soul delight. Deeply inspired by the aesthetics of Wat Phumin, acclaimed architect Lek Bunnag has mastered here a fine melting of culture and nature. Exquisiteness of color, shape, texture, and even fragrance is to be found in every single element used here, from rooms design to candle lighting. Relaxing in your private Spa suite, indulge yourself with the wide range of exotic treatments and beauty secrets, magic rainshower massages, outdoor showers, or tropical garden scented baths.

Unfold your senses and fly into a blissful world. This is what the Regent in Chiang Mai is all about.

THE REGENT CHIANG MAI RESORT AND SPA

Mae Rim-Samoeng Old Road,
Mae Rim, Chiang Mai 50180
Tel 66 (053) 298-181
Fax 66 (053) 298-190
66 (053) 298-189
E-mail *rcm.reservations@
fourseasons.com*
Web *www.regenthotels.com*

1. By air and land (1 hour and 40 minutes) ***Plane*** 1 hour and 10 minutes flight from Bangkok to Chiang Mai on Thai Airways (11 daily flights) or on Bangkok Airways. ***Car*** 30 minutes drive from airport to the resort.
2. By land (12 ½ hours) ***Train*** 11 to 12 hours (about 700 kilometers) by Special Express train leaving from Hua Lamphong railway station every evening (air-conditioned cabins with sleeping berths). ***Car*** 30 minutes from railway station.
Note: Chauffeured limousine service is available for airport transfers.

80 Units
64 Pavilion suites with garden, mountain, or rice terrace view. Each suite offers a spacious living space (70 m^2) composed of a bedroom with sitting area, a dressing/bathroom area with double vanity, an oversized bathtub and separate shower overlooking a secluded garden, and an outdoor sitting pavilion · 16 one, two, or three bedrooms Residence suites, 'home away from home' style (350 m^2 and 524 m^2).

Food and Beverage Outlets
Restaurants: Sala Mae Rim (elegant with fine cuisine) · Pool Terrace Restaurant and Bar (pool-side casual meals) Also picnic baskets to take on day-expeditions and even freshly packed "meals to go" for those leaving the resort.
Cuisine Offered: Northern Thai · Western · Vegetarian and light
Quality: Excellent food and service
Bar: Elephant Bar (for afternoon tea, sunset cocktails and after dinner drinks)

Other services: Business services with free e-mail access · Babysitting · Kids club · Complimentary shuttle service to and from downtown Chiang Mai runs four times daily.

Water sports and Activities
Swimming pool · Lanna-Spa · Fitness studio · Library · Lanna Cooking School · Tennis on two floodlit courts · Complimentary mountain bikes · Golf at nearby courses · Tropical garden tours · Sightseeing and short distance expeditions (overnight treks to hilltribe villages or the Golden Triangle Region · Jungle treks by elephant riding · Orchid farms · Bamboo river rafting · Visit to temples in the city of Chiang Mai, etc.)

Per room per night not inclusive of breakfast

Hmong Hilltribe Lodge

The sun's last rays play upon the rice paddies while the soft chiming of bells announces that the buffalo herder is going home for the evening. The area, encircled with wooded hills is deliciously bucolic. Although you are only about 30 kilometers from Chiang Mai, the lifestyle of the Hmongs seems to have changed very little.

When the resort, popular with small ecotourist groups, was first constructed in 1988, getting there was rather an ordeal, especially during the rainy season. Since then, a narrow asphalt road has been built and it does render the expedition definitely less arduous, despite the fact that certain stretches of it are in a piteous condition.

The prevailing concept in Hmong Hilltribe is to offer travelers a closer contact with the Hmong tribes and the surrounding natural environment, while assuring them comfortable accommodation. Thus, it is the Hmongs from a nearby village who serve the guests at dinner, dressed in their traditional costumes. To tell the truth, oral communication is difficult as the Hmongs speak very little English.

In front of the restaurant, a great flat expanse of grass faces the rice paddies, the colors of which vary with the seasons. Here you will see farmers going about their daily tasks. The surrounding hills are made up of dense forest and the national park of Doi Suthep, is actually very close. Along the road that leads to the resort, you can also stop and see one of the park's many waterfalls. From the resort it is easy to find one of the narrow paths, which cross through the countryside and the forest.

The lodge offers simple comfort but is perfectly maintained. The bungalows were modeled on the traditional Hmong houses, whose architecture is sparing: a large bamboo rectangle with a thatched roof—although some adjustments have been made in order to cater to the need for modern comforts.

Each bungalow houses four rooms and a spacious central common area made up of bamboo armchairs grouped around an open hearth. The nights can get quite chilly and damp in winter, sometimes the temperature drops to 6°C, but you will be provided with blankets. On winter mornings, the rice paddies and lawns are covered in a thick mantle of dew, while the last vestiges of opal mist clinging to the trees vanish into the air.

A small terrace extends the lounge in each bungalow, where one has a lovely view of the rice paddies or the garden. This has been purposely left in its natural state with only a few beautiful trees scattered across the green lawns.

Within the rather dark interiors of the rooms, lovely quilts and traditional curtains made of black, white and red geometric patterns contrast with the bamboo walls and the wooden floorboards. The doors and windows, without glass, are furnished with mosquito nets.

Dinner is served at a fixed hour every evening. When it is busy, you are served a friendly outside barbeque. A large fire is lit and, after dinner, you may enjoy a performance of traditional dance, which lasts about 20 minutes.

HMONG HILLTRIBE LODGE

111 Moo 4 Mearam, Maerim, Chiang Mai 50200
Mobile 66 (0) 1 460-0209
Booking Office in Bangkok
133/14 Ratchaprarop Road, Makkasan, Phayathai, Bangkok 10400
Tel 66 (0) 2 642-6361
 642-5497
Fax 66 (0) 2 246-5679
E-mail info@riverkwaifloatel.com
 flortel@samart.co.th
Booking Office in Chiang Mai
301/8 Soi Sbun-Nga Nimman Hae Min Road, Chiang Mai 50200
Tel/Fax 66 (0) 53 215-072
Web www.riverkwaifloatel.com

 1. By air and land (2 ½ hours)
Plane 1 hour and 10 minutes flight from Bangkok to Chiang Mai on Thai Airways (11 daily flights) or on Bangkok Airways. ***Car*** 1 hour from airport (42 kilometers); take Maerim–Samoeng Road, 5 kilometers after Maerim turn right (before the gas station), then continue for 15 kilometers: you will see a signboard on the left.
2. By land (12 hours)
Train 11 to 12 hours (about 700 kilometers) by Special Express train leaving from Hua Lamphong railway station every evening (air-conditioned cabins with sleeping berths). ***Car*** 1 hour from railway station (40 kilometers).
Note: *Transfer from Chiang Mai can be arranged by the resort*

 40 Units
10 Bungalows with 40 rooms.
All rooms have private bathroom (shower, hot water). There is a common terrace and a common living room with a coffee/tea maker at your disposal.

 Food and Beverage Outlets
1 Restaurant and 1 bar
Cuisine Offered: BBQ • Thai • International
Quality: Familial

 Water sports and Activities
Tours can be organized. It is advisable to book them when making your reservation (Rafting trips, mountain bike, forest treks, elephants safaris).

 Per room per night, half board

Mae-Sa Valley Craft Village

Flowers can be seen everywhere in Thailand. But nowhere in such abundance, in such variety of species, and so extensively grown as at the Mae-Sa Valley Craft Village. Nestled in the Mae-Sa valley's misty mountains, this resort is one-of-a-kind. Not only its spectacular flowery theme, but also its amazing traditional 'Craft Village' make this place a very popular destination for both resort guests and daily visitors, all coming to learn how to practice hands-on the traditional arts and crafts, with the help of talented local artisans.

The Craft Village sits at the foot of a hill, by the clear waters of a rushing stream. In a busy workshop atmosphere, participants try their skills, with much dedication and fun, on parasol or ceramic painting, 'Sa' paper making, or Batik dyeing. Wearing professional-looking aprons and head covers, others throw unknown spices into sizzling *woks* at the Thai cooking school, preparing exotic delicacies to be savored at the end of the class. These activities, all wonderfully designed and organized, are a hit with everyone, parents and children alike.

By crossing the rough wooden bridge overpassing the stream, guests walk into the resort's land, which extends up to the top of the rather steep hill. As one walks up the winding path, an unbelievable flower world slowly unfolds before one's flabbergasted eyes! Flowers bloom e.v.e.r.y.w.h.e.r.e. They're stretching out like thick but delicate carpets over all slopes and terraces; weeping down cottages' thatched roofs; trailing up pillars of the romantic summerhouses scattered amidst this Alice in Wonderland's huge parkland. For real garden lovers, the November to February period should not be missed, when Mae Sa radiates with all-around colorful flower works.

Traditional bamboo cottages and thatched-roof houses cling to the hillside, up to the top. Amidst this spectacular garden, each accommodation unit has been individually designed; hence one gets the pleasant feeling of walking through a village rather than through a resort. Yet, it is as if most care and attention had been focused on the exterior: the rooms' interior decoration is not of any very elaborate nor trendy style. Standard rooms are very simply furnished, but in rather folk and fun fashion: beds lay on a wood platform with colorful native bedcovers, large sitting cushions are thrown on the wooden floor, and kitsch checked orange curtains hang by the window. As every cottage's decoration is unique, some look more sophisticated and offer better comfort than others, as the 10 'concept rooms' do. Depending on your own personal taste, you can chose from the hilltribe, the farmer, or even the fisherman's cottage! The honeymoon cottage is an obvious choice, with its bamboo-paneled walls and a romantic mosquito net topping a king-size bed, and rough white curtains made of Chiang Mai hand-woven cotton to create a soft cocoon-like room. Children will definitely want to stay in the cottage displaying the most entertaining bathroom, where most amenities have been given an animal's shape. The highest cottage on the hill is one of the prettiest. But make sure you have strong legs and a good heart for walking to the top.

Mrs. Chinda, owner of the resort, says her love of nature was her only source of inspiration to create this very unique place, some 20 years ago. And as though proof of this dedication to nature had not been made sufficiently clear, guests will fully appreciate it in the resort restaurant, where a homemade cuisine is served offering fabulously fresh vegetables and spices, all grown at the resort's kitchen garden.

MAE-SA VALLEY CRAFT VILLAGE

P.O. Box 5, Mae Rim,
Chiang Mai 50180
Tel 66 (0) 53 290-051 to 52
Fax 66 (0) 53 290-017
E-mail *maesa1@ksc.th.com*
Web *www.thailandhotels.net/ chiang-mai-hotel*

Booking Office in Bangkok
41 Sukhumvit Soi 4,
Bangkok 10110
Tel 66 (0) 2 251-1704
656-9175 to 77
Fax 66 (0) 2 254-8865
251-1702

1. By air and land (2 hours) *Plane* 1 hour and 10 minutes flight from Bangkok to Chiang Mai on Thai Airways, (11 daily flights) or on Bangkok Airways. *Car* 45 minutes from airport (37 kilometers) on Mae Rim-Samoeng Road.
2. By land (12 hours) *Train* 11 to 12 hours (about 700 kilometers) by Special Express train leaving from Hua Lamphong railway station every evening (air-conditioned cabins with sleeping berths). *Car* 45 minutes from railway station (36 kilometers).
Note: Transfer from Chiang Mai can be arranged by the resort.

40 Units
30 Standard rooms (with fan only) • 10 Concept rooms (with air-conditioning)
All rooms have private terrace, private bathroom (hot shower) and mosquito net.

Food and Beverage Outlets
1 Restaurant with terrace overlooking the property
Cuisine Offered: Thai • some Western using garden vegetables
Quality: Good

Other services: Excursions can be organized with the help of Khun Somchart, manager of Mae-Sa Valley Craft Village.

Water sports and Activities
Health center for herbal steam room and massage in open sala • Trekking to Doi Suthep • Visits to San Kamphaeng hot springs • Mae Sa elephant camp nearby Queen Sirikit botanical gardens • Jungle elephant ride.

Activities provided by the Craft Village: Thai cookery school • Parasol and fan painting • Sa' papermaking • Batik dyeing • Ceramic painting

Per room per night not inclusive of breakfast

Pong Yang Garden Resort

A spectacular waterfall cascades down the slope of the hill of the Pong Yang Garden, and becomes a torrent as it reaches the valley below, surrounded by forests.

The restaurant, perched on the heights, is very popular in the region, partly for its dramatic surroundings but also for its innovative and spicy northern Thai cuisine. It is composed of a covered area and several wooden terraces on three different levels that have views of the waterfall and the gardens below. The rustic decor, with terracotta-tiled floors, wicker furniture, and several agrarian objects, lends a warm atmosphere to the whole place. At the base of the restaurant, a massif of frangipanis clings to the steep incline of the terrain. When in bloom, the trees give off an exquisite scent and, during winter, the strange silhouette of their naked and twisted branches is beautiful.

The Pong Yang gardens occupy the entire hillside right down to a flat expanse of grass at the edge of the swiftly running river, where a small lake has been created. The gardens were designed in such a way as to best conserve their natural aspect and keep them in harmony with the surrounding forest. Groves of massive bamboo trunks punctuate the space. Ox carts, decorated with red poinsettias, and large earthenware jars have been placed along the pathways; nestled within the foliage, they add a lovely rustic touch.

The gardens take on a magical atmosphere in the evenings, lit up by many tiny lights in the trees and the waterfall itself is illuminated.

The duplex bungalows are distributed between the bottom of the valley, along the river, and high up near the restaurant. Those situated near the river are almost completely engulfed in tropical vegetation. With a large wooden terrace overhanging the torrent and looking into the forest, they are somewhat dark and damp because of the dense greenery, but are also very tranquil; only the rhythm of rushing water will lull your nights.

The architecture of the bungalows is simple: a wooden structure set on wooden stilts with pointed roofs, unfortunately covered in corrugated iron. The interiors, including the ceilings, are completely covered with plaited bamboo. The mattresses are placed atop wooden platforms and are made up with warm blankets, as the nights can be especially cold in winter. At night the dim lighting makes the rooms a little sad. Each bungalow has its own clean and functional bathroom.

The reception at Pong Yang Garden Resort is efficient. Transfer to and from Chiang Mai can be organized, as well as various excursions if you ask in advance.

The incline and many steps make the resort rather difficult for elderly guests, unless they can arrange accommodation in one of the bungalows at the top.

PONG YANG GARDEN RESORT

49/3 Moo 2, T. Pong Yang, Mae Rim, Chiang Mai 50180
Tel 66 (0) 53 879-151 to 52
Fax 66 (0) 53 879-153
E-mail
pongyangangdoi@hotmail.com

 1. By air and land (2 hours)
Plane 1 hour and 10 minutes flight from Bangkok to Chiang Mai on Thai Airways (11 daily flights) or on Bangkok Airways. *Car* 45 minutes from airport (36 kilometers) on Mae Rim–Samoeng Road.
2. By land (12 hours)
Train 11 to 12 hours (about 700 kilometers) by Special Express train leaving from Hua Lamphong railway station every evening (air-conditioned cabins with sleeping berths). *Car* 45 minutes from railway station (35 kilometers).
Note: *Transfer from Chiang Mai can be arranged by the resort.*

 19 Units
16 rooms in 8 Duplex bungalows • 3 Private bungalows
All rooms have private terrace, private bathroom (shower, hot water), air-conditioning, TV, minibar and coffee/tea maker.

 Food and Beverage Outlets
1 Restaurant and bar
Cuisine Offered: Thai
Quality: Very good and very spicy
Friendly service.

Other services: Internet • Telephone (reception)

 Water sports and Activities
The resort can organize excursions (request in advance), visit to Queen Sirikit botanical gardens (5 minutes by car).

 Per room per night

Ban Klang Doi Hotel and Resort

At Ban Klang Doi you will stay in a traditional Lanna house and benefit from all modern comforts and competent service. The resort offers several types of accommodation, but the most pleasing by far are the seven Lanna houses, situated apart from the others in a beautiful garden of trees and flowers, on an undulating landscape facing forested hills. A small brook meanders to one side.

The teak Lanna houses have a rather imposing aspect; they are supported by massive pillars, designing a beautiful trapezoidal structure. Their roofs are covered with shingles made of gray wood. Each house is different in size as well as in decoration. Some are individual, while others are semi-detached, but even the latter are nonetheless private as their terraces are separated by a common platform.

Rooms number 39 and 40 boast original bathrooms made up of a verdant open-roofed patio, protected by a mosquito net. An enormous tree trunk has been incorporated into one of the terraces. The "Deluxe Thai House," number 35, is a large and very attractive family-sized house with three rooms and a lovely spacious terrace overhanging the garden, which is decorated with one of the superb natural rocks that grace Ban Klang Doi. The house also offers a spacious lounge, furnished in an attractive wooden furniture from Burma and well illuminated thanks to large bay windows.

The "Mini Thai Private House," Number 38, is perfect for a couple; it is perched, well isolated at the end of the garden. Its terrace, made up of a sofa and a low Thai table, is a place where you will enjoy relaxing, soothed by the murmuring of a small waterfall and the somewhat hoarse calls of the frogs in the evening. The interior decoration is rather disparate: a mixture of traditional objects and the rather incongruous aspect of a washstand facing the bed. The overall effect is nonetheless rather pleasant. For those who have their own car, there is also parking space just below the house.

At the back there is another building of more ordinary architecture, which houses ten rooms. These are of good size, and not without character, with half-timbered white walls, original wooden bathtubs made of teak in bathrooms lined with black stones. The rooms on the upper floor offer a more open view than those on the ground floor and have balconies.

In another area of the grounds, completely separate from the Lanna houses, Ban Klang Doi offers "VIP Houses" and "Junior Suites;" the immense rooms are rather sad, decorated in an overdone "European style." They are also excessively expensive.

Breakfasts and lunches are served in a large pavilion at the entrance of the resort or in the individual Lanna pavilions along the water. The second restaurant where dinner is served is not especially attractive in the evenings as it is rather dark; it is infinitely more pleasant to have your dinner served in your Lanna villa. The resort offers a swimming pool and a small spa. The personnel at the reception speak good English and are very competent; they can arrange anything from answering simple information requests to transfers or excursions.

BAN KLANG DOI HOTEL AND RESORT

190 Hang Dong-Samoeng Road, Banpong, Hang Dong, Chiang Mai
Tel   66 (0) 53 365-306 to 07
             565-350 to 01
Fax   66 (0) 53 365-307
E-mail
baanklangdoi@yahoo.com
Booking Office in Bangkok
2272/100-1 Ramkhamhaeng Soi 42, Huamak, Bangkapi, Bangkok 10240
Tel/Fax 66 (0) 2 732-1876 to 77

1. By air and land (2 hours)
Plane 1 hour and 10 minutes flight from Bangkok to Chiang Mai on Thai Airways (11 daily flights) or on Bangkok Airways. ***Car*** 30 minutes from airport (23 kilometers) on Hang Dong–Samoeng Road.
2. By land (11 ½ to 12 hours)
Train 11 to 12 hours (about 700 kilometers) by Special Express train leaving from Hua Lamphong railway station every evening (air-conditioned cabins with sleeping berths). ***Car*** 45 minutes from railway station (30 kilometers).
Note: *Transfer from Chiang Mai can be arranged by the resort (free of charge).*

20 Units
(in the Lanna part of the resort)
3 Mini Thai houses (1 bedroom) • 4 Deluxe Mini Thai houses (duplex houses with 2 bedrooms that can be rented separately) • 2 Deluxe Thai houses (1 with 3 bedrooms—only 1 bedroom with air-conditioning, 1 with 4 bedrooms) • 10 rooms in a 2-story building
All rooms have private terrace, private bathroom (shower, hot water), air-conditioning, phone, TV and minibar.

Food and Beverage Outlets
2 Restaurants and 1 bar
Quality: Familial
Other services: Babysitting (request in advance) • Car rental

Water sports and Activities
Swimming pool • Spa • Thai massage • Mountain biking

 Per room per night

Lanna Resort

There is a timeless beauty about the grounds of the Lanna Resort, set deep between the bamboo-covered slopes of a wild valley. The park is so often deserted, it seems as though the vibrant natural surroundings have been arranged, or brought under control, by a magician.

Trees, hundreds of years old, ficus, with their tentacle-like vines, border the paths, along which attractive wooden Lanna pavilions are perched on stilts, the peaks of their roofs adorned with the traditional cross-shaped *kalae.*

The wide lawns are dotted with numerous trimmed shrubs, colorful bougainvillea, ficus trees and hedges of "golden tea" with their yellowy-gold foliage. Cypress groves raise their elongated silhouettes, adding a European note to the gardens. Daturas, adorned with their white hanging trumpet flowers, suc-culent agaves, euphorbias abound, surrounded by colorful beds of calendula, Busy Lizzies, amaranths, red salvias and roses. An enormous cycad massif adds a spectacular touch to the garden. The flowers are at their best during the winter months, from December to March.

Strangely, while the gardens are meticulously and lovingly tended by the proprietors, the pavilions show some signs of wear (weathered, scratched wood on the terraces, slightly shabby interiors).

The Lanna pavilions are generally semi-detached, each room opening on a pleasant terrace. Most enjoy a superb view of the grounds (especially pavilions 1 to 6); others look over the small free-form swimming pool or a stream.

The resort also offers two family-sized pavilions.

The rooms are small, simply furnished and provided with minuscule

The North • Around Chiang Mai

bathrooms. Nevertheless, for a very reasonable price, you have the essential elements of comfort: air-conditioning (although, in winter, the blankets are more useful!), a telephone, a small television, and hot water.

The reception and restaurant are situated in a large and attractive Lanna-style pavilion with its roof of old wooden shingles, smoothed and burnished by time, extended by a wide terrace. The interior decoration is pleasantly rustic with its massive wooden pillars and high, latticed wicker ceilings, from which cartwheels hang down, serving as suspensions.

The restaurant closes at 8 p.m. and not a sound, other than those of the abundant nature around you, will trouble your sleep.

You will wake rested and refreshed in the morning, ready to begin another day in the valley. How magnificent to see the sun emerging over the hill, illuminating the dewy grounds with a soft pink wash of light!

During your stay at the Lanna Resort, you will need your own car, as they do not organize excursions. If it were renovated, Lanna Resort, with the unparalleled beauty of its gardens, could be one of the most appealing in this region.

LANNA RESORT

1 Moo 4 Hang Dong-Samoeng Road, T. Banpong Amphoe Hang Dong, Chiang Mai 50230
Tel 66 (0) 53 365-222 to 23
Fax 66 (0) 53 365-224

1. By air and land (2 hours)
Plane 1 hour and 10 minutes flight from Bangkok to Chiang Mai on Thai Airways (11 daily flights) or on Bangkok Airways. *Car* 30 minutes from airport (18 kilometers).
2. By land (11 ½ hours)
Train 11 to 12 hours (about 700 kilometers) by Special Express train leaving from Hua Lamphong railway station every evening (air-conditioned cabins with sleeping berths). *Car* 35 minutes from railway station (25 kilometers).
Note: *Transfer from Chiang Mai can be arranged by the resort.*

47 Units
45 Rooms
All rooms have private terrace, private bathroom (shower, hot water), air-conditioning and phone and TV.
2 Family cottages (2 bedrooms, living room and one Big House for 12 people near the pool)

Food and Beverage Outlets
1 Restaurant (closes at 8 p.m.)
Quality: Average

Water sports and Activities
Swimming pool • Massage

 Per room per night

Kao Mai Lanna Resort Hotel

Kao Mai Lanna was born out of Mr. Thawat Cherdsthirakul's determination to preserve the rapidly disappearing tobacco barns that were so numerous in the region fifty years ago.

What a surprise, leaving the bustling road from Chiang Mai to San Pa Tong, to go through a spectacular wooden porch, into a large six-hectare wooded park to discover there 52 tobacco barns!

Eighteen barns have been converted into thirty-six rooms, offering on two levels luxurious lodging space, brimming with character. The exteriors, characterized by high red brick walls and corrugated iron roofs, have been left deliberately as they were; only windows with wooden crossbars have been pierced.

On the fringes of the park, you can see the old barns in their original state, the oldest made of brick, others of whitewashed bamboo. The grounds are overrun by vegetation and have a strange, rather melancholic atmosphere. The proprietor once kept a nursery, which is now abandoned, and you can find all around hundreds of varnished jars and plants. This is where a beautiful swimming pool has just been built; its cool waters reflect the towering trees, alive with birdsongs in the mornings.

The idea of converting the barns into a hotel was a rather audacious one, since originally, the three lines of six barns could have had a rather austere aspect. Mr. Thawat Cherdsthirakul, seeking to break the monotony, created a labyrinth of alleys and wooden walkways to connect the buildings, parts of which are covered with arbors, heavy with entangled passion fruits and vines. Creeping ficus vines have almost completely covered some facades of the buildings with their small round leaves, giving the place a truly romantic aspect.

The interiors have been entirely remodeled with exquisite taste and particular attention to detail. The rooms are spacious and each is decorated in its own unique style. The beautiful white leaded teak furniture is from Burma, where it was made by English cabinetmakers. Depending on the room, there are four-poster beds, wooden chests, dressing tables, and colonial-style cane armchairs.

Each room comprises a spacious entrance and, a few steps above, the bedroom area with superb red wooden parquet floors. The harmonious colors in room, well lit in the evenings, are made up of soft tones: walls painted pale gray and white, crocheted curtains and bedspreads in a gentle ecru. Altogether, it is very cozy with an English-cottage look tinged with a hint of the orient.

The bathrooms are an original and inventive blend of ceruse wood, wooden shingles, handcrafted tiles on the floors and colored ceramic splinters inlaid around the bath and shower.

Unfortunately located slightly too close to the busy road, but opened onto the garden, the restaurant is housed in a large Lanna pavilion, whose roof is covered with wooden shingle. It is decorated with various agrarian objects and jars.

Apart from its charm and history, Kao Mai Lanna is a good base from which to explore the region and, especially, the superb Doi Inthanon National Park and its unique cloud forest.

KAO MAI LANNA RESORT HOTEL

1 Moo 6 Chiang Mai-Hod Road,
Baan-glang Sanpatong,
Chiang Mai 50120
Tel   66 (0) 53 834-470 to 75
Fax   66 (0) 53 834-480
E-mail
         service@kaomailanna.com
Web   *www.kaomailanna.com*

1. By air and land (2 hours)
Plane 1 hour and 10 minutes flight from Bangkok to Chiang Mai on Thai Airways (11 daily flights) or on Bangkok Airways. *Car* 45 minutes from airport (29 kilometers) on the Chiang Mai–San Pa Tong Road.
2. By land (11 ½ hours)
Train 11 to 12 hours (about 700 kilometers) by Special Express train leaving from Hua Lamphong railway station every evening (air-conditioned cabins with sleeping berths). *Car* 35 minutes from railway station (37 kilometers)
Note: *Transfer from Chiang Mai by the resort minibus can be arranged free-of-charge.*

36 Units
36 Rooms in two-story tobacco barns
All rooms have private bathroom (separate bathtub and shower, hot water), air-conditioning, IDD phone, cable, TV and minibar.

Food and Beverage Outlets
1 Restaurant and bar
Quality: Familial • Friendly service
Cuisine Offered: Thai
Other services: Baan Boran shop • Car rental • Excursions

Water sports and Activities
Swimming pool • Ruins of the 800-year-old town of Viang Tha Karn (3 kilometers) • Doi Inthanon (the entrance of the park is about 30 kilometers away) • Rafting in the jungle stream of Mae Wang (the site is 26 kilometers west of San Pa Tong) • Elephant camp at Ban Kad • Sunday market at Ban Viang (water buffalo and cattle) • Ban Thawai wooden handicraft center

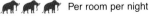   Per room per night

The Golden Triangle

Naga protecting a temple

The mountainous region between Mae Taeng up to Fang and Thaton has become more and more popular in recent years, especially with trekkers visiting the hilltribe villages.

The quiet and rural village of **Thaton** is a pretty place from where to enjoy different travel adventures, ranging from simple walks along the Mae Nam Kok's banks to more exciting rafting excursions on the river's tumultuous waters right after the rainy season. Lahu villages are easily reachable by bike or even on foot.

The welcoming **Thaton River View Resort** sits along the river's banks. From there, the hotel will efficiently arrange 1-, 2- or even 3-day rafting journeys down the river with as many stops as you wish to explore the Palaung, Lahu, and Akha hilltribe villages.

A half-a-day journey in a long-tail boat along the picturesque Mae Nam Kok River is the most exotic available transportation to reach the nearby city of Chiang Rai.

Chiang Rai is a rather small city offering an easy-going ambiance, a few interesting *wats* worth discovering and a small Night Market.

Those looking for a perfect relaxing nature retreat outside the city will enjoy the unique design of the **Phu Chaisai Resort** located less than 1 hour drive from

Detail, Chiang Rai Temple

Chiang Rai Festivals

Sakura Flowers Blooming Fair: End of January—held at Doi Mae Salong. This festival features exhibitions and performances from the area's hilltribes.
Wild Flowers Blooming Fair: From January 13th to 15th—held at Fah Thai village. The fair features several hilltribe performances and various sports events.
Strawberries and Flowers Blooming Fair: Early February—in the village of Mae Sai.
Chiang Saen Songkran Festival and Boat Racing: From the 16th to the 18th of April. In Chiang Rai province, Songkran is best celebrated at the village of Chiang Saen.

Floating market in Chiang Rai

Chiang Rai's center and a hub to many beautiful excursions. On the Chiang Mai–Chiang Rai Road is the elegant and also isolated **Suanthip Vana Resort**.

The Golden Triangle has long been a fascinating spot to many worldwide visitors, mostly because of its poisonous fame related to the opium industry. Its fame also comes from its location right at the confluence of two huge Asian rivers— the Mekong and the Mae Ruak—and three countries—Thailand, Laos and Myanmar.

Although the Thai government has massively cleaned up the drug business in the region, this northernmost point of the country remains a very popular area for visitors. Buses can be seen lining up the River's banks during the tourism high season, next to the too many souvenirs shops selling T-shirts and postcards.

Yet this region has remained extremely attractive to nature lovers and trekkers as it offers a huge variety of jungles and forested areas to explore. As a consequence of this attraction, too many villages have become tourist traps. To

Detail, Chiang Rai Temple

avoid them, it is advisable to arrange your treks or river cruise through travel agencies located within the most renowned hotels and resorts. For serious treks and genuine encounters with hilltribe villages, we highly recommend the one- to four-day journeys around the Golden Triangle Area offered by the Hilltribe Museum in Chiang Rai. A huge range of excursions — treks on foot, aboard 4-wheel drive vans, elephant, bamboo rafts or longtail boats — into the homelands of hill tribe villagers can be organized within small groups.

Reaching the Golden Triangle by bike or motorbike from the small village of **Chiang Saen** is a very enjoyable experience. This village has been kept relatively untouched, with a colorful morning market, and its riverbank busy with boats unloading goods coming all the way from China. A few ancient and ruined wats are worth a walk or two up the hill, to embrace the very romantic feeling exuded by these vanishing monuments: **Wat Phratat Chedi Luang, Wat Mun Muang,** protected by a huge teak tree, and **Wat Roi Kho. Wat Pa Sak,** located in the middle of a teak forest, is one of the most artistically striking *wats* in the area, showing common features with the wonderful temples to be seen in Sukhothai or Pagan in Myanmar.

Right at the heart of the Golden Triangle, beside the Sop Ruak–Mae Sai Road is the Lanna-style **Baan Boran Resort,** undoubtedly the best resort in the whole area, set amidst a huge and scenic park.

Mae Hong Son

(6 hours drive from Chiang Mai) The province of Mae Hong Son remained totally isolated from the travelers' crowds until very recent years. Although it can now be reached by plane — if visibility allows so — the 6-hour car journey through Pai (or the 8- to 9-hour journey through Mae Sarian) is an unforgettable sinuous mountain drive (with 1,864 curves) disclosing the most unbelievable scenic views all along the way.

At the end of the road, Mae Hong Son is an extremely peaceful and picturesque small town. Built originally as an elephant center around the calm waters of a tiny lake by Burmese-Shan people, it has so far kept its 19th-century charm and genuine atmosphere untouched, with old teak houses and shops, and a lovely morning market. In the middle of the town, many beautiful Shan-style *wats* are worth seeing: **Wat Chong Klan** and **Wat Chong Kham** around the lake and **Wat Plai Doi** at the summit of Doi Kong Mon. The latter is best visited during the early morning hours when fog evaporates over the rice fields and teak forests and discloses plunging views onto Mae Hong Son's roofs.

Longneck girl, Karen tribes

Wat Chong Kham

Although Mae Hong Son is an extremely quiet village where you cannot expect any of Chiang Mai's night life entertainment, do not miss a relaxing after-dinner drink at the Lakeside Bar, to enjoy the friendly local band playing old R&B standards, on the terrace around the tiny lake.

Padaung villages have become a major attraction around Mae Hong Son to discover the so-called longneck women wearing traditional tall gold collars. So, if you accept to enter the rather zoo-like atmosphere of the Padaung villages, you will be impressed to meet these aristocratic people belonging to the **Karen tribes** who have been expelled into Thailand by Myanmar's regime.

Beside the town of Mae Hong Son, isolated at the foot of **Mae Surin National Park**, the **Fern Resort** is a perfect place to rest and organize fabulous nature treks around the region with very experienced and friendly guides.

Mae Hong Son Festivals

Poi Sang Long Festival: Late March to early April; lasts for 3 days. Poi Sang Long is a Buddhist novice ordination ceremony, attracting people from far and wide.

Chong Pa Ra Procession: October—at the end of the rainy season. Locals build elaborate models of castles and place them in front of temples and their homes.

Wild-Sunflower Blossom Fair: November/December—held at Doi Mae U-Kho and Doi Mae Hoh when the sunflowers blossom and carpet the surrounding countryside for miles in each direction.

Thaton River View Resort

Tha Ton is a small and quiet rural town stretching along the banks of the Mae Nam Kok, at the foot of misty hills. It has become very popular with visitors departing for treks along the nearby Yao and Karen villages and for river cruises to and from Chiang Rai aboard bamboo rafts or long-tail boats. With the increase of such adventure-tourism, many hotels and guest houses have bloomed in the area for the last 15 years. A sparkle lies hidden within one of them: the Thaton River View Resort, owned by Khun Chantana Indragarjita, fairy godmother of this rustic and cheerful Shan-style place.

As the river is the beating heart of the landscape, the hotel's entire structure deliberately extends along the shore of the Mae Nam Kok as if naturally blending into the natural surrounding of flowing waters and morning hazy hills. A serpentine wooden pontoon connects the guest rooms and cottages, making the way to one's room a pleasant walk. All rooms and cottages face the river, except the more recent ones built around the large open-air barbecue area. Although the bungalows are aligned in quite a stiff manner, a feeling of homely privacy floats around these simple and country-styled bungalows. This is probably because of the charm of their individual terrace—a perfect spot for whispering night secrets under the stars—, because of their spaciousness as well, their wooden floor soft to the feet, and their unsophisticated yet pleasant inside fitting, all using native materials. With amenities kept to a minimum, bathrooms are perfectly clean and provide standard comfort. The real magic of the place performs at night though. At the time of switching off the bedside lamp, the murmurs of the flowing river and the calls of the *gecko* start the most exotic lullaby behind the window's mosquito net.

Meals at the resort are a time for real enjoyment, not restricted to hotel guests. The restaurant is actually highly rated in the region. As a matter of fact, it proudly displays the 19 awards received to date from the famous Shell Chuan Chim guide for its best homemade dishes—all taught to kitchen staff by Khun Chantana in person. As a consequence of such celebrity, local gourmets may pretty well fill up the huge dining room located under the high-vaulted ceiling of the main building. The restaurant terrace glows at night with special charm, as garlands of multicolored lights create a festive and unpretentious decor, reflected in the river's waters. At the time of early morning breakfast, with birds as only table neighbors on the still deserted terrace, the tangerine marmalade is an unforgettable flight into paradise!

On the other side of the main building, a lovely garden stretches out with a plantation of *litchi* trees and a profusion of flowers. It is the setting of an unusual jogging trail. This side of the property also leads to a low-rise wooden construction housing a herbal sauna and rooms for Thai massage. Finally, Khun Chantana welcomes hilltribe people from the neighborhood for a daily handicraft market outside the resort lobby.

THATON RIVER VIEW RESORT

302 Baan Thaton, Mae Ai,
Chiang Mai 50280
Tel　66 (0) 53 373-173 to 76
Fax　66 (0) 53 418-900
E-mail
thatonriverview@ hotmail.com

　1. By air and land (2 hours and 45 minutes)　*Plane* 1 hour and 10 minutes flight on Thai Airways (11 daily flights) from Bangkok to Chiang Mai.　*Car* 1 ½ hour drive over 90 kilometers of hilly and scenic highway up to the resort.
2. By land (12 hours)　*Car* 3 daily air-conditioned buses from Bangkok to Tha Ton (with New Wiriya Tour or 999-Tour bus companies).
Note: Airport transfer can be arranged by the resort.

　35 Units
22 Standard rooms · 13 Cottages (displayed along three different wings—8 rooms by the Litchi wing, 20 rooms facing the river by the River wing and 7 rooms by the 'Barbecue wing')
All rooms have private balcony, private bathroom (hot shower), air-conditioning, telephone, satellite TV.

Food and Beverage Outlets
Best restaurant in the area, awarded by famous Shell Chuan Chim guide. Excellent seafood supplied daily, and fabulous fruits in season (own mangoes plantation and litchi orchard). Food and drinks can be arranged at the 'Barbecue wing' for casual/private groups upon request.
Casual bar for snacks and drinks.
Cuisine Offered: Thai · Chinese · International · Seafood
Quality: Excellent (the best in the area)
Other services: Gift shop

Water sports and Activities
Sauna · Traditional Thai massage on request · Jogging trail within litchi orchard · Hilltribe daily market in front of lobby · Boat excursions to Chiang Rai (3 hours) or to close-by hilltribes (1 hour) · Bamboo-rafting adventure to Chiang Rai (1 to 3 days) · Visits by car to hilltribes around Thaton · Various trekking programs

　Per room per night inclusive of breakfast

Phu Chaisai Resort and Spa

Have you ever, as a child, dreamt of a wooden hut? A hiding place where you could only listen to the amazing sounds of nature? Famous Thai architect and high society designer M.L. Sudavadee Kriangkrai has created, with immense talent, such a nest for people longing for simple and soul-filled nature communing.

On this land owned by her family, Sudavadee has left behind her skills in creating wealthy urban buildings. Here, her inspiration is led by her love of the way the hilltribe people build their homes around this rural region of Chiang Rai. Located eight kilometers uphill from the road to Mae Sai, Phu Chaisai—'Mountain of Clear Heart'—sets an exceptional nature-friendly resort, nearly entirely built and decorated with bamboo. Other materials used are all traditional, like red-colored mud for walls and lanes, raw cotton for fabrics and teak leaves for the topping of peak-roofed pavilions.

This peaceful place, seated on top of the hill, offers 28 rustic suite-type cottages, each of them with a unique interior design, and all connected by narrow paths and intricate bamboo walkways. Widely opened to the mountains' backdrop, each cottage welcomes guests with a large private verandah, where a cushioned bamboo divan is an invitation to indulgent hours. Inside the hut, the layout of the spacious room is a clear demonstration of how perfect taste and comfort can be achieved by pure simplicity. Bamboo is everywhere: from ceiling to walls and floors, from furniture to door handles, lamps, and even clothes hangers and electric wall switches! Within room 701—our favorite room—a large canopy bed with nicely draped four-sided mosquito nets stands on a smooth and glossy bamboo floor. Uncomplicated furniture make this room a very special place to relax, nap, and dream. Large windows on three out of the four walls of the room create a fascinating openness to the surrounding lush tropical nature, while at the same time reinforcing the coddling feeling of being nestled inside a cocoon. At the back of the room, a sky-lighted bathroom with bathtub and separate shower offers all expected amenities, set in a beautiful rustic decor. Hidden into the greenery, a fanciful love nest, an untraditional suite with a huge open-air garden-bathroom, is much in demand by honeymooners and requires booking well in advance.

On the highest point of the hill, an open-sided pavilion restaurant and a charming circular terrace surround an ornamental pool reflecting the twisted shapes of a frangipani tree. Beside this dining venue—unfortunately providing a limited but quite pricey menu—, lies a friendly-decorated open bar and sitting area which lead to a homely library. Garden lovers much enjoy walking up and down the resort's alleys, as they discover a rich variety of plants, flowers and bushes, duly name-tagged as if in a botanical garden.

Phu Chaisai is unquestionably an isolated haven within a beautiful region, a special retreat to savor a simpler world.

PHU CHAISAI RESORT AND SPA

 388 Moo 4, Ban Mae Salong Nai, Mae Chan, Chiang Rai 57110

Tel	66 (0) 53 918-333
	(0) 53 918-636
	(0) 53 918-637
Fax	66 (0) 53 918-333
E-mail	phu_chaisai@hotmail.com
Web	www.phu-chaisai.com

Booking Office in Bangkok
Tel	66 (0) 2 260-2646
	66 (0) 2 661-5898 to 99
Fax	66 (0) 2 260-2645
	66 (0) 2 661-5897

 By air and land (2 ½ hours)
Plane 1 hour and 10 minutes flight on Thai Airways (11 daily flights) from Bangkok to Chiang Mai. ***Car*** 50 minutes drive over 34 kilometres to reach the resort.
Note: Airport transfer can be arranged by the resort. Drive to Chiang Rai's city center takes approximately 1 hour.

 28 Units
12 Superior cottages • 10 Deluxe cottages • 5 Executive Suite cottages 1 Honeymoon suite • 2 Special Villas (for special guests renting only)
All rooms have private terrace, private bathroom (shower only in Superior, separate bathtub and shower in the other rooms, hot water), air-conditioning, minibar, and coffee/tea maker.
Note: A TV set can be installed in the room on request.

 Food and Beverage Outlets
Restaurant: Phu View Restaurant (with scenic circular terrace)
Cuisine Offered: Thai • International
Bars: Phu View Barlu • Phu View Underground Club (enjoy drinks in two different totally relaxed atmospheres)
Quality: Average

Other services: Telephone (available through reception) • Nice native gift shop

 Water sports and Activities
Outdoor pool for relaxing swim • Spa offering body massages and treatments • Large library • Painting and Thai cooking classes for small groups • Golf at Santiburi Golf Club • Tour programs to Doi Tun Mae Sai • Boat trip to Karen, Lahu and Akha villages and elephant camp, and extensive visit of Chiang Rai.

 Per room per night inclusive of breakfast

Suanthip Vana Resort

If a blend of isolation and total relaxation in the middle of forested hills, with elaborate and modern amenities, is what you are looking for, this is a place for you. Located by the main road some 70 kilometers south from Chiang Rai and 107 kilometers north of Chiang Mai, the fairly recent Suanthip Vana Resort is quite an unusual spot to be found in such a remote and wild area.

Initially, the Suanthip Vana Resort was not meant to be a resort. The original project of its owner was to build a property to welcome his family and friends. His dream estate property was to be inspired by the most luxurious Lanna-styled resort of the Chiang Mai area. But, as the project moved to construction, it so expanded in size and scope that, ultimately, it overcame its first compass and became a resort.

From the main road into Suanthip Vana, a majestic private alley climbs up the hill to reach the resort's main entrance. An imposing flight of stairs takes you up to the huge, open air lobby, offering a spectacular view on the surrounding forest, expanding in all tones of green. Under a lofty vaulted ceiling supported by massive teak pillars, reception staff greet guests with professional manners. The impeccable setting of the lounge—though slightly formal—and the affability of the staff illustrate how hospitality is highly regarded by the resort's management.

Five two-story pavilions house the 30 deluxe rooms of the resort, scattered around a perfectly maintained tropical garden. These five houses are elegantly designed, with out-bricks frontage and Lanna-styled roofs. Privacy is well protected and guests can hardly believe that each pavilion shelters six rooms, three on the ground floor and three on the second floor, the latter accessed by a private external staircase. Each room offers an extremely commodious and bright living space serving as an entrance hall which leads to a large bedroom, extending to a vast sitting area. Room style is fresh, clean, but resolutely functional. Some simple decorative touches are subtly used to warm up the room's atmosphere. Bathrooms, very functional too, scrupulously clean, and open to morning sunlight, provide only the best in a refined setting: carved wood mirror frame, marble basin top, and an environment-friendly items galore like superior quality cotton towels, natural Thai herbs' soap and shampoo… An outside terrace complements the rooms' comfort.

In the main house, a well supplied reading room is located on a tranquil area of the upper floor covered terrace. A small bar, a snooker room, and even a karaoke bar are the after-dinner favorites with guests. At the center of the garden, the large and pleasant lagoon-shaped swimming pool is surrounded by high-rise trees shading the pool deck.

The terrace of the Toke Kham restaurant is a lovely setting for Thai or international candle-lit dinners, in the absolute silence of this remote world. Candle light is actually the magic wand of Suanthip Vana to be discovered when all the resort's garden alleys are lit in sheer magic for the eyes as you walk back to your room, under a black velvet sky studded with stars.

SUANTHIP VANA RESORT

49 Chiang Mai–Chiang Rai Road, Tambon Takok, Amphur Mae Suay, Chiang Rai 57180
Tel 66 (0) 1 224-6984 to 86
Fax 66 (0) 1 213-9821
E-mail *sale@suanthipresort.com*

Booking Office in Bangkok
14/F Phaholyothin Place,
408/55 Phaholyothin Road,
Samsennai, Phayathai,
Bangkok 10400
Tel 66 (0) 2 619-0363 to 64
619-0368 to 69
Fax 66 (0) 2 619-0208
E-mail *rsvn@suanthipresort.com*
Web *www.suanthipresort.com*

 By air and land
1. From Bangkok via Chiang Rai (2 ½ hours) *Plane* 1 hour and 15 minutes flight on Thai Airways (4 daily flights) from Bangkok to Chiang Rai. *Car* 1 hour drive over 75 kilometers to reach the resort.
2. From Bangkok via Chiang Mai (3 hours) *Plane* 1 hour and 10 minutes flight from Bangkok to Chiang Mai on Thai Airways (11 daily flights) or on Bangkok Airway. *Car* 1 hour and 45 minutes drive over 107 kilometers.
Note: Transfer from Chiang Rai or Chiang Mai airport can be arranged by the resort.

 30 Units
30 Deluxe rooms (with sitting area and private terrace located in 5 Lanna-styled pavilions, fully equipped with individually controlled air-conditioning, minibar/fridge, coffee maker, telephone voice mail and cable TV. Bathroom with bathtub and Thai herbal toiletries.

 Food and Beverage Outlets
Restaurants: 2 dining rooms; Toke Khum • Juer Jan
Campfire barbecue on request, 1 pool-bar and 1 karaoke bar
Cuisine Offered: Thai and international
Quality: Very good

Other services: 2 Function rooms with capacity for 50 to 100 people • Tours and travel arrangements at the tour desk

 Water sports and Activities
Swimming pool • Fitness center • Sauna • Snooker room • Library with reading room • Thai cooking class • Free mountain bike • Jogging trail

 Per room per night not inclusive of breakfast

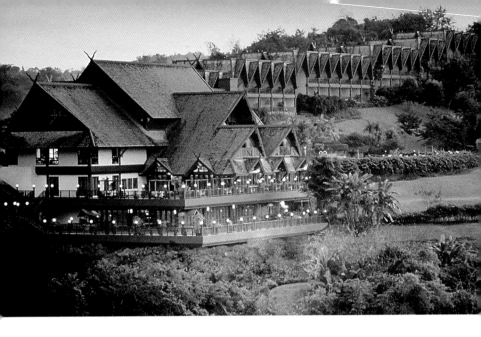

Baan Boran Resort

In the middle of the legendary and infamous Golden Triangle, where the Nam Ruak river meets the giant MeKong, stands, oddly enough, a Lanna-style modern palace. Formerly known as 'Le Méridien Baan Boran' when it opened in 1991, it is now called the 'Baan Boran Resort' since its acquisition by the Royal Garden Resorts group in April 2002. Perched atop a hill planted with thousands of teak trees, the five-star Baan Boran Resort offers the very best accommodation of this northernmost region of Thailand, whose appeal lies in visiting the opium-trading hilltribes; and having the family picture taken at this crossroads where Thailand, Myanmar and Laos meet.

What dazzles any newcomer to Baan Boran is the imposing architectural complex both embodying the heritage of Northern Thailand and blending harmoniously with its environment. The resort has been widely praised by connoisseurs as a perfect example of ecotourism. Designed by famous architect and mem-

ber of the royal family, M.L. Tridhosyuth Devakul, the hotel welcomes guests with a stunning monumental Thai building connecting two low-rise accommodation buildings. The style of Baan Boran is sumptuously displayed inside the huge lobby. Here, three gigantic 'Glong Yao' (long drums) create a cultural as well as a decorative imposing centerpiece. Other samples of northern art treasures are displayed everywhere under the immense vaulted ceiling lobby, making one wonder if this is indeed the Baan Boran Resort, or a Lanna culture heritage museum.

Accommodation is distributed along two-story buildings, running along the ridge, and topped with sharp-pointed wooden roofs. These are home to 110 deluxe rooms and suites all appointed with their own balconies offering magnificent views on Laos and Myanmar scenery. The atmosphere of the rooms is rather conventional, although ethnic materials and designs are extensively used for decoration; modern amenities fully provide the level of comfort expected in such high standard hotel.

Dining at the resort is a diversified experience, with no less than six different venues and styles: from early morning buffet breakfast enjoyed on the sunbathed terrace of the main restaurant overviewing the Ruak River to pleasant campfire barbecue dinners at the 'Hill Top,' and not to mention the inviting and well-named 'Trafficker Rendez-Vous' bar for sipping cocktails by the library and the huge fireplace.

What makes the Baan Boran Resort such a relaxing oasis is the wide variety of activities, to please both parents and children after a day's excursion in the area. The resort is located within a huge property of 64 hectares, beautifully cared for and planted with a wide variety of flora. A jogging trail runs along 64 hectares of a bamboo and teak plantation, another token of the serious eco-tourism commitment of the resort. Birdwatching expeditions and elephant safaris are favorites amidst the 'exotic' activities proposed at the resort like mountain biking, hiking, and long-tail boat on the Mekong river. More traditional sports like tennis, squash, and swimming in the huge bean-shaped outdoor pool definitely make the Baan Boran Resort the very best place to stay at when visiting the Golden Triangle.

BAAN BORAN RESORT

 The Golden Triangle, Chiang Saen, Chiang Rai 57150
Tel 66 (0) 53 784-084
Fax 66 (0) 53 784-090
E-mail *info@baanboran.com*
Web *www.baanboran.com*

 By air and land (2 ½ hours)
Plane 1 hour and 10 minutes flight on Thai Airways (11 daily flights) from Bangkok to Chiang Mai. *Car* 1-hour drive over 74 kilometers to reach the resort.

Note: Transfer from and to the airport can be arranged by shuttle bus or by private limousine.

 107 Units
62 Superior rooms · 42 Deluxe rooms · 3 Suites
All rooms have private bathroom (separate bathtub and shower, hot water), air-conditioning, IDD phone, cable TV, minibar and safety box. Coffee/tea maker in all deluxe rooms.

Food and Beverage Outlets
Restaurants: Yuan Lue Lao (the main open air dining room, serving breakfast, lunches and dinners) · Opium Den (Italian pizza and pasta) · Trafficker Rendez-Vous (for cocktails) · Triangle Deck (snacks and drinks by the pool) · Suan Fin (traditional Northern Thai Khantoke) · Hill Top (campfire barbecues)
Cuisine Offered: Thai and European
Quality: Very good food and service

Other services: Internet · Well-appointed gift shop · Babysitting · In-house 'Diethelm Travel' office desk

 Water sports and Activities
Large swimming pool with garden pool side · Fitness center with sauna and Jacuzzi · Game room with karaoke · Movies and snooker at the 'Opium Den' · Squash and tennis courts · Mountain bike rental · Birdwatching · Trekking · Elephant safari · Long-tail boat cruises along the Mekong

Note: *Baan Boran will have been named the Anantara Resort and Spa Chiang Saen by 2004.*

 Per room per night

Fern Resort ♥

Nestled within an untouched hilly woodland, the quiet town of Mae Hong Son was unknown to travelers until trekking and rafting adventures boomed a few years ago and made it a favorite destination for nature lovers. Hence an airport was built. And travel agencies, restaurants, hotels and guest houses alike. One resort, though, stands out of them all with its absolute commitment to preserve nature, while providing a welcoming and comfortable environment for inspiring relaxation and great sightseeing adventures.

The Fern Resort is hidden on a hill at the foot of the Mae Surin national park, 7 kilometers southeast of Mae Hong Son. A serpentine country road surrounded by old rice fields is the bucolic introduction to the resort. And as you walk into the plain yet charming reception-and-lobby lodge, you understand that this place is going to gently take you by the hand into an indeed rustic world ... so far away from life in the city's daily grind.

The resort was created in 1992 with government funding for developing eco-tourism in this remote region. And so it successfully did, and still does more than 10 years later, with a set of lovely Shan-style leaf-roofed bungalows scattered around a vast parkland, lavishly planted with beautiful flora. An added natural and uncommon feature highlights the strong ecology character of this isolated retreat. The crystal-clear waters of a nearby stream run across the property through a network of bamboo pipes. This is a traditional irrigation system for the land which also creates a pleasant background noise of whispering running water around the resort.

The specific 'geography' of Fern Resort offers a number of options, would your preference go for a hill or a garden cottage, or for the recent suites located by the stream. All of them blend in perfect harmony with the forest environment, as only wood, bamboo, and leaves have been used for building material.

The standard bungalows are the most isolated ones, clinging to the hillside and slightly hidden from one another by a wild mix of trees and bushes. Although they offer a rather limited living space compared to other options at the resort, they are probably the most charming little wood houses of all with their small terrace, homey furniture and functional bathroom.

The rice paddy farm, not far from the unpretentious but pleasant swimming pool, presents a set of five larger deluxe bungalows with two rooms each—a favorite to families or friends wanting to enjoy a subtle mix of both privacy and social life.

Deluxe bungalows and suites were recently added by the streamside. With a more spacious and modern comfort setting, they lack some of the rustic charm of the original bungalows: tiled floors instead of warmer wooden floors, beautifully equipped bath and dressing room, and a large bedroom with peaceful views of the garden or the front rice paddy, and the rushing stream.

Despite a cozy setting and gracious and joyful staff, the restaurant at the resort does not stand the comparison with the excellent downtown Fern restaurant, also owned by Mr. Thawatchai. A free shuttle service will take you there for dinner on request.

Excellently guided tours—along with a friendly and expert dog-guide!—can be arranged by the resort to discover untouched nature spots. Back at the resort after a full day hiking, there is no better place to recline with a drink than on the pocket-size terrace overviewing the silent rice paddies sparkling under a golden sunset. This is our recommended place at the Fern Resort for a flighty sip of paradise.

FERN RESORT

64, Baan Hua Num, Maesakhut, Mae Hong Son 58000
Tel 66 (0) 53 686-110
Tel/Fax 66 (0) 53 686-111
E-mail *ferngroup@softhome.net*
Web *www.maehongson-tourism.net/fernresort.htm*
(a very informative and quite amazing site)

1. By air (2 ½ hours)
Plane 2 hours and 15 minutes flight on Thai Airways from Bangkok to Mae Hong Son via Chiang Mai (4 daily flights).
Car 15 minutes drive to the resort.
Note: Be aware of possible late flight cancellations due to weather conditions. Round trip transfers from airport with Fern Resort's private car can be arranged, free of charge.

2. By land from Chiang Mai (6 to 9 hours) Depending on your transportation—by bus or by car—and the chosen road coming from Chiang Mai—via Pai or Mae Sariang—the journey may take more or less time, as indicated. The route via Pai takes less time, allows stops at several very nice viewpoints.

26 Units
26 Rooms set in 21 bungalows (all with individual terrace or balcony, air conditioning and bathroom with hot water) •
7 Standard bungalows • 7 Deluxe bungalows (12 rooms) • 7 Suite bungalows
No TV and no telephone inside the rooms for a closer contact with nature!

Food and Beverage Outlets
Open-air restaurant with bamboo terrace. Barbecue at the campfire.
Cuisine Offered: Thai • Western
Quality: Average

Other services: Free shuttle to Fern Restaurant located downtown which is a much better choice (87 Khunlumprapas Road, Amphur Muang, Mae Hong Son) • Tour desk

Water sports and Activities
Large swimming pool with garden poolside • Mountain bike rental • Walks around nearby trails • Birdwatching • Very wide range of nature-related activities can be arranged at the resort's tour desk • Treks to waterfalls • Hiking to hilltribe villages A very good map of nature-trail offerings around the resort can be found on the website.

Per room per night inclusive of breakfast

The Southwest Peninsula

Koh Yao

Painting by Lily Yousry-Jouve

The Southwest Peninsula

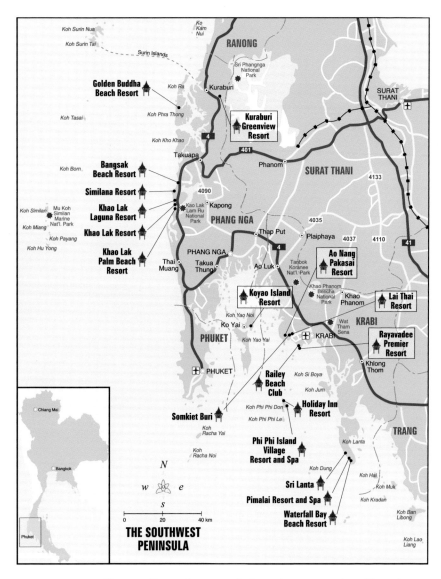

THE SOUTHWEST PENINSULA

Climate   Dry and comparatively coolest season from November to March. The hottest month is April (37°C).
Rainy season from May to October (showers alternating with sunshine). From June to August, sea currents may be dangerous, and, on the beaches, you should look at the flags.

Phuket

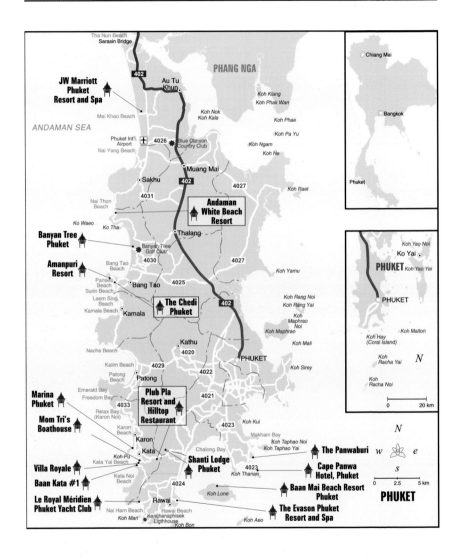

Tha Nun Beach
Sarasin Bridge

PHANG NGA

JW Marriott Phuket Resort and Spa

402

Au Tu Khun

Koh Klang
Koh Phak Wan

Mai Khao Beach

Koh Nok
Koh Kala

Koh Phae

ANDAMAN SEA

Phuket Int'l. Airport
Nai Yang Beach

4026

Blue Canyon Country Club

Koh Pa Yu

Koh Ngam

Koh He

Sakhu

Muang Mai

402

4031

4027

Koh Raet

Nai Thon Beach

Ko Waeo

Ko Tha

Andaman White Beach Resort

Banyan Tree Phuket

Thalang

Banyan Tree Golf Club

4030

4027

Amanpuri Resort

Bang Tao Beach

Koh Yamu

Pansea Beach
Surin Beach

Bang Tao

4025

Koh Rang Noi
Koh Rang Yai

Laem Sing Beach
Kamala Beach

Kamala

The Chedi Phuket

402

Koh Maphrao Noi
Koh Maphrao

Kathu

4020

Koh Mali

Nacha Beach

Kalim Beach

4029

4022

PHUKET

Koh Sirey

Patong Beach

Patong

Emerald Bay
Freedom Bay

4033

4021

Marina Phuket

Relax Bay
(Karon Noi)

Mom Tri's Boathouse

Karon Beach

Plub Pla Resort and Hilltop Restaurant

4023

Koh Kui

Karon

Makham Bay
Koh Taphao Noi
Koh Taphao Yai

The Panwaburi

Koh Pu

Kata

Chalong Bay

Shanti Lodge Phuket

4023
Koh Thanan

Cape Panwa Hotel, Phuket

Villa Royale

Kata Yai Beach

Kata Noi Beach

Baan Kata #1

4024

Koh Lone

Baan Mai Beach Resort Phuket

Le Royal Méridien Phuket Yacht Club

Rawai

Nai Harn Beach

Rawai Beach
Kanchanaphisek Lighthouse

The Evason Phuket Resort and Spa

Koh Man

Koh Bon

Koh Aeo

Chiang Mai

Bangkok

Phuket

Koh Yao Noi

Ko Yai

PHUKET Koh Yao Yai

PHUKET

Koh Maiton

Koh Hay
(Coral Island)

Koh Racha Yai

Koh Racha Noi

N

0   20 km

N

w   e

s

0   2.5   5 km

PHUKET

Vegetarian festival: On the first day of the ninth month in the Chinese calendar—for 9 days, the Chinese community turns to vegetarian food, seeking purification. A procession takes place, during which people in a trance have their cheeks pierced and walk on ladders made of knives.

Sea turtle hatchling: April 13—many children participate in this nice event, which takes place on several beaches, under the supervision of the Marine Biology Research Center of Cape Panwa.

Bangtao Beach

Phuket

The island of Phuket, with more than three million visitors a year, is one of the most popular Asian and world destinations. This success has led to the multiplication of hotels along the west coast that boasts the most attractive beaches. These are generally high-priced, sizeable, contemporary buildings. On the better-known beaches, in an unremitting manner, lounge chairs and parasols are aligned and available for hire. Having said this, it is undeniable that an aura of *dolce vita* pervades the whole island which accommodates, in secluded areas, some of the most sumptuous hotels in Thailand. With rare exceptions, residing in the exclusive hotels of Phuket implies big spending.

Besides, you are always at liberty to escape from the madding crowd to certain not-so-frequented beaches or to the less visited, and in fact, not so spectacular inland region of the island, or to explore the neighboring islands in long-tail boats with streamlined prows. The island of

Phuket which extends over 50 kilometers is easily crossed in one day and is linked to the mainland by a 700-meter long bridge.

THE SIRINAT MARINE NATIONAL PARK AND THE MANGROVE FOREST *(15 minutes from the airport)* The park, situated to the north of the island, near the airport, covers an area of 90 square kilometers and includes a mangrove forest, the three beaches of Mai Khao, Nai Yang and Nai Thon and a small part of the marine habitat. The mangrove forest is at the extreme northern tip of the isle near Ta Chatchai. A nature trail has been built, made of a wooden footbridge on stilts, zigzagging through the strange and inextricable aerial roots of the trees. It is a good observation place for birdwatching.

The Beaches

MAI KHAO *(10 minutes from the airport)* Nine kilometers of deserted beach fringed

177

by casuarinas trees stretch out for your pleasure, but the strong currents are not propitious to swimming, notably during the rainy season. Sea turtles come to lay their eggs here from December to February. The elegant **JW Marriott Hotel** is the only hotel on this beach.

NAI YANG *(15 minutes from the airport)* The beach, shaded with casuarinas trees, is situated in a lovely curved shore with a coral reef. It is the location for the park offices and sea turtles also come here to lay their eggs.

NAI THON *(15 minutes from the airport)* A naturally paradisiacal site with a striking beach of fine sand bathed by turquoise crystalline waters lies curved in a creek encircled by deserted wild wooded hills. Only one hotel is located here—the attractive **Andaman White Beach Resort**.

the equipment and facilities of the other four. As such, you may have dinner in any of the hotels and be billed in your own hotel, or be driven, free of charge, from one hotel to another.

The complex comprises an 18-hole golf course, four spas — notably the well-renowned **Banyan Tree Spa**—and the "Canal Village" commercial shopping center.

The complex was built on an old mining site, partially rehabilitating the devastated environment. Numerous trees have been planted, excavations have been converted into lagoons, and a sophisticated system for treating used water and waste recycling has been realized.

SURIN AND PANSEA *(30 minutes from the airport)* The little powdery white sandy beach of Pansea, in the extension of Surin, lies in a tranquil little wooded creek, on the edge of an extraordinarily blue transparent sea. It is the site of the **Chedi Hotel** and the very exclusive **Amanpuri.**

KAMALA *(30 minutes from the airport)* This is a pretty beach where only a few bungalows have been set up.

PATONG *(35 minutes from the airport)* The road that runs along the beach is lined with hotels, small restaurants, travel agencies and discotheque clubs. Moreover, neither the beach nor the ocean are attractive.

KARON *(45 minutes from the airport)* Karon beach is less developed than the neighboring Patong Beach. At its extreme southern end, the attractively rustic cottages of the **Marina Hotel** are spread out over a vast jungle terrain on a rocky promontory. **Marina Sports** is a well-equipped diving center.

KATA *(45 minutes from the airport)* The long Kata Beach, framed by partially forested hills, is also developed. At the extreme south of Kata Noi, near a rocky promontory, the discreet but nevertheless renowned **Boathouse,** with its excellent

Nai Harn

BANGTAO *(25 minutes from the airport)* The sandy beach of Bangtao, eight kilometers long, lies in a sheltered cove but the water is not as clear as at Nai Thon. Several hotels and bungalows are constructed here and, in the north, the very vast Laguna complex is made up of five luxury hotels—the extravagantly sumptuous **Banyan Tree**, Laguna Beach, Dusit, Sheraton Grande Laguna, and Allamanda. Residents of these hotels can benefit from

restaurant, is a good spot for relaxation therapy. On an escarpment to one side, you can rent one of the superb villas of **Villa Royale** run by the Boathouse or the charming private home of **Baan Kata #1.**

NAI HARN (*50 minutes from the airport*) This part of the island is the quietest and the undulating scenery picturesque. Nai Harn is in a very sheltered bay serving as an anchoring point for many sailboats. The southern end of the bay is closed by the Prom Thep cape, known for its magnificent sunsets. A few drink stalls and bungalows are constructed along the beach and the **Le Royal Méridien Yacht Club** is located at the extreme north at the foot of a wooded hill.

RAWAI (*45 minutes from the airport*) Rawai, on the southern coast, is not very touristic due to the turbid seawaters, but just in front are the lovely islands of Koh Bone and Koh Lone, and their deserted beaches of golden sand surrounded by coral reefs. A little farther on, are the Coral and Racha islands. The imposing, original and futuristic **Evason Hotel** is isolated on a vast green hill facing the isles.

THE CAPE OF LAEM PANWA (*45 minutes from the airport*) On the Cape, nestling in peaceful creeks of golden sand, are the **Cape Panwa Hotel** and the **Panwaburi Hotel**. From here it is easy to take a long-tail boat to the surrounding islands. The aquarium of the **Marine Biology Research Center of Cape Panwa,** next door, can be visited from 8:30 a.m. to 4 p.m.

The Nearby Islands

KOH BON (*15 minutes from Rawai*) The small untamed island of Koh Bon comprises a lovely beach often visited by the clients of the Evason Hotel.

KOH LONE (*15 minutes from Rawai*) On this peaceful wooded island, along a deserted beach, the charming little hotel of **Baan-Mai** is the best value for money in Phuket.

CORAL (*45 minutes from Rawai*) The beach is of unbelievably fine, soft pure white sand and, from the shore, you can snorkel on the coral reef, a few meters away. The peacefulness of the surroundings is nevertheless disturbed by the numerous boats and waterski enthusiasts who come here during the day.

RACHA YAI AND RACHA NAI (*respectively 75 minutes and 2 hours from the coast of Phuket*) Racha Noi, 25 kilometers from Phuket, offers spectacular coral reefs said to be comparable to those in Similan with a visibility at 20 to 40 meters underwater. Only confirmed divers should attempt to venture into the strong ocean currents. A small golden beach is concealed at the southern end of the isle.

At Racha Yai, diving is easier, with the Andaman wreck to explore at the northeastern tip and the pretty sandy bay on the west coast.

MAITON (*1 hour from the port of Phuket*) The island belongs to the luxurious Maiton resort and no one, unless a client, can visit it. The beach is effectively quite superb, a short way from the coral reef in the pure blue sea. The architecture is a bit oddly assorted, but the resort, nevertheless, deserves to be mentioned: Maiton Island Phuket, Central Reservation and Sales and Marketing, 43/22 Moo 5, T Rawai, A. Muang, Phuket 83000. Tel: 66 (0) 76 281-434, 281-435, 281-436 Fax: 66 (0) 76 281-437; E-mail: *resv@maitonisland.com.*

Apart from the diving sites around the above-mentioned islands, there are other diving sites around Phuket, notably Koh Doc Mai (60 minutes) with interesting diving along a wall of 30 meters; Shark Point (90 minutes) where only a rock emerges from the sea and where, with a little luck, one can observe the leopard shark; Anemone Reef (90 minutes), 10 minutes by boat from Shark Point; the King Cruiser (90 minutes).

— *Phi Phi* (about 2 hours from Phuket): see **Krabi province.**
— *Similan and Surin* (plan preferably a couple of days' excursion): see **Phang Nga province**.
— *The Bay of Phang Nga* (day excursion): this excursion is an absolute must, it would be a pity to leave Phuket without having contemplated this magnificent bay. See Phang Nga province.

The Town of Phuket
(35 minutes from the airport)

Apart from the few ancient buildings in Sino-Portuguese architecture dating back to the time, a century ago, when the town was prosperous due to the tin-mining activities, the town is uninteresting. The most noticeable houses are on the following streets: Talang, Krabi, Dibuk, Ranong and Phang Nga. The main market

and the Taoist Chinese Temple of Put Jaw are on Ranong street.

There are a few **antique shops** to visit such as the "Loft" at 36 Talang (decorations, ceramics, *objets d'art*). "Ancient Art gallery" on Yaowarat (ceramics); "Touch Wood Antique Furniture" at 27 Yaowarat (colonial furniture); "Baan Boran Antiques" at 39 Yaowarat; "Baan Boran Textiles" at 51 Yaowarat; "Puk Shop" at 7 Phang Nga Road (second-hand curio-dealer), "Antique Arts" at 68 Phang Nga (Chinese objects and furniture).

The Natural Royal Reserve of Phao Phra Thaw
(northeast of the isle)

This tiny 23-hectare reserve shelters the last surviving rainforest of Phuket where two small waterfalls named Ton Ai and Bang Pae can be seen cascading down. Next door is the Center for the Rehabilitation of Gibbons bred in captivity, with the objective of gradually reintroducing them into the wild (open from 10 a.m. to 4 p.m. with one hour break for lunch).

Kata Beach

JW Marriott Phuket Resort & Spa

As dusk falls, the façade of JW Marriott is bathed in the sun's dying rays and, when the torches around the large stone lotus ornamental lake light up in response, the effect is sheer magic. The superb perspective of an initial vast pool looking onto a second one facing the sea renders the arrival at the reception, open to the exterior, absolutely spectacular. Around the expanse of water, wooden-tiled two-tiered roofs adorn low, pure white buildings whose sober lines evoke Tibetan temples. Huge, originally designed woven metal lamps hang down from the lofty teak ceiling of the sumptuous reception. It is a pleasure to linger here and enjoy the sunset.

This extensive hotel comprise no less than 265 rooms distributed among numerous three-story buildings, but those are well spaced out within an 11-hectare coconut grove.

Spacious bright rooms skillfully combining modernism and Thai traditionalism display elegance and character. An original interior sala in a glass-walled alcove open onto the gardens and a small balcony. Reproductions of ancient engravings and Burmese lacquered lamps add that delicate individual touch. Attractive materials have been used throughout: aged tiles for the floor, dark teak wood for the furniture, as well as for walls paneling of the entrance hall—also serving as dressing room—and shot silk fabrics in red and gold tones. The luxurious bathrooms are visible from the bedrooms through sculpted wooden shutters.

JW Marriott runs along the 17-kilometer long deserted Mai Khao beach, by the Marine Park of Sirinath. Turtles come here to lay their eggs from November to February. Strong sea-currents make swimming not advisable here but two magnificent swimming pools, one of which is 127 meters long, amply make up for this inconvenience. Right on the beach, the latter, hemmed in by rocks and frangipani trees, is extremely attractive. Pink sandstone statues portraying a bestiary beautifully adorn this spot, where deck chairs are arranged so as to preserve guest's privacy. One part of the shallow, stone-polished swimming pool is just the thing for children.

The treatment rooms at the lavishly romantic Mandara Spa's are stylish suites, comprising of a massage parlor and a patio enclosed by walls where a sala crowned with a cloth canopy sprawls in the middle of a pond.

The most pleasant restaurant is the Sala Rim Talay, serving Thai delicacies and seafood presented in market-style baskets for your choosing. It is a wooden pavilion with a traditional architecture, which faces the beach. In the evening, diners are entertained by musicians playing classical Thai music.

A special mention must be made for the Kid's Club: the abundance of games and computers in a vast and bright room looking onto the gardens almost makes one long for those happy-go-lucky childhood days again!

JW MARRIOTT PHUKET RESORT & SPA

Marriott International Hotels Management
231 Moo 3, Mai Khao,
Phuket, Talang 83110
Tel 66 (0) 76 338-000
Fax 66 (0) 76 348-348
E-mail
jwmarriott.phuket@marriott.com
Web *www.marriott.com*

By air and land (1 ½ hour)
Plane 1 hour and 20 minutes flight on Thai Airways from Bangkok to Phuket (12 daily flights). *Car* 15 minutes from Phuket airport to GW Marriott.
Note: *Transfer from Phuket airport can be arranged by the resort.*

266 Units
253 rooms: Garden View rooms • Sea View • Deluxe Terrace (ground floor) • 12 One-bedroom suites • 1 Royal suite (2 bedrooms, dining pavilion, private pool)
All rooms have private balcony or terrace, indoor sala, private bathroom (separate bathtub and shower, hot water, hairdryer), air-conditioning, 2 phone lines (IDD, voice mail), cable flat screen TV (in-room movies), DVD player, minibar, coffee/tea maker, safety box.
Note: *There is an elevator in each building.*

Food and Beverage Outlets
Restaurants: Sala Rim Talay (on the beach) • Cucina • Marriott Café (breakfast buffet, overlooking the beach) • Kabuki Sushi Bar (in the gallery) • Siam Deli (pastries, sandwiches—in the gallery)
Cuisine Offered: Thai • Seafood • Italian East and west cuisine • Japanese
Quality: Very good
Bar: Sala Sawasdee lobby bar (music during evening)

Other services: Business center • Shopping arcade • Babysitting • Kids pavilion with little turtles activities • Desk excursions • Shuttle service to Phuket and Patong

Water sports and Activities
2 Swimming pools with kiddie pool • Beach (it is not advised to swim because of strong currents) • Sea Canoeing nearby • Diving • Snorkeling (in others places, closest departure point to Similan island) • Boat trips to nearby islands

Other sports and activities
Mandara spa • Fitness center • Lighted tennis courts • 36-hole golf course (10 minutes drive) • Table tennis • Elephant trekking

 Per room per night

Andaman White Beach Resort

I t is intriguing to discover a wooded coastline, still secret and untamed, where long beaches of golden sand skirt turquoise waters, at only a 15 minutes' drive from Phuket airport.

Andaman White Beach was inaugurated in 2002. It is the only hotel set in an ancient coconut grove along the enticing Nai Thon Beach. It is an excellent option for those who fancy remote, calm places without having to forfeit their comfort.

The natural, untamed surroundings are outstanding. The hotel overhangs a deserted creek a few meters below, encircled by rocks at the foot of forested hills. The shore of white powdery sand, fringed by clear blue seawaters, retains the beauty of a lost paradise. You will feel as if you were very far from everything, while you actually just landed a short while ago.

The elegant and welcoming reception, near the small coastal road, is an open pavilion towering above the sea, with a high wooden platform and inviting sofas arranged on a floor of polished tiles. Individual villas, all spruced up with white walls topped with green tiled roofs, make up the hotel. They are gently tiered all the way to the beach, linked by wooden bridges on stilts amidst bushes. Generally, they all have terraces, where, while lolling on your lounge chair, you can admire the marvelous seaview.

The duplex Sea View villas are closely aligned below the reception, whereas the individual Beach villas are directly on the beach. The rooms are all very comfortable and vibrant, in tones of pale yellow contrasting with the fine flooring in dark wood. They possess a refined Thai décor with beautiful furniture in light-colored wood, sculpted panels, enameled lamps and sofas spread with silk cushions in various hues. Luxurious bathrooms have original tiled bathtubs embedded in the ground.

The long, deep blue tiled swimming pool bordering the beach, sparkles under the reflections of the sun, rendering it particularly striking and attractive.

Near the reception, a stylish pavilion with high ceilings in blond wood accommodates the restaurant and overlooks the sea. You can chose between dining under the stars on the terrace or indoors in air-conditioned comfort. On the edge of the beach, near the pavilion housing the bar, cozy tables are also displayed on a teak terrace.

If you wish to leave the allure of this location for a while, the Laguna complex with its luxury hotels, its restaurants, its boutiques, and its golf course, is only a 20 minutes' drive away. The drive along the winding coastal road leading there is particularly picturesque. Rubber plantations and rainforests go by and glorious vistas through the trees to the ocean below are exhilarating.

ANDAMAN WHITE BEACH RESORT

28/8 Moo 4, Tambon Sakoo, Amphur Talang, Phuket 83110
Tel 66 (0) 76 316-300
Fax 66 (0) 76 316-399
E-mail
info@andamanwhitebeach.com
Web
www.andamanwhitebeach.com
Contact Luciano Lazzarin, General Manager

Booking Office in Bangkok
Grand Building,
538 Ratchadapisek Road,
Huay Kwang, Bangkok 10310
Tel 66 (0) 2 541-5275 to 77
Fax 66 (0) 2 541-5278
E-mail
swst.bkk@suriwonghotels.com

By air and land (1 ½ hour)
Plane 1 hour and 20 minutes flight on Thai Airways from Bangkok to Phuket (12 daily flights). *Car* 15 minutes from Phuket airport to Andaman White Beach.
Note: *Transfer from Phuket airport can be arranged by the resort.*

50 Units
16 Beachfront villas • 24 Sea View villas • 10 Sea rooms (with sea view—a bit smaller, no balcony but nice view) All rooms have private balcony (except Sea rooms), private bathroom (bathtub, hot water, hairdryer), air-conditioning, IDD telephone, cable TV, minibar, and safety box. Beachfront villas have coffee/ tea maker.

Food and Beverage Outlets
Restaurants: The Dining Room • Coconut bar and terrace (barbecue, snacks)
Cuisine Offered: Seafood • Thai • Western

Other services: Business services • Laptop computer rental • Souvenir shop • Babysitting • On site car rental • Tour desk

Water sports and Activities
Swimming pool • Beach • Diving and water sports facilities with Aquadivers on Nai Thon beach (*www.aquadivers.com*)

Other sports and activities
Spa • Sauna • Jacuzzi • Fitness center (free of charge) • Golf (20 minutes away)

 Per room per night

Banyan Tree Phuket

Indisputably the most attractive of the five hotels in the Laguna complex, along Bangtao Beach, Banyan Tree flaunts luxurious settings bordering extravagance.

An imposing centenarian Banyan tree, with myriads of aerial roots, marks the entrance to the sophisticated splendor of the immense reception area, which comprises several salas opening onto the gardens linked by ponds. White columns sustain precious wooden capitals, and sunlight floods in through light wells in the roof. An aura of infinite peace and tranquility radiates all around, as only the rustling of trees and twittering of birds break into the silence.

The hotel is composed of exceptionally plush individual villas scattered in an extensive and magnificent park along the Bangtao beach, around an artificial lagoon. White walls, enclosing gardens, over which only the pointed red-tiled rooftops are visible, protect the majestic villas, ensuring residents perfect privacy.

Traditional Thai architecture characterizes the very first Jacuzzi and Pool villas. Though slightly less luxurious than the Spa Pool villas – though in this context, luxury is hard to measure – they are very appealing. The Jacuzzi Villas comprise an open-air Jacuzzi in a garden, whereas the Pool Spa Villas boast a swimming pool and a sala. Virtually identical décors with paneled walls and teak flooring epitomize the tasteful interiors embellished by a few exquisite Thai objects. The beds lie on wooden platforms, slightly raised above the lounge area, displaying rattan pieces of furniture. Eye-catching bathrooms have bathtubs innovatively nestled in planted patios.

The brand new Spa Pool villas are of supreme sumptuousness, comprising a swimming pool, a Jacuzzi and a hammam. The swimming pool, under the gaze of a Buddha statue, is sublime, with a spa pavilion facing the lagoon. Two all-glass pavilions lie in the heart of a nymphea-strewn pond, one sheltering the bedroom, and the other the dining room. Contemporary, refined interior décor displays a clever interaction of colors between white floors and walls, black and gold. Though quite stunning, these villas retain a rather impersonal ambiance when compared to the older ones.

The Banyan Tree Spa is one of Asia's most renowned, and a treatment session there is a memorable experience. Surrounded by trees, vegetation and ponds, the various individual and very romantic pavilions of the spa, decorated with Thai statues, are secluded in an immense patio, at the entrance of which is an agreeable swimming pool. Only the sea breezes waft over the high walls and diffuse through the room. The massage beds placed on wooden stands appear to be floating in the middle of the ponds. The murmuring of the fountains, the trills of the birds and the sweet, melodic refrains of the traditional Thai music, softly soothes, relaxes and transports you into reverie.

The thought of venturing out from this all-embracing luxury rarely enters the mind, if not, perhaps, for a stroll along the long sandy beach of Bangtao that stretches alongside the park. As a resident of one of the five Laguna hotels, it is possible to take advantage of the services provided by the other hotels and be transported free-of-charge by boat or shuttle to any of them. The swimming pool of the Sheraton Grand Laguna meanders around the resort to the delight of the kids—young and not so young! That of the Laguna Beach decorated with bas-relief reproductions of the Angkor Temples is quite breathtaking. Ruenthai, the reputed Thai restaurant of the Dusit Laguna Resort, is also well worth a visit, while golf enthusiasts will be in their element at Banyan Tree's 18-hole golf course.

BANYAN TREE PHUKET

33 Moo 4, Srisoonthorn Road, Cherngtalay, Amphur Talang, Phuket 83110
Tel 66 (0) 76 324-374
Fax 66 (0) 76 324-356
E-mail phuket@banyantree.com
Web www.banyantree.com

Booking Office in Bangkok
Banyan Tree Bangkok
21/100 South Sathon Road,
10/F, Thai Wah Tower II Building,
Sathon, Bangkok 10120
Tel 66 (0) 2 679-1200
Fax 66 (0) 2 679-1199
E-mail bangkok@banyantree.com

 By air and land (2 hours)
Plane 1 hour and 20 minutes flight on Thai Airways from Bangkok to Phuket (12 daily flights). **Car** 25 minutes from Phuket airport to Banyan Tree.
Note: Transfer from Phuket airport can be arranged by the resort.

 101 Villas
40 Jacuzzi Villas (with outdoor Jacuzzi) • 36 Pool villas (with pool, dining area, video system) • 14 Spa pool villas (with pool, Jacuzzi, sauna, steam room, massage outdoor pavilion, dining pavilion, video system) • 11 Two-bedroom pool villas (with 2 bedrooms, 2 bathrooms, living and dining areas, kitchen, pool, Jacuzzi, outdoor sala, video system) All villas have private patio, private bathroom (shower and outdoor sunken bathtub, hot water, hairdryer), air-conditioning, IDD phone, cable TV, audio system, minibar, coffee/tea maker, safety box.

 Food and Beverage Outlets
Restaurants: Saffron (traditional interior) • Watercourt (buffet breakfast) • Sala Terrace (above the lagoon) • Tamarind Spa restaurant (by the pool—salads, snacks) • The Sanya Rak dinner cruise (for 2); in-villa dining
Cuisine Offered: Thai • Southeast Asian • Mediterranean • Seafood
Quality: Excellent
Bars: Wine Rack (fine wines, once a week special dinner) • Banyan Café (at the golf club— snacks) • The pool bar
Other services: Business services • Banyan Tree Gallery • Laguna tours • Wedding facilities

 Water sports and Activities
2 Swimming pools • Beach • Lessons in scuba diving, sailing, canoeing and windsurfing

Other sports and Activities
Banyan Tree Phuket Spa • Aerobics • Aqua toning • Tennis courts • 18-hole golf course • Cycling • Yoga • Body and beauty treatments • Meditation • Tai Chi • Library • Cooking class • Batik painting

 Per room per night

Marina Phuket

Perched on a jungle-swathed promontory, the Marina Phuket lies at one extreme of Karon Beach in total contrast to the other resorts of Karon, located within a much more mineral environment.

Eighteen years ago, the owner, Mr. Somchai Silaparont, fell in love with this site, named the "Mermaid Beach" by fishermen in days gone by. The place was little known then, surrounded by marshes and rice paddies, and accessible only by the sea. Mr. Silaparont progressively bought the land that today covers an area of seven hectares. By planting scores of trees and plants, he transformed the site into an exuberant jungle where no less than one hundred cottages were constructed. Residing in Kata, he personally oversees the running of the establishment, with much thought and consideration. The clientele, frequently regulars who come back year after year,

appreciates the warm and relaxed atmosphere of the resort where, to quote the owner, "nature and culture, not disco" are given precedence.

On arrival at the small reception lounge, where the tiled flooring and turquoise blue rattan armchairs bring a Mediterranean touch, you are stricken by the pervading atmosphere of quietness which reigns here, and the exuberance of the vegetation.

Cottages are linked by an amusing network of wooden footbridges on stilts, winding amidst ficus trees, climbers, cannas, and other trees hemmed by philodendrons. Those behind the ocean, entirely in wood, and inspired by traditional southern Thai architecture, have got more character. Completely buried beneath the jungle, you can spot only the peaks of the high red-tiled roofs that, like ship prows, soar out of the greenery. The cottages are decorated with fine-looking sculpted wooded facades and offer a terrace from where you have a good chance to spot a variety of birds.

The duplex cottages near the sea have a less original architecture with their wooden half-timbered white walls, but enjoy a lovely view of the Karon Bay from their small wooden terraces overhanging the sea. Suitable for families, with a communicating door between the two terraces, the plan is to eventually replace them in the future by traditional Thai villas.

Similarly styled, but less spacious, the standard cottages are scattered on an emerald lawn in a large coconut grove, above the reception area. Interiors are simple but comfortable, painted in white with rosewood flooring and cane furniture. All cottages have bay windows, but those located in the forest are somewhat dim due to the thick vegetation.

A few steps away from the reception lies the beach of golden sand, tranquil at this end, where you can rent a lounge chair and parasol to spend the day in total *farniente*.

For that romantic dinner, reserve one of the tables set apart in the rocks at the "On the Rocks" restaurant. The resort also comprises another restaurant in the more wooded part, above an entertaining swimming pool surrounded by rocks and a tiny waterfall, where dance and traditional music concerts are organized.

A few meters from the resort, the very well equipped Marina Sports Diving Center organizes numerous excursions to the neighboring islands for the day or longer periods, depending on clients' request.

MARINA PHUKET

47 Karon Road, Karon Beach, Phuket 83100
Tel 66 (0) 76 330-625
330-493 to 97
Fax 66 (0) 76 330-516
330-999
E-mail *info@marinaphuket.com*
Web *www.marinaphuket.com*
Contact Mr. Somchai Silaparont

By air and land (2 hours)
Plane 1 hour and 20 minutes flight on Thai Airways from Bangkok to Phuket (12 daily flights). *Car* 45 minutes from Phuket airport to Marina Phuket.
Note: *Transfer from Phuket airport can be arranged by the resort.*

104 Units
24 Standard cottages (garden view) • 48 Superior cottages (in jungle) • 32 Ocean View cottages
All rooms have private terrace, private bathroom (bathtub, hot water; Standard cottages have shower), air-conditioning, telephone, minibar, safety box.

Food and Beverage Outlets
Restaurants: On the Rock • Sala Thai (cultural show three times a week)
Cuisine Offered: Seafood • Thai
Quality: Good and friendly service
Other services: Business center • Babysitting • Excursions center

Water sports and Activities
Swimming pool • Beach • Snorkeling (in front but not the best) • Diving in the islands with Marina Sports Ltd, Part. 47 Karon Road, Karon Beach (e-mail: *info@marinadivers.com*, web: *www.marinadivers.com*)

Other sports and activities
Minigolf and Dino park for children (next in Karon)

 Per room per night

Mom Tri's Boathouse

There is something indefinable about the atmosphere at Boathouse making it a very special place. Merely 30 rooms and an exclusive regular clientele guarantee perfect tranquility. With celebrity guests making this a getaway hideout, it has acquired an established renown.

Here there is no display of ostentatious luxury, but a quality of life and a remarkable hospitality. Everything is at close range: the fine, sandy beach, limpid seawaters ideal for swimming even at low tide, an excellent terrace restaurant, and roadside animation if desired, are only a few meters away from the rooms.

Breakfasts opposite an azure blue ocean, on a shady terrace, followed by a voluptuous recline on the lounge chairs disposed on the beach, are sublime. Deliciously ice-cold water, fruit skewers and cool perfumed towels are presented without even asking for it.

From this very place, you will enjoy the sunset, when the deserted beach rings only with the laughter of children selling jasmine garlands, while a hungry ocean laps up the blazing disc of the sun.

The "Mom Tri's Boathouse" restaurant is one of Phuket's best, with its cellar preserving more than 400 wines from all over the world at perfect temperature: dining here in the evenings, under the trees lit by large linen lanterns hanging from the branches, lulled by the breaking waves, is another unique moment not to be missed!

The narrow strip of land between the small road and the beach that The Boathouse occupies means that there is no garden, but the renowned architect and owner, M.L. Tri Devakul, has created an unquestionable ambiance here that amply makes up for this. The lofty pointed red-tiled roofs of the traditionally-styled Thai pavilions emerging amidst the majestic trees provide a harmonious view. A profusion of pink, orange and red bougainvilleas that surround the pavilions add a touch of sheer exuberance. The interior décor evokes that of a luxury liner: muffled atmosphere of the paneled restaurant with its copper and wooden counter and marine maps, corridors resembling gangways with portholes as windows, and rooms with boat furniture and ladders leaning against the walls. An ocean theme characterizes the bathrooms, amusingly decorated with friezes representing crabs or fish.

The rooms are situated in a large three-story pavilion forming an angle around a patio. All have sea views from their small balconies. The views are more direct from the Suites.

Trees, among which tall palm trees holding heavy bunches of red fruits, have been planted along the building, and the rooms on the ground floor are buried under vegetation.

MOM TRI'S BOATHOUSE

Kata Beach, Phuket 83100
Tel   66 (0) 76 330-015 to 17
Fax   66 (0) 76 330-561
E-mail
info@boathousephuket.com
Web
www.boathousephuket.com
Contact: Richard Bronner,
    General Manager

By air and land (2 hours)
Plane 1 hour and 20 minutes flight on Thai Airways from Bangkok to Phuket (12 daily flights). *Car* 45 minutes from Phuket airport to Mom Tri's Boathouse.
Note: *Transfer from Phuket airport can be arranged by the resort.*

36 Units
33 Deluxe rooms • 3 Suites
All rooms have private balcony, private bathroom (with bathtub, hot water, hairdryer) air-conditioning, cable TV, radio, IDD telephone, minibar, coffee/ tea maker, safety box.

Food and Beverage Outlets
Restaurants: Mom Tri's Boathouse wine and grill (air-conditioned in a Verandah) • Gung café (more casual beach bar and restaurant); cellar with a choice of over 400 worldwide labels
Cuisine Offered: Thai • European • Seafood
Quality: Excellent cuisine, wine and service
1 Bar

Other services: Boutique • Babysitting (request in advance) • Car rental • Tour desk

Water sports and Activities
Swimming pool • Jacuzzi • Beach

Other sports and activities
Health and fitness center • Thai cooking classes every Saturday and Sunday with chef Tamanoon Punchun • Some happenings such as monthly art gallery, cultural events.

 Per room per night

Villa Royale

Villa Royale is architect M.L. Tri Devakul's family property that he only recently opened to the public. Over the years, he built six private Thai-designed homes, on a steep land that commands a spectacular view of the Andaman Sea, for use by his family and friends.

As of late 2003, twelve studios with spa facilities were being added.

The place has a lot of charm: the garden is a joyful abundance of bougainvillea, barringtonia, pandanus with aerial roots, and hibiscus to mention only but a few plant varieties. Each part of the garden has a specific ambiance: here, a pathway leads to a small unobtrusive altar where rests a stone Buddha, hemmed in with philodendrons, while at the far end of the garden, in the middle of a lawn, dramatically rises the façade of an ancient temple with an elongated silhouette and a finely sculpted wooden pediment.

Lower down, near the sea, the track leading to M.L. Tri Devakul's collection of modern sculptures is trimmed with ficus trees whose tentacles clasp big rocks in a timeless embrace. Finally the ocean, till now only barely discernible through the foliage, becomes the central element of the landscape.

You can enjoy the beauty of the site by dining at the "Mom Tri's Kitchen" restaurant located at the entrance of the property where Wanchai Buranakit, the personal chef of M.L. Tri Devakul, officiates. Though no rival to the Mom Tri's Boathouse restaurant, the surroundings are deliciously romantic. Concealed in a part of the garden with a jungle-like atmosphere, where gigantic tree trunks literally disappear under philodendrons, bird nest and staghorn ferns, a few intimate tables are disposed, near ponds, on a terracotta-tiled terrace. *Chao fa*, ornaments in the form of slender flames—in fact, stylized representations of birds that decorate the temple roofs—adorn the restaurant in perfect harmony with nature and the sober furniture in wood.

Access to the residential area is through a porch from where a track descends to an overhang above the ocean. A small saltwater swimming pool, with large round rocks from the shore integrated in its décor, is located here. However, it must be mentioned that there is no direct access to the beach.

Being all different in size and decoration, furnished with antiques or personal creations, each of the six villas has its own character. The most agreeable ones are numbers 5 and 6 facing the ocean, as those behind are somewhat dark.

The favorite is "Toy Talay," whose pleasant terrace overlooks the escarpment. It has specially designed unique bamboo furniture and very pretty Thai cabinets, in red and gold lacquered wood, as well as a secret cellar. The beautiful bathroom is incredible, with paintings representing landscapes on the bamboo-paneled walls, and a bathtub in a Japanese garden adorned with bonsai.

Mom Tri's Boathouse and Villa Royale being at five minutes' driving distance from each other, you can avail of the facilities of the former while staying at the latter.

VILLA ROYALE

Kata Beach, Phuket 83100
Tel 66 (0) 76 330-015 to 17
Fax 66 (0) 76 330-561
E-mail
info@boathousephuket.com
Web
www.boathousephuket.com
Contact Richard Bronner,
General Manager

By air and land (2 hours)
Plane 1 hour and 20 minutes flight on Thai Airways from Bangkok to Phuket (12 daily flights). *Car* 40 minutes from Phuket airport to Villa Royale.
Note: *Transfer from Phuket airport can be arranged by the resort.*

18 Units
6 villas have living room and bedroom, private terrace, private bathroom (separate bathtub and shower, hot water), air-conditioning, IDD telephone, cable TV, CD and VCD player, minibar, coffee/tea maker, safety box. There is a private cellar in Villa number 5.
Note: *12 Studio units with spa added late 2003.*

Food and Beverage Outlets
Restaurant: Mom Tri's Kitchen (meals can also be served in the villas)
Cuisine Offered: European • Thai
Quality: Good

Other services: All of Boathouse's services are available

Water sports and Activities
Small swimming pool

Others sports and activities
Guests of Villa Royale have full access to The Boathouse's facilities, including beach access and service. The two properties are just minutes away by shuttle bus.

 Per room per night

Baan Kata # 1

A Javanese entrance porch made of carved stone screens a cheerful private home, concealed in an exuberant garden, with a spectacular view of the sea. The owner's wife, a Japanese interior designer, artistically created the interior décor that contributes much to the charisma of the place, while architect M.L. Tri Devakul was its talented designer.

Located in a residential block of flats occupying a promontory above Kata beach, it is nonetheless completely independent from the other houses. A staircase, edged by twisted trees and a lotus pond, leads to different pavilions that make up the house. The pretty garden is decorated with stone statues partially masked by the foliage.

Baan Kata incorporates three pavilions. One at the back of the garden houses a bedroom and a bathroom. The two single-story pavilions overlooking the sea are particularly attractive. Each story comprises a bedroom extended by a large terrace. The dining room terrace is quite surrealistic with its balustrade from where stone frogs and an abstract statue, with an enigmatic smiling face, gaze at you against the timeless background of the sea. The view onto the coastline, trimmed with gigantic rounded polished rocks, is fabulous. Three bedrooms are at your disposal, each with its own private bathroom, as well as a dining room and a music room. Original and precious are words which best describe the interior décor, particularly the Balinese wooden doors, the dining room furniture inlaid with egg shell inspired by the 1920s, and ostrich egg lamps adorned with unusual lampshades crafted with porcupine quills!

The bathrooms are equally fantastic: one on the main bedroom has a bathtub embedded with sparkling stones and two large glazed shower cabins, whose interiors are plastered with pebbles and open onto a patio flourishing with plant life.

The swimming pool can be found close by down below the pavilions on a grassy platform. A *sala* with wooden tiled roofs juts out onto the rocks facing the ocean. Relishing the sunsets, while lying on the cushions and mattresses arranged here, is an experience not to be missed.

Their services included in the renting of the house, Bee, the cook, and a housekeeper will wait on you with kindness and cheerfulness during your stay.

It is advisable to have your own car to go to the shore, as there is no direct access to the ocean from the house.

Note: *Asian Sky also organizes the renting of several private luxury houses in Phuket: Baan Kata Keeree (6 rooms); Talay Sawan (6 rooms) near the Surin beach; Naka Wanna at Kamala (3 villas in Thai style around a large swimming pool with a total of 5 rooms) on a wooded hill above the village of Karon.*

Koh Pak Bai

BAAN KATA #1

 In a compound overlooking Kata beach

Lakeside Offices
8/25 New Rachadapisek Road (opposite Sukhumvit Soi 16), Bangkok
Tel   66 (0) 1 832-2172
Fax   66 (0) 2 229-4315
E-mail
asiansky@britishacorn.com
Web
www.britishacorn.com/tourism

 By air and land (2 hours)
Plane 1 hour and 20 minutes flight on Thai Airways from Bangkok to Phuket (12 daily flights). ***Car*** 45 minutes from Phuket airport to Baan Kata 1.
Note: *There is parking at the entrance of the compound.*

 Private house
3 Pavilions (good for 6 people) • 1 Pavilion (including a bedroom with bathroom) • 1 Pavilion (including the master bedroom; first floor) with bathroom (separate bathtub and shower) and the study room (music and TV) • 1 Pavilion (including 1 bedroom with bathroom and 1 dining room). Kitchen in a separate pavilion.
All rooms have private terrace, private bathroom (hot water), air-conditioning, cable TV, stereo equipment, and computer, sala overlooking the sea.

 Food and Beverage Outlets
You have the services of a cook and a cleaner who visit daily. There are shopping facilities in Kata nearby. You have easy access to Mom Tri's Boathouse and Villa Royale restaurants nearby.

Other services: Securicor provide with 24-hour site surveillance.

 Water sports and Activities
Small swimming pool—swimming in the sea is not easy because it is steep and rocky. Kata beach is walking distance (15 minutes).

 Per room per night

Plub Pla Resort

Lonely perched atop a wooded cliff, far from the hustle and bustle of the coast, Plub Pla commands spectacular views on Kata Beach on one side and the Chalong Bay on the other.

This is the perfect place for those seeking for tranquility and communion with nature, though Kata is only a 15-minute drive away. A former rubber plantation, this immense land planted with numerous species starts right at the foot of the hills, thus assuring full privacy.

A flight of steps leads to the large bay-windowed vast reception, followed by a ridged track swerving to a terrace with panoramic views of Kata beach, as well as to the swimming pool and to the rooms.

On the top of the cliff, the site of the swimming pool, nestled among trees filled with multicolored butterflies, iridescent green insects and flying lizards, is truly magnificent.

From here, serenely installed in deck chairs, you have a breathtaking view of the coast. The swimming pool is small but, with its imitation sand base and waterfall in the hollow of the rocks, quite original. A dip in the deliciously cool waters, while caressed by the lulling sea breezes, is particularly refreshing after the sweltering heat of the beach.

The project initially embraced a hotel section, a conference room, and some houses for sale. A young architect, Mr. Pakorn, is now striving to bring some design unity to the initial buildings, which were constructed in relative disharmony.

When we visited, four rooms and two suites had been completed, in a modern single-story building facing the distant Chalon Bay. The additional rooms being located in completely independent buildings, ongoing constructions works should definitely not prevent staying at Plub Pla.

Very sober, the rooms are superb and airy, with two immense white beds on wooden bases, a sofa, a large designer cupboard in beautiful blond teak that conceals the closet, a minibar, and a safe box.

The bathtub is embedded in a bow window which, when opened on the garden close by, allows you to enjoy your morning bath, contemplating the rising sun.

Then, just before breakfast, you can relax in the small Jacuzzi surrounded by bougainvillea located on the common wooden terrace overlooking the hill.

The suites have an enhanced Zen atmosphere. The Junior suite, enclosed in a patio, offers a semicircular bow window with a panoramic view on the grounds, while the entrance to the Honeymoon suite is via gravel flooring lit by a glass roof. Each suite has its own private exterior Jacuzzi surrounded by plants, with a waterfall cascading from a wall covered with vegetation in the Honeymoon suite.

Surprisingly enough, the place is little patronized. This is probably due either to the ongoing renovation work or the fact that it is advisable to have a car or a motorbike to go to the beach. If requested in advance, Plub Pla can provide a shuttle service or call a taxi for you. The privilege of returning in the evenings to these cool, peaceful surroundings and contemplating this marvellous view, amply justifies the short wait…

PLUB PLA RESORT

137/6-7 Patak Road, Karon, Phuket 83100
Tel 66 (0) 76 285-167 to 69
Fax 66 (0) 76 285-170
E-mail *info@plubpla.com*
Web *www.plubpla.com*

By air and land (2 hours)
Plane 1 hour and 20 minutes flight on Thai Airways from Bangkok to Phuket (12 daily flights). *Car* 45 minutes from Phuket airport to Plub Pla Resort and Hilltop Restaurant.
Note: *Transfer from Phuket airport can be arranged by the resort.*

6 Units
4 Rooms • 2 Suites
All rooms have private terrace, private bathroom (hot water, bathtub, hairdryer), air-conditioning, IDD telephone, minibar, coffee/tea maker, safety box. The suites have private patio, living area, bathroom with separate bathtub/shower, Jacuzzi.

Food and Beverage Outlets
1 Restaurant and 1 bar
Cuisine Offered: Thai • European
Quality: Familial
Other services: Car rental • Taxi service • Shuttle to beaches (only upon request: it is advisable to book in advance)

Water sports and Activities
Small swimming pool

 Per room per night

Amanpuri

You will notice the quality of silence in Amanpuri, or "place of peace." It is an ultra-exclusive resort where, right from the entrance, the tone of elegance, serenity and sobriety is set.

It is marvelously isolated on its forested hill overlooking the secret, rock-encircled Pansea creek that it shares with the Chedi Hotel. Nowhere else in Phuket are the sand so soft, so powdery white, nor the seawaters so pure, where turquoise reflections dance in the sun and dazzle the eye.

American architect Ed Tuttle, the brain behind the majority of Aman's hotels, derived his inspiration from the Ayutthaya Palace that he has stylized and perfected in consistence with his own personal artistic sensibility. Transparence is the theme in the reception, where a vast pavilion opens onto the exterior and appears floating in the middle of lotus pools facing the spectacular black-bedded swimming pool overlooking the sea.

A pleasant terrace restaurant and a bar are situated around the swimming pool and non-residents are also welcome to dine here. A monumental stone staircase goes right down to the creek, where a beach surrounded by tall palm trees curls up.

Amanpuri offers a choice between individual Pavilions and private villas.

The sea-facing pavilions rise in terraces on the hill at one end of the creek. Each possesses a garden, and a sala where dinner can be served. Though a high level of luxury is only to be expected from an Aman hotel, it is one of refined sobriety which, combined with spaces of geometric precision, draws attention to the beauty of the material and the furniture, such as the remarkable teak flooring and ceilings, and precious Thai objects on the shelves. The pavilions are all endowed with superb bathrooms in teak and mirrors.

The villas, located on the other crest of the hill, are very secluded. They are set in large patios surrounded by cascading bougainvillea, and composed of separate pavilions: a sala, a kitchen, a transparent glass salon furnished with antiques, and the bedrooms. Each villa possesses an astounding black-tiled swimming pool, its water flowing over the edges. The most spectacular villas are those that overhang the sea. Capable, yet unobtrusive staff tends to the cooking and cleaning.

The geometrical architecture of the Spa evokes German new-art. Traditional architecture has been reserved for the exterior salas only, laying in tiers on the hill, with spectacular views onto Bangtao bay.

A fleet of ships, sailboats and junk boats are at your service to help you discover the region.

AMANPURI

Pansea Beach, Phuket 83000
Tel 66 (0) 76 324-333
Fax 66 (0) 76 324-100
E-mail
amanpuri@lamanresorts.com
Amanresorts Global
Reservations Office
Tel 65 6887-3337
Fax 65 6887-3338
E-mail *info@amanresorts.com*
reservations@amanresorts.com
Web *www.amanresorts.com*

By air and land (2 hours)
Plane 1 hour and 20 minutes flight on Thai Airways from Bangkok to Phuket airport (12 daily flights). *Car* 30 minutes from Phuket airport to Amanpuri.
Note: *Transfer from Phuket airport can be arranged by the resort.*

70 Units
40 Pavilions
6 Garden pavilions • 25 Superior Garden pavilions • 4 Superior partial Ocean pavilions • 5 Deluxe Ocean pavilions (105 and 103 have best view)
All rooms have outdoor sala, (sundeck and dining terrace), private bathroom (with separate shower and bathtub, hot water, hairdryer), air-conditioning, IDD phone, no TV, CD stereo, minibar, coffee/tea maker, safety box.
30 Villas with garden or ocean view
Each villa consists of 2 to 6 separate bedrooms with private bathroom, separate living and dining salas, pool, kitchen, a live-in maid and cook.
Note: *Transfers by electric car between pavilions, villas and lobby, 24-hour room service.*

Food and Beverage Outlets
Restaurants: The Restaurant • The Terrace • Beach (barbecue and beach restaurant)
Cuisine Offered: Italian • Thai • Western
Quality: Excellent cuisine and service
1 Bar

Other services: Internet (complimentary) • Secretarial services • Shops • Babysitting • Tailor • Medical assistance • Car rental • Airline reservation • Buddhist wedding

Water sports and Activities
Swimming pool • Beach • Snorkeling • Diving in islands • Fish feeding • Sailing • Hobie cat • Windsurfing • Water skiing • Aman cruises (more than 20 boats from dinghies to 60-foot cruiser!) to Phang Nga Bay, Kai Nok and Phi Phi islands.
Other sports and activities
Spa • Gym • Tennis courts • Golf (40 minutes away) • Library (over 1000 books and CD)

 Per room per night

The Chedi Phuket

Quite secluded on a forested hill, the Chedi, together with Amanpuri, shares the tranquil Pansea Bay of white sand, above an utterly transparent azure blue ocean.

Ed Tuttle, the renowned architect of both resorts, ingeniously blends Thai art with the refined geometrically linear 1920s European Art Nouveau, in an innovative manner.

The imposing buildings perched at the summit of the hill that shelter the reception, the boutiques, and the restaurants, are all hexagonal in shape. The interior structural framework of the lofty marquee sustained by massive wooden columns is amazingly outstanding, as it gives you the impression of standing under a gigantic unfurled umbrella. Breakfasts are pleasant in one of the Lomtalay Restaurant's two very airy hexagonal rooms that overhang the gardens and the sea. Very sober interiors are an effective blend of beautiful natural materials, gray granite and wood, with Art Nouveau furniture, particularly the original chairs with long backrests in checkered wood.

The well-spaced cottages, with half-timbered white walls surmounted by thatched roofs, amidst coconut trees, frangipanis, and palm trees that rustle in the morning with the singing of birds, are set in terraced rows on the hillside, down to the beach. A real labyrinth of footbridges and staircases links them, making the place quite unsuitable for the elderly.

In contrast with their rustic-styled exteriors, the cottages interiors blend timeless simplicity and modern sophistication. Rooms are particularly relaxing and harmonious. Shining white walls emphasize the dark patina of the floor made of beautiful wood. Arched white ceilings are highlighted by wooden beams, as are the doors and window frames. Elegant streamlined wooden furniture, silk-covered sofas, and beautiful abstract Thai prints framing the white bed surmounted by a dais, add to the ambiance of comfort. Huge dressings and luxuriously paneled teak bathrooms extend them. The alignment of the folding doors connecting the terrace, the bedroom and the bathroom broadens the area.

With the exception of the Hillside cottages that have a view onto the trees, all other cottages have sea views. The black-tiled hexagonal swimming pool on the beach contrasts somewhat surrealistically with the white sand and turquoise sea. Quiet *farniente* can be indulged in under the parasols along the swimming pool or on the beach, with a spa treatment at the romantic small spa, perched on the heights, providing a unique climax to the day.

THE CHEDI PHUKET

Pansea Bay 118 Moo 3,
Choeng Talay, Talang,
Phuket 83110
Tel   66 (0) 76 324-017 to 20
Fax   66 (0) 76 324-252
E-mail
chedipht@ghmhotels.com
Web   *www.ghmhotels.com*

By air and land (2 hours)
Plane 1 hour and 20 minutes flight on Thai Airways from Bangkok to Phuket (12 daily flights). *Car* 30 minutes from Phuket airport to The Chedi.
Note: *Transfer from Phuket airport can be arranged by the resort.*

108 Units
34 Hillside cottages • 37 Superior cottages • 20 Deluxe cottages • 16 Beach cottages (some two-bedrooms cottages) • 1 Spa cottage
All rooms have private sundeck, private bathroom (separate shower and bathtub, hot water, hairdryer), air-conditioning, IDD telephone, satellite TV, minibar, coffee/tea maker, safety box.

Food and Beverage Outlets
Restaurants: Lomtamay Restaurant • Beach restaurant
Cuisine Offered: Thai • Seafood
Quality: Very good cuisine and service
Bars: Poolside and sunset bar

Other services: Business services • Boutiques • Babysitting • Kid's corner • Tour information desk • Car rental • Shuttle bus service to Phuket town (30 minutes) and to Patong beach (20 minutes)

Water sports and Activities
Swimming pool • Beach • Kiddie pool • Beach games • Snorkeling • Diving • Catamarans • Hobie cat • Water skiing • Windsurfing • Charter boats from Amancruise

Other sports and activities
Spa (yoga available) • Tennis courts • Table tennis • Badminton • Volleyball • Golf course (40 minutes away) • Library • Thai culinary cooking class (twice per month only)

 Per room per night

Cape Panwa Hotel, Phuket

Cape Panwa Hotel stands on top of a wooded headland overlooking the sea. From the terrace, amidst swaying palm trees, you can see the small tramway leading to the beach below, and the sea lashed by iridescent waves. Lounge chairs abandoned near the deserted beach by the coconut grove lie, ready to welcome regular clients who can enjoy the encompassing peace and calm in total security.

Though the architecture and the interior décor are quite unremarkable, Cape Panwa exudes a feeling of a joyous well-being, as it adroitly sustains its relaxed family ambiance despite its large size. It also benefits from a privilcged location. As a matter of fact, the hotel is isolated on a vast hill whose vegetation has been preserved. At the foot of the hill, a rocky cove surrounds a pretty private white sand beach.

The different well-spaced multi-storied buildings are on the heights amidst the trees, hence enjoying a panoramic view of the ocean. The large private terraces of the vast suites are sea-facing and bedecked with bougainvillea. The standard rooms with tiny balconies are in the buildings on the other side of the reception, near the swimming pool and the restaurants.

The pleasing traditionally styled bungalows lie tiered on the flanks and stretch right to the beach. Possessing two comfortable bedrooms each with a balcony facing the sea and a high-ceilinged hall lit up by a large glass roof, they are ideal for families.

The fact that the hotel sits on a hillside is no obstacle for elderly persons as the tramway—quite an outright hit even with the younger generation—ensures regular trips to the beach.

An adorable house in Sino-Portuguese architecture with a white façade, green shutters, and a portico crowned with a framework of finely sculpted wood, can be reserved on the beach. It nestles amidst the surrounding vegetation and has its own tiny swimming pool.

Close by, a second large Sino-Portuguese house shelters the Thai restaurant where the cuisine is excellent. Its white columns, overhanging terrace with a panoramic view, antique furniture, and ceramic tiles from the 1920s, create a decidedly romantic setting. The Thai owner has reconstructed both these houses with antique items acquired from another region.

He also owns the less remarkable Bay Hotel that overlooks the bay of Chalon, on the other side of the hill near the harbor. A free shuttle service will transport you to visit its shopping gallery and its several restaurants or even to the town of Phuket. You can also benefit from a free day-excursion by boat to the Coral Island and its coral reef, good for snorkeling.

Panwa House Restaurant

CAPE PANWA HOTEL, PHUKET
27, Moo 8, Sakdidej Road,
Cape Panwa, Phuket 83000
Tel 66 (0) 76 391-123 to 5
Fax 66 (0) 76 391-177
E-mail *gm@capepanwa.com*

Bangkok Sales Office
and Group Reservations
4/F, Kasemkij Building,
120 Silom Road, Bangkok 10500
Tel 66 (0) 2 233-3433
2 233-9560
Fax 66 (0) 2 238-2988
E-mail *sales@capepanwa.com*
Web *www.capepanwa.com*

 By air and land (2 ½ hours)
Plane 1 hour and 20 minutes flight on Thai Airways from Bangkok to Phuket (12 daily flights). *Car* 45 minutes from Phuket airport to Cap Panwa Hotel.
Note: *Transfer from Phuket airport can be arranged by the resort.*

245 Units
211 Superior rooms • 13 Triple rooms (with living room) • 14 Suites • 6 Bungalows (2 bedrooms, living room, kitchenette) • 1 Villa (3 bedrooms, living room, private swimming pool)
All rooms have private balcony, private bathroom (hot water, hairdryer) air-conditioning, IDD telephone, cable TV, minibar, and safety box. Suites and Bungalows have coffee/tea maker.
Note: *There is an elevator in "L" and "S" buildings.*

 Food and Beverage Outlets
Restaurants: Panwa House • Top of the Reef • Cafe Andaman (breakfast)
Cuisine Offered: Thai • Western • Seafood
Quality: Good
Bars: Light House pub (hillside) • Otter's bar (next to Top of the Reef)
Note: *You can try also one of the 2 restaurants in Panwa Bay Village (free shuttle), taste the grand marnier soufflé of French chef Philippe, in Uncle Nan's restaurant (Italian cuisine)!*
Other services: Internet • Shops (in Panwa Bay Village) • Babysitting • Children's corner • Excursions desk • Car rental • Free shuttle bus to Phuket

 Water sports and Activities
2 Swimming pools (with kiddie pool) • Beach • Jacuzzi • Scuba diving lesson • Windsurfing • Panwa Princess II yacht • Long-tail boats (boat pier) • Free day trip to Coral island 15 minutes away (snorkeling • beach)
Other sports and activities
Exercise room • Tennis courts • Volleyball • Game room • Day's activities and sauna

 Per room per night

The Panwaburi

Panwaburi's sophisticated, lavish reception in Sino-Portuguese architecture is a spectacle that conjures up visions of a small palace from the 1001 nights. Isolated on an immense exclusive 4-hectare hill, the hotel dominates Cape Panwa, near the Cape Panwa Hotel. Nevertheless, the two hotels are not interlinked.

The architect has definitely made a statement with octagonal geometry by repeating this theme inside the common buildings and those providing accommodation. As such, the reception and the restaurant, in superb redwood, are large high-ceilinged octagonal pavilions opening onto beautiful gardens and the sea.

Sustaining the restaurant pavilion is a quadruple circle of columns linked by wooden sculpted arcades in geometric patterns. Stone elephants adorn the terrace dotted with a few inviting tables. White marble floors throw out sparkles.

The select décor set with striking furniture, white and blue antique pottery, gracefully shaped *chao fa*, and orchid-filled bowls creates a romantic ambiance in the evenings under the light of small wooden Chinese lanterns.

The restaurant dominates the free-form swimming pool and its two round Jacuzzis embedded in a teak platform, overhanging a waterfall cascading down to the beach. Swimmers have the luxury of ordering drinks, without leaving the pool, from the amusing bar overwhelmed under a bower of pink bindweed. An entirely paneled teak pavilion with comfortable leather sofas shelters the library and the internet corner.

Meticulously conceived, the garden is filled with innumerable species of foliage and flora—acajou trees whose ripening fruit exude an overpowering odor, banana, papaya, pandanus, cycads, traveler palm trees, and balisiers—and the reverberating sounds of mocking mynahs and cooing pigeons.

The rooms are either located on the heights in the honeycomb-shaped two-story buildings or in the downhill terraced octagonal villas reaching the small private beach.

Distinguished elegance is the hallmark of the interior décor, no matter what category of room you choose: superb dark wood floorings, and stylish wooden colonial furniture. Bathrooms attractively blend wood and green hand-crafted tiles. All rooms have sea-facing terraces with a vista onto the distant islets. The astutely conceived balconies in a staggered zigzag pattern, surrounded by vegetation, guarantees intimacy even in the buildings. Attention to detail is conspicuous all over the resort.

The Angsana spa, where the secret red and gold lacquered wooden doors of the individual pavilions lead to the vast sumptuously decorated massage parlors and stone-sculpted patios, is a haven of serenity.

On the other hillside, along with the tennis court, is Panwaburi's second renowned restaurant. It is a long traditional Thai pavilion topped by a striking gray wooden-tiled roof, with a view onto a pretty deserted bay filled with mangroves. By a simple call from your room, the services of an electric car can be availed of to drive you there.

THE PANWABURI

84 Moo 8, Sakdidej Road,
Tambon Vichit, Amphur Muang,
Phuket 83000
Tel   66 (0) 76 200-800
Fax   66 (0) 76 200-819
E-mail
executive@panwaburi.com
Contact M. Lukas,
            General Manager

Booking Office in Bangkok
252/117 Muang Thai-Phatra
Complex Building 2 Ratchadapisek
Road, Huay Kwang, Bangkok 10320
Tel   66 (0) 2 645-1400 to 04
Fax   66 (0) 2 645-1409
Web
www.phuket.com/panwaburi

By air and land (2 hours)
Plane 1 hour and 20 minutes flight on Thai Airways from Bangkok to Phuket (12 daily flights).   *Car* 45 minutes from Phuket airport to Panwaburi.
Note: *Transfer from airport can be arranged by the resort.*

79 Units
12 Beach villas • 27 Seaview villas • 40 Seaview Deluxe guest rooms
All rooms have private balcony, private bathroom (bathtub, hot water, hairdryer), air-conditioning, IDD telephone, satellite TV, minibar, safety box, coffee/tea maker. Beach villas have CDs.

Food and Beverage Outlets
Restaurants: The Cashewnut • The Bay (seafood and steak— beautiful restaurant accessible by shuttle car, on the other side of the bay, for dinner only)
Cuisine Offered: Thai • International
Quality: Good
Bar: The Cascade (pool bar and snack)

Other services: Internet • Shops • Babysitting • Doctor • Tour counter • Car rental

Water sports and Activities
Swimming pool • Small beach • Jacuzzi • Scuba diving (not available in-house but it can be arranged for at tour counter) • Free shuttle boat once a day to Coral Island, 15 minutes away (snorkeling, beach)

Other sports and activities
Spa • Tennis court • Golf (about 40 kilometers away) • Library • Thai cooking class

 Per room per night

The Evason Resort & Spa

With minimalist and surrealistic architecture, Evason is an ode to imagination. As if in a weird dream, you will need to walk through a long and dim white rough cast tunnel, until you reach a vast terrace overhanging an aquamarine blue ocean. Almost ethereally, four *salas* float on a seemingly boundless pond whose water, flowing over the edges, appears to spill endlessly into the sea.

Nothing in the view from the distance of the imposing and archetypical buildings atop the hill gives any hint whatsoever of this wondrous sight that finally greets the eye. Minimalism is the defining character of the resort with every space — walls and floors — in immaculate white highlighting the purity of lines. This austerity also shows in the inspirational interior décor of the rooms inciting relaxation and meditation. The large bed over which floats the mosquito netting suspended from a bamboo grid is the core of the décor,

while the only dash of color originates from the orange and red fabrics and dark wood of the contemporary furniture. The hotel offers a variety of rooms where even the standard ones are quite attractive, with mirrored windows opening into pretty bathrooms. The latter are ornamented with sponge painted walls, sparkling hammered-metal washbasins, and opalescent glass low-hanging lamps.

The two stories of the very original Duplex suites are linked by a winding staircase and comprise a bedroom, a salon, and a sublime bathroom where the bathtub is coiled in an exterior verdant patio. The salon opens onto a small private garden where a *sala* has been erected amidst a profusion of foliage.

The rooms are scattered in various buildings spread out over a hilly wooded 26-hectare park. A shuttle serves them all. The Garden Wing rooms are best located in proximity to the sea, to the superb main swimming pool and to the restaurants all at once.

The concept of tasteful simplicity is also displayed in the restaurants with a panoramic view onto the sea, the bar and the spa. The architect's talent is fully patent in his mastery for staging the water element. With every area overhanging the sea, he designed ornamental ponds to create a breach between earth and water, thus provoking an impression of vertigo or, conversely, one of equilibrium and serenity.

Among the several swimming pools at Evason, the small triangular one is strikingly spectacular, as it appears to merge with the sea down below, both showing identical blue waters and the same foamy waves created by sea breezes.

The picture of the sea-facing spa, where romantic *salas* topped with white dais appear like floating above the surface of a stretched lotus pond, is absolutely stunning. The Spartan facet of the spa's several massage parlors may seem to border on the excessive, if it were not for the outstandingly sumptuous scenery framed by the bay windows opening to the sea and wooded hills.

Though Evason does not have a beach, long-tailed boats anchored at the small landing-jetty will take you free of charge to Bon Island and its golden sandy beach.

THE EVASON RESORT AND SPA

Six Senses Hotels, Resorts and Spas
100, Vised Road, Tambon Rawai,
Muang District, Phuket 83130
Tel   66 76 381-010 to 17
Fax   66 76 381-018
E-mail rsvn@evasonphuket.com
Web   www.six-senses.com

Booking Office in Bangkok
Six Senses Hotels, Resorts and Spas
12/F One Pacific Building,
140 Sukhumvit Road, Klongtoey,
Bangkok 10110
Tel   66 (0) 2 631-9777
Fax   66 (0) 2 631-9799
E-mail steven@sixsenses.com

By air and land (2 hours)
Plane 1 hour and 20 minutes flight on Thai Airways from Bangkok to Phuket airport (12 daily flights). **Car** 45 minutes from Phuket airport to Evason.
Note: *Transfer from airport can be arranged by the resort.*

282 Units (in 5 buildings)
46 Standard suites • 122 Studios • 101 Deluxe suites • 7 Junior suites • 5 Duplex suites • 1 Presidential suite
All rooms have private balcony, private bathroom (separate bathtub and shower except in Standard, hot water, hairdryer), air-conditioning, IDD telephone, cable TV, CD player (on request) minibar, tea/coffee maker, and safety box. Duplex suites have a separate living room and a private sala in garden.

Food and Beverage Outlets
Restaurants: Into The View • Onto the Island • Into Fusion • Onto The Room • Into Thai
Cuisine Offered: Asian • International • Thai • European
Quality: Good

Bars: Into Pondering • Into Spirits • Into Wines • Pool Bars (three pool bars for the family pool, garden pool and infinity edge pool offering a wide range of drinks and light snacks)

Other services: Business center • Shops • Babysitting • Kid's club • In house clinic • Shuttle bus to Phuket town (20 minutes) • Tour desk

Water sports and Activities
3 Swimming pools • No beach in front (but private beach on Bon island, 15 minutes away by free shuttle boat) • Snorkeling (on Bon island) • Dive center • Sailboards • Canoeing

Other sports and activities
Six Senses spa • Fitness center • Tennis (night-lit) • Volleyball • Snooker table • Library

 Per room per night

Shanti Lodge Phuket

A rare charming guest house in the beach-tourism capital island of Thailand, Shanti Lodge turns out to be a joyful experience: a very friendly-run guest house with aqua walls and metallic blue roofs raising amidst a fluorescent exotic garden, located just a stones' throw away from the main road.

Shanti Lodge in Phuket is the younger sister of Shanti Lodge in Bangkok. They share the same unique sense of hospitality, as well as a number of accented physical features: fish ponds and the sound of flowing water, bright colors everywhere, creative tile designs breaking the rule of straight lines on walls and floors, a scrupulous care to cleanliness in private as well as communal areas, a generous free-and-easy living style… Yet, Shanti Lodge in Phuket has developed its own vigorous and inspired character as a back-to-nature tropical islander family house. It also expresses, with incredible power and free style, the soul of its owner, designer, and manager South-African citizen and Thai hearted young Kim.

In this spacious property cooled by fresh sea breezes, Kim has built a dazzling multilevel and multiperspective architectural environment surrounded by abundant blooming trees, bushes, and flowers, a passion-fruit orchard and even a small chicken farm. The first building shelters the beating heart of the house: a radiant sitting-dining-chatting-drinking area set in a vast room with practically no walls, but arches and wooden traceried windows instead, opening onto the garden in all directions. A huge 'Shanti' sign centers the floor right under the silhouette of a Latino-styled dancing couple outlined in colored light-tubes on the ceiling. These two are just a sample of

Kim's spontaneous artworks expressing her love to life and joy everywhere in the house. Sinuous terrazzo pathways tattooed with other Kim's fluid figures lead to the garden scattered with waterfalls overlooked by terracotta bas-reliefs and reflected by mirrors, small bridges overpassing fish ponds. You'll even find a hidden sauna if you carefully put your feet onto a set of mysterious foot-shaped stepping stones close to the 'Alice in Wonderland' garden-shower area located under a fragrant frangipani tree…

Ultimately, the main pathway leads to a two-story house located at the back of the property, which accommodates the guest rooms. The ground floor houses five spacious rooms with creatively designed open-to-garden bathrooms. Kim let her talent fully express itself in this private, yet open to the nature space. The floor looks like seashore, with cement treated like solid sand with inlaid shells, as if abandoned by the tide. A tiny but thick tropical garden in full open air surrounds a fishpond running along the five interconnected bathrooms. The washing corner is an exuberant creation with various shapes and sizes of vibrant colored tiles artfully mixed with black stones and mirror splinters. Such fantasy of textures, hues, and forms turns any shower into quite a new sensory experience! The very large rooms on the upper floor, all without bathrooms, are set in a more classical décor, with traditional bamboo wall panels and polished wooden floors. The communal bathroom though is another originally conceived and decorated area à la Shanti with vivid and contrasting colors.

With its fabulous riot of colors and shapes and its warm and easy family-feel atmosphere, the Shanti Lodge is undoubtedly a very precious guest house —and excellent value for money—whose name you'll only want to share with your best friends.

SHANTI LODGE PHUKET
1/2 Soi Bang Rae,
Chaofa Nok Road,
(Ao Chalong) A. Muang,
Phuket 83130
Tel 66 (0) 76 280-233
E-mail shantilodge@hotmail.com
Web www.shantilodge.com

Booking Office in Bangkok
Booking can also be arranged through Shanti Lodge in Bangkok
Tel 66 (0) 2 281-2497
628-7626
Note: *It is not advisable to use e-mail for short notice bookings, use for advanced booking only; it is highly recommended to book with 1 week notice (not earlier) and to confirm stay one day before arrival.*

 By air and land (2 hours)
Plane 1 hour and 20 minutes flight on Thai Airways from Bangkok to Phuket airport (12 daily flights). **Car** 45 minutes from Phuket airport to Shanti Lodge.
Note: *Taxi can be reserved through Shanti Lodge for pick-up at the airport or you can take the airport shuttle to Phuket town where Shanti Lodge arranges free pick-ups if advised early enough.*

 18 Units
Ground Floor: 5 Double rooms (with garden-bathroom—cold shower) • 2 Double rooms (without bathroom) • 1 Communal (cold shower and toilet) Second Floor: 7 Double rooms • 1 Dormitory (with 4 single beds, without bathroom) • 2 Communal (cold showers and 2 toilets) All rooms are equipped with electric fan and mosquito net. No telephone in rooms.

Food and Beverage Outlets
1 Family-type restaurant and bar
Cuisine Offered: Vegetarian • Western and Southern Thai. Not to be missed are the excellent fruit as well as alcoholic cocktails.
Quality: Excellent and healthy food using non-organic vegetables as well as eggs from in-house chicken farm. Very friendly service.
Other services: Internet services
Kim, the owner, is a precious information provider for all available activities and sightseeing around Phuket, which can be arranged through Shanti Lodge.

 Water sports and Activities
Sauna (free access) • Tree-house library and reading room

 Per room per night
Note: *Payment in cash and Baht only.*

Baan-Mai Beach Resort

An undeniable favorite, this delightful little hotel, isolated on its serene island, combines many qualities. Eight secluded cottages, in a tranquil yet easily accessible and naturally preserved environment, boast distinctive architecture and décor. Moreover, the warm, inviting welcome makes it excellent value-for-money—quite an exception in Phuket.

A 15-minute journey by long-tail boat from the port of Chalon up to the small undulating wooded island of Koh Lone brings you to Baan-Mai. The resort becomes visible only on arrival at the island, with the pointed rooftops emerging discreetly from the treetops being the only signs of its presence. The cottages lying against a backdrop of forested hill are concealed in the green-

ery of a former coconut grove that has since been planted with a profusion of trees and flowers. The beauty of the garden reaches its zenith in April when the ground is carpeted with a superb coat of red lilies.

Baan-Mai is the harmonious fusion of a variety of Southeast Asian architectures, mainly Thai, Burmese and Balinese. The warm ochre-red cottages and their polished tiled roofs brilliantly contrast with the green symphony of lush vegetation.

The restaurant and the cottages are suitably distanced from each other and scattered along a lawn smooth as silk, facing the sea and the golden beach.

The Burmese-inspired rooms in paneled teak are very appealing. Immaculate white curtains and mosquito netting in muslin contrast with the dark polished wood. Canopy beds, chests, and antique cupboards exude a romantic aura. Original bathrooms, in a Balinese style, lie in exterior white patios decorated with pebbles and pot plants. Under the shower

you can hear the unremitting breaking of the waves, the rasping chirping of the cicadas and the joyful twittering of the birds. Each cottage has a terrace sheltered by a portico, looking onto the sea.

Set slightly back from the beach, right at the foothills, lies a splendid and extensive Thai wooden house on stilts. Its teak interior and stylish antique furniture endow it with a special atmosphere. All the rooms have access to a terrace that runs along the house and from where the sea view is aspiring.

Also behind the beach, concealed in a green setting, lies an attractive free-form swimming pool around which deck chairs invite you to savor the calm of the place.

The spacious restaurant pavilion opening wide onto the garden and the sea has a welcoming interior in the same harmony of warm tones as the cottages, with terracotta floors and partially paneled walls. Eyecatching decoration includes a large counter in blond wood, wooden colonial furniture and opalescent glass low-hanging lamps from the 1930s. Large earthen jars containing evergreens, and pretty botanical watercolors decorate the area.

Two young very enthusiastic French managers, Nawel and Didier, efficiently run the resort. An excellent chef, Nawel personally cooks the freshly baked bread and croissants, delicious soufflés and appetizing tropical fruit

tarts! If you can bear to depart from this blissful oasis for a while, Baan-Mai is an excellent starting point for a trip to the nearby Coral Island and the Racha islands, renowned for diving.

BAAN-MAI BEACH RESORT

35/1 Moo 3 Koh Lone,
Phuket 83130
Tel 66 (0) 76 223-095 to 097
Mobile 66 (0) 1 626-8212
66 (0) 9 873-7845
E-mail *baan_mai@yahoo.co.uk*
Web *www.baanmai.com*
Contact Didier Gruel,
General Manager

By air, land and sea (2 ½ hours)
Plane 1 hour and 20 minutes flight on Thai Airways from Bangkok to Phuket (12 daily flights). ***Car*** 45 minutes from Phuket airport to Chamlon pier. ***Boat*** 15 minutes from Chamlon pier to Koh Lone by long-tail boat.

Note: *Transfer from Phuket airport can be arranged by the resort.*

9 Units
8 Bungalows · 1 Villa (with sundeck, 3 bedrooms, 2 bathrooms, 1 living room and kitchen. The villa is fan-cooled only).
All bungalows have private balcony, private bathroom (shower, hot water), air-conditioning, and minibar.

Food and Beverage Outlets
Restaurant and bar
Cuisine Offered: European · Thai
Quality: Excellent family-type food and friendly service

Other services: Phone and Internet at the reception

Water sports and Activities
Swimming pool · Beach · Snorkeling and diving (in others places) · Kayaking · Fishing · Boat trips to Coral island (20 minutes in long-tail boat), to Racha Island (1 hour and 15 minutes in long-tail boat)

Other sports and activities
Trekking to waterfall (1 ½ hour one way) · Excursions to Phang Nga Bay and to Phi Phi islands (40 minutes in speedboat) can be organized · Parascending (in Cruiser island resort next to Baan Mai) · Climbing · Bungee jumping · Massage

 Per room per night

Le Royal Méridien Phuket Yacht Club

The gleaming white tiered terraces of the hotel, against which pink bougainvilleas stand out clearly, face the tranquil Nai Harn bay and Cape Phrom Thep, a narrow spit planted with palm trees, reaching far into the sea, famous for its glorious sunsets. The sheltered bay is a moorage for sailboats.

The hotel's extensive trapezoidal building was built on a small headland, extending a wooded hill, at one extremity of the bay. You can get to the yet uncrowned Nai Harn Beach through a few steps. Modest stalls and a handful of bungalows have been set up along the beach, but no big hotel.

The superb terraces extending the bedrooms and commanding panoramic sea-view are a distinctive attraction of this hotel. A Mediterranean touch is manifest in the high white walls that ensure complete privacy, the red terracotta floor tiles, and the huge glazed bougainvillea-crammed jars.

The bedrooms are spacious and comfortable, and Suites comprise a sizeable lounge area where it is possible to have meals served.

An artistic blend of Thai traditionalism and modernism characterizes the interior décor where much research and study has been put into the layout of large canopy beds, nice rattan furniture, yellow and blue porcelain lamps, miniature models of ships and reproductions of ancient bells.

In a harmony of pale marble, black granite and wood, distinctive bathrooms in the Deluxe rooms and Suites are endowed with amusing bright yellow tiled bathtubs embedded in the ground and washbasins resting on pretty semicircular pieces of furniture.

With it polished terracotta flooring and numerous pots plants, the small reception is welcoming. It gives access to a huge and superb pavilion, open onto the sea, with a tall wooden marquee held up by columns embellished with finely carved sculptures.

Etched on the horizon is the elegant abstract silhouette of a *chao fa* in wood, the traditional decoration element of Thai roofs. Burmese lacquered boxes, lamps, and antique blue and white potteries render the setting ideal for a relaxing moment while having a drink, lounging in one of the comfortable sofas or armchairs. Next to one side of the pavilion, the "Regatta Restaurant," open onto the bay as well, has a pleasant décor. Multicolored bougainvilleas adorn the free-form swimming pool overhanging the sea, with enticing lounge chairs. Access to the beach is from here, the spa, extended by exterior relaxation patios, is a bit further off.

The intimate and personal Méridien Yacht Club is more appealing than the rather monumental, concrete Méridien of Patong. Nevertheless, it has to be acknowledged that the latter has special amenities for handicapped persons, a particularly attractive beach and a gigantic swimming pool.

LE ROYAL MÉRIDIEN PHUKET YACHT CLUB

23/3 Vises Road, Naiharn Beach, Phuket 83130
Tel 66 (0) 76 381-156 to 63
Fax 66 (0) 76 381-164
E-mail *pycrsvn@meridien.co.th*
Web www.lemeridien-yachtclub.com

Booking Office in Bangkok
Tel 66 (0) 2 653-2201 to 07
Fax 66 (0) 2 653-2208 to 09
E-mail *meridien@samart.co.th*
lmresort@bkk.loxinfo.co.th
Web *www. lemeridien.com*

 By air and land (about 2 hours)
Plane 1 hour and 20 minutes flight on Thai Airways from Bangkok to Phuket (12 daily flights). ***Car*** 50 minutes from Phuket airport to Le Royal Méridien.
Note: *Transfer from Phuket airport can be arranged by the resort.*

 110 Units
19 Superior rooms • 65 Deluxe rooms • 16 Royal rooms • 10 Suites
All rooms have private patio with sea view, private bathroom (separate bathtub and shower, hot water, hairdryer), air-conditioning, IDD telephone, satellite TV, CD player, minibar, coffee/tea maker, safety box, 24-hour room service.

 Food and Beverage Outlets
Restaurants: The Regatta (sea view) • The Quarterdeck (open-air terrace with nightly dancing) • La Promenade
Cuisine Offered: Italian • Asian • International • Mediterranean • Seafood
Quality: Good cuisine and service
3 Bars

Other services: Internet • Souvenir shop • Babysitting • Hotel tour desk

 Water sports and Activities
Swimming pool • Beach • Snorkeling (in other places) • Windsurfing • Hobie cat • Kayaking • Body boards • Sailing with Margaret Lee, a 65-feet cruise boat (day and sunset cruise) • Excursions to Phang Nga Bay (3 hours by boat), Phi Phi Islands (2 hours from Chalong Bay)

Others sports and activities
Spa • Fitness center • Tennis • Mountain biking

 Per room per night

Phang Nga Bay and the Islands of Koh Yao

Phang Nga Bay

PHANG NGA BAY *(95 kilometers north of Phuket, day excursion)* The sight of the hundreds of limestone cliffs and peaks that loom dramatically out of the Phang Nga Bay is stunningly spectacular. Certain peaks reach a height of 350 meters with clinging vegetation forming spectacular hanging gardens. The unremitting battering of the waves has worn the bases of some cliffs and given them bizarre, phantasmagoric forms that impose upon you a world of ogres, fairies, monsters and beasts.

One comes across a number of touristic sites here, such as the village on stilts of the Muslim fishermen of **Koh Panyi** or **Koh Phing Kan** and the peak of **Koh Tapu,** the location of a James Bond movie. **Khao Khian**, the painted mountain, is a cavern that conceals cave art portraying men and animals. Accessible through mysterious tunnels, several grottos such as **Tham Lot, Tham Nak** and **Koh Thalu** abound with stalactites, hidden in the cliff hollows. You can get there with long-tailed boats or kayaks.

A whole day is necessary to visit the most remarkable part of this immense 400-square-kilometer bay. Any of Phuket's numerous hotels can organize this excursion, either directly by sea from Phuket or over land, by first reaching the small town of Phang Nga and then, 7 kilometers away, renting a boat which goes into a canal bordered by mangroves before emptying onto the sea.

Depending on the means of transport used, this excursion can be a pleasant memory or a disappointment, as it is a fact that tourists, who flock, can hinder discovering the splendor of the environment. From Phuket, a ride aboard one of the bulging junk boats with rusty-colored sails, such as June Bahtra or Nakalay Junk, fitted with kayaks, is quite a treat. If leaving from the town of Phang Nga, it is possible to rent your own personal long-tail boat to explore the wilder limestone islands and emerald colored lagoons at your leisure. **June Bahtra**, the junk boat with a capacity to transport 25 persons, leaves from the Tilok Jetty, near the town of Phuket. Sunset cruises are possible on certain days. Tel: 66 (0) 76 340-912, 341-987, 341-209; Fax: 341-188. E-mail: *hktmkt@east-west-siam.com.* Web: *www.east-west.com.*

Nakalay-Junk: e-mail: *info@nakalayjunk.com.* Web: *www.nakalayjunk.com* **Sea Gypsy** is a 10-seat motor yacht that departs from Yacht Haven Marina. Laguna Travel and Tours has a desk at the Laguna Hotel complex at Bangtao. Tel : 66 (0) 76 324-453 to 7 (ext. 228).

The Islands of Koh Yao Noi and Koh Yao Yai *(1 ½ hour from the airport of Phuket by road and boat)*

Lying in the heart of Phang Nga Bay, the islands of Koh Yao Noi and Koh Yao Yai are

Phang Nga Bay

less visited than those in the north, even though the **karstic** scenery is equally beautiful. To explore these islands, the charming **Koyao Island Resort,** on the island of Koh Khao Noi is ideal. Aboard a slender-prowed boat, discover in solitude a strange, extraordinary world. High cliffs, evoking stone goddesses, draped in a forested cloak clasp secret lagoons to their breasts and gaze upon you with enigmatic smiles. The rocks are sometimes striped with long, red and orange streaks. Trees heave up from the stone and raise their twisted silhouettes against a clear blue sky. Golden sandy beaches nestled in the solitary creeks invitingly tempt you to take a break.

KOH YAO NOI   A small road goes round the 10 by 12 kilometers island which has pretty sandy beaches: the tree-fringed Hat Pasai with its view of Krabi in the distance, Hat Thak Khao and its strange colored rocks and the islet of Koh Nok accessible on foot during low tide. To the north of Koh Yao, facing Koh Ku Du Yai, a 10-minute track leads to a splendid 200-year old tree standing in a narrow luxuriant valley.

KOH YAO YAI   Several interesting beaches make up the isle: the little bay of Tikood lined by casuarinas trees, Ao Klong Son and its corals, Ao Sai, Ao Larn bordered by cliffs, Ao Hin Go and the forest of Mai Kiem (not recommended for swimming) and Lo Pa Raed.

Koh Pak Bia

Koh Hong

The Archipelago of The Bileh Islands *(to the east of Koh Yao Noi)*

KOH HONG AND THANBOKE KHORANEE MARINE PARK *(30 minutes from Koyao Island resort)*   It is the most spectacular of the isles, possessing two beaches of powdery white sand. High wooded cliffs, outlining an almost circular lagoon, enclose one of the beaches. You may swim in the tranquil waters while the silence of the surroundings is occasionally disturbed by the furtive slide of a monitor lizard on the shore. On the isle you will find only a small Marine Park Office where an entrance fee is compulsory.

KOH PAK BIA AND KOH KA MIT *(15 minutes from Koyao island resort)*   These two little forested rocky isles, trimmed by a strip of golden sand, lie opposite each other.

KOH PA HU SIA   The long-tail boat penetrates into a small lagoon enshrined by high cliffs with numerous thorny euphorbia trees clinging to its walls.

KOH ROI   A few meters from the beach, you penetrate a lagoon whose mangroves with inextricable roots are inhabited by secretive birds.

LAEM SAK   *(1 ½ hour from Koyao Island resort)*   Situated in the bay of Ao Lok on the continent, the coast is bordered by a rather impenetrable mangrove forest.

Koyao Island Resort

Nestled in peaceful seclusion on Koh Yao Noi, in the middle of Phang Nga Bay, facing the magical limestone cliffs of the Bileh archipelago, and not far from Phuket, lies Koyao Island Resort, a charming hideaway you would like to keep as a secret. Indeed, few resorts in this region combine so many qualities: the tranquil beauty of the site, the pleasant villas, the family

lagoons scattered in the bay, landscapes of ethereal beauty far from the throng of tourists. The most visited islands in Phang Nga Bay are in fact those accessible from the small village of Phang Nga to the north, while the lesser-known Bileh islands are equally beautiful.

The 15 villas comprising the little resort, well concealed amidst a coconut grove, are barely visible from the sea. Here, French manager, architect and trained ethnologist Georges Cortez has reinterpreted the local architecture of the south and designed spacious villas in sober style. White walls with thatched roofs contain comfortable interiors. Large wooden sliding doors open out onto the garden or the sea enabling the villas to amply benefit from the outside environment. They all possess a large covered sea-facing terrace equipped with cane furniture where you can even have your meals served. Though smaller, the standard villas are the most inviting, since the bedrooms face the sea. Family villas include a second bed well protected by a mosquito net on the terrace. There is little need for air-conditioning as the space created between the walls and

ambiance, the numerous possibilities for excursions in the traditional long-tail boats and an good value for money.

Set your own pace and leisurely explore the multiple islands and their

the ceiling allows the sea breeze to ventilate the villas; the murmuring of the wind and the breaking of the waves will lull you to sleep.

Rooms are airy with cream-washed walls in clean contrast to high bamboo structures and yellow-ochre tile flooring. The king-size bed draped in its mosquito net rests on a wide wooden platform. In the evenings, the softened light filtering from the bamboo creates a decidedly romantic atmosphere. The tiled bathrooms in blue handcrafted ceramic from the north are accessible from the terrace. They open directly onto the garden and there are no windowpanes to isolate you from the sounds of nature.

Deck chairs in bamboo are arranged on the green, velvety lawn in front of each villa facing the Bileh islands.

Whether at twilight when the silhouettes of the isles adorned with watered colors, take on an enigmatic aspect or at dawn, when only the early-riser can delight in the magnificent sunrise behind the cliffs, the magic of the spectacle is captivating. The private golden sandy beach, just a few steps away, is an invitation to swim, facing this idyllic landscape. As the bay is always protected you can swim here whatever the tide or season.

In the heart of the coconut grove, facing the sea, on either side of a basin, two pavilions on bamboo stilts with double thatched roofs shelter the restaurant and the bar.

They are pleasant and attractive, soberly furnished with tables and chairs in bamboo and wood, and prettily adorned with turtle dove cages.

Georges Cortez and his assistant Jano will be happy to provide you with any information you may desire to help you better understand the inhabitants of the region and organize your excursions.

KOYAO ISLAND RESORT

Bay of Phuket, 24/2, Moo 5, Tambon Koh Yao Noi, Koh Yao, Phang Nga, 82160

Tel 66 (0) 1 606-1517
Fax 66 (0) 1 606-1518
E-mail *info@koyao.com*
Web *www.koyao.com*
Contact Georges Cortez or Jano

By air, land and boat (3 hours)
Plane 1 hour and 20 minutes flight on Thai Airways from Bangkok to Phuket (12 daily flights). **Car** 15 minutes from Phuket airport to Bangroong pier. **Boat** 1 ½ hour from Bangroong pier to Koh Yao by long-tail boat or small ferry.

Note: *Transfer from Phuket airport can be arranged by the resort.*

15 Units
12 Villas • 3 Familial villas (with 1 bedroom and 1 bed on the terrace)
All rooms have private terrace, private bathroom (shower, hot water), fan only, telephone (connected only to reception or room to room), cable TV, minibar, coffee/tea maker, safety box.

Food and Beverage Outlets
1 Restaurant and 1 Bar
Cuisine Offered: Thai • International
Quality: Familial

Other services: Telephone (reception) • Fax and Internet

Water sports and Activities
Beach • Snorkeling (around nearby islands) • Sea canoeing • Fishing • Islands hopping by long-tail boats or speedboat

Other sports and activities
Small spa • Bike • Motorbike or tuk-tuk

 Per room per night

Khao Lak, Takuapa, Kuraburi, Similan and Surin Islands

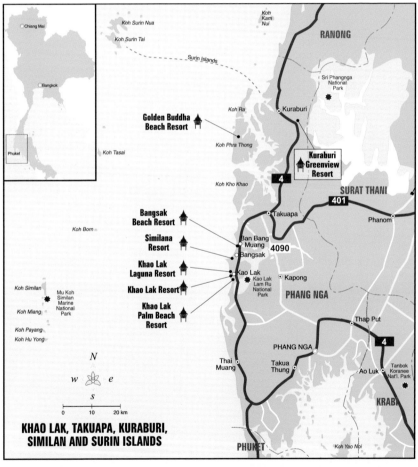

KHAO LAK, TAKUAPA, KURABURI,
SIMILAN AND SURIN ISLANDS

Climate   *Season special note:* The best season to go to Similan and
Surin is from November to April, as the monsoon rains from
May to October render the crossing impossible. Even in sea-
son, the crossing could be canceled if the sea is too rough.

The entire thus far unspoiled region between Khao Lak and Kuraburi is marvelously breathtaking. Rainforests cascade down the hill flanks that overlook the sea, to the boundless secluded beaches. Merely a dozen hotels, full of charm, have sprung up along the beaches, while several national parks have been created here. It is a real pleasure to discover the natural beauty of the region. What is more, the roads are excellent and not very frequented! Access to the hitherto virgin isles of Similan and Surin, and their renowned coral reefs, is easiest from Khao Lak.

Khao Lak

KHAO LAK BEACH *(80 kilometers from the airport of Phuket; 1 ½ hour)* Rocks border the attractive Khao Lak beach and a 45-minute boat ride out to sea brings you to a coral reef barrier favorable to diving. **The Khao Lak Palm Beach, Khao Lak Laguna, Similana** and **Khao Lak Resorts**

fringe the long deserted sandy beaches, framed by primary forest.

Khao Lak Lam Ru National Park

Covering an area of 125 square kilometers, the park has a small visitors' center along route no. 4. The only path that crosses the park (5-hour walk over 7 kilometers) does not leave from the visitors' center but slightly further on from the other side of the road. Being not very well indicated, the services of a guide are indispensable.

The waterfall of **Ton Chong Fah** can be reached by car. The path crossing the park ends up there. From the headquarters of the park, you must continue along road no. 4 in the direction of Takuapa for about 10 kilometers, and branch off inland when you get to Wat Phanat Nikhom. The small road stops five kilometers further on at the Rangers' station, where it gives way to a track. It is preferable to leave the car here

Khao Lak Beach

Khao Lak Lam Ru National Park

simply for those who cherish deserted solitary areas. The natural setting of these islands is well worth a visit on its own.

From Khao Lak, the crossing is by a sizeable speedboat in one and a half hour. Despite offers from some agencies, it is not reasonable to do the return trip to Similan from Phuket in a single day. It is more sensible to travel by diving boat and stay for two or three days.

SIMILAN *(60 kilometers from Tap Lamu on Khao Lak coast, 1½-hour crossing; 100 kilometers to the northwest of Phuket)*

Similan National Park covers 128 square kilometers. It has two offices — one on Koh Similan, the other on Koh Miang — and a few basic bungalows for sleeping.

and continue on foot into the forest (30-minute walk). The waterfall is not very interesting in itself but the surrounding jungle is.

Similan and Surin Isles

Situated about a hundred kilometers apart, the islands were given the status of national park in 1980. These are the most isolated islands of Thailand and, as a result, the coral reef has remained protected. It is a haven for divers and snorkelers, or

Similan or "nine islands" in Malaysian, is a wild forested archipelago lying in crystal-clear waters, where all shades of blue blend in a superb palette of turquoise, beryl, cerulean, ultramarine, and azure. Little creeks of fine white sand lie, coiled along the coasts, dotted with weird gray round polished granite blocks.

Similan is considered as one of the best diving sites in Asia. It has a considerably diverse range of fauna, corals of all forms and colors and underwater caverns. In season, you may have a good chance to see a whale shark or a giant manta ray. Khao Lak's hotels generally organize the visit.

SURIN *(1½ hour, 50 kilometers from Kuraburi)* Lying to the north of Similan and composed of five islets, Surin boasts of good diving spots and has the advantage of permitting snorkeling. There are walking trails, a village of sea gypsies and a small office of the Koh Surin Neua National Park at Ao Mari Yai, where boats anchor.

If the sea is not rough, Kuraburi Greenview Resort can organize the one-day excursion by fast boat for 25 persons; Kuraburi Greenview Travel, 129 Moo 5 Banwan, Kuraburi, Phang Nga; 140/12 Moo 3 Kura, Kuraburi; P.O. Box 14 Kuraburi, Phang Nga. Tel. /Fax: 66 (0) 76 491-414, 421-360, 421-477 to 78; (0) 1 229-6866 to 67.

TAKUAPA *(1½ hour, 130 kilometers from Phuket)* The **Bangsak Resort**, situated here on flatter terrain, 14 kilometers to the south of Takuapa, is very pleasant along the sandy beach of Bangsak, fringed with slender casuarinas trees.

KURABURI *(2½ hours from Phuket)* The excellent, practically deserted road penetrates into the cove of a superb forested massif. Situated along the road, **Kuraburi Greenview Resort** is built right up jungle-shrouded hills. One-day excursion to the Surin islands or visits to the neighboring national parks from this point are easy to arrange.

SRI PHANG NGA NATIONAL PARK *(17 kilometers from Kuraburi Greenview resort)* The 250-square-kilometer park comprises several small waterfalls: Nam Tok Tam Nang (4.5 kilometers from headquarters, 500 meters only on foot, Nam Tok Tohn Sai (15 minutes' walk), Nam Tohn Ton Teui and Nam Tok Tohn Ton Tuei Noy (3 hours' walk).

KHAO YA *(day excursion from Kuraburi Greenview)* The resort organizes land rover safaris through landscapes of hills and jungle, marked by several river crossings and the visit of the small waterfalls along the way, including those of Tonekhing.

KHAO WAN *(20 minutes by car from Kuraburi Greenview and 4 hours' walk)* Khao Wan is one of the sites where you can admire the spectacular blossoming of a certain species of rafflesia. The best season to observe this gigantic flower in bloom is from the end of December to the beginning of January. The resort will tell you when the rafflesias are in bloom, though it must be mentioned that the walk through the forest to reach the site is quite difficult.

KOH PHRA THONG ISLE *(1 hour by long-tail boat)* Situated in a vast bay, the isle of Koh Phra Thong is easily accessible and its diverse landscapes of mangroves, forests, savannahs, as well as a beautiful sandy beach, render the place particularly attractive. One-day excursions or overnight stays at one of the private villas of the **Golden Buddha Beach Resort** are possible. There is a small restaurant on site.

Hevea plantations, Takuapa

225

Khao Lak Palm Beach Resort

Along the picturesque coastal road with cascading rainforest, Khao Lak Palm Beach resort is the first hotel you come across on the Khao Lak coast upon arrival from Phuket. An aura of luxury, elegance and quality exudes from the resort right from the superb reception. This is a vast Thai pavilion, opening onto the gardens overhanging the sea, its high rooftop supported by white sculpted columns. Comfortable cane sofas and armchairs adorned in beige material are agreeable to sit in and admire the rays of the setting sun, shimmering on thousands of specks in the gray granite floor.

The hotel is in traditional Thai style with multi-paneled roofs covered in green-varnished terracotta tiles artistically contrasting with the whiteness of the walls.

The slightly compact setting of the hotel buildings is compensated by the fact that a profusion of trees, bushes, plants and flowers, of all varieties and colors surround them. Particular care and attention is manifest in the landscaped garden. Research and thought for details are evident in the stone *apsaras*, the petal-filled bowls along the sinuous alleys linking the cottages and the small bridges spanning streams and ponds.

The resort gradually slopes down to the beach, and immediately below the reception; a first swimming pool embedded in a terrace surrounded by palm trees overhangs the sea. Several large white two-story four-room pavilions are set out around the area.

The other rooms are in the white individual traditionally styled bungalows. Bright and spacious, they open onto private terraces through large French-windows. Regardless of the category they are comfortable and well designed with a sober décor in light tones. They have parquets or terracotta floorings and furniture in wood or cane. The bathrooms are comfortable, with sunken bathtubs in the Deluxe Seaview rooms.

Not far from the beach, in an elegant two-story pavilion, is the restaurant. Its terrace, opening onto a second swimming pool and the sea, is attractive. The interior is warm and lively, with an exposed beam structure in superb red wood, a polished terracotta floor and wooden tables draped with red and white tablecloths. The Mookda Spa is a beautiful circular teak paneled room opening via large bay windows onto the garden and the sea. It is sheer luxury to unwind and relax in the superb round Jacuzzi that lies enthroned in the middle of the room. Afternoons are the best time to recline here and soak in the warm rays of the setting sun.

KHAO LAK PALM BEACH RESORT

26/14 Moo 7, Takuapa,
Phang Nga 82190
Tel   66 (0) 76 420-099 to 102
Fax   66 (0) 76 420-095
E-mail
info@khaolakpalmbeach.com
Web
www.khaolakpalmbeach.com

By plane and land (2 ½ hours)
Plane 1 hour and 20 minutes flight on Thai Airways from Bangkok to Phuket (12 daily flights).   *Car* About 50 minutes from airport to Khao Lak Palm Beach (72 kilometers).

Note: *Transfer from Phuket airport can be arranged by the resort.*

60 Units
24 Deluxe Mountain rooms (in buildings up the hill) • 26 Deluxe Garden rooms • 8 Deluxe Seaview rooms • 2 Deluxe Ocean suites
All rooms have private balcony, private bathroom (bathtub, hot water, hairdryer), air-conditioning, IDD telephone, satellite TV, minibar. Deluxe Ocean suite have a living room and coffee/ tea maker.

Food and Beverage Outlets
1 Restaurant and 2 bars
Cuisine Offered: Thai •
International

Other services: Internet • Shop • Babysitting • Tailor • Tour counter • Car/jeep/motorbike rental • Safety box (at front cashier)

Water sports and Activities
2 Swimming pools with kiddie pool and Jacuzzi • Beach • Snorkeling (in front or in Na Yak island, 30 minutes by boat) • Windsurfing • Canoeing • Bamboo rafting • Excursion to Similan island (by big boat: 35/50 people or by speedboat: 8/12 people) for day trip or several days

Other sports and activities
Spa • Fitness room • Golf (in Thai Mueng Golf Club at about 33 kilometers or in Thap Lamu Golf at 14 kilometers) • Mountain biking • Elephant trekking • Jungle walking

 Per room per night

Khao Lak Resort 🍃

Of all the very attractive hotels along the coast of Khao Lak, Khao Lak Resort has the most character and appeal. Situated in a forested hill escarpment, slightly behind the coastal road that leads to the other establishments, it enjoys a commanding view of the ocean.

When arriving at the reception, a tall ochre pavilion supported by massive wooden columns, you may have the feeling that you enter a small temple dedicated to a sylvan god.

The rustic flooring in wood and stone, sculptured panels, a superb gong and the antique furniture create a special atmosphere, enhanced by the presence of the gigantic, august trees encircling the pavilion.

From the reception, a steep stairway through the natural vegetation of the hill leads to a lagoon shaped like a sinuous river. It is separated from the beach by a grassy stretch and small bridges cross over it here and there. The duplex pavilions are of traditional architecture, bright and sunny, adorned with green-tiled roofs with their walls painted in this ochre color so characteristic of the resort. Suitably spaced, they directly overlook the golden sandy beach surrounded by rounded rocks or the lagoon. Some of the pavilions are even romantically isolated on grassy islets surrounded by vegetation and accessible by the footbridges.

Bright spacious rooms open onto the trees through large bay windows and are painted in light, cheerful yellow. Originality in the decoration is discernible in the bow windows where sofas are embedded, in the small entrances with their pebbled floors, and in the interior structure of the conical roof with exposed beams. The bathrooms are also imaginative with gray walls studded with diamond-shaped white porcelain, large angled bathtubs, and brackets lamps with shell-shaped frosted glass.

Accessible by a wooden staircase, certain rooms are in various isolated buildings on top of the hill. A Moresque atmosphere reigns in the buildings with golden ochre walls, arcaded windows and dark wooden shutters. The rooms here are particularly spacious, with large terraces enjoying superb sea views. However, access is not easy as you must undertake climbing a wooden staircase to get to the different areas, there being no direct communication with the reception or the restaurants. Its location on a hill-flank makes Khao Lak Resort unsuitable for the very young or the elderly.

You have a choice of restaurants at the resort. One perched on the heights, at treetop level, is a beautiful open pavilion supported by posts and lighted in the evenings by small wooden Chinese lanterns. Two others in the middle of a lagoon facing the sea are octagonal pavilions on stilts covered by a white canopy. An amusing small wooden boat on the grass shelters the Thai restaurant.

KHAO LAK RESORT

158 Sritakuapa Road, Takuapa, Phang Nga 82110
Tel 66 (0) 76 420-060 to 03
Fax 66 (0) 76 420-636
E-mail
center@khaolakresort.com
khaolak-resort@hotmail.com
Web *www.khaolakresort.com*

By air and land (2 ½ hours)
Plane 1 hour and 20 minutes flight on Thai Airways from Bangkok to Phuket (12 daily flights). *Car* 1 hour from Phuket airport to Khao Lak Resort (75 kilometers).
Note: *Transfer from Phuket airport can be arranged by the resort.*

80 Units
29 rooms (Superior and Deluxe) and 1 Suite in 4 buildings • 50 bungalows (32 Superior and 18 Deluxe on the beach front)
All rooms have private terrace with sea view, private bathroom (hot water, bathtub), air-conditioning, telephone, cable TV, minibar.

Food and Beverage Outlets
Restaurants: The Jasmine • Kumpan Boat
Cuisine Offered: Thai • International • Seafood
Quality: Good
1 Bar

Other services: Internet • Small shop • Beauty saloon

Water sports and Activities
Swimming pool • Beach • Snorkeling and diving (in Similan and Surin islands)

Other sports and activities
Snooker room • Trekking in Khao Lak National Park

 Per room per night

Khao Lak Laguna Resort

Created in the style of an ancient Thai city, Khao Lak Laguna is located in a sprawling wooded park bordering a long sandy beach, swathed in rainforest. When dusk falls and the mist envelopes the nearby forest, the night resounding with chirping cicadas and croaking frogs, Laguna acquires the allure of an enchanted kingdom.

A spectacular labyrinth of bridges on high stilts connects the buildings, gracefully crowned with weathered tiled roofs. From the road, a long footbridge leads to the reception, then spans the river flowing through the park, while other bridges meander near the rooms situated in the main building, themselves connected by small private bridges.

There are enormous old trees in the huge, romantic park, with streams and ponds swarming with lotus. In the center, a magnificent and extensive wooden

Thai house on stilts, covered by pointed roofs, accommodates the restaurant. It comprises various levels and terraces for dining. Finely sculpted wooden panels create a tasteful interior décor. On the edge of a small stream, wooden tables are laid out in an intimate manner on teak platforms in the garden. It is a real treat to dine here in the evenings in the glimmer of countless little lights hanging from the trees. Cocktails at the bar made up of many wooden terraces floating on a large pond near the sea are an equally pleasant experience.

The rooms are distributed between the Chalet Hotel and the individual cottages. The Chalet Hotel is a recent, long, white two-story building near the reception, and is a skilful blend of contemporary and ancient Thai design. The spacious and sparklingly clean rooms have an abundance of natural light streaming in from large bay windows. These open out onto a wooden terrace from where you have a sweeping view of the park. The interior is very cheerful with nice parquet floor, bright colored curtains in contrast with white walls, attractive furniture in sculpted wood and rattan and tiled bathrooms.

The slightly older, entirely wooden individual pavilions are huddled, gathered in the center of the park. The interior is more rustic, but comfortable and pleasing. The French windows of the pavilions open out onto a small terrace having either a sea or garden view. The most attractive pavilions are the Beachfront cottages and the Family suites. These are brighter and more spacious with an entrance, a dressing room and amusing small glass-roofed bathrooms hidden in the foliage. The warmth of the paneled interior and the 1930s glass hanging give them a cozy allure. The terrace commands a wonderful view onto the beach and sunset gazing is inspiring.

Unlike the other established hotels in Khao Lak, generally located on the hills, this hotel is ideal for families with children or elder persons. The hotel's small shopping center, the night bazaar with a variety of shops, the excursion center and a second air-conditioned Thai restaurant, with a traditional paneled interior, are all less than a 5-minute walk away.

KHAO LAK LAGUNA RESORT

27/3 Moo 1
Bang Naisee, Takuapa
Phang Nga, 82110
Tel 66 (0) 76 420-200 to 02
Fax 66 (0) 76 420-206
E-mail *info@khaolaklaguna.net*
message@khaolaklaguna.net
reservation@khaolaklaguna.net
Web *www.khaolaklaguna.net*

By plane and land (2 ½ hours)
Plane 1 hour and 20 minutes flight on Thai Airways from Bangkok to Phuket (12 daily flights). *Car* 1 hour from Phuket airport to Khao Lak Laguna (80 kilometers).
Note: *Transfer from Phuket airport can be arranged by the resort.*

110 Units
54 Rooms (with garden or lagoon view; 1 Suite with 2 bedrooms and 2 bathrooms in Hotel Chalet—a two-story building • 44 Deluxe cottages • 10 Beachfront cottages • 2 Beachfront family suites cottages (with 1 bedroom and 1 living room)
All rooms have private balcony or terrace, private bathroom (bathtub in Hotel Chalet, shower in Deluxe and Beachfront cottages, hot water), air-conditioning, telephone, minibar.
Note: *Only the suite has TV.*

Food and Beverage Outlets
Restaurants: Grill Hutte (in the garden by the lagoon side) • RuenThai Restaurant • Old Siam (in night bazaar)
Cuisine Offered: Seafood • Thai • International
Quality: Very good
Bars: Moken bar • The Lobby bar

Other services: Internet • Night bazaar • Minimart • Souvenir shops • Tailor

Water sports and Activities
Swimming pool • Beach • Snorkeling and diving with Kon Tiki Dive Center (day trip to Similan islands, 1 hour by speedboat) • Canoeing in Phang Nga Bay (day excursion, 1 hour by road) • Kon Tiki dive center *(www.kontiki-khaolak.com)*

Other sports and activities
Golf (in Thai Mueng golf club at about 33 km) • TV room • Billiards • Children playground • Thai massage and beauty saloon • Library • Excursions to Sri Phang Nga National Park with elephant trekking, to Krabi and Phuket, to Khao Sok National Park.

 Per room per night

Similana Resort

Isolated amidst rainforest on a sea-facing hill, the resort's main attraction is its natural setting and the rustic serenity of its pavilions. Similana lies at the end of a secondary trail traversing a hevea plantation. The sun penetrating the dense undergrowth creates a strange optical illusion on the regularly aligned trees with trunks notched by rosy spirals.

Perched on the hill, the reception opens onto the forest and its antique wooden furniture creates a special ambiance. A few steps away are airy wooden pavilions sheltering the restaurants with a lovely view of the ocean. The small wooden terrace of the Sunset Bar nestles in the foliage and, as its name suggests, sundowners are an unspoken rule!

Some of the rooms are in the rather ordinary two-story building on the hilltop and though the rooms are pleasing and spacious with sea-facing terraces, it is better to stay in the individual pavilions concealed in the natural surroundings.

Stone alleyways lit by pretty wooden lanterns lead to the traditionally Thai-styled Deluxe bungalows lying on the flank of the hill itself. Being independent and secluded by the tropical vegetation, they enjoy unspoiled serenity. Only glimpses of the weathered red-tiled roofs peeking out from the greenery can be had. Some of the pavilions, the most pleasant ones, directly overhang the sea.

The warm interiors are a combination of wood and woven nipa with cane furniture and sofas recessed in alcoves. Numerous windows, with small window-panes, open onto the sea and the trees.

Lingering on the terrace in relaxed reverie, facing the crystal blue ocean while listening to the forest resounding with echoes and cries, can become a welcome ritual.

Situated on a promontory benefiting from a spectacular view of the sea through the bay windows, the library provides a contemplative atmosphere in its romantic little wooden Thai pavilion extended by a terrace. Wooden steps descend to the rock-encircled, pretty, deserted beach of white sand where you can relax on the comfortable lounge chairs available. The free-form swimming pool is just behind, under the foliage of impressive old ancient trees.

It is at this level that the more rustic thatched-roofed Tree houses are constructed. A number of them are facing the sea while others are somewhat receding in the rather dark mangroves. The high wooden stilt structures that prop up these pavilions, mingle with the inextricably entwined trunks and roots. Numerous birds enliven the place. The paneled rooms, though slightly smaller than those of the Deluxe bungalows, strangely enough, evoke cozy mountain chalets.

Trips to and from the bungalows to the restaurants and the beach invariably involve encounters with stairways and staircases rendering Similana unsuitable for the elderly.

SIMILANA RESORT

4/7 Moo 1, Kuk-Kak, Takuapa, Phang Nga 82190
Tel   66 (0) 76 420-166 to 67
Fax   66 (0) 76 420-169
E-mail *info@similanaresort.com*
similananature@hotmail.com
Web   *www.similanaresort.com*

Booking Office in Bangkok
Tel   66 (0) 2 379-4586
            379-4560
            731-6889
Fax   66 (0) 2 731-6844
E-mail
similana@asiaaccess.net.th

By plane and car (3 hours)
Plane 1 hour and 20 minutes flight on Thai Airways from Bangkok to Phuket airport (12 daily flights). *Car* 1 ½ hour (84 kilometers) from Phuket airport to Similana.
Note: *Transfer from Phuket airport can be arranged by the resort.*

61 Units
12 Deluxe bungalows (located on the hillside; with 2 double duplex bungalows) • 31 Tree houses (in rain forest near beach) • 18 Deluxe hotel rooms in a building
All rooms have private terrace, private bathroom (hot water, shower except in the Deluxe hotel rooms with bathtub), air-conditioning, telephone, minibar.

Food and Beverage Outlets
1 Thai restaurant and 1 Italian restaurant
Quality: Familial
Bar: Sunset Bar

Other services: Internet • Shops • Babysitting • Safety box (front desk) • Tour counter • Car and motorbike rental

Water sports and Activities
Swimming pool • Beach • Diving • Snorkeling (in Similan islands, day trip) • Excursions to Phang Nga Bay

Other sports and activities
Small spa • Fitness room • Tennis • Golf (Thap Lamu golf, 10 kilometers away and Thai Mueng golf, 45 kilometers away) • Billiards • Recreation room (video/TV/games) • Library

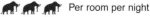 Per room per night

Bangsak Beach Resort

Set in a sprawling deserted bay, bordered by 17 kilometers of golden sand, Bangsak cleverly combines eye-catching, traditional rustic architecture with a good level of comfort. Attention to quality, even in small details, is evident everywhere.

Arriving by a quiet road, you will discover an elegantly imposing semi-circular Thai pavilion perched on lofty stilts and open on both sides. It harbors the reception and one of the restaurants. Once you have got over a flight of stairs to reach it, the others constructions are easily accessible. The pavilion towers over the azure-blue sea and a beautiful swimming pool embedded in a vast wooden terrace. Creative oriental sofas in wood face the ocean. The restaurant is enticing and its two small round separated pavilions make an ideal setting for an intimate dinner.

From there, a green lawn slopes gently down to the beach, trimmed with tumbleweed, where the large thatched-roof pavilion embodying the Thai restaurant is located. Dining in the cool sea breeze at one of the tables that dot the terrace is quite a pleasure.

The access to the cottages is through a wooden footbridge, edged with tall broad-leaved pandan trees, which disappear into an archway of mingling trees.

The standard cottages on stilts are constructed purely from natural materials—woven palm leaves, wood and straw. They have a rotund and cozy appearance under their large, thatched roofs adorned with nests of weaver birds.

The standard cottages are aligned, well spaced and set in the vegetation, along a large, sinuous stone alley where creepers snaking down from gigantic trees provide a natural backdrop. Each is equipped with a small terrace accessible via a large French window. The flawless cottage interiors are decorated with tasteful sobriety, the white walls in keen contrast with comfortable bamboo furniture, fine blond flooring, interior shutters, and brightly colored fabrics.

The more independent cottages situated on the beach are stunning with their large square terraces facing the sea, merely a stones' throw away. They are spacious and on two separate levels connected by few steps. The hall room is on one level while the other contains the bedroom. The high ceiling with its deliberately exposed wooden beams enhances the impression of spaciousness. The Deluxe cottages enjoy the added luxury of a paneled kitchenette. Light pours abundantly into the comfortable bathrooms through windows with mini-balconies.

The national parks of Sri Phang Nga and Khao Lak, 20 kilometers away from the resort, can be visited during the day. It is also possible to visit Khao Sok National Park from Bangsak but the park deserves more than a one-day visit.

BANGSAK BEACH RESORT

31 Moo 7, Petchkasem Road,
Bangmuang, Takuapa,
Phang Nga 82190
Tel 66 (0) 76 593-408
Fax 66 (0) 76 593-406
E-mail
bbr@bangsakbeachresort.de
Web
www.bangsakbeachresort.de

By plane and land (3 hours)
Plane 1 hour and 20 minutes flight on Thai Airways from Bangkok to Phuket (12 daily flights). *Car* 1 ½ hour (130 kilometers) from Phuket airport to Bangsak Beach resort.
Note: *Transfer from airport can be arranged by the resort.*

39 Units
34 Standard bungalows • 3 Superior bungalows (living room, bathtub, coffee/tea maker) • 2 Deluxe bungalows (living room, kitchen, bathtub, coffee/tea maker)
All rooms have private terrace, private bathroom (hot water, shower in Standard bungalows), air-conditioning, telephone, minibar.

Food and Beverage Outlets
Restaurants: Inle seafood (on the beach) • Sun Rise
Cuisine Offered: International • Thai
3 Bars
Quality: Good

Other services: Internet and fax • Small shop • Babysitting (on request only) • Safety box • Exchange • Beauty saloon • Car and motorbike rental • Excursions (reception)

Water sports and Activities
Swimming pool with kiddie pool • Beach • Snorkeling (in Similan and Surin islands) • Mini-surfboards

Other activities
Spa • Volleyball • Badminton • Golf (in Thai Muang golf and in Tap Lamu golf) • Library • Excursions to Krabi, Phang Nga National Park, Phuket, Sri Phang Nga National Park with elephant riding, Khao Sok National Park

 Per room per night

Kuraburi Greenview Resort

The road from Takuapa passes through stunning landscapes of hills covered with primary forest, before arriving at Kuraburi Greenview resort with its welcoming features of a mountain refuge. Nature lovers will be in their element, given the tranquil environment and the proximity of the tropical rainforest. The extreme comfort of the chalets and the multiple possibilities for excursions in the forest or on the coast make it all the more appealing.

From the fairly unfrequented road, the large pink and ochre multi-story building that houses the reception is visible. It dominates a lush green valley around a large expanse of jade-colored waters. The chalets are constructed either in the valley or on the flanks of the opposite forested hills and you can reach them by car. The stone Deluxe chalets on high stilts, covered with tiled roofs with cut-off corners, stand along a pebbled alley near the stretch of water. They offer agreeable views of the hills and its tall trees, through French and bay windows.

The xylophone song of the frogs that venture into the alleys in the evenings will keep you company as you sip cocktails on the terrace.

A portion of the spacious rooms consists of a mezzanine. The rooms are very snug and warm, with beautiful red flooring, wooden beams and white lime-washed walls plastered with pebbles. At nightfall, with a little imagination, you can almost hear the crackling of a good fireplace. A large bed nestles in an elevated alcove and two mattresses are at your disposal in the mezzanine, which is accessible by a wooden ladder. Much attention has been paid to the decoration with pretty cane furniture, vibrant batik materials, traditional Indonesian puppets and suspensions in opalescent glass.

The more rustic standard chalets, built in round billets, line the wooded hill. Quite independent and concealed in the trees, each one is isolated on a private small stone terrace. Though not less comfortable than the Deluxe chalets, they are not advisable for elderly people, being accessible only by a staircase.

The original feature of the chalets is the amusing bathroom with slate walls where the water gushes out from a rocky wall, giving you the impression of having a shower under a cascade framed with plants.

The Superior rooms and the Junior suites situated in a two-story building close to the stretch of water, though more spacious and better fitted, don't have the charm of the chalets.

The owner, who is an avid lover of plants, has built a short botanic track in the garden, which leads out from near the swimming pool.

From the resort you can make a number of excursions: the national parks of Sri Phang Nga (17 kilometers), Khao Sok (45 minutes), or Khao Wan when in season, you can go and gaze at the rafflesias (20 minutes by car and a 4-hour walk) or even go to the islands of Koh Phra Thong and Surin (one-day excursion).

KURABURI GREENVIEW RESORT

129 Moo 5, Bangwan, Kuraburi,
Phang Nga, 82150
Tel/Fax 66 (0) 76 421-360
412-794 to 96
1 229-6866 to 67
E-mail
pom@kuraburigreenview.com
Web
www.kuraburigreenview.com
www.phuket.com/kuraburi/

 1. Via Phuket (4 hours)
Plane 1 hour and 20 minutes flight on Thai Airways from Bangkok to Phuket (12 daily flights). **Car** 2 ½ hours from Phuket airport to Kuraburi Greenview resort.
2. Via Ranong (2 hours)
Plane 1 hour and 10 minutes on Thai Airways or Phuket Air from Bangkok to Ranong (daily flight). **Car** 1 hour from Ranong airport to Kuraburi Greenview Resort.
3. Via Surat Thani (2 ½ hours)
Plane 1 hour and 15 minutes on Thai Airways from Bangkok to Surat Thani (2 daily flights). **Car** 2 hours from Surat Thani airport to Kuraburi Greenview Resort.
Note: *Transfer from airport can be arranged by the resort.*

 35 Units
10 Superior rooms • 2 Junior suites • 17 Deluxe Cabin bungalows • 6 Standard bungalows
All rooms have private balcony, private bathroom (hot water, shower), air-conditioning, telephone, satellite TV, minibar. Superior rooms and Junior suites are in a building.

 Food and Beverage Outlets
1 Restaurant
Cuisine Offered: Thai • International
Quality: Familial

Other services: Excursions (reception)

Other sports and activities
Small golf putting green • Day trip excursions to the national parks of Khao Sok, Khao Ya, Sri Phang Nga and Khao Wan

 Water sports and Activities
Swimming pool • Snorkeling (in Phra Thong Island, 1 ½ hour away by long-tail boat and in Similan and Surin islands, 1 hour away by speedboat (day trip).

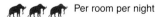 Per room per night

Golden Buddha Beach Resort

From the terrace of the villa, the tranquility of the surrounding forest is disturbed only by the furtive flight of a kingfisher bird and waves breaking on the sand of the secret isle, so rich in natural diversities, of Koh Phra Thong, Isle of the Golden Buddha.

The resort is situated on a narrow forested isthmus of the isle, accessible by boat from the coast across a vast lagoon. The isthmus is fringed on one side by a deserted, golden, sandy beach of seven kilometers and on the other by a little sheltered cove.

Behind a littoral forest, the vegetation on the isle of Phra Thong consists of a coastline bordered by a beautiful mangrove and an amazing savannah conjuring up African landscapes, inhabited by deer, wild boar and colored birds—rollers, bee-eaters and shrikes. Incidentally, the resort organizes jeep safaris to the interior. The ecological abundance of the isle has attracted scientists, and there is a small center for the conservation of tur-

tles. The laying season is from December to January while the hatching period is from February to March.

An Italian manager runs the resort, composed of several cottages in a coconut grove near the reception. More striking are the very independent, sometimes sea-facing private villas that can be rented in the absence of the owners. Dispersed in the forest, they are linked by a large tree-lined alley through which it is pleasant to stroll.

The villas are constructed in traditional Thai style, in wooden stilts, crowned with thatched roofs or terracotta tiles, with attractive exterior terraces. They all have distinguishing individual characteristics with simple, essential furniture. In the jungle, Baab Sabai enjoys an unbelievable view from its terrace onto an inextricable weaving of climbers and creepers. Gaby House is the spruced up smart one, while Baab Toke is a decidedly superb composition of three pavilions. Tree House, as its name suggests, is literally shrouded by the trees and looks onto the sea. The villas have bathrooms opening onto the forest and bathing in the evenings to the sound of cicadas is an enjoyable experience. There is neither hot water nor electricity during the day, but a generator works in the evenings.

Simple meals in a self-service buffet style are served at fixed times in the large pavilion perched above the bay.

The atmosphere is relaxed and informal there, and there is no dearth of things to do. Kilometers of beach wait to be explored, and just in front of the restaurant is an islet around which you can snorkel. Walks through the forest and further on in the bushy savannah are ideal for discovering the natural richness of the island and its fauna.

As the island of Phra Thong lies on the way to the island of Surin from Kuraburi, the speedboats that leave from the coast are able to make a pick-up stop to take you there in one hour, fine weather permitting of course.

Nature nature lover will revel in Golden Buddha Beach's charming, rustic setting, its pristine beaches and its rich marine, bird, and animal life.

GOLDEN BUDDHA BEACH RESORT

131 Moo 2, Koh Phra Thong, Kuraburi, Phang Nga 82150
Tel 66 (0) 1 894-7195
66 (0) 1 892-2208
E-mail *franzi@bluewin.ch*
reservations@
goldenbuddhabeach.com
Web
www.goldenbuddhabeach.com
Contact Lory Follador or Francesca

1. Via Phuket (5 hours)
Plane 1 hour and 20 minutes flight on Thai Airways from Bangkok to Phuket (12 daily flights). *Car* 2 ½ hours from Phuket airport to Kuraburi pier. *Boat* 1 hour and 15 minutes (7 kilometers) from Kuraburi pier to the resort.
2. Via Ranong (3 ½ hours)
Plane 1 hour and 10 minutes flight on Thai Airways or Phuket Air from Bangkok to Ranong (daily flight). *Car* 1 hour from Ranong to Kuraburi pier. *Boat* 1 hour and 15 minutes from Kuraburi pier to the resort.
3. Via Surat Thani (4 ½ hours)
Plane 1 hour and 15 minutes flight on Thai Airways (2 daily flights). *Car* 2 hours from Surat Thani airport to Kuraburi pier *Boat* 1 hour and 15 minutes (7 kilometers) from Kuraburi pier to the resort.
Note: *Transfer from airport or bus station can be arranged by the resort.*

25 Units
3 Small bungalows (1 bedroom) • 22 private villas (beachfront or facing the forest: 2 Houses with 1 bedroom and a small kitchen, 11 Houses with 2 bedrooms and a kitchen, 9 Houses with 2 bedrooms and no kitchen).
All bungalows and villas have balconies or terraces, private bathroom (running water and cold shower), electric fans.
Note: *Electricity is powered by a generator between 6:00 p.m.–11:00 p.m. As there is no pier at the resort, you have to leave the boat in knee-deep water.*

Food and Beverage Outlets
1 Restaurant (buffet style)
Cuisine Offered: Thai • Seafood • Western • Vegetarian
Quality: Familial

Other services: Small shop • Excursions

Water sports and Activities
Beach • Snorkeling (5 minutes away in Phra Tong island) • Diving (in Surin islands, 1 hour by speedboat) • Canoeing along mangroves • Fishing
Other sports and activities
Table tennis • Yoga and massage • Library • Birdwatching • Trekking (Koh Ra rain forest, 30 minutes away by boat) • Jeep safari in the island's interior • Stilt village tour. (There is a sea turtle project: *www.naucrates.org*)

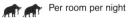 Per room per night

Note: *Cash or payment by traveler's checks is preferred.*

Krabi

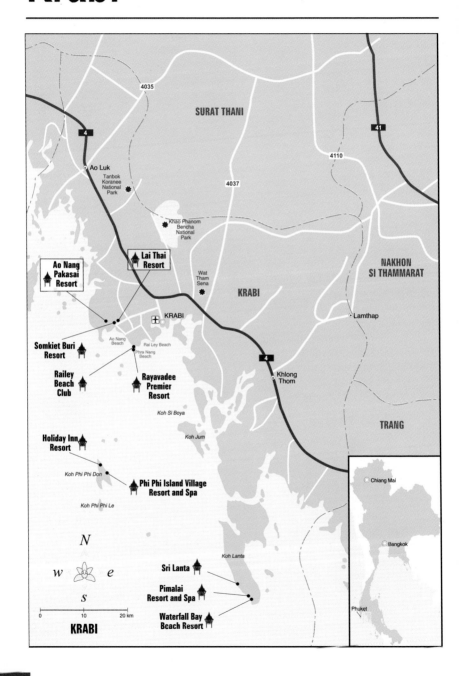

SURAT THANI

4035

4

41

4110

Ao Luk

Tanbok
Koranee
National
Park

4037

Khao Phanom
Bencha
National
Park

**Lai Thai
Resort**

**Ao Nang
Pakasai
Resort**

Wat
Tham
Sena

KRABI

NAKHON
SI THAMMARAT

KRABI

Lamthap

Ao Nang
Beach

Rai Ley Beach

Phra Nang
Beach

**Somkiet Buri
Resort**

4

Khlong
Thom

**Railey
Beach
Club**

**Rayavadee
Premier
Resort**

Koh Si Boya

TRANG

Koh Jum

**Holiday Inn
Resort**

Koh Phi Phi Don

**Phi Phi Island Village
Resort and Spa**

Chiang Mai

Koh Phi Phi Le

N

Bangkok

w   *e*

s

Koh Lanta

Sri Lanta

0   10   20 km

**Pimalai
Resort and Spa**

Phuket

KRABI

**Waterfall Bay
Beach Resort**

Krabi

High limestone cliffs on land and sea in the forested mountainous province of Krabi, whose rugged coastline conceals beaches of fine sand bordering a sheer blue shimmering sea, create a stunning panorama. Thanks to an airport, tourism began and developed here but in a reasonably balanced manner showing greater respect to the environment than in Koh Phi Phi.

The Beaches

THE BEACH AND VILLAGE OF AO NANG *(22 kilometers from the airport of Krabi)* Several hotels and restaurants are located along the small road that separates them from the beach. Situated in a nice park, but with a heterogeneous architecture, **Krabi Resort** is the only hotel in Ao Nang with direct access to the beach. Here, the hotels are still modestly sized, comprising mainly of bungalows. Further inland, on the heights, more monumental hotel buildings are being constructed.

Unfortunately, the numerous long-tail boats anchored here and the murky waters do not make Ao Nang beach very attractive for swimming. Nevertheless, apart from this inconvenience, staying in the relaxed atmosphere of Ao Nang is rather pleasant and it makes an excellent starting point for discovering the region. From here it is easy to rent a boat by the hour or the day to explore the nearby beaches of Railay and Phra Nang or the neighboring isles.

Pakasai Resort, on the heights, is a 10-minute walk away whereas a five-minute car drive along the road to Krabi leads to **Lai Thai** and **Somkiet Buri** resorts

THE EAST AND WEST RAILAY BEACHES *(10 minutes by boat from Ao Nang)* Railay beach West is accessible only by boat from

Ao Phra Nang Beach

Railay Cliffs

Ao Nang. As the afternoon draws to a close, a boat ride, alongside the dizzyingly towering limestone cliffs facing the setting sun, is the most beautiful you can have in the region. The high ledges are cloaked in jungle cascading down to the aquamarine sea. The oxidized rock reflects colors from a painter's palette ranging from pure white to red, swarthy brown or orange, while aerial stalactites hang suspended, like tears of stone.

The site of West Railay is fabulous : a long paradisiacal beach of white powdery sand, coiled in an amphitheater of cliffs. To the extreme north of the beach, the **Railay Beach Club,** with its traditional Thai houses spread out in a beautiful park at the foot of the cliff, is incontestably the "place with a heart" of Krabi.

Otherwise, **Sand and Sea Resort,** an unpretentious yet comfortable resort, composed of small bungalows, is the best choice on the beach.

Sand and Sea Resort: 39 Moo Ao Nang Muang Krabi 81000, Tel: 66 (0) 75 622-608 to 09 Tel/Fax: 66 (0) 75 622-608 E-mail: *sandsearesort@hotmail.com* or *info@krabisandsea.com.* Web: *www.krabisandsea.com* Via a small path from Railay West, a 10-minute walk leads to the mangrove-fringed Railay East beach, which is not good for swimming. There are several

small resorts, whose main leisure activity is rock climbing as the cliffs of Krabi are among the most well known in Thailand.

PHRA NANG BEACH *(20 minutes by boat from Ao Nang)* Situated just after Railay beach, and with the same radiant beauty, Phra Nang Beach is also only accessible by boat. It takes its name from a princess of legend, whose boat went down here in days gone by. At the extreme end of the beach, high cliffs conceal a circular emerald lagoon, "the Princess Lagoon." A good hour's fairly steep walk is necessary to reach it but the magnificent panorama is rewarding. Lying at the foot of this cliff is the luxurious and exclusive **Rayavadee resort.**

Inland Region

Winding inland roads twist and turn amidst the beautiful limestone cliffs.

WAT THAM SENA *(9 kilometers to the north)* This forest temple, whose monks live in troglodyte cells, occupies a vale in the middle of high limestone cliffs. A half hour climb up 1,300 steps leads to a panoramic view from the summit, where a Golden Buddha lies.

KHAO PHANOM BENCHA NATIONAL PARK *(30 minutes, 20 kilometers north)* The national park covers-50 square kilometers of forest with a massif culminating at 1350 meters. There are only two paths leading to two small waterfalls, one at 500 meters from the headquarter and the other at 1.2 kilometer, and this can be quite a frustrating detail. The entrance to the park is a popular picnic site at weekends. Prior to the park entrance is the Tam Khao Phung cave containing stalagmites and stalactites.

TANBOK KORANEE NATIONAL PARK *(40 minutes west)* The attraction of this pretty park, enclosed in a karstic landscape, is a river running on a stone platform creating pretty small waterfalls, amidst large trees and jungle where wild gardenia bloom. The reservoir is a good spot for birdwatching.

The Islands

A day excursion to the neighboring limestone isles of Koh Rang Nok, Koh Poda and Koh Hua Kwan with its strange chicken head rock formation, is pleasant. You can anchor your boat at one of the deserted creeks and relax. The isles are often fringed by small coral reefs but snorkeling is not something to write home about!

Koh Hua Kwan Island

Ao Nang Pakasai Resort

Strelitzia, heliconias and gingers mingle with giant Tarot leaves on the 10.5 hectares of wooded hill where Pakasai has been built, overlooking the distant Ao Nang beach. The forest that swathes the hilltops begins behind the very last buildings.

The resort succeeds in being a haven of peace, only a short walk away from the bustle of Ao Nang, with its street stalls and roadside vendors.

A labyrinth of alleys and stairways connects the constructions, cleverly concealed in the vegetation whose exuberance is carefully nurtured. An enigmatic, mysterious ambiance pervades at twilight, when countless small lamps twinkle in the foliage and the surrounding forest echoes with shrill cicada calls.

Sobriety characterizes the architecture and interior décor. White two- or three-story thatch-roofed houses shelter the comfortable rooms. The décor is relaxing and the arrangement allow maximum privacy.

Up on the heights, the suites enjoy a panoramic view of the bay speckled with islets and the hills. Elegantly simple, spacious and bright, their bay windows open onto large terraces. Evenings here in togetherness with the reverberating forest sounds, are a particularly pleasant experience.

The sizeable bed, sprawled on a wooden platform, enhanced by bright walls and superb parquet floors, promises nights of deep reviving sleep. Sliding panels give access to the large functional bathroom.

For the elderly or very young, the Superior rooms situated in the long buildings, near the reception and the swimming pool, would be more appropriate.

Classic décor is displayed in the wooden reception.

Romantic candlelight *tête-à-tête* dinners are perfect at the tranquil terrace restaurant, where attractive Thai umbrellas grace the intimate tables set along a small stream, murmuring in a jungle setting.

On the roof, just above the restaurant, lies a crescent swimming pool with water flowing over the edges, spectacularly overhanging the vegetation and the distant ocean. Reclining here on the lounge chairs while marveling at the setting sun can be a real treat.

From the resort, it is easy to take a boat excursion and explore the coastal beaches or the neighboring isles.

AO NANG PAKASAI RESORT

88 Moo 3, Tambon Ao Nang, Amphur Muang, Krabi 81000
Tel   66 (0) 75 637-777
Fax   66 (0) 75 637-637
E-mail apakasai@loxinfo.co.th

Bangkok Sales office
14 Soi 9 Seri 2 Road,
Hua Mark, Bankabi
Tel   66 (0) 2 719-0034 to 39
Fax   66 (0) 2 318-7687
E-mail krabi@asianet.co.th
Web   www.pakasai.com

1. Via Krabi (2 hours)
Plane 1 hour and 20 minutes flight on Thai Airways (3 daily flights), from Bangkok to Krabi or on PBAir (2 weekly flights). *Car* 30 minutes from Krabi airport to Ao Nang beach (34 kilometers).
2. Via Phuket (3 ½ hours)
Plane 1 hour and 20 minutes flight on Thai Airways from Bangkok to Phuket (12 daily flights). *Car* 2 hours from Phuket airport to Ao Nang beach.
Note: *Transfer from airport can be arranged by the resort.*

77 Units
34 Superior rooms • 19 Deluxe rooms • 12 Japanese Deluxe rooms • 8 Thara Deluxe suites • 4 Suites
All rooms have private balcony, private bathroom (hot water, shower, bathtub only in Japanese Deluxe suites and in 2 other suites, hairdryer), air-conditioning, IDD telephone, satellite TV, minibar. Japanese Deluxe rooms and suites have coffee/tea maker.

Food and Beverage Outlets
1 Restaurant and 2 bars
Cuisine Offered: Thai • International
Quality: Good

Other services: Babysitting • Safety box (reception) • Tour counter

Water sports and Activities
Swimming pool • Excursions (island tours, long-tail boats, speedboat, snorkeling or diving) • Mountain biking • Game room • Massage

 Per room per night

Lai Thai Resort

What makes Lai Thai special is its warm, relaxed and familial atmosphere. The lone traveler will soon begin to feel at ease and at home.

Robert Reynold, an American who came to settle in Krabi with his wife and family, natives of Chiang Mai, constructed the hotel comprising 10 villas, ten years ago.

Contrary to the popular trend of constructing along the Ao Nang beach, he built his hotel inland, facing a cliff, slightly removed from the road leading to the beach. This proved to be a shrewd alternative as the Ao Nang beach is now dotted with numerous small hotels along the road which generally separates them from the shore. The constant heavy traffic of the boats churning up the murky waters does not make swimming engaging there.

Lai Thai is only a five minute-drive by car from the center of Ao Nang, from where is no problem getting a boat ride to explore the archipelago and its neighboring coasts. Robert knows the region perfectly well and is ever ready with advice and suggestions, even willing to organize your activities on request.

Maintenance and attention to detail are apparent everywhere. Robert's wife is a passionate gardener and this can be observed in the profusion of orchids, including some rare species, hibiscus and other foliage and flora thriving everywhere in her little garden. The villas, inspired by the style of northern Thailand, are spread around the swimming pool surrounded by bougainvillea. Spruced up, freshly painted in white with red tiles, they dispose of a small terrace surrounded by a columned railing.

Inside, the rooms are comfortable, classically styled, with some rustic furniture and sculpted wooden objects from the north. Each has a well equipped tiled bathroom.

The small dining area with views onto the garden and the swimming pool is close to the reception area at the entrance of the resort. The pointed roofs of the villas peeping out from the bright pink bougainvillea are outlined against a backdrop of towering cliffs and offer a very pretty sight. You can enjoy Thai classical music while you dine under soft, subdued lighting in a slightly heteroclite décor of tree trunks, seeds, and wooden sculptures of fish and turtles.

LAI THAI RESORT

25/1 Moo 2, Tambon Ao Nang, Muang, Krabi, 81000
Tel   66 (0) 75 637-281
Fax   66 (0) 75 637-282
E-mail info@laithai-resort.com
Web   www.laithai-resort.com
Owners Robert and Pat Reynolds

1. Via Krabi (2 hours)
Plane 1 hour and 20 minutes flight on Thai Airways (3 daily flights) from Bangkok to Krabi or on PBAir (2 weekly flights). *Car* 30 minutes from Krabi airport to Ao Nang beach (34 kilometers).
2. Via Phuket (3 ½ hours)
Plane 1 hour and 20 minutes flight on Thai Airways from Bangkok to Phuket (12 daily flights). *Car* 2 hours from Phuket airport to Ao Nang beach.
Note: *Transfer from airport can be arranged by the resort.*

20 Units
10 Standard rooms • 10 Deluxe rooms
All rooms have private balcony, private bathroom (hot water, shower—bathtub in Deluxe), air-conditioning, minibar, satellite TV, and safety box.

Food and Beverage Outlets
1 Restaurant and bar
Cuisine Offered: Thai • Mexican
Quality: Familial and friendly service

Other services: Car rental
Many activities can be booked through the resort (snorkeling and diving, long-tail boats, kayaking, rock climbing, excursions to Tiger cave/Wat Tam Suea or national parks).

Water sports and Activities
Swimming pool • Excursions

 Per room per night

Somkiet Buri Resort

This resort is evidently the long-nurtured dream of Mr. Somkiet Kayanram come true. A plant and nature lover, he himself designed the resort and the garden, giving free rein to his fantasy.

The result is sheer fairy tale enchantment. He has made a deliberate effort to make conspicuous the originality of the southern culture and it is smiling gracious women in traditional Muslim costume who greet you at the reception.

The setting, a two-hectare terrain situated inland, close to marshland, at the foot of vertiginous lime cliffs, is magnif-icent. The hotel is slightly set back from the road to Ao Nang and only a few minutes away by car. Particular attention has been paid to landscape gardening and Mr. Kayanram has sometimes himself planted the incredible variety of trees, plants and flowers. Tiny wooden foot-bridges extend over marshes and ponds, creepers embrace knotted wooden bow-ers, and sinuous tracks border the brooks buried beneath the flowers. Emphasis is on the use of natural materials, some of which have been collected over the years by the owner, such as old stumps and roots of trees, ancient timber rail tracks and stones. An assortment of small round pavilions—large wooden beams supporting straw roofs—lie along the principal footpath and house the various restaurants. You must tread over the small footbridges concealed in the vegetation to get to them. For a dinner *tête-à-tête*, individual bamboo tables in patios surrounded by a profusion of plants provide an intimate setting.

The rooms are situated in several two-story buildings at the back of the terrain with views of either the swimming pool or a pond. Each is equipped with a large terrace from where the garden view is enjoyable. Light streams into the spacious interiors through large bay windows. The sometimes slightly kitsch décor of beige granite flooring with large colorful flowery motifs is nevertheless attractive. The comfortable rooms include beautiful bathrooms with walls covered in superbly crafted tiles from the north.

The outstanding view of the limestone cliffs from the sizeable free-form swimming pool, embedded in a teak terrace surrounded by luxuriant vegetation, is breathtaking.

SOMKIET BURI RESORT

236 Moo 2, Ao Nang, Muang, Krabi 81000
Tel (66) 75 637-990
Tel/Fax (66) 75 637-320
E-mail *somkietburi@yahoo.com*
info@somkietburiresort.com
Web *www.somkietburi.com*

 1. Via Krabi (2 hours)
Plane 1 hour and 20 minutes flight on Thai Airways (3 daily flights) from Bangkok to Krabi or on PBAir (2 weekly flights). *Car* 30 minutes from Krabi airport to Ao Nang beach (34 kilometers).
2. Via Phuket (3 ½ hours)
Plane 1 hour and 10 minutes flight on Thai Airways from Bangkok to Phuket (12 daily flights). *Car* 2 hours from Phuket airport to Ao Nang beach.

 26 Units
16 Superior rooms • 10 Deluxe rooms
All rooms with private balcony, private bathroom (bathtub, hot water), air-conditioning, telephone, TV, minibar.

 Food and Beverage Outlets
1 Restaurant
Cuisine Offered: Thai • Seafood International
Quality: Familial

Other services: Internet and fax • Safety box • Tour counter • Parking

Water sports and Activities
Swimming pool • Jacuzzi • Massage • Excursions

 Per room per night

Rayavadee Premier Resort

Unparalleled setting and imaginative architecture characterize Rayavadee, situated on the forested cape of Phra Nang. Towering wooded limestone cliffs mirrored in the turquoise, beryl-green waters fringed by white fine sand render the natural environment awe-inspiring.

Cape Phra Nang shelters the remarkable beaches of Railay West and Ao Phra Nang as well as the more melancholic Nam Mao beach bordered by mangroves. No different from all of Thailand's public beaches, these three attract countless tourists whose main interest is to sunbathe and bask in the hotel front, much to the chagrin of those in quest of peace and solitude. Despite this, however, the reputation of Rayavadee's site and architecture has remained intact, earning it praise including for environmental protection.

Its polygonal yellow-ochre habitations crowned with gently rounded roofs evoke a hamlet of elves. These are nestled in the lush gardens teeming with trees, plants, birds, butterflies, ponds of water lilies and streams. The pavilions are spread out in the park. Those near the swimming pool behind Railay beach are slightly crammed together and devoid of any surrounding vegetation. While this allows you to better appreciate the architecture, it gives you less privacy. The other pavilions in the gardens are very independent, either near the cliffs and the Phra Nang beach, or at Nam Mao, behind the reception and the restaurant.

The single-story pavilions, all designed in the same way, have a winding staircase visible from the outside, and interiors featuring sheer refined luxury. On the ground floor, a round, well-lit living room, opens onto the exterior via a bay window. The central element of the décor is a large and comfortable wooden swing, piled with silk cushions, suspended from the ceiling. It is an ideal spot from which to watch television or listen to music. On the second floor, the room and the bathroom each occupy a semicircular area under a domed ceiling. Rooms are brightly painted in a harmonious concord of beige and yellow that highlights the attractive furniture. Access to the balconies is via large bay windows.

Sophisticated bathrooms feature round bathtubs and basins encrusted in polished teak. Romantic siestas or relaxing meditations in unison with nature can be experienced in the exterior hexagonal *salas* available in some pavilions. Other ones, enclosed in a private garden, have a swimming pool, Jacuzzi or sauna. Incredible tree trunks sculpted with meticulously detailed scenes prop up the reception's sizeable, glazed pavilion. A universe of trees, flowers and elephants has been brought to life under the skilful hand of a talented artist. Breakfast is served at the Raya restaurant near the reception on a shaded terrace facing the Nam Mao beach. The interior décor displays a harmonious combination of wood, dark silk and whitewashed walls. Creative abstract compositions of flowers and large seeds evoke the natural environment. Dining after a sundowner at the Krua Phra Nang restaurant, romantically set overhanging the distant Phra Nang beach, is a pleasure not to be missed.

RAYAVADEE PREMIER RESORT

214 Moo 2, Tambon Ao Nang,
Amphur Muang, Krabi 81000
Tel   66 (0) 75 620-740 to 43
Fax   66 (0) 75 620-630
E-mail   rayavadee@rayavadee.com
Web   www.rayavadee.com

Booking Office in Bangkok
59/3 Soi Akkaphat,
Sukhumvit 49-4 Bangkok 10110
Tel   66 (0) 2 712-5506 to 09
Fax   66 (0) 2 712-5512
E-mail   sales@rayavadee.com

1. Via Krabi (2 ½ hours)
Plane 1 hour and 20 minutes 3 daily flights on Thai Airways from Bangkok to Krabi or on PBAir (2 weekly flights). **Car** 30 minutes from Krabi airport to Ao Nang beach. **Boat** 15 minutes.
2. Via Phuket by land (4 hours)
Plane 1 hour and 20 minutes flight on Thai Airways from Bangkok to Phuket (12 daily flights). **Car** 2 hours from Phuket airport to Ao Nang beach. **Boat** 15 minutes.
3. Via Phuket by boat (3 ½ hours)
Plane 1 hour and 20 minutes flight on Thai Airways from Bangkok to Phuket (12 daily flights). **Car** 30 minutes to the pier. **Boat** 1 ½ hour private transfer by speedboat from Phuket to the resort.
Note: *Transfer from airport can be arranged by the resort.*

101 Units
55 Garden pavilions • 22 Village pavilions • 8 Spa pavilions (garden Jacuzzi, sala) • 9 Deluxe pavilions (hydro pool in fenced garden) • 4 two-bedroom pavilions (one attached ground-level bedroom unit, some with hydro pool) • 3 Villas (2 or 3 bedrooms, dining and living room, one villa with hydro pool, one with swimming pool, sauna and Jacuzzi)
All rooms have private terrace or garden, ground floor lounge, upper floor bedroom with en suite bathroom (separate bathtub and shower, hot water, hairdryer), air-conditioning, 2 IDD telephones, 2 TV, video tape and CD player, minibar, tea/coffee maker, safety box.

Food and Beverage Outlets
Restaurants: Raya Restaurant • Krua Phra Nang
Note: *Private dinning service in your pavilion.*
Cuisine Offered: International • Asian • Thai • Seafood
2 Bars
Other services: Internet/fax services • Gift shop • Tailor • Babysitting (on request) • First-aid clinic • Beauty saloon • Tour and travel assistance • 24-hour room service

Water sports and Activities
Swimming pool • Beach • Snorkeling and diving (in other places) • Non-motorized water sports • Speedboat charter • Siamese junk (sunset cruise)
Other sports and activities
Spa • Fitness center • Tennis • Table tennis • Volleyball • Squash • Snooker • Video and CD library • Trekking to Princess Lagoon hidden beside the Resort (1 hour one way) • Rock climbing

 Per room per night

Railay Beach Club

Nestled in the mesmerizing setting of a wide forested park,
at the foot of towering cliffs
fringed by a white sandy beach, the
Railay Beach club is indisputably the
ultimate venue at Krabi. It is located at
one end of the Railay beach, accessible
only from the sea, opposite the very
exclusive Rayavadee Club. Inexplicably,
people rarely come to this part of the
beach that remains serene and calm
whereas they throng to the vicinity of
Rayavadee.

Sheer cliffs at dizzying heights
dominate this extremity of the beach.
Cycads and other plants cling to the rock

faces from where peculiar limestone
blobs dangle in the form of tears.

A manager, who undertakes the
renting of the homes while the owners
are away, runs the club. He lives on the
premises, in a small wooden building
that serves as a club, and is there to assist
you if you so wish.

The well-spaced villas, hidden in the
vegetation, lie on emerald lawns in the
middle of a splendid park where primeval
trees intermingle with the coconut palms,
frangipanis, and bougainvillea. With the
exception of a Balinese-styled villa, all the
other ones are constructed in traditional
Thai style on stilts, with emphasis being

given to natural materials such as wood, bamboo, and red earthen or polished tiles. Generally opening onto the park through windows and sliding panels, they all have terraces or exterior bridges that allow the passage from one room to another.

No two villas are alike and with each one having its own particular appeal you can choose according to size and budget. In order to give you an idea of a few: "Deborah" lies facing the sea and is endowed with a very beautiful wooden facade finely sculpted under its red pointed roof. "Solly" is the transparent one with its glass tower looking out onto the sea. At the back, accessible by a tiny bridge, the huge and magnificent "Bridge House" attempts to hide in the vegeta-

tion. It is composed of several Thai pavilions connected to each other by terraces and drawbridges. An ideal hideaway for two, "Cliff House," is dwarfed by the imposing cliff at the foot of which it lies.

Interiors are decorated with flair, with ancient teak and bamboo furniture, sofas filled with shimmering silk cushions, and large mosquito nets draped over the beds. Each house has a kitchen and you can shop at Ao Nang, 10 minutes away by boat, or at Krabi, 45 minutes away. However, there is nothing to stop you from varying the pleasure and trying some of the delicacies on offer at the numerous small restaurants on the Railay Beach.

The club provides sheets and towels and the villas are cleaned daily. Ice for

the cool box, available in each villa, can be bought on the spot. There is no air-conditioning and the generator only works from 6 p.m. to 6 a.m., but what a small price to pay for the privilege of experiencing such a wonderful setting!

Visualize waking up each morning in idyllic surroundings to the twittering of the birds and the calls of the monkeys who watch you from the trees above! Imagine, only a few steps away from your villa, a beach of soft, powdery sand beneath your feet. Picture the aquamarine sea readily waiting to embrace you in this bay surrounded by cliffs of unimaginable beauty. A fleet of long-tail boats awaits you at the center of the beach to take you to Krabi or on

RAILAY BEACH CLUB

P.O. Box 8 Krabi 81000

Tel   66 (0) 75 622-582
          (from 8 a.m. to 6 p.m.)
Fax   66 (0) 75 622-596
          (from 8 a.m. to 6 p.m.)
E-mail   *info@railay.com*
Web   *www.railay.com*

1. Via Krabi (2 ½ hours)
Plane 1 hour and 20 minutes flight on Thai Airways (daily flight) from Bangkok to Krabi or on PBAir (2 weekly flights). *Car* 30 minutes from Krabi airport to Ao Nang beach (34 kilometers). *Boat* 15 minutes.
2. Via Phuket (4 hours)
Plane 1 hour and 20 minutes flight on Thai Airways from Bangkok to Phuket (12 daily flights). *Car* 2 hours from Phuket airport to Ao Nang beach. *Boat* 15 minutes

Note: *Transfer from airport can be arranged by the resort.*

28 Units
The villas vary in size and range from 1- to 3-bedroom homes. The manager can send you a list of the different houses with their characteristics by mail or fax. The clubhouse provides sheets and towels (but not beach towels). All villas have large deck spaces, living room, bathrooms (cold water), fan, kitchen, ice cooler chest.

Note: *No electricity but generator from 6 p.m. to 6 a.m.*

Food and Beverage Outlets: In other restaurants in Railay Beach

Other services: On site manager to assist you • House keeping services daily • Linen changed every 3 days • Drinking water provided in each house • Beverage and ice available at the club • Complementary tea and coffee available at the clubhouse

Water sports and Activities
Beach • Excursions in long-tail boats

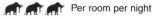 Per room per night

Note: *Minimum stay of 3 days—cash only.*

excursion to the surrounding areas. The only understandable drawback of this little paradise is that it is always fully booked, thus making long-term advance bookings a must—especially during the vacation period.

Phi Phi Islands

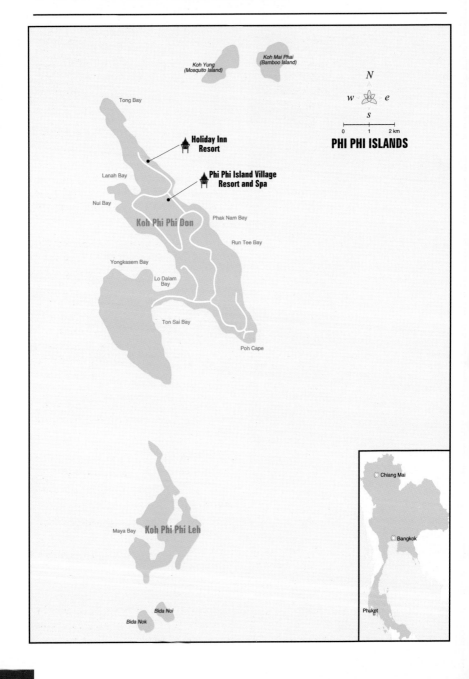

Koh Yung
(Mosquito Island)

Koh Mai Phai
(Bamboo Island)

Tong Bay

**Holiday Inn
Resort**

**Phi Phi Island Village
Resort and Spa**

Lanah Bay

Nui Bay

Koh Phi Phi Don

Phak Nam Bay

Run Tee Bay

Yongkasem Bay

Lo Dalam
Bay

Ton Sai Bay

Poh Cape

N

w — e

s

0   1   2 km

PHI PHI ISLANDS

Maya Bay   Koh Phi Phi Leh

Bida Noi

Bida Nok

Chiang Mai

Bangkok

Phuket

Koh Phi Phi is made up of two islands. The hotels are concentrated on the larger isle of Phi Phi Don (8 km by 2 ½ km) which faces the high limestone cliffs sheltering several paradisiacal lagoons on the smaller untamed isle of Phi Phi Leh (3 km by 1 km).

PHI PHI DON ISLAND *(40 kilometers from Krabi out at sea, 1½ hours by ferry (1 ½–2 hours by ferry from Phuket depending on the Company).* The natural, exceptionally picturesque surroundings of Phi Phi Don have been scarred by the frenzied construction of small hotels, without the slightest consideration for the aesthetics or the environment. Serving as a jetty for ferryboats and crammed with a large number of constructions, this is particularly true of Ao Ton Sai where there is hardly a square meter that is not occupied by bungalows, boutiques, souvenir shops or cafes. In addition, rubbish sometimes piles up just behind the bungalows! Ao Ton Sai beach where numerous long-tail boats anchor resembles more a murky waterfront than a beach.

The site, situated on a sandy isthmus forming two semi-circles, was nevertheless exceptional. One side looks out onto Phi Phi Leh, while the other has a view onto the almost encircled Ao Lo Dalam. Going from one side to the other takes only a few minutes.

Lodgings situated in more serene surroundings, such as **Phi Phi Island Village**

Koh Phi Phi Don

Resort or **Holiday Inn Resort,** are located further along the east coast.

The west coast of the isle is also better protected, with limestone cliffs bordering a translucent sea where snorkeling is possible. Boats are the isles' only means of transport.

PHI PHI LEH ISLAND *(40 minutes from Phi Phi Don)* Phi Phi Leh is absolutely stunning with high wooded sugar loaf limestone cliffs lying huddled around the marvelous emerald waters of Phi Leh Bay, a swallow's realm.

You can visit one of the white-sanded beaches, swim in the crystal-clear waters, practice diving and snorkeling in the Ao Maya bay, or even observe the cave paintings in the Viking Grottos.

Unfortunately, the isle being a popular tourist attraction, there is little chance of being alone there.

The neighboring islands

Several neighboring isles offer various opportunities for jaunts and escapades as well as snorkeling:

MOSQUITO ISLE (KOH YUNG) AND BAMBOO ISLE (KOH MAI PHAI), to the north of the east coast of Koh Phi Phi Don.

GOAT'S ROCK (HIN PAE), to the south of Phi Phi Don.

BIDA NOK AND BIDA NOI (50 minutes by long-tail boat) These two rocky isles to the south of Koh Phi Phi Leh are diving sites.

Koh Phi Phi Don

Phi Phi Island Village

High cliffs limestone stand out at the back of the magnificent bay of golden sand where Phi Phi Island Village lies in peaceful seclusion. It is the only hotel in Koh Phi Phi Don enjoying such a situation.

The undeniable appeal of this hotel is its advantageous location, its local architecture privileging only natural materials and its relaxed atmosphere.

The strikingly soft-sanded beach is irresistible to swimmers. At low tide, however, you have to walk for a while, since the sea recedes rather far away. A small pastoral track starts off from one extremity of the bay, beyond a small bridge that spans an arm of the sea lined with beautiful mangroves. It crosses the isle and you can reach a vast, very secluded circular bay in fifteen minutes, from where you can embark for Tonsay on windy days. Swimming is also possible here. With the exception of a small hotel that was under construction when we visited, this part of the coast is also deserted. Another track on the side leads to a pretty viewing point on the top of a wooded hill.

Phi Phi Island Village is constructed in bamboo, wood and nipa, in accordance with the traditional Thai style. Nestled in the frangipanis and multi-colored bougainvillea, with tortuous branches, is the reception area built on stilts. Floral compositions of ephemeral beauty are created daily with flower petals in the large earthen bowls. From the reception, wooden bridges link the small activity center, the bar, the restaurant, the large boutique, and the inviting swimming pool facing the sea, draped in a cloak of vegetation. On the other side are the diving center and the Coconut bar.

An extremely appealing grand terrace restaurant, on a wooden platform surrounded by bushes, proposes a variety of delectable Thai dishes. A romantic ambiance created by multiple small pearly lights reigns in the evenings. Wooden bungalows on stilts, with graceful thatched pointed roofs, are spread out on immaculately emerald manicured lawns in the large coconut grove. They are well spaced, among groves and colorful flowers. The two terraces situated at different levels in the seafront Deluxe bungalows allow you to enjoy the marvelous view of the ocean. One terrace has lounge chairs, while the other is fitted with armchairs—the choice is yours.

The rustic exterior aspect of the bungalows belies the very comfortable décor of the interior. Spacious rooms, with striking wooden floors, whitewashed walls partly plastered with plaited palms, colorful fabrics and cane furniture, are equipped with large bay windows. The Superior bungalows, at the immediate rear end of the sea, are identical in size but have only one terrace. Free of walls separating the spaces between the living room, study, dressing room and bathrooms, their concept is different.

The bathrooms are a successful harmony of colors in either crafted ceramic tiles of blue, green and yellow or sponge painted walls. In the Deluxe bungalows, a marble shower opens onto a verdant patio, whereas the Superior bungalows have amusing round washbasins in granite resting on natural stone. The Standard bungalows, more simple though comfortable, are about to be phased out.

Phi Phi Island Village offers to organize your activities on request and, after a hectic, activity-filled day, it is sheer bliss to return to this haven of calm and tranquility where natural surroundings have been respected.

PHI PHI ISLAND VILLAGE

Loa Ba Gao Bay, Phi Phi Island
Tel 66 (0) 75 612-915

Booking Office in Bangkok
7 Inthamara, 34 Suttisarn Road, Bangkok 10320
Tel 66 (0) 2 277-0038
      277-0704
      276-6056
Fax 66 (0) 2 277-3990
E-mail *info@ppisland.com*
Web *www.ppisland.com*
Booking Office in Phuket
Tel 66 (0) 76 215-014
      66 (0) 76 222-784
Fax 66 (0) 76 214-918

1. Via Phuket (4 ½ hours or 3 hours with speedboat). *Plane* 1 hour and 20 minutes on Thai Airways from Bangkok to Phuket (12 daily flights). *Car* 1 hour from Phuket airport to Phuket pier. *Ferry* 1 ½ hour from Phuket pier to Tonsai bay (2 times daily). *Boat* ½ hour by long-tail boat from Tonsai bay to the resort.

Note: *From Phuket you have the option to have a 1 ½ hour special transfer by speedboat to Phi Phi Island Village.*

2. Via Krabi (4 hours)
Plane 1 hour and 20 minutes flight on Thai Airways from Bangkok to Krabi (3 daily flights). *Car* 20 minutes from Krabi airport to Choa Fah Krabi pier. *Ferry* 2 hours by PP Family ferry from Choa Fah Krabi pier (2 times daily) to Tonsai bay. *Boat* ½ hour by long-tail boat from Tonsai to the resort.

Note: *Transfer could be arranged by the resort.*

84 Units
28 Deluxe bungalows • 31 Superior bungalows • 25 Standard bungalows
All rooms have private balcony, private bathroom (hot water, shower), air-conditioning, minibar Deluxe and Superior bungalows have cable TV, coffee/tea maker, hairdryer.

Food and Beverage Outlets
Restaurants: Marlin • Dolphin (breakfast)
Cuisine Offered: Thai • Seafood • Chinese • Western • Asian
Bars: Coffee corner (on the terrace) • Coconut Pub (on the beach)
Quality: Excellent Thai cuisine

Other services: Internet • Gift shop • Babysitting (on request) • Satelllite TV lounge • Safety deposit box (reception) • Tour info center

Water sports and Activities
Swimming pool with kiddie pool • Beach • Snorkeling (on other places) • Dive center • Kayaking • Water skiing • Fishing • Island hopping with long-tail boat or speedboat (Phi Phi Leh, Mai-Phai and Yung islands)
Other sports and activities
Spa • Tennis courts • Beach volleyball

 Per room per night

Holiday Inn Resort
Phi Phi Island

Holiday Inn Resort Phi Phi Island is part of the international chain and lives up to its reputation for hospitality and attentive service. It occupies a large wooded terrain situated on the narrow northeast point of the isle, at the end of a large sandy creek that it shares with two other hotels, the Phi Phi Natural Resort and the Coral Resort.

The hotel is set along the length of the Laem Tong beach or on its immediate rear, at the foot of a hill. In a few minutes, you can reach the very steep west coast via a flight of stairs. The site is more rugged and the view below onto the limpid seawaters is stunning. A small pavilion bar, perched on a high cliff, allows a spectacular view of the sunset.

The hotel's architecture successfully combines traditional Thai style with modernism. The exuberant gardens filled with bougainvillea, frangipanis, and pandan trees are particularly delightful.

One can observe everywhere a sense of detail, a concern for refinement in the décor and an effort to ensure maximum comfort to passing guests.

A Thai-styled lofty pavilion in wood, with a floor in polished stones, serves as the reception. The interior decoration is refined—large jars teeming with water lilies mark the entrance, Thai-styled statues in painted wood stand at the feet of white columns, and bowls filled with flowers are placed near the comfortable cane sofas. Nearby is a free-form pool surrounded by vegetation, as well as an activity center.

Two restaurants constructed on wooden platforms are located in the midst of the coconut palm trees whose

trunks sometimes rip through the flooring. Plants in attractive polished earthen
jars decorate the terrace, and evenings,
in the glow of lamps flickering in the
trees, are in an atmosphere of starry
romance. Table arrangements ensure
privacy, but for that special dinner *tête-
à-tête*, reserve the small Thai-styled
pavilion at the heart of the restaurant.

The rooms are situated in individual
cottages constructed on stilts, all spruced
up with their white walls topped with
the traditional pointed red-tiled roofs.
Identical in size and decoration, they
differ only in location. The more spaced
out seafront cottages have the added
advantage of being only a few steps
away from the golden sandy beach and
the turquoise waters. Nevertheless, in
the garden, ablaze with bougainvillea
and accessible by a set of platforms and
wooden bridges on stilts, the rear cottages going right up to the foothills are
equally attractive.

The cottage interiors are not very
large, though comfortable and pleasant.
Bright, luminous rooms, painted in
light colors to contrast with the wooden
flooring, are soberly decorated. A small
dressing room and a blue tiled bathroom with washbasins in marble are
quite attractive. Each cottage has a little
wooden terrace where you can sit in
comfort and absorb the beauty of the sea
or the gardens.

HOLIDAY INN RESORT PHI PHI ISLAND

Phi Phi Island, Laem Tong Beach
Tel   66 (0) 1 476-3787
           66 (0)   676-7317 to 18
           66 (0) 75 621-334
           75 620-798
E-mail
resort@phiphi-palmbeach.com
Booking Office in Phuket
196/1-3 Phuket Road, Phuket 83000
Tel   66 (0) 76 214-654
           217-105
Fax   66 (0) 76 215-090
E-mail
reserv@phiphi-palmbeach.com
Web   *www.phiphi-palmbeach.com*

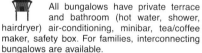

By air, land and sea
1. Via Phuket (4 ½ hours or 3 hours
with speedboat).   **Plane** 1 hour and 20 minutes
flight on Thai Airways from Bangkok to Phuket (12
daily flights).   **Car** 1 hour from Phuket airport to
Phuket pier.   **Ferry** 1 ½ hour from Phuket pier
to Tonsai bay by ferry (2 times daily).   **Boat** ½
hour by long-tail boat from Tonsai to the resort.
Note: *From Phuket you have the option to have
a 1 ½-hour special transfer by speedboat
to Holiday Inn Resort.*

2. Via Krabi (4 hours)
Plane 1 hour and 20 minutes flight on Thai
Airways from Bangkok to Krabi airport (3 daily
flights).   **Car** 20 minutes run from Krabi airport to
Choa Fah Krabi pier.   **Ferry** 2 hours by PP
Family ferry from Choa Fah Krabi pier to Tonsai
Bay (2 times daily).   **Boat** ½ hour by long-tail
boat from Tonsai to the resort.
Note: *Transfer could be arranged by the resort.
The resort is accessible only by boat.*

80 Units
All bungalows have private terrace
and bathroom (hot water, shower,
hairdryer) air-conditioning, minibar, tea/coffee
maker, safety box. For families, interconnecting
bungalows are available.

Food and Beverage Outlets
Restaurants: Tai Rom Prao • Cha-Bah
Seafood Barbeque (on the beach)
Cuisine Offered: Thai • Chinese • European
Bars: Mong Thalay Bar Sunset • Satay Bar
Quality: Good cuisine and service

Other services: Fax • Gift shop • Babysitting •
Tour desk

Water sports and Activities
Swimming pool and Jacuzzi • Beach •
Snorkeling (in other places) • Wind-
surfing • Canoeing • Water sport center

Other sports and activities
Tennis • Billiards • Television room • Game room •
Massage on the beach • Sauna

 Per room per night

Koh Lanta

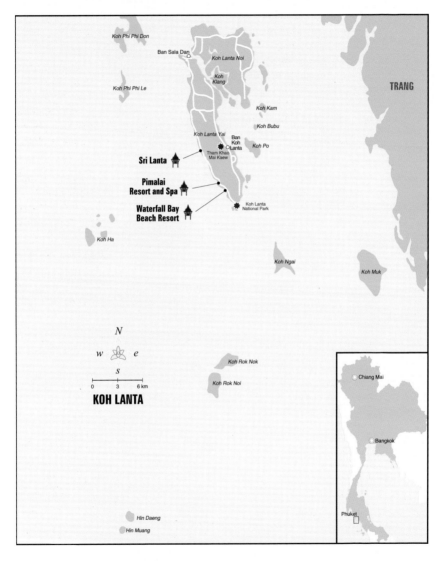

The Setting Adrift of the Chao Le Boats: During the full moon night of the sixth and eleventh lunar months. This is a religious rite performed by Sea Gypsies or "Chao Le" who gather on the beach near Ban Sala Dan Village. Ceremonies feature singing and dancing. The reason for the feast is to bring prosperity and happiness to the participants.

The archipelago of Koh Lanta is composed of 52 islands and islets, 15 of which are part of the Koh Lanta National Marine Park renowned for diving. The hotels are situated on the larger undulating isle of Koh Lanta Yai (26 by 4 kilometers). With the exception of the northern part of the isle near the Ban Sala Dan quay where a multitude of little bungalows have sprung up, tourism is not yet fully developed here. Koh Lanta remains, in its southern end, wooded and untamed, an isle full of charm. It is here that the beautiful hotels of **Sri Lanta** and **Pimalai,** as well as the little **Waterfall Bay** are situated. For those seeking ambiances of remote islands at the ends of the earth, and a certain measure of solitude, Koh Lanta is undeniably irresistible.

The Beaches

On the west coast of the isle are the more attractive beaches, while to the south, the shores are fringed by wooded hills. A single road links the different beaches but means of transport are scarce.

THAM KHAO MAI KAEW *(2-hour excursion)* The limestone caves at the heart of the isle can be reached via a track weaving through hevea plantations and jungle. Access to the caves is through a hole in the rocks and the family that lives nearby will provide you with a guide.

Koh Lanta National Park

At the southern tip of Koh Lanta Yai, the park consists partly of mainland forest and 15 isles out at sea surrounded by beautiful coral reefs. There is no restaurant but a small office in the park rents out tents. A track leads from here along the beach trimmed by a grassy stretch,

where beautiful palm trees grow and looks out over a disconcerting lighthouse, before disappearing into a relatively dark jungle. With a little luck and patience birds, squirrels and monkeys can be spotted here (1 ½-hour walk).

In the Marine Park, the isles more renowned for diving are:

KOH ROK *(south: 2½-hour crossing)* Two islets, Koh Rok Nok and Koh Rok Nai, make up Koh Rok, fringed by paradisiacal beaches of golden powdery sand framed by wooded limestone cliffs. The islands are surrounded by magnificent coral gardens teeming with multicolored fish.

KOH HA *(southwest: 1½-hour crossing)* This is a group of five small limestone islands where you can dive and discover the underwater caves and marine life equipped with mask and tuba.

HIN DAENG AND HIN MUANG *(southwest: 4-hour crossing)* These two rocks, though quite isolated and remote, are reputed as being among the best diving sites in Thailand.

Among the diving centers, one of the oldest and most renowned is: Koh Lanta Diving Center, Koh Lanta, Sala Dan, 81150 Krabi; web: *www.kolantadivingcenter.com*; e-mail: *info@kolantadivingcenter.com*.

Koh Lanta

Pimalai Resort and Spa 💚💚

P imalai stands guard like a sentinel facing the Andaman Sea, terraced on a forested hill of over 40 hectares. Leaving the main road, the red-earthed track penetrates into the untamed part of Koh Lanta, to reach the spellbinding hotel. Here, where the rain forest still shrouds the hills, on certain mornings the descending mist from the gigantic surrounding trees renders Pimalai, the "wild flower," sensually captivating.

Inaugurated towards the end of 2001, the hotel has an architecture that is resolutely contemporary in strict geometric lines. Visual harmony is achieved from an expert blend of robust stones, slating of walls and roofs with the smooth, polished, blond teak floor and furniture, and shimmering

Pimalai's Spa

surrounding environment was made during construction.

The suites, enclosed by a stonewall, except on the side of the nearby beach, are composed of two pavilions separated by a rectangular pond. Being completely independent, they can be occupied by one large family or two couples holidaying together. The pavilions are very spacious and luxurious, with towering, exposed roof timber work. Ample bay windows give exposure to the sea on one side and a verdant patio on the other. Each comprises of one room, a hall extended by a lovely wooden terrace, and a sumptuous bathroom fitted with a bathtub in a glass alcove opening onto the green courtyard. The ensemble exudes an exquisite aura of intimacy.

The modeling and decoration of the rooms situated in the buildings uphill are also well done. You may prefer those on the second floor which command a more sweeping view of the sea. The rooms comprise a large paneled entrance in teak wood and a luxurious bathroom, covered in ochre-colored gold, opening into the room by a window that can be closed when necessary. A large bay window opens onto the sea-facing terrace hidden in the foliage.

In elegant simplicity, the interior decoration of the rooms is a harmony of light saffron and gold. The bed, sofa, desk and mirror, exclusively designed for

colors of the glossy artisan tiles from northern Thailand. A sense of space and liberty is created by deliberately steering clear of partitioning the various living areas.

The rooms are airy and sophisticated, spread out in the different two-storied buildings situated amidst the trees on the sea-facing hill, or in individual suites. Every attempt to preserve the

Pimalai, cleverly combine a modernism influenced by the 1920s and the traditional Thai style.

The spa of Pimalai reflects the inventive spirit of its architect, Khum Gib Gharorn. Totally different and absolutely unique, it seems to have transpired from a book of fairytales. In the hollow of a vale, on either side of a rustling torrent that cascades onto pink ochre stones, individual pavilions crowned with pointed thatched roofs dot the area enclosed in a bamboo patio. They are accessible by a geometric set of footbridges assembled with ropes and cords. Gib has emphasized the use of natural materials, like wood from Kiam, bamboo, river pebbles, fishing anchors, and cords.

An immense and spectacular swimming pool seems to flow endlessly towards the sea below. At one end of the pool a sculptured stonewall spurts out jets of water.

Countless moments render your stay at Pimalai unforgettable: flamboyant sunsets at the Rak Talay beach bar, nights

adorned with a myriad of lights dispersed in the trees and alleys, the strident rasping of the cicadas, and romantic candlelight dinners at the sea-facing restaurant are only a select few.

Numerous activities can be organized in the nearby forest or in the marine park renowned for its diving, but it is an undeniable dilemma to tear yourself away from the enchantment of Pimalai and the fragrance of this wildflower will without doubt linger with you for a long, long while.

PIMALAI RESORT AND SPA

 99 Moo 5, Ba Kan Tiang Beach, Lanta Yai Island, Krabi 81150
Tel   66 (0) 75 607-999
Fax   66 (0) 75 607-998
E-mail   reservation@pimalai.com
Web   www.pimalai.com
Contact Franck de Lestapis, General Manager

 1. Via Krabi by Pimalai speedboat (3 hours) **Plane** 1 hour and 20 minutes flight from Bangkok to Krabi on Thai Airways (3 daily flights). **Van** 50 minutes drive from airport to Ba Hua Hin pier. **Boat** 50 minutes to Pimalai by speedboat.
2. Via Krabi by ferry (4 ½ hours) **Plane** 1 hour and 20 minutes flight from Bangkok to Krabi. **Car** 20 minutes from airport to Krabi Chaofa Pier. **Ferry** 2 hours to Sala Dan on Lanta Yai north. **Van** 40 minutes to Pimalai.
Note: *In low season (May – Oct.) add 30 minutes more.*

3. Via Trang (4 hours) **Plane** 1 ½ hour flight on Thai Airways (daily flight) from Bangkok to Trang **Van** 1 hour and 20 minutes from Trang to Ba Hua Hin pier **Boat** 50 minutes to Pimalai by speedboat.
Note: *The transfer could be organized by the resort. Pimalai could organize also a transfer via Phuket with speedboat (5 ½ hours).*

 82 Units
64 Hillside Superior rooms • 4 Bay Front Deluxe rooms • 7 Pavilion suites (2 bedrooms) • 7 Beach villas (1 to 3 bedrooms, private pool)
All rooms have private balcony or terrace, private bathroom (hot water, separate bathtub and shower, hairdryer), air-conditioning, IDD telephone, cable TV, piped-in music, minibar, coffee/tea maker, safety box. Suites have CD/DVD equipment.

 Food and Beverage Outlets
Restaurants: Baan Pimalai (breakfast) • Spice 'N Rice Thai
Cuisine Offered: Thai • Western
Quality: Good cuisine and service
Bars: Rak Talay Beach Bar (provide snacks and grilled seafood) • The Lounge bar • The Pool bar
Other services: Business center • Shop • Babysitting • Tour desk • Car rental

Water sports and Activities
Swimming pool (with Jacuzzi) • Beach • Snorkeling • Diving (in other places) • Dive center • Kayaking • Windsurfing • Sailing boat • Private speedboat • Sunset cruise

Other sports and Activities
Spa • Fitness center • Library • Mountain biking • Jungle trekking • Elephant trekking

 Per room per night

Sri Lanta ♥

The minimalist, sober architecture of Sri Lanta, along with the numerous inspirational sayings dispersed all over the garden, create an atmosphere conducive to rest, relaxation and meditation. The resort blends in well with the natural environment of a vast hilly forested sea-facing terrain. Low wood and bamboo structures with thatched roofs exhibit a distinct partiality for natural materials.

It is slightly regrettable that the resort is split in two by the small main road. The communal areas are situated on the seafront, while the cottages are on the other side, terraced on the hillock behind. Given that traffic in Koh Lanta so far is not very busy, this does not present any real inconvenience for the moment.

The reception, where hostesses clad in Japanese costume greet you on arrival, is an open wooden pavilion surrounded by ponds decorated by earthen jars. A pavilion "for contemplation" floats, rather unrealistically, on the opposite side, in the middle of another pond: on a superb platform of dark wood lie two white mats and a beautiful, ancient red-lacquered Chinese cupboard. Antique armchairs are disposed along a path under an arcade that leads to different areas, such as the boutique, excursions office, and the Japanese restaurant. The restaurant is stylishly designed, in a harmony of dark red colors with tables separated by unique partitions in wooden fretwork.

The black-tiled swimming pool, whose water flows over the edges, is right on the long deserted sandy beach. On one side small *salas*, with double thatched roofs used for massages and yoga practice, align the shore laced with blue bindweeds.

Massive round wooden pillars hold up a thatched roof sheltering the sea-facing restaurant. A large pond teeming with papyrus occupies the middle of the terrace outside. Babbling water soothe the atmosphere at mealtimes. The architect imagined a strange gray slate wall fountain enclosing one side of the terrace, from which cascades a thin sheet of water. Black granite tables with legs in bamboo and chairs assembled from roots of trees make up the unusual furniture of the restaurant.

On the other side of the road, a large alley, made with old wooden rail sleepers, leads to the individual, well-spaced cottages on stilts, which rise in tiers on the wooded hillocks, tucked in a the luxurious vegetation of heliconias, banana, palm and a variety of other trees.

The rustic-decorated cottage interiors, full of charm, are quite unconventional. The room is a dream-inspiring ship: white sails float at the windows as well as above the large, immaculate bed. The walls are plastered with blond rattan and the floor is made of attractive planks of teak. Antique wooden cupboards and chests furnish the room. The walls are large wooden sliding shutters that, in addition to the glazed windows, allow almost complete openings onto the gardens. The equally Spartan-styled little bathroom with floor and walls in unrefined cement and bamboo partly opens onto the natural surroundings. The songs of cicadas and birds will provide accompaniment as you take your shower, in a verdant patio with a pebbled floor!

SRI LANTA

111 Moo 6, Klongnin Beach,
Koh Lanta Yai, Krabi 81150
Tel   66 (0) 75 697-288
Fax   66 (0) 75 697-289
E-mail   srilanta@srilanta.com
Web   www.srilanta.com

 1. Via Krabi by speedboat (3 hours)
Plane 1 hour and 20 minutes flight from Bangkok to Krabi via Thai Airways (3 daily flights). *Van* 50 minutes from airport to Ban Hua Hin Pier. *Boat* 45 minutes from Ban Hua Hin Pier to Sri Lanta by speedboat.

2. Via Krabi by ferry (4 hours)
Plane 1 hour and 20 minutes flight from Bangkok to Krabi. *Car* 20 minutes from airport to Krabi Chaofa Pier. *Ferry* 2 hours to Sala Dan on Lanta Yai north. *Van* 20 minutes to Sri Lanta.

Note: *In low season (May–Oct) add 30 minutes to travel time.*

3. Via Trang by speedboat (4 hours)
Plane 1 ½ hour flight on Thai Airways (daily flight) from Bangkok to Trang. *Van* 1 ½ hour from Trang airport to Ban Hua Hin Pier. *Boat* 45 minutes from Ban Hua Hin Pier to Sri Lanta Resort by speedboat.

Note: *Transfer can be arranged by the resort.*

 49 Units
36 Hillside villas • 10 Sea View villas • 3 Suites
All rooms have private bathroom (hot water, shower), IDD telephone, air-conditioning, minibar, coffee/tea maker. Suites have bathtub, DVD and TV. Only some villas have a terrace.

 Food and Beverage Outlets
Restaurants: Surya Chandra
Cuisine Offered: Thai • Western • Japanese
Quality: Good
2 Bars

Other services: Internet • TV corner • Shop • Tour desk • Car rental

Water sports and Activities
Swimming pool • Beach • Windsurfing • Sailing • Kayaking • Snorkeling • Island excursions

Other sports and activities
Volleyball • Petanque • Darts • Library • Yoga • Massage • Jungle tours

 Per room per night

Waterfall Bay Beach Resort

Nature lovers in search of peace and tranquility traveling on a shoestring budget will find the Waterfall Bay just what they are looking for.

Situated at the southern tip of Koh Lanta, it lies in the wildest part of the island, surrounded by secondary forest. It is slightly beyond the luxurious Pimalai resort, set back from the red-earth track that continues up to the national park. Near the junction leading to it is a small wooden kiosk that serves as a shelter for elephants waiting for those looking to explore the forest on elephant back! A path going up to the waterfalls, hidden in the jungle 40 minutes away, also begins here.

The resort nestles in a very striking, serene bay, outlined by rocks on the edge of a large golden-sanded beach.

It has extremely various categories of rather disparate bungalows under renovation when we visited. The owners have large-scale extension plans which, given the scenic beauty of the site, is only to be expected. The most recently built bungalows aligned just behind the beach, along an alley amidst the trees, are the most appealing. It would be advisable to avoid, if possible, the older, simpler, slightly decrepit bungalows that have yet to be renovated. They do, however, have the advantage of being a good deal cheaper, while still having the benefit of the magnificent surroundings.

The new constructions evoke mountain chalets, smart in yellow wood, with large pointed thatched roofs. They contain one room on the ground floor with an attached bathroom. A bay window gives access to the garden and a terrace fitted with bamboo furniture. The second floor has a small room with a balcony and is quite independent, being accessible by an exterior staircase.

On the beach shaded by large trees, wooden tables and chairs entice you to relax and enjoy the sea breeze. The small restaurant in bamboo is situated just on the shoreline onto which it overlooks. Another larger one, with a carefully laid out architecture, was under construction when we visited.

A great setting, a relaxed and low-key atmosphere and affordable prices are all key plus points of the Waterfall Bay and you would do well to benefit from this marvelous cove while it is still undisturbed by the developing tourism industry, though one supposes not for long.

WATERFALL BAY BEACH RESORT

7-7/1 Sukon Road, Krabi, 81000
Mobile   66 (0) 1 228-4014
                    (0) 1 397-7529
E-mail   waterfallbayus@yahoo.com
Note: *As it is difficult to contact the resort, it is advisable to book through a travel agency.*

1. Via Krabi (4 ½ hours)
Plane 1 hour and 20 minutes flight from Bangkok to Krabi via Thai Airways (3 daily flights)   **Car** 20 minutes from airport to Krabi Chaofa Pier   **Ferry** 2 hours to Sala Dan on Lanta Yai north.
Note: *In low season (May–Oct) add 30 minutes travel time.*
Car   50 minutes to Waterfall Bay.
2. Via Trang (5 ½ hours)
Plane 1 ½ hours flight on Thai Airways (daily flight) from Bangkok to Trang.   **Car/Ferry** 2 ½ hours from Trang to Ba Hua Hin pier/Koh Lanta pier.   **Car** 50 minutes to Waterfall Bay.
Note: *Transfer from Sala Dan pier can be arranged by the resort.*

30 Units
22 Deluxe bungalows (some are fan-cooled, others with air-conditioning) • 8 Superior bungalows (two-story with air-conditioning—the best choice).
All rooms have private small terrace and private bathroom (shower, hot water).

Food and Beverage Outlets
1 Restaurant and bar
Cuisine Offered: Thai • Western
Quality: Average

Water sports and Activities
Beach • Fishing • Snorkeling • Diving • Cycling (could be organized) • Trekking (waterfalls, 40 minutes away)

 Per room per night

Note: *Cash only.*

The Southeast Peninsula

Cheow Lake

Painting by Lily Yousry-Jouve

The Southeast Peninsula

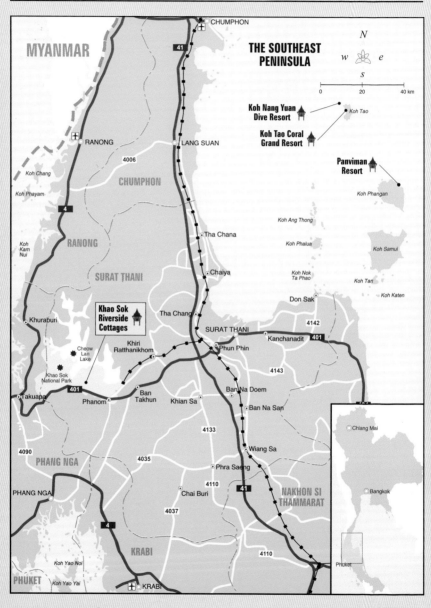

THE SOUTHEAST PENINSULA

N
w · e
s

0   20   40 km

MYANMAR

CHUMPHON

41

Koh Nang Yuan
Dive Resort

Koh Tao

Koh Tao Coral
Grand Resort

RANONG

LANG SUAN

4006

Panviman
Resort

CHUMPHON

Koh Phangan

Koh Chang

Koh Phayam

4

Koh Ang Thong

Koh
Kam
Nui

RANONG

Tha Chana

Koh Phalua

Koh Samui

SURAT THANI

Chaiya

Koh Nok
Ta Phao

Koh Tan

Koh Katen

Khao Sok
Riverside
Cottages

Tha Chang

Don Sak

Khuraburi

4142

Cheow
Lan Lake

Khiri
Ratthanikhom

SURAT THANI

Kanchanadit

401

Phun Phin

Khao Sok
National Park

401

Ban
Takhun

Khian Sa

Ban Na Doem

4143

Takuapa

Phanom

Ban Na San

Chiang Mai

4133

4090

PHANG NGA

4035

Wiang Sa

Phra Saeng

Bangkok

PHANG NGA

4110

Chai Buri

41

NAKHON SI
THAMMARAT

4037

4

KRABI

4110

Phuket

Koh Yao Noi

PHUKET

Koh Yao Yai

KRABI

Climate **Khao Sok National Park:** Subject to the summer and winter monsoons, the best season to visit the park is between December and the beginning of May.

Khao Sok National Park

Khao Sok National Park (35 kilometers from Takuapa; 109 kilometers from Surat Thani) Together with the surrounding parks of Si Phang Nga and Kaeng Krung and the Khlong Nakha and Khlong Saen natural reserves, Khao Sok, an area of a mere 650 square kilometers, protects the largest stretch of virgin forest in southern Thailand, totaling 40,000 square kilometers. Culminating at 960 meters, it is home to a few rarely spotted large mammals and remarkable plants such as the langkow palm and rafflesia, whose giant parasite flower can attain a diameter of 80 centimeters during the flowering period between January and February. The guides know where the flowering sites are, but it takes often a 4-hour walk through the jungle to reach them. Majestic wooded limestone cliffs highlight an exceptionally picturesque landscape. In fact, there are only two paths in the park:

— The path along the Sok River, which branches into a few secondary paths, leads to several waterfalls: Wing Hin (2.8 kilometers from the Park's Center), Bag Le Ap Nam (4.5 kilometers), Tan Sawan (6 kilometers — quite difficult and slippery especially during the last kilometer in the torrent), the narrow Tong Nam gorge hollowed into a limestone cliff and its freshwater pool (6 kilometers, accessible by a bypass), Tong Gloy and its freshwater pool (7 kilometers).

— The path along the Bang Laen River leads from behind the restaurant of the Khao Sok Riverside Cottages to the 11-level Sip and Chan Waterfall (4 kilometers). There are several river crossings to contend with after an easy trek through a bamboo forest.

Khao Sok Region

CHEOW LAN LAKE *(65 kilometers from the headquarters of Khao Sok National Park)* The high cliffs of Cheow Lake are among these landscapes that remain engraved in our memory, haunting our dreams. A boat that disappears into the morning mist shrouding the cliffs with a pearly veil takes you on a timeless journey to a land of fantasy. The landscape's almost unreal, breathtaking beauty captivates the eye that never tires of gazing at the limestone peaks suffused with clouds, gracious silhouettes of an occasional tree clinging precariously to a cliff face, or the inert underwater forest whose trunks melancholically emerge here and there. Then the rising sun unveils one of the most strange and marvelous visions in Thailand—hundreds of dizzyingly high cliffs raise their sharp walls from the midst of the lake's dark waters, and openings into the rocks lead to secret lagoons. The silence is broken only by the raucous calls of hornbills or the mocking chortles of the monkeys, the only visible inhabi-

Cheow Lake

tants of the cliffs and the impenetrable jungle that swathe the lake's edges. Given the vastness of the lake, a one-day trip may not seem enough, as it doesn't allow a full discovery of the site. Formed by the construction of the Rachabrapha dam in 1982, the lake enfolds hundreds of isles and, for enthusiasts, caverns to visit. Two clean and very basic floating houses are available for meals or an overnight stay.

Access: On road 401, from Takuapa to Surat Thani, at Ban Takhum (58–59 kilo-meters) after Phanom, turn left in the direction of the Rachabrapha dam, 12 kilometers away. The road between Khao Sok National Park and the lake is sumptuous, going through wooded limestone massifs that are easier to admire from here than from inside the forest.

It is preferable to organize the excursion beforehand from the hotel as the boats at the lake's jetty are not always available and bargaining for a good rate becomes trickier.

Khao Sok Riverside Cottages

On the edge of Khao Sok National Park, in a beautiful and peaceful natural setting along the river, the rustic little Khao Sok Riverside Cottages is the most comfortable of the many simple and fairly cheap resorts available in the park's vicinity. Perfect tranquility is assured by the small track that terminates here after coursing from the main road through the countryside.

The location can pose a relative problem if you do not have a car, as it is slightly far off from the park's entrance five kilometers away. In any case, a visit to Lake Cheow, 65 kilometers from the park's center, necessitates hiring a vehicle.

Surrounding hedges and flowers brighten the reception, a large thatch-roofed wooden pavilion equipped with a billiard table. A long footbridge on stilts made from trunks of unrefined wood leads to the dining area overlooking the river, and decorated with earthen jars, roots and creepers. Huge trees, which have been left untouched, randomly rip through the floor and roof of the vast open wooden pavilion where bamboo tables and chairs are disposed. The setting is agreeable with the spreading canopies of other old gigantic trees providing cool and pleasurable shade.

The shallow river, where kayaking is possible, is safe enough for children to wade and splash in. Some wooden cottages perched on stilts are spread out in the forest criss-crossed by twisted creepers where a variety of ferns hang decoratively on the trunks, while others lie on the riverbanks. With walls in large rounded logs and windows with small window panes, they bear a resemblance to mountain lodgings.

Simple interiors accommodate a nice bed protected by a mosquito net and bamboo lamps diffuse a dim light. The linoleum imitating wood that covers the ground unfortunately mars somewhat the whole thing. Each bungalow has a terrace, from where you can try to decipher forest echoes and sounds.

It is regrettable that certain visitors content themselves with the one-day visit to the national park from Phuket or from Khao Lak as they miss out on the trip to the magic Cheow Lake dotted with high limestone cliffs. This most beautiful and astonishing landscape of Southern Thailand is even more worthy of a visit than the park.

Other alternatives:

Pantoorat Mountain Lodge, a kilometer from the park, is run by young Englishwoman Sue and her Thai husband Toy, both staunch defenders of the environment. Situated 100 meters from the bifurcation, in a flowery terrain along the road leading to the park, it has four cottages with electricity (fans) and a bathroom. A small restaurant is available for meals. It is very simple but well maintained, the welcome is warm, and excursions can be organized according to your wishes.

E-mail: *pantoorat@yahoo.com*
Web: *www.pantoorat.lovesnature.com*

Tree Trop River Huts Very close to the principal entrance of the park, this is the only resort inside the park itself. The ensemble is quite disparate and several cottages are run-down, but the eight new bungalows are satisfactory, with electricity and bathrooms. There is also a large restaurant.

Tel.: 66 (0) 77 299-150 ext. 518

KHAO SOK RIVERSIDE COTTAGES

136 Moo 6 Soi Natai, Phanom, Surat Thani 84250
Tel   66 (0) 1 229-3750
Fax   66 (0) 7 739-5027
E-mail *khao_sok@hotmail.com*
Web   *www.khaosok.net*
Note: *As it is may be difficult to contact the resort, it is advisable to book through a travel agency.*
E-mail *info@khaosok.com*

All by plane and land
1. Via Phuket (4 ½ hours)
Plane 1 hour and 20 minutes flight on Thai Airways from Bangkok to Phuket (12 daily flights). *Car* 3 hours from Phuket airport to Khao Sok Riverside Cottages.
2. Via Surat Thani (3 hours)
Plane 1 hour and 15 minutes flight on Thai Airways from Bangkok to Surat Thani (2 daily flights). *Car* 1 ½ hour from Surat Thani airport to Khao Sok Riverside Cottages.
Note: *Transfer from airport can be arranged by the resort.*

12 Units
All rooms have private balcony, private bathroom (cold water, shower), fan and mosquito nets.

Food and Beverages
1 Restaurant and 1 small bar
Cuisine Offered: Thai
Quality: Familial

Other services: Excursions

Water sports and Activities
Billiards • Kayaking • Inflatable canoes on the river (just in front) • Excursions by car to Khao Sok National Park • Trekking in the national park or to rafflesia sites • Elephant trekking • Caves

Per room per night

Note: *Cash only.*

Koh Samui

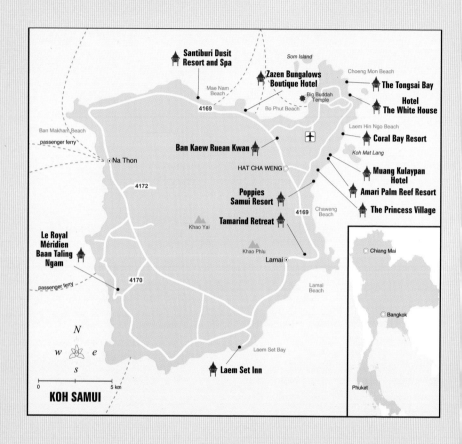

Santiburi Dusit Resort and Spa

Zazen Bungalows Boutique Hotel

Som Island

Choeng Mon Beach

Mae Nam Beach

4169

Bo Phut Beach

Big Buddah Temple

The Tongsai Bay

Hotel The White House

Ban Makham Beach

passenger ferry

Na Thon

Laem Hin Ngo Beach

Coral Bay Resort

Ban Kaew Ruean Kwan

Koh Mat Lang

HAT CHA WENG

Muang Kulaypan Hotel

4172

Poppies Samui Resort

Amari Palm Reef Resort

The Princess Village

Tamarind Retreat

4169

Chaweng Beach

Khao Yai

Le Royal Méridien Baan Taling Ngam

Khao Phlu

Lamai

Chiang Mai

passenger ferry

4170

Lamai Beach

Bangkok

N
w   e
s

Laem Set Bay

0   5 km

Laem Set Inn

Phuket

KOH SAMUI

Climate   Dry season from February to June; rainy season from July to November, but it rains only occasionally except in November that experiences heavy rains. Strong winds from October to January

Full Moon Party (in Koh Phang Nga): Once a month at Haad Rin Beach, more than 10,000 people make it a party from dusk 'till dawn and even beyond with Thai and western DJ's.

The Fishermen Village Festival: Bophut (Koh Samui)—From the 22nd–26th of August. It is a new festival with lots of live music including pop music and Thai rock played by local bands and artists from Bangkok.

A more peaceable seaside resort island than Phuket, Koh Samui nevertheless accounts for over 900,000 visitors annually. Urbanization has developed mainly on the east and partially on the northern coasts. The route leading to the beaches of Chaweng and Lama is a recurrent sequence of hotels, boutiques, agencies, restaurants and cybercafes. Fortunately the impression of saturation completely disappears on the beach where hotels are well concealed in the vegetation. Koh Samui's urban regulations limit the heights of constructions along the shore so, contrary to Phuket, hotels are mostly low-rise bungalows.

The 21 by 25 kilometers isle is small and undulating and the coast is scattered with odd granite formations weathered by the elements. The mountainous interior is essentially the realm of coconut trees, palm trees and durian trees and hardly any forest remains on the isle.

Cat lovers will notice the princely treatment reserved for the numerous cats of Koh Samui, comfortably curled up in the stalls on soft cushions.

The Beaches

Chaweng Beach on the east coast is the longest and most attractive. Seven kilometers of white fine sand border an azure ocean. It is the most visited beach but the activity is concentrated along the coastal road, leaving the beach quite calm and serene. Some areas are more propitious to swimming.

Poppies and **Princess Village** are situated at the center of the beach and here you can swim at any time whatever the tide. A lagoon enfolding tranquil waters lies to the north and is ideal for children, but from June to September, it is not possible to swim at low tide. It is here that the astonishing **Muang Kulaypan** and its neighboring **Amari** resorts are situated.

Lamai Beach, also on the east coast, generally hosts more modest bungalows. It is more mountainous with notably nice rock formations to the south that go up to the top of the slopes in the vicinity of the attractive **Tamarind Retreat.**

Koh Samui

Koh Samui

Laem Set Bay, to the southeast, is spotted by a superb chaos of granite rocks. The charming **Laem Set Inn** nestles on a pretty quiet beach. From June to September swimming is possible only at high tide.

The west coast is not touristic. Wooded cliffs border the deserted beaches near the **Méridien Baan Taling Ngam** positioned in spectacular fashion on a promontory. The presence of rocks renders swimming impossible except on a tiny portion of the beach.

Maenam Beach to the north of the isle is tranquil and very pleasant for swimming. Here the **Santiburi Dusit** is situated in the heart of an immense park.

Bophut Beach, near the former, is bordered by the homes of fishermen and a few small bungalows—like the attractive **Zazen.** The ambiance is more authentic than on the touristic beaches but the waters are less clear.

At the northeastern point, a cape separates Bophut from Chaweng. Several isolated untamed creeks lie coiled here, such as the Tongsai creek with thick grainy sand where the **Tongsai Bay** Resort is located. Swimming is possible irrespective of the tide.

Chengmon Bay, to the south of Tongsai, conceals a 600-meter beach of white sand along which numerous hotels are situated such as **White House.** Swimming is not easy during low tide from June to September.

Laem Hin Ngo Beach. Just before arriving at Chaweng, this tranquil beach of rocky sands and romantic charm shelters the **Coral Bay Resort**, nestled in a vast coconut grove.

INLAND *(one day excursion)* The most interesting excursion at Koh Samui is the discovery, by all-terrain vehicle, of the mountains at the center of the island, crossed only by a few tracks edged by abundant coconut, durian, and pineapple plantations. There are several scenic viewpoints along the coast. At the end of the rainy season, a ramble through the tropical vegetation up to the Na Muang waterfall in the center of the isle is interesting. This excursion is offered at most of the hotels and travel agencies and generally includes lunch at one of the nice small restaurants on the heights.

ANG THONG NATIONAL MARINE PARK *(2 hours by boat – day excursion)* Situated 20 kilometers to the northwest of Koh Samui, the park extends over approximately fifty limestone islets covered with vegetation, resting like emeralds in the middle of a turquoise beryl ocean. Some islets, such as Koh Wua Talab, harbor idyllic creeks of fine white sand, good for swimming. There are several short treks options: in Koh Wua Talab up to the 400-meter high viewpoint and in Mae Koh to a lagoon enshrined by sheer cliffs.

Snorkeling is, on the other hand, disappointing. Several companies organize excursions on boats with a capacity for 40 persons such as Blue Stars and Samui Ocean Sports. The latter also organizes tours of Koh Samui or to Koh Phang Nga by sailboat.

Residents of the Méridien Baan Taling, opposite Ang Thong Park, have the privilege of venturing out on a smaller, more exclusive motorboat.

DIVING AT KOH TAO *(one day excursion)* Diving is mainly at Koh Tao. Several centers organize dives for the day. Among them are:

— *Samui International Diving* (Tel: 66 (0) 77 422-386 or 413-050; Fax: 66 (0) 77 231-242); E-mail: *info@planet-scuba.net* Web: *www.planet-scuba.net*

— *Easy Divers Koh Samui* (Tel.: 66 (0) 77 231-190; Fax: 66 (0) 77 230-486); E-mail: *easydivers@sawadee.com* Web: *www.thaidive.com*

Koh Samui

Tamarind Retreat 💕

Nestled on an extensively forested hill strewn with outlandish rocks, Tamarind Retreat, with its charming villas, is a peaceful place in harmony with its surroundings.

The association of two nature enthusiasts and admirers of Asian art, one Thai, the other German, resulted in the concept of the villas in 1987, and, later on, in the creation of the "Tamarind Spring" spa. Equally renowned for its cures as for its setting, massages can be enjoyed in a large circular pavilion perched on stilts, with a breathtaking view, while the *hammam* lies concealed among impressive granite blocks.

The very private villas, rented when their owners are absent, rise in tiers right up to the middle of the hill, well camouflaged in the trees and exuberant bougainvillea.

Inspired by traditional Thai style, they have been constructed taking into consideration the granitic chaos

feeling that you are part of the environment around you.

The bathrooms are in verdant patios, partially open to the sky, where you can bathe in the hollow of the rocks and listen to the birds singing. Similarly, some kitchens are wide open onto the garden. Stone, wood and terracotta are the natural construction materials used and beautiful ancient furniture is customary in most villas. Choosing a house is not easy, as they all have their own special charm. Tamarind Suite is a romantic ochre pink villa continued by a vast wooden terrace, while Rock'n Wood nestles between two gigantic blocks of granite with a room perched at canopy level.

Wind House has a distinctive bathroom built around a fig tree with tentacular roots, whereas Octavio's spacious terrace makes an ideal lookout point for birds and multicolored butterflies. Fifty-seven species of birds have been sighted and catalogued by amateur birdwatchers. With its bed embedded in the rocks, the bedroom is truly spectacular. This is the only house with air-conditioning, though this is by no means a necessity, as the villas have been constructed in a manner that effectively allows the sea breezes to circulate and ventilate.

Pond House is in a Japanese décor with sliding partitions, elegant oriental furniture and rooms with a view onto a

The Spa

dispersed all over the domain that has become part of the architecture. These occasionally jut and protrude out of the most unpredictable places, such as at the foot of the bed or in the bathrooms.

With the concept of blending interior and exterior boundaries, the garden becomes a visual extension of the villas from the numerous bay windows, terraces and open-air spaces. It creates a sense of space and light, a

The Pond House

The Suite House

pond inhabited by carps and toads that unleash their xylophone sounds into the night. Spectacular views are the assets of Monica Ocean View and Sala Dhawan, higher up on the hill, but nothing equals the fabulous panorama you have from the terrace of Baan Fah Sai, high above, with triple exposure onto mountains, sea and the Lamai beach. These last two houses are accessible by car.

From behind the spa, amidst trees and rocks, a track leads to the top of the hill from where the panoramic view is pleasing. If you really wish to drag yourself away from the charm of the site, a car can be hired at the reception for a beach trip or on an excursion.

There is no restaurant on site yet, but copious and savory breakfasts are served in the rooms in the mornings,

TAMARIND RETREAT

205/3 Thong Takian,
Koh Samui 84310
Tel   66 (0) 77 424-221
Fax   66 (0) 77 424-311
E-mail *info@tamarindretreat.com*
Web   *www.tamarindretreat.com*

1. By air and land (1 ½ hour)
Plane 1 hour and 10 minutes flight on Bangkok Airways (10 daily flights) from Bangkok to Koh Samui. **Car** 25 minutes from airport to the hotel.
2. By air, sea and land via Surat Thani (5 hours)
Plane 1 hour and 15 minutes flight on Thai Airways from Bangkok to Surat Thani (2 daily flights) **Car** 1 hour from airport to Donsak pier **Boat** 2 hours on Seatran Express in Donsak (most recommended) to Nathon pier or on Raga ferry. You may have to wait for a while. **Car** 30 minutes from Nathon to the resort.

Note: Transfer from airport or Nathon can be arranged by the resort. Transport from Bangkok to Surat Thani by bus or train is possible but more time-consuming.

8 Units
All villas have private terrace and garden, bathroom (hot water, shower, some with bathtub), fan, fully-equipped kitchen, IDD telephone, CD player.
Tamarind Suite • Pond House • Wind House • Rock'n Wood (good for 2) • Baan Fah Sai (good for 6 with 2 bedrooms and living room) • Sala Dhawan (good for 6 with 1 bedroom, 1 loft and futon on the open deck) • Octavio (good for 6 with 2 bedrooms and futon in the living room) • Monika's Ocean View (good for 4 with 1 bedroom and living room)

Note: *Daily maid service; because of its unprotected decks and steep stairs, or ponds, houses may not be suitable for elderly people or very young children; only Octavio has air-conditioning.*

Food and Beverage Outlets
No Restaurant, only breakfast is served in your house but delivery service is available (see menus at reception). Coffee, tea, drinking water and fruits are supplied daily.
1 bar at Tamarind Springs (snacks)

Other services: For car/jeep/motorbike rental ask at the reception.

Water sports and Activities
One beach a 200-meter walk away for sunbathing only • Another one for swimming (20-minute walk); Lamai beach (5-minute drive)
Other sports and Activities
Tamarind Springs Spa (unlimited use of steam sauna and 20% off all massage) • Walks • Birdwatching

  Per room per night

Note: Minimum of 5-night booking required. Rate includes free airport roundtrip transfer, one spa treatment and breakfast served in your villa.

and should you wish to avoid the hassle of cooking, menus of a nearby restaurant are available at the reception and takeaway are no trouble to order.

The Princess Village

Princess Village is one of the rare hotels in Southern Thailand that offers the privilege of residing in an ancient house of Ayutthaya. Located in an exuberant tropical garden, on the edge of a paradisiacal white-sanded powdery beach, it is composed of only 12 rooms. The beach here is tranquil and you can swim in the transparent waters, whatever the tide. At the foot of the hotel's small restaurant, deck chairs are available on the shore.

Cross over the threshold of Princess Village from the busy commercial road with its numerous stalls, cybercafes and restaurants, only a few steps away, and enter a world apart where echoes of the past resound. A collection of diverse objects decorates the warm reception— bamboo sofas, bookshelves, strelitzia-filled jars, parasols and above all, the cat of the house blissfully curled up on his cushion.

The houses were dismantled and brought from the region of Ayutthaya to be meticulously reconstituted on site. Their gracious wooden silhouettes, with streamlined roofs in red half-moon tiles, stand on high stilts. The "Sea View" villas are scattered on a green lawn, near the sea, that is at any rate never far away. The "Garden View" villas are situated at the back of the garden, bedecked by an aerial curtain of banyan tree roots, around a lotus-filled square basin. A romantic timber *sala* accessible by footbridge was constructed in the middle of the basin.

Certain villas are individual, while others consist of two rooms separated by a large wooden veranda, thus allowing complete privacy. All rooms have nice private terraces, equipped with sofas and lounge chairs and partially sheltered. Reclining here, in the beauty of the garden whose quietude is interrupted only by the happy singing of the birds in the foliage, is sheer bliss.

As in the olden days, you make your way into the rooms through a small trapezoid paneled door. The wooden interiors, with antique furniture, beds draped in muslin dais, dressing tables and cupboards create a warm atmosphere. Air-conditioning required that the openings be glazed.

With the exception of the Family suites, rooms are relatively small, in identical size. The bathrooms in the "Sea View" suites are better equipped than those in the "Garden View," though renovation plans for these are underway.

Two spacious and bright suites near the sea open via bay windows onto large terraces. Right on the beach, the "Rojana Beach" suite, has a salon, while the "Pra Luksa Family Beach" suite, just behind, has two bedrooms. Both suites are well equipped with modern bathrooms.

It is to be noted that though the two suites are easily accessible, the "Garden View" and "Sea View" villas are unsuitable for the elderly and very young, due to the high steps leading to them.

At Princess Village homey touches are evident in the fresh hibiscus that decorates the beds on arrival and the afternoon tea served on the terrace in delicately woven baskets containing porcelain tea sets.

THE PRINCESS VILLAGE

101/1 Moo 3, Chaweng Beach, Koh Samui 84320
Tel 66 (0) 77 422-216
Fax 66 (0) 77 422-382
E-mail
pvl@samuidreamholiday.com
Web
www.samuidreamholiday.com
For reservation
P.O. Box 25, Koh Samui
Tel 66 (0) 77 245-315 to 7
Fax 66 (0) 77 245-318
E-mail *htwhite@loxinfo.co.th*
Contact Thomas Andereggen, General Manager

1. By air and land (1 ½ hour)
Plane 1 hour and 10 minutes flight on Bangkok Airways (10 daily flights) from Bangkok to Koh Samui. *Car* 20 minutes from airport to the hotel.
2. By air, sea and land, via Surat Thani (5 hours) *Plane* 1 hour and 15 minutes flight on Thai Airways from Bangkok to Surat Thani (2 daily flights). *Car* 1 hour from airport to Donsak pier. *Boat* 2 hours on Seatran Express in Donsak (most recommended) to Nathon pier or on Raga ferry. You may have to wait for a while. *Car* 30 minutes from Nathon to the resort.

Note: *Transfer from airport or Nathon can be arranged by the resort. Transport from Bangkok to Surat Thani by bus or train is possible but more time-consuming.*

12 Units
6 rooms in Garden View Thai houses
• 4 Sea View houses • 2 Family suites
All rooms have private terrace, private bathroom (hot water, shower, hairdryer), air-conditioning, telephone, cable TV, radio, minibar, coffee/tea maker and safety box.
Rojana Beach suite has saloon, 1 bedroom and 1 bathroom (shower and bathtub).
Pra Luksa Family Beach suite has 2 bedrooms and 1 bathroom (shower).

Food and Beverage Outlets
Seaside Restaurant
Cuisine Offered: Thai • International and seafood BBQ
Quality: Familial

Other services: Internet service • Babysitting (on request) • Excursions counter • Massage

Water sports and Activities
Beach

 Per room per night

Poppies Samui 💚

Intimate and attractive Poppies Samui lies discreetly to the south of Chaweng, where the beach is the prettiest, on a long spit of white, powdery sand, fringed with turquoise, aquamarine waters. Since 1999, the hotel is in the capable hands of the dynamic British couple Michael Holehouse and his wife Susan.

Poppies conceals some secrets: on arrival, only the elegant little oriental reception with its marble floor and white columns, prettily furnished with antiques, is apparent. You have to walk through an initiatory passage, a narrow cavern-like corridor, to reach a delightful garden, enclosed by stonewalls, where the villas are spread out. A winding track, over small bridges spanning streams, leads to the beach. The other's Poppie's secret is a hidden underground passage that runs beneath the garden and accommodates the kitchens and the entire logistical infrastructure.

The architect effectively put to good use a relatively small piece of land, while guaranteeing the clientele's intimacy and tranquility.

Each villa, linked by a private path, is hidden in a skillfully orchestrated tangle of plants, mixing cheerfully cycads, palm trees, frangipanis, strelitzia, and bougainvillea among others. Inspired by traditional Thai style, they have shining white walls and streamlined red tiled roofs, protruding out from the foliage. Equal in size, the villas are cheerful and cozy, the light flowing in through windows and door-windows opening onto a nice independent small terrace.

Customer suggestions were taken into account during the renovations made in 2002 and particular attention was given to detail and quality in the interior arrangement of the rooms. Some of the suggestions included deck chairs on the terraces to replace the existing chairs and halogen bulbs above the dressing tables rather than a subdued lighting. Interiors are not large, but well designed, with a salon apart in a recess of the room. White walls, the corner unit concealing the bar, as well as decorative objects such as sculptured panels, silk paintings and red lacquered Burmese lamps enhance beautiful wooden floors.

Colorful tribal tapestry brightens the white bed and built-in ceiling spotlights diffuse a pleasant light. Pastel crafted tiles from the north decorate the attractive bathroom that has a patio dotted with plants lit by a glass roof.

In an Ayutthaya-styled pavilion, the décor of the restaurant is as noteworthy as its cuisine. One of Koh Samui's most renowned restaurants, the delicious international and Thai cuisine served here results in it often being fully booked. A Thai chef and an American chef rustle up a variety of specialities with flair and imagination. The entirely teak wood interior, with soared ceiling held up by massive wooden pillars, is decorated with sculpted bas-reliefs. It is also possible to relish candlelight dinners under a starry sky, at one of the tables set up near the swimming pool or on the seashore. Guitar, piano or traditional Thai-dancing concerts and shows are performed every evening and add a pleasant touch to the prevailing ambience.

The tranquil, exclusive setting, superb beach, comfortable rooms and excellent cuisine make a sojourn at Poppies relaxing and revitalizing.

POPPIES SAMUI

P.O. Box 1, Chaweng,
Koh Samui, Surat Thani 84320
Tel 66 (0) 77 422-419
Fax 66 (0) 77 422-420
E-mail *info@poppiessamui.com*
Web *www.poppiessamui.com*
Contact Michael R. Holehouse, General Manager
E-mail *gm@poppiessamui.com*

1. By air and land (1 ½ hour)
Plane 1 hour and 10 minutes flight on Bangkok Airways (10 daily flights) from Bangkok to Koh Samui. *Car* 20 minutes from airport to the hotel.
2. By air, sea and land, via Surat Thani (5 hours) *Plane* 1 hour and 15 minutes flight on Thai Airways from Bangkok to Surat Thani (2 daily flights). *Car* 1 hour from airport to Donsak pier. *Boat* 2 hours on Seatran Express in Donsak (most recommended) to Nathon pier or Raga ferry. You may have to wait for a while.
Car 40 minutes from Nathon to the resort.
Note: *Transfer from airport or Nathon can be arranged by the resort. Transport from Bangkok to Surat Thani by bus or train is possible but more time-consuming.*

24 Units
All villas have private terrace, private bathroom (hot water, sunken bathtub and shower, hairdryer), air-conditioning, telephone, cable TV, minibar, coffee/tea maker, and safety box.

 Food and Beverage Outlets
1 Restaurant and 1 bar
Cuisine Offered: Thai • International
Quality: Excellent cuisine and service

Other services: Shop • Babysitting (on request but take note that Poppies is more for couples) • Guest relations for all activities and excursions

 Water sports and Activities
Swimming pool • Beach • All water sport activities could be booked at the reception.

Other sports and Activities
Small spa

🐘 🐘 🐘 🐘 🐘 Per room per night

Muang Kulaypan Hotel

Resembling no other hotel on Koh Samui, Muang Kulaypan, with its imposing personality, leaves nobody indifferent. Its minimalist architecture is the result of elaborate reflection and sheer audacity inspired by history and symbols.

Kulaypan was the name of the province where the legendary Prince Inao lived during the reign of Sri Vijaya. The love between Prince Panyee and Princess Budsaba was the main inspirational theme for architect M.L. Archava Varavana. Traditional culture characterizes the hotel and is evident everywhere. At the height of the main staircase, mirrors have the task of warding away evil spirits, while the stone lotus is destined to attract the good ones. Rabbit-shaped topiaries gaze upward at the sky in a quest for the impossible love while children's sculptures adorn the roof's frontage, epitomizing purity and innocence.

Straight off the road, the arrival at the reception is astonishing, where a long corridor of cemented walls assumes an almost austere aspect. The area gives way to a huge mowed lawn stretching to the seafront that, apart from a few original coconut trees, has intentionally been left empty, preferring the beauty and purity of space to that of exuberant tropical luxuriance.

The sky and tree silhouettes are reflected in the waters of the black-tiled swimming pool. As in bygone days, small lumber salas with palm roofs, on the edge of a sandy beach, serve as meeting places for discussions, writing, eating or drinking, while comfortably installed in the handy cushions. Several evenings during the week, a musical concert or classical Thai dance show is performed in a sala on the lawn.

The few rooms are discreetly sheltered in the white, very sober two-story constructions framing the lawn. Chairs in driftwood or modern materials are arranged in the connecting corridors. The low roof compels visitors to bend down as a sign of respect for the house owners in accordance with Thai custom. Magnificent bonsai decorate the vast wooden terrace that leads to the ocean-facing construction accommodating the Standard and Superior rooms. The rooms display evidence of the same meticulous attention to sobriety that enhances the finer points of the original furniture. Whatever the category, the rooms are equally spacious and enticing, differing only in the décor. Various extracts from love poems and black and white photos representing Prince Panyee and his Princess Budsaba embellish the walls. The Deluxe rooms are in a Japanese-inspired décor with mats resting on a platform of polished wood, whereas the Honeymoon rooms have romantic canopy beds draped with white muslin or in the case of the "Honeymoon Inao," black, as tradition required that the young couple be protected from the indiscreet eye.

Only the "VIP Inao" is much larger, independent, and furnished with antiques such as the splendid sculpted bed of King Rama IV.

In the evenings, a mesmerizing play of shadows and light, emanating from the metal torches in the entrance corridors, accentuate the surreal aspect of the perspective. "Serenity" is the recurring word engraved in Sanskrit on the pillars and takes on a new connotation at this hour, after a day spent at Muang Kulaypan. It is, in fact, one of these rare places that successfully go beyond providing material well-being, to move the soul and spirit.

MUANG KULAYPAN HOTEL
100 Moo 2 Chaweng Beach,
Koh Samui, Surat Thani 84320
Tel 66 (0) 77 230-84951
77 422-305
Tel Reservations
66 (0) 77 230-036
Fax 66 (0) 77 230-031
66 (0) 77 230-034
E-mail serenity@kulaypan.com
reservations@kulaypan.com
Web www.kulaypan.com

 1. By air and land (1 ½ hour)
Plane 1 hour and 10 minutes flight on Bangkok Airways (10 daily flights) from Bangkok to Koh Samui **Car** 15 minutes from airport to the hotel
2. By air, sea and land, via Surat Thani (5 hours) **Plane** 1 hour and 15 minutes flight on Thai Airways from Bangkok to Surat Thani (2 daily flights). **Car** 1 hour from airport to Donsak pier. **Boat** 2 hours on Seatran Express in Donsak (most recommended) to Nathon pier or Raga ferry. You may have to wait for a while. **Car** 40 minutes from Nathon to the resort.
Note: _Transfer from airport or Nathon can be arranged by the resort. Transport from Bangkok to Surat Thani by bus or train is possible but more time-consuming._

 41 Units
4 Standard rooms • 20 Superior rooms • 6 Deluxe rooms • 3 Deluxe Inao • 5 Honeymoon Inao • 2 Honeymoon (connecting room) • 1 VIP Inao
All rooms have private balcony, private bathroom (hot water, shower), air-conditioning, IDD telephone, satellite TV (in-house movie channel), minibar, safety box.

 Food and Beverage Outlets
Restaurant: Budsaba Restaurant (private salas)
Cuisine Offered: Thai • Sea food
Quality: Excellent
Bar: Panyee bar

Other services: Fax and internet access • Shop (clothes designed by architect M.L. Varavana) • Babysitting (upon request) • Tour services (guest relation officer)

 Water sports and Activities
Swimming pool • Beach (no swimming at low tide from June to September)

 Per room per night

Amari Palm Reef Resort

High-quality service, tasteful and discreet luxury character-ize this exclusive hotel.

Elegant multi-tiered roofs extended by gracious *chao fa* crown the teak wood constructions in traditional Thai-style architecture. In an atmosphere of warmth and finesse, a lofty pavilion shelters the reception with a vista onto the sea-facing garden. Around this area are located the restaurant and the pavilion accommodat-ing the eight suites whose facades are screened by a profusion of bougainvillea. During the day, the hub of activities is near the sea around the large free-form swimming pool with Jacuzzi.

Swimming at the pleasant beach shaded by coconut trees is possible, dur-ing certain times of the year, only at high tide, due the shallow waters, less limpid than in other parts of the coast. A boat ride to a solitary islet situated just oppo-site is on offer.

Under the watchful eye of the guard you will cross the small road to another much larger garden where the majority of the rooms is located.

Lodgings have been built in accor-dance with the organization of a tradi-tional Thai village. The "Family Houses" are a series of well-spaced individual lumber pavilions, on a vast wooden platform built on various levels, linked by gangways and terraces. The mezzanine provides an ideal sleeping area for kids.

Further on, two-story pavilions accommodate a series of four "Deluxe" rooms and are clustered around a second swimming pool. Both the Family houses and Deluxe rooms are bright and spacious with a pleasant traditional décor.

Less distinctive, but functionally furnished rooms are situated in a long building near the reception. Those which look out onto the nearby hotel's wall, at the back, are less agreeable.

Suites have a very modern refined style. Shining white walls convey a feeling of coolness despite the sultry heat and, in the evenings, sophisticated halogen lights accentuate this sensation. Wooden *chao fa* and eyecatching photos of plants soberly decorate the walls, while the bathrooms are particularly well conceived, in black granite and wood. The ground floor suites are even more immense and attractive with direct access to the swimming pool. All suites have well equipped terraces, and those at the ground floor have a private miniature Japanese garden.

Quality cuisine also plays its part in boosting Amari's esteem. The restaurant on a terrace, in agreeable surroundings, projects out over the distant sea, while the interior Thai restaurant is nicely paneled in teak wood.

AMARI PALM REEF RESORT

Chaweng Beach, Koh Samui 84320
Tel 66 (0) 77 422-015
Fax 66 (0) 77 422-394
E-mail *palmreef@amari.com*
Web *www.amari.com*

Booking Office in Bangkok
847 Phetchaburi Road,
Bangkok 10400
Tel 66 (0) 2 255-3767
Fax 66 (0) 2 255-3718
E-mail *sales@amari.com*

1. By air and land (1 ½ hour)
Plane 1 hour and 10 minutes flight on Bangkok Airways (10 daily flights) from Bangkok to Koh Samui. *Car* 15 minutes from airport to the hotel.
2. By air, sea and land via Surat Thani (5 hours) *Plane* 1 hour and 15 minutes flight on Thai Airways from Bangkok to Surat Thani (2 daily flights). *Car* 1 hour from airport to Donsak pier. *Boat* 2 hours on Seatran Express in Donsak (most recommended) to Nathon pier or on Raga ferry. You may have to wait for a while. *Car* 40 minutes from Nathon to the resort.
Note: *Transfer from airport or Nathon can be arranged by the resort. Transport from Bangkok to Surat Thani by bus or train is possible but more time-consuming.*

104 Units
33 Standard rooms • 40 Deluxe rooms • 23 Family houses • 8 Suites
All rooms have private balcony, private bathroom (hot water, shower, hairdryer), IDD telephone, air-conditioning, cable TV, safety box. Deluxe rooms and suites have separate shower and bathtub, coffee/tea maker.

Food and Beverage Outlets
1 Restaurant and 1 bar
Cuisine Offered: Thai • Seafood • International
Quality: Very good cuisine and service

Other services: Shop • Babysitting • Tour desk

Water sports and Activities
2 Swimming pools with 1 kiddie pool and Jacuzzi • Beach (no swimming at low tide from June to September) • Dive center • Water sports (available nearby)

Other sports and Activities
Tennis • Squash • Mountain biking

Per room per night

Coral Bay Resort ♥

Brimming with ideas and enthusiasm, Doris and Oradee, the hotel managers for 20 years, are fervent protectors of the environment. They have built an extremely pleasant resort in a vast four-hectare coconut grove, enclosed by a stonewall, and set apart from the touristic places of Koh Samui. The original coconut grove has been planted with more than 500 different species of trees and plants. With a fertile imagination, Doris skillfully uses unusual natural materials for the décor and furniture, such as flowers, coconuts, shells, cut bamboo, and driftwood.

All over the garden reigns a joyous fantasy: sinuous winding stone alleys edged by scented ylang-ylang trees and no less than 20 varieties of heliconias, footbridges spanning streams, arbors weighed down by morning glory and bougainvillea, orchids, ferns and philodendrons entwining the tree trunks where birds, butterflies and squirrels abound.

Passionately fond of her garden, Doris cultivates cuttings in a large greenhouse.

The success of the resort rests in the harmony between the appealing natural setting and the architecture of the constructions for which only natural materials such as stone, wood and straw have been used.

From the reception, in the middle of which blooms a frangipani tree, a stairway leads to the swimming pool framed by bougainvillea, then to the sandy shore strewn with rocks, exuding a solitary and melancholic charm. The rather mysterious forested islet of Matlang in front of the resort is accessible at low tide.

Near the beach, a fantastic, vast private villa in wood, with its own garden, can be rented out. In duplex, it comprises an ultra-modern American-style kitchen and three bedrooms. The master bedroom has a spectacular view onto the sea. The interior design is an interesting combination of teak, pebbles and black stone. The strikingly original furniture was conceived by Doris, such as canopy beds with twisted tree trunks, sofas in driftwood, and hanging wardrobes inlaid with coconut flowers.

There are several varieties of individual wooden thatch-roofed bungalows spread out in the coconut grove. For the view, the most pleasant ones are The Deluxe Family bungalows on the shoreline, very luminous thanks to the large bay windows. Each of their two rooms has its own private entrance onto a spacious terrace and share a large black and white bathroom. Inside, the canopy beds of tortuous tree trunks are the preponderant elements of the décor. The dais of colorful material that covers them brings a touch of brightness in the paneled rooms with high ceilings in plaited plant material. The Superior Family bungalows, slightly less vast, look onto the profuse garden. The Deluxe bungalows are very attractive, extended by a pretty terrace in russet red teak boards, well equipped, and with a large bathroom brightened by a stained glass roof. The Standard bungalows, aligned along an alley concealed in the vegetation, are smaller and more simple, but not less appealing. Eventually, they will be renovated and upgraded to the Deluxe category and the result should be promising, with mural frescos.

Next to the reception, an airy restaurant overhangs the beach, whereas another one, more intimate and cozy, is situated on the seashore.

CORAL BAY RESORT

9 Moo 2, Tambon Bophut, Chaweng Beach, Koh Samui, Surat Thani, 84320
Tel 66 (0) 77 422-224
Fax 66 (0) 77 422-392
E-mail info@coralbay.net
coralbay@samart.co.th
Web www.coralbay.net
Contact Doris Chiatanasen or Oradee Pornwiwadh, General Managers

1. By air and land (1 ½ hour)
Plane 1 hour and 10 minutes flight on Bangkok Airways (10 daily flights) from Bangkok to Koh Samui. *Car* 5 minutes from airport to the hotel
2. By air, sea and land via Surat Thani (5 hours)
Plane 1 hour and 15 minutes flight on Thai Airways from Bangkok to Surat Thani (2 daily flights). *Car* 1 hour from airport to Donsak pier. *Boat* 2 hours on Seatran Express in Donsak (most recommended) to Nathon pier or on Raga ferry. You may have to wait for a while. *Car* 45 minutes from Nathon to the resort.
Note: Transfer from airport or Nathon can be arranged by the resort. Transport from Bangkok to Surat Thani by bus or train is possible but more time-consuming.

54 Units
18 Standard bungalows • 22 Deluxe bungalows • 7 Superior Family bungalows • 6 Deluxe family bungalows with 2 bedrooms • 1 Private villa
All bungalows have private terrace, private bathroom (hot water, shower), air-conditioning, minibar, and safety box. Baan Chomjan Villa has terrace and balcony, living room, fully-equipped kitchen, dining area, 3 bedrooms, 2 convertible beds in TV room, 3 bathrooms, toilet, den area with projection TV, air-conditioning.

Food and Beverage Outlets
2 Restaurants and 1 bar
Cuisine Offered: Thai • Continental
Quality: Good
Other services: Internet • Babysitting • Tour desk activities

Water sports and Activities
Swimming pool • Beach (no swimming at low tide from June to September) • Snorkeling (in front in Matlang island) • Kayaking • Water sports activities (in nearby Chaweng beach)
Other sports and Activities
Spa • Gym • Video theater

 Per room per night

White House

Hotel The White House

The reception area at Hotel The White House evokes the splendor of a small Thai Palace. Several halls and a library are located around an attractive central open-air patio, embellished with plants, large jars, Thai umbrellas, and a papyrus-filled pond. They are stylishly decorated, furnished with antiques, precious sofas, lacquered screens and delicate silk paintings. On the second floor, a Thai restaurant opens onto the patio, with tables on a terrace and several cozy air-conditioned rooms.

Hotel The White House belongs to the same owner and shares the same manager as Princess Village. Despite the narrow site, it succeeds in maintaining an enticingly secluded atmosphere and the comfort and quality of the services are excellent.

The two-story buildings accommodating the rooms are aligned along a central alley, up to the beach. Numerous hedges and flowers have been planted and magnificent varnished jars and Thai umbrellas have been placed at the entrances to brighten up the area. As a result, you have a pleasant feeling of a verdant profusion out of which point the slender silhouettes of the rooftops.

The two more prestigious Superior rooms on the ground floor of each building have more character, but are less luminous than the two Deluxe rooms on the second floor that are the best choice. The vast, bright, pastel painted rooms with an entrance hall are equipped with contemporary Thai furniture and decorated with watercolors representing butterflies, birds, and plants. The Junior suites, near the beach, are of similar size and décor.

Near the entrance, two distinctive traditional Thai suites are situated in an Ayutthaya-styled house on high stilts. Quite private, they are composed of a hall, a room and a luxurious bathroom combining pink sandstone and wood. Rooms are furnished with antiques, canopy beds and precious chests, while iridescent silks float at the windows. The pretty terraces have view onto the roofs of Hotel The White House and the vegetation.

Other accommodation option: If more privacy and seclusion is desired, Hotel The White House rents two private villas named **Ban Kaew Ruean Kwan**, in the village of Bohput, one kilometer from the beach. Perched on stilts in the Ayutthaya style, the villas have been built in an enclosed garden. Elegantly refined interiors reveal superb wooden floorings, beautiful ancient furniture, silk cushions and tapestries. Hot water, air-conditioning, telephone, television, stereo, safety box, supervised parking, a daily cleaning service and a swimming pool ensure that every comfort is catered to.

Ban Kaew Ruean Kwan

HOTEL THE WHITE HOUSE

59/3 Moo 5, Chengmon Beach, Koh Samui 84320
Tel   66 (0) 77 245-315
Fax   66 (0) 77 245-318
E-mail
wh@samuidreamholiday.com
Web
www.samuidreamholiday.com
Contact Thomas Andereggen, General Manager
For reservation
P.O. Box 25, Koh Samui
Tel   66 (0) 77 245-315 to 17
Fax   66 (0) 77 245-318
E-mail   *htwhite@loxinfo.co.th*

1. By air and land (1 ½ hour)
Plane 1 hour and 10 minutes flight on Bangkok Airways (10 daily flights) from Bangkok to Koh Samui.   *Car* 10 minutes from airport to the hotel.
2. By air, sea and land via Surat Thani (5 hours)
Plane 1 hour and 15 minutes flight on Thai Airways from Bangkok to Surat Thani (2 daily flights).   *Car* 1 hour from airport to Donsak pier *Boat* 2 hours on Seatran Express in Donsak (most recommended) to Nathon pier or on Raga ferry. You may have to wait for a while.   *Car* 40 minutes from Nathon to the resort.

Note: *Transfer from airport can be arranged by the resort. Transport from Bangkok to Surat Thani by bus or train is possible but more time-consuming.*

42 Units
16 Superior rooms (ground floor) • 16 Deluxe rooms (upper floor) • 8 Junior suites (ground floor) • 2 Thai suites Ruean Chomdao and Ruean Chomduean (upper floor) with private patio, saloon, 1 bedroom.
All rooms have private bathroom (hot water, shower, hairdryer only in Deluxe rooms and suites), air-conditioning, IDD telephone, cable TV, minibar, coffee/tea maker, safety box.

Food and Beverage Outlets
2 Restaurants
Ruean Sai Lom Terrace • Four Seasons • 1 pool bar
Cuisine Offered: Thai • International
Quality: Good

Other services: Boutique • Babysitting (on request) • Tour counter and car rental

Water sports and Activities
Swimming pool with Jacuzzi • Beach (no swimming at low tide from June to September)
Other sports and Activities
Spa

   Per room per night

Zazen Bungalows
Boutique Hotel

The innovative Zazen Bungalows Boutique Hotel, with its congenial and hospitable atmosphere, is a good value for money. The young, dynamic owners, Alex, of Belgian origin and Ti, his Thai companion, have put all their hearts in designing the architecture and interior décor of their resort, successfully bringing out the best from a relatively small piece of land, situated between a *klong* fringed by mangroves and the sea.

They have happily combined their favorite Mediterranean, Thai and Balinese styles and, somewhat uncharacteristically for Koh Samui, used warm bright colors such as superb ochre-yellows and sponge-painted oranges that evoke antique frescos.

Bungalows in a rather disparate style border the track leading to the resort, but once you cross the threshold of Zazen, an impression of joyful harmony pervades the setting. The interior design of the rooms is elaborate, in various shades of warm tones—a blend of terracotta and wood for the floors, plant fibers for the ceilings and orange walls. Numerous details convey a personal touch in each room: alcoves decorated with beautiful objects, exquisite statues of Buddha, pretty paper parasols, vividly colored tapestries and striking traditional wooden furniture. Sprawling large white beds lie on stone or wooden platforms. Some bungalows have attractive exterior bathrooms in Balinese style.

The sea-facing bungalows are the most appealing, brightened by bay windows opening onto the terraces with colonial furniture. The bungalows with a view of the mangroves are also pleasantly tranquil.

The restaurant, along the beach, has a warm Mediterranean appearance with its terrace sheltered from the sun by a pergola, its red terracotta floor tiles, and wrought-iron furniture. The excellent Thai and Mediterranean cuisine served here even attracts clients from outside the hotel. A bar with an outdoor billiard table is nearby. The swimming pool shaded by coconut trees and frangipanis is small but attractive with amusing Thai parasols and deck chairs in modern design.

The Bophut beach is certainly not Koh Samui's best but it is peaceful and the fishermen's dwellings along the banks retain that feeling of days gone by.

Surfboards and kayaks are at your disposal to reach the tiny islet of Koh Som just in front of Zazen. Alex knows the region well and will give you all the tips and advice you may need for the organization of your excursions.

ZAZEN BUNGALOWS BOUTIQUE HOTEL

Samui Ring Road, Bophut
177 Moo 1, Tambon Mae Nam,
Koh Samui, Surat Thani 84320
Tel 66 (0) 77 425-085
Mobile 66 (0) 1 891-6035
9 866-8931
Fax 66 (0) 77 425-177
E-mail *info@samuizazen.com*
Web *www.samuizazen.com*
Contact Ti and Alex

1. By air and land (1 ½ hour)
Plane 1 hour and 10 minutes flight on Bangkok Airways (10 daily flights) from Bangkok to Koh Samui. *Car* 10 minutes from airport to the hotel.
2. By air, sea and land via Surat Thani (5 hours) *Plane* 1 hour and 15 minutes flight on Thai Airways from Bangkok to Surat Thani (2 daily flights). *Car* 1 hour from airport to Donsak pier. *Boat* 2 hours on Seatran Express in Donsak (most recommended) to Nathon pier or on Raga ferry. You may have to wait for a while. *Car* 40 minutes from Nathon to the resort.

Note: Transfer from airport can be arranged by the resort. Transport from Bangkok to Surat Thani by bus or train is possible but more time-consuming.

16 Units
4 Beach Front rooms · 12 Garden View rooms
All rooms have private terrace, private bathroom (hot water, shower, hairdryer), air-conditioning, TV and DVD, minibar, coffee/tea maker, safety box.

Food and Beverage Outlets
1 Restaurant and 1 beach bar
Cuisine Offered: Thai · Seafood · International
Quality: Good food and friendly service

Other services: Internet · Babysitting · Tour counter

Water sports and Activities
Swimming pool · Beach · Windsurf · Kayaking (Koh Som island in front) · Water skiing (on request)

Other sports and Activities
Spa · Billiards · Table tennis · Football · Darts · Petanque

 Per room per night

The Tongsai Bay

I solated on a large forested hill sloping down to a private sandy creek, Tongsai Bay is the brainchild of Akorn Hootrakul. When it was constructed, it was the first luxury hotel in Koh Samui.

The management is now in the capable hands of his son and his daughter-in-law, a young dynamic couple, motivated by the same love for the resort and its environment.

In addition to the beauty of the natural surroundings, what contributes to the attractiveness of the site and causes it to retain its family atmosphere despite the large size of the resort, is the diversity and fantasy in the styles of the lodgings and the decoration. An interior renovation project is considered and it is hoped that it will retain this non-conformist aspect.

The architecture has a Mediterranean touch perceptible in the red-roofed white villas and the reception area. The latter evokes a Spanish hacienda with its cubic forms in white roughcast, its arcades, and wooden balustrades. The Thai restaurant that dominates the bay is contiguous, copious breakfasts with succulent croissants are served here.

The hotel is composed of villas and cottages that are scattered along the slopes of the hills on both sides of the beach, while rooms in a multi-storied building are situated directly on the beach. Given the distances, especially for those cottages lying high on the slopes, the service of the small electric cars that can be ordered directly from the room is greatly appreciated.

The "Grand Villas" on stilts are the preferred accommodations at Tongsai Bay. Large and comfortable, they are famous for their extravagant wooden terraces that succeed to fuse together the limits between the inside and the outside. Immense, they accommodate a shining white bathtub and a romantic canopy bed draped in immaculate muslin floating in the sea breeze.

Soaking in the bath to the twittering of the birds, gazing at the extraordinary sea view, is a deliciously unexpected treat. Meals can also be served on the terraces that have a dining area and a counter well equipped with cold drinks.

The "Beach Front" suites in a three-story building in the hollow of the bay, are well-situated vis-à-vis the swimming pool, the sea and the restaurants. Ground floor rooms are recommended for the elderly.

The cottages on the other slope include an array of diverse lodging. Poised on the rocks overhanging the sea lie the "Sea Front" cottages, and the romantic "Special Cottage" suites. Almost all cottages have a style, shape, view and furnishings that differentiate them from each other. They are smaller than the rather huge villas and very cozy. The cottages on the heights are quite private and have a wonderful view of the sea but access via a flight of steps may discourage some.

The beach is the focal point of the activities where the seawater swimming pool, two bars and a big restaurant are situated. The "Butler" restaurant in an intimate setting as well as a second swimming pool overhanging the sea are to the rear. Slightly above the beach is an enjoyable spa.

Although the grainy sand may be unfriendly to your feet, swimming in the clear blue waters of Tongsai Bay is always possible irrespective of the tide schedule.

THE TONGSAI BAY

84 Moo 5 Bophut, Koh Samui, Surat Thani 84320
Tel 66 (0) 77 24-5480
66 (0) 77 24-5544
Fax 66 (0) 77 42-5462
E-mail *info@tongsaibay.co.th*
Web *www.tongsaibay.co.th*
www.tongsaibay.com

1. By air and land (1 ½ hour)
Plane 1 hour and 10 minutes flight on Bangkok Airways (10 daily flights) from Bangkok to Koh Samui. *Car* 10 minutes from airport to the hotel.
2. By air, sea and land via Surat Thani (5 hours) *Plane* 1 hour and 15 minutes flight on Thai Airways from Bangkok to Surat Thani (2 daily flights). *Car* 1 hour from airport to Donsak pier *Boat* 2 hours on Seatran Express in Donsak (most recommended) to Nathon pier or on Raga ferry. You may have to wait for a while. *Car* 45 minutes from Nathon to the resort.
Note: Transfer from airport can be arranged by the resort. Transport from Bangkok to Surat Thani by bus or train is possible but more time-consuming.

83 Units
15 Tongsai Grand villas • 44 Cottage suites • 24 Beachfront suites (in a 3-story building)
All rooms have private terrace (with bathtub except in 5 cottages, which have bathtub in private garden), private bathroom (hot water, shower, hairdryer), air-conditioning, IDD telephone, cable TV, video player, minibar, safety box, coffee/tea maker. Grand Villas have gazebo on the terrace (where you can sleep with mosquito net).

Food and Beverage Outlets
Restaurants: Chef Chom's Thai • The Butler's • Floyd's Beach Bistro (on the beach—seafoods, stir-fries and noodles)
Cuisine Offered: Thai • European
Quality: Good
Bars: Floyd's Beach Bar • Lobby Bar • Sip (for coffee/tea/cakes)

Other services: Internet • Shop • Babysitting (ask in advance) • Tour desk and jeep rental • Taxi service • Room service

Water sports and Activities
2 Swimming pools • Kiddie pool • Jacuzzi • Beach • Water sports (catamaran, canoes, windsurf, sailing and snorkeling gear)
Other sports and Activities
Spa • Exercise room • Tennis court • Snooker • Video library

Per room per night

Santiburi Dusit Resort and Spa

Located in a beautiful eight-hectare park in a peaceful part of Koh Samui, the Santiburi Dusit Resort and Spa is one of the most luxurious hotels on the island along with the Le Royal Méridien Baan Taling. It stretches along the pretty Maenam white sandy beach shaded by numerous palm trees. Hammocks and deck chairs tempt to sweet torpor. It is probably here, or around the large swimming pool surrounded by traveler and red-trunk palm trees, that you will spend most of the day in *farniente*.

An atmosphere of luxury emanates from the place as soon as you arrive at the elegant reception with shining marble flooring, arcades, walls adorned with striking sculptures and sparkling silk-draped sofas. Soft traditional music plays to the accompaniment of the fountain's cascading waters, while a discreet hostess awaits to lead guests to their room in the park.

The rich flora of the park evokes a botanical garden. A river flows through and lotus-filled ponds are scattered here and there. Squirrels leap and bound in the alleys from the large surrounding trees.

With its two-tiered roofs, and sculpted stone pediments, Santiburi's architecture is inspired from Phra Nakhon, the summer palace of King Rama IV, in Phetchaburi.

The most pleasant lodgings are provided by the villas, which are identical in size and décor, varying only in location, either on the sea front or in the park. Well spaced from each other, and enclosed by low hedges, they give a sensation of privacy. Interior decoration resourcefully blends tradition with sober modernity. Notice the amusing basketry at the entrance where your morning newspaper will be placed, as well as the wooden and metal umbrella stand.

A feeling of elegant simplicity and cheerfulness emanates from the villas. Pale-colored rooms are bathed in light streaming through large bay windows screened by Japanese blinds in fabric. Originality is evident in the glass and wooden panels separating the hall from the bedroom, superb floral compositions, ledges under the windows embellished with beautiful objects, and the sculpture nestling in the alcove at the head of the bed. The sizeable adjoining bathrooms combine the warmth of the wood with the dramatic black color of the tiles, the round bathtub and the washbasins.

The other rooms are in a rather banal two-story building near the reception. Situated on the second floor, they have a view of the sea or the park. Designed as a duplex, with a large hall at the entrance and a small bedroom on the mezzanine level, they are pleasant and offer the same facilities as the villas, but are decorated in a much more classical manner.

There is no dearth of activities here and with nautical sports, tennis, squash, ping-pong, gym, an appealing spa at the far end of the park, Tibetan massages, and excursions, there is enough to fill the day at the end of which you may be tempted to take a romantic cruise on the hotel's magnificent sailboat, looking out for the setting sun.

SANTIBURI DUSIT RESORT AND SPA

12/12 Moo 1, Tambol Mae Nam,
Amphur Koh Samui,
Surat Thani 84330
Tel 66 (0) 7742-5031 to 8
Fax 66 (0) 7742-5040
E-mail santiburi@dusit.com
Web www.samui.dusit.com
Central reservation Bangkok
Tel 66 (0) 2 636-3333
Fax 66 (0) 2 636-3562
E-mail booking@dusit.com

1. By air and land (1 ½ hour)
Plane 1 hour and 10 minutes flight on Bangkok Airways (10 daily flights) from Bangkok to Koh Samui *Car* 20 minutes from airport to the hotel.
2. By air, sea and land via Surat Thani (5 hours)
Plane 1 hour and 15 minutes flight on Thai Airways from Bangkok to Surat Thani (2 daily flights) *Car* 1 hour from airport to Donsak pier *Boat* 2 hours on Seatran Express in Donsak (most recommended) to Nathon pier or on Raga ferry. You may have to wait for a while *Car* 40 minutes from Nathon to the resort.

Note: *Transfer from airport can be arranged by the resort. Transport from Bangkok to Surat Thani by bus or train is possible but more time-consuming.*

71 Units
57 villas • 12 Duplex rooms • 2 Deluxe Santiburi suites (2 bedrooms)
All rooms have private terrace, private bathroom (hot water, separate shower and bathtub, hairdryer, IDD telephone, satellite TV, video and CD player, minibar, tea/coffee maker, safety box.

Food and Beverage Outlets
Restaurants: Sala Thai (traditional dance or music) • Vimarnmek (garden, near-the-pool breakfast)
Cuisine Offered: Thai • Asian • Western • Seafood
Quality: Very good cuisine and service
3 Bars

Other services: Internet services • Shops • Babysitting • Doctor on call • Tour and travel service • Car rental • 24-hour room service • Wedding facilities

Water sports and Activities
Beach • Swimming pool • Kiddie pool • Water sports (windsurf, Catamaran, sailing) • Cruises (sunset cruise)

Other sports and Activities
Spa • Fitness center • Tennis • Table tennis • Squash • Golf putting practice • Tibetan massage • Beauty salon • Library

 Per room per night

Le Royal Méridien Baan Taling Ngam

Dramatically perched like an eagle's nest in splendid isolation on a promontory towering over an untamed coast, Le Méridien Baan Taling Ngam faces the Ang Thong Marine National Park discernible in the distance. Leaving behind the hustle of Chaweng and Lamai, you will discover a part of Koh Samui still unscathed by building constructions. The road, after having passed along the hills, climbs up to the summit of the escarpment where the reception is built. A spectacular view greets your arrival. The limestone islets of Ang Thong, the bluish cliffs of the Surat Thani coast, and the neighboring islets of Koh Tan and Koh Matsum stand out on the horizon. Below the reception, the vertiginous swimming pool, hanging over the aquamarine ocean is the emblematic image of the Le Méridien Baan Taling Ngam. Wherever you turn eyes, you will see only long deserted beaches fringed by palm trees and framed by wooded hills.

The hotel was designed in such a way that all rooms and villas benefit from this splendid view, nurturing an exhilarating feeling of space and freedom.

Open to the ocean, the soaring pavilion in traditional architecture housing the reception has the splendor of a small palace where numerous statues of Buddha and ancient bronze bells lie. A central lotus-filled pond demarcates the "Lom Talay" restaurant from the lounge, furnished with Thai sofas and pretty bamboo tables with voluted feet. An original arrangement of handcrafted tiles in assorted shades makes up the flooring. It is an ideal setting for evening drinks at sunset. The cuisine is excellent, be it at Lom Talay or Baan Chatra, a pretty private pavilion in traditional velvety décor where you can dine, sitting on cushions at a low table. The third terrace restaurant down below on the beach, near a second swimming pool, is very pleasant at lunchtime.

There is a choice of lodgings between the rooms in the buildings near the reception or the villas set in tiers along the hills down to the beach. The numerous steps and stairways leading to some are not suitable for the elderly, despite the fact that electric cars serve the different areas.

The very spacious Deluxe suite rooms have private terraces facing the sea. Interiors are elegant and warm with a penchant for beautiful yellow amber pale wood. Revolving doors open on to bathrooms in shining black stone with an original sunken green mosaic bathtub, a bas-relief, celadons and shells: you may feel as if you were in an underwater cavern.

The Villas are of a slightly extravagant size and luxury. The two-story ones on high stilts lie on the hill slopes. The immense salon with a high ceiling opens via large sliding doors onto the terrace that commands some breathtaking view on the ocean. Sober white walls enhance

the wooden floors and attractive colonial furniture. A staircase leads to the bedrooms situated below.

Equally sumptuous, the Beach Villas, framed by the foliage, face the ocean along the beach. They are composed of two private pavilions, one sheltering the salon, the other the rooms.

Should you be able to tear yourself away from these splendid surroundings, there is no shortage of activities and things to do. Notably, there is the possibility of a day excursion to discover the Ang Thong Marine National Park, aboard a speedboat where you have the privilege of being a select few. The 2.5-kilometer deserted beach of golden sand is superb, but swimming is not easy, due to the presence of rocks. Swimming however is possible beyond the diving center at the extreme left of the beach or on the nearby islets of Koh Tan and Koh Matsum.

LE ROYAL MÉRIDIEN BAAN TALING NGAM
295 Moo 3, Taling Ngam Beach, Koh Samui, Surat Thani 84140
Tel 66 (0) 77 429-100
Fax 66 (0) 423-220
E-mail talingng@samart.co.th
Web www.meridien-samui.com
Contact Samir Wildemann, General Manager

Booking Office in Bangkok
Tel 66 (0) 2 653-2201 to 07
Fax 66 (0) 2 653-2208 to 09
E-mail meridien@samart.co.th
lmresort@bkk.loxinfo.co.th
Web www.lemeridien.com

1. By air and land (2 hours)
Plane 1 hour and 10 minutes flight on Bangkok Airways (10 daily flights) from Bangkok to Koh Samui. *Car* 45 minutes from airport to the hotel.
2. By air, sea and land via Surat Thani (4 ½ hours)
Plane 1 hour and 15 minutes flight on Thai Airways from Bangkok to Surat Thani (2 daily flights). *Car* 1 hour from airport to Donsak pier *Boat* 2 hours on Seatran Express in Donsak (most recommended) to Nathon pier or on Raga ferry. You may have to wait for a while. *Car* 15 minutes from Nathon to the resort.
Note: *Transfer from airport can be arranged by the resort. Transport from Bangkok to Surat Thani by bus or train is possible but more time-consuming.*

72 Units
34 Deluxe rooms • 6 Deluxe Sala rooms • 2 Deluxe suites in main building • 22 villas and 7 Beach villas (veranda, living room, kitchen, 2 or 3 bedrooms, 2 or 3 bathrooms) • 1 Royal villa
All rooms have private balcony, private bathroom (hot water, separate shower and bathtub), air-conditioning, IDD telephone, satellite TV, DVD player, CD and stereo system, minibar, coffee/ tea maker, safety box.

Food and Beverage Outlets
Restaurants: Lom Talay (lobby) • The Promenade (near the beach) • Baan Chantra
Cuisine Offered: Thai • Western • Mediterranean • Seafood • Royal Thai
Quality: Excellent cuisine and service
Bars: Verandah bar • Pool bar
Other services: Internet • Boutiques • Babysitting (ask in advance) • Car rental • Library • Medical service (on call) • 24-hour room service • Shuttle bus to Nathon and Chaweng

Water sports and Activities
Beach • 2 main pools and 5 pools near villas • Jacuzzi • Dive center • Windsurf • Water skiing • Kayaking • Sailing • Excursions to neighboring islands (Koh Tan, Koh Matsum with snorkeling, Ang Thong and Koh Tao by speedboat)
Other sports and Activities
Sauna • Massage • Fitness center • Tennis • Beach volleyball • Golf driving range • Mountain biking • Thai cooking • Sightseeing excursions in jeep • Elephant trekking

Per room per night

Laem Set Inn

L aem Set Inn has as much character and personality as its owner,
David Parry, an Englishman who
settled in Koh Samui twenty years ago.
David's fertile imagination gave birth to
this haven imbued with culture and conceived with minimal effects on the surrounding environment—of which he is a
fierce defender. He has set his heart on
this spellbinding natural site full of
charm: the resort lies in a deserted sandy
creek, studded with polished rock formations with phantasmagoric shapes, at
the foot of a forested hill. The largest
part of the land, realm of the kingfishers,
sunbirds and flower peckers, has been
left wild. The lodgings, constructed
uniquely from natural materials, have an
original architecture full of fantasy that
blends well with the surroundings.

For those who yearn to return to
simple living, or those traveling on a
shoestring, the tiny thatch-roofed nipa
bungalows on the beach framed by beautiful trees are best. Despite their rustic
appearance, they offer the same elements
of comfort as the rest of the resort with the
exception of the air-conditioning.

The very attractive suites are ancient
wooden houses that were left in ruin and
abandon, that David scrupulously dismantled and brought in from the neighboring islands to reassemble facing the
ocean. Certain suites, like "Koh Tan" and
"Ma-ret," even have private swimming
pools and all benefit from a magnificent
view of the sea, notably from the large
terraces they possess.

"Koh Tan" and "Honeymoon" suites
are on the hill slopes. "Koh Tan" is
in rosewood and composed of two
pavilions. Its hall brings to mind Jim
Thompson's Bangkok house with its velvety atmosphere, dark woodwork and

Chinese furniture in lacquered wood. Specially designed for couples, the intimately romantic "Honeymoon" suites are airy and bright with ample exposure to the sea. They are gaily decorated in yellow lacquered furniture that contrasts with the dark wood. Ancient houses on slightly elevated positions with sea views, the "Studio" suites are similar to the "Honeymoon" suites.

On the ocean shores, the rooms of "Hua Thanon" have direct access to the beach via full-length sliding glazed doors. "Ma-ret," isolated in its own private creek, just a few meters above the beach, is a large two-story house with a huge attic lounge under its glazed roof, perfect for children.

The standard rooms, in pretty wooden constructions situated near the beach or around a pond, though more conventional, are very comfortable. Some are two-story, others on two levels linked by a few steps, and they differ slightly from each other in the furniture or décor.

There is no shortage of things to do at Laem Set Inn. Walk along the sandy coastal beaches and explore the property. Find your way to the bar at dusk and enjoy the sunsets. As night falls, go right up to the observatory and admire the starry sky (or birds during the day), through the telescope or just laze around and pore over the numerous books on fauna and flora at your disposal in the library.

The beach is of fine white sand but the dead coral in the shallow waters make swimming at low tide from April to October difficult. Water bicycles are used to go down the canal where you can anchor onto a platform, beyond the reef. For the rest of the year, there is generally enough water to bathe at all times. Children are particularly welcome and many games, fittings and amenities have been created especially for them. A picnic excursion to one of the neighboring isles visible from the coast is possible on one of David's boats. He can also organize any other excursion you desire and possesses a wealth of knowledge and good recommendations. His website is particularly detailed.

 LAEM SET INN
110 Moo 2, Hua Thanon,
Koh Samui, Surat Thani, 84310
Tel 66 (0) 77 424-393
233-299
233-300
Fax 66 (0) 77 424-394
233-301
E-mail inn@laemset.com
Web www.laemset.com
Contact David Parry

 1. By air and land (2 hours)
Plane 1 hour and 10 minutes flight on Bangkok Airways (10 daily flights) from Bangkok to Koh Samui. *Car* 40 minutes from airport to the hotel.
2. By air, sea and land via Surat Thani (5 hours)
Plane 1 hour and 15 minutes flight on Thai Airways from Bangkok to Surat Thani (2 daily flights). *Car* 1 hour from airport to Donsak pier. *Boat* 2 hours on Seatran Express in Donsak (most recommended) to Nathon pier or Raga ferry. You may have to wait for a while.
Car 30 minutes from Nathon to the resort.
Note: *Transfer from airport can be arranged by the resort. Transport from Bangkok to Surat Thani by bus or train is possible but more time-consuming.*

 30 Units
6 Bungalows (with fan) • 16 Standard rooms (1 bed and bunk beds) • Koh Tan suite (with pool, living room, kitchen, 2 bedrooms and attic) • Honeymoon suite (with living room, 1 bedroom, bathtub) • 4 Studio suites (with living room, 2 bedrooms) • Hua Thanon suite (with lounge, 3 bedrooms) • Ma-ret suite (with pool • 2 bedrooms, attic)
All rooms have private balcony or terrace, private bathroom (hot water, shower, hairdryer), air-conditioning (except in bungalows), IDD telephone, minibar, coffee/tea maker, safety box.

 Food and Beverage Outlets
Restaurant: 1, barbecue dining facility
Cuisine Offered: Thai and Western
Quality: Familial food and friendly service
Bar: Sunset bar

Other services: Internet (free of charge) • Laptop computer connections in rooms • Shop • Babysitting • Facilities for nannies • Laem Set car rental • For excursions or diving ask reception

 Water sports and Activities
Swimming pool • Kiddie pool • Beach (no swimming at low tide from April to October but there is an offshore raft) • Snorkeling (100 meters offshore) • Glass-bottom pedal boats • Kayaking • Sailing dinghy

Other sports and Activities
Small spa • Playgrounds for children • Children center (December to May) • Celestial observatory • Mountain bikes • Birdwatching • Cookery courses (request in advance)

 Per room per night

Koh Phang Nga
and Koh Tao

Koh Phang Nga

To the north of Koh Samui, accessible in half an hour by fast ferry, the island is still very natural and wild. It is absolutely sumptuous, with hills swathed in jungle, the coastline interspersed by fantastic weathered rock formations and deserted sandy beaches.

An uneven landscape together with the absence of a proper road infrastructure and airport have preserved it from the onslaught of mass tourism. The ferry arrives at Tong Sala where a few shops and travel agencies are located.

The island only comprises small modest resorts concentrated on the Hat Rin Beach on the southwest part of the island that it is advisable to avoid. Here, once a month, the "Full Moon Party" attracts hundreds of youth, tourists and Thais alike, for a night of frenzied music.

The **Panviman,** in a fabulous location, is the only really comfortable hotel on the island. Situated on a promontory to the northeast, it lies between the beautiful beaches of Tong Nai Pan and Ton Pan Noi.

The way to Panviman, across the island by *songtao,* on a bad track, allows you to discover the steep inner island covered in some parts with dense jungle. From Panviman, the most enjoyable excursion is to skirt the coastland and its astonishing granite chaos in a long-tailed boat, halting at will to swim in a lonely creek.

Koh Phang Nga island coast

Koh Tao

Koh Tao is a small undulating and forested island of 21 square kilometers, lost in the middle of the sea, 50 kilometers away from Koh Phang Nga and 75 kilometers from Chumpon on the mainland. Access to it can therefore be difficult in inclement weather.

The village of Ban Mae Hat bustles with verve and vivacity on the arrival of the ferry and then slips slides back into gentle reverie. It is true that at Koh Tao, life is easygoing and unhurried with a total disregard

Tong Nai Pan Beach, Koh Phang Nga

for time and the rest of the world. Only one road suitable for vehicles that discontinues serves a few houses, and then, after a very short while, ends abruptly.

Koh Tao, with its considerable diversity of coral and other marine fauna, is a diver's paradise. Nang Yuan, Red Rock, Sail Rock between Koh Tao and Koh Phang Nga, South West Pinnacle, Chumpon Pinnacle and Green Rock are among the most reputed spots. Divers even come from Koh Samui for the day even though there are several good diving spots on site.

The very recent **Koh Tao Coral Grand Resort** is well equipped for diving and the most comfortable of the island's resorts with the added luxury of a small swimming pool. This is most appreciable as the beaches of Koh Tao are, in general, not favorable for swimming, especially at low tide, the seabed being quite shallow and rocky. The three islets of Nang Yuan are linked at low tide by strips of golden sand disposed in the form of a starfish. They conceal fascinating marine depths that can be discovered by deep-sea diving or snorkeling. The isles are home to the Nang Yuan resort, equipped with a diving center.

It is pleasurable to go round the island by boat, as the coast also comprises enthralling polished weather-beaten rock formations and sandy deserted creeks.

Koh Tao Coral Grand Resort

J ust newly open, Koh Tao Coral Grand Resort is the most comfortable of the hotels in Koh Tao island, with the best scuba diving facilities. Run by a Danish manager, the diving center employs five instructors, three master divers and possesses three reliable fast diving boats.

The hotel is situated at the tranquil extremity of Sairee beach, the longest in Koh Tao. The beach bends in a gentle curve of almost-white fine sand, right up to a small rocky promontory. The rocks in front of the coral reef, unfortunately, render the beautifully azure ocean inappropriate for swimming at low tide. The island's only little swimming pool has resourcefully been constructed to compensate for this inconvenience.

Octagonal, the ochre-painted wood bungalows are topped with a two-tiered roof, whose aspect imitates tiles. In such a captivating setting, it is unfortunate that they have been constructed at such close proximity to each other. However, their alignment in stagger rows allows for relative privacy on the minute balcony equipped with a table and chairs.

The most attractive bungalows, "Deluxe Pirate" and "Captain" suites have views of the swimming pool or the sea.

The bungalows are relatively small and simple, but warm and bright, with their interiors painted in light pastel colors, their bamboo-plaited ceilings and wooden floor, and with a good lighting for reading in the evening. There is a rather large bathroom a few steps below.

There are rooms for divers, less expensive than the bungalows, in a building near the reception. The small seafront thatch-roofed bar is the most alluring spot, where red wooden tables are arranged under the trees and deck chairs are set out on the shore. Plans for a future dining area here are underway as meals are currently served in a large rather impersonal room situated in a building near the entrance.

During our visit, the resort had only recently opened and the island had experienced a period of drought. Consequently the garden had not yet been created and only the surviving coconut trees remained. Welcoming helpful staff is on hand at the reception and will be glad to help you hire a taxi and boat or organize the excursions if you wish.

Note: Koh Tao Palace, just next door at the end of the beach, is a pleasing resort with its vast white circular villas built in terraced rows, on a green hill. The original interiors consist of alcoves and curved whitewashed walls delimitate the spaces —entrance, bedroom, and bathroom. The villa has several bay windows opening onto a circular terrace. However, the resort does not have many facilities and even lacks a restaurant. Rooms are equipped with fans, private bathrooms with cold water, a minibar and a safe.

Tel: 66 (0) 77 456-504 to 05
Bangkok office : 66 (0) 2 621-7890

KOH TAO CORAL GRAND RESORT

Sairee Beach, Koh Tao
Tel 66 (0) 77 456-431 to 34
Fax 66 (0) 77 456-430
E-mail info@kohtaocoral.com
Web www.kohtaocoral.com
www.coralgranddivers.com

Bangkok Sales office
133/137 Kaoosan Road, Kwang Taladyod, Phranalorn, Bangkok 11200
Tel 66 (0) 2 629-2916
Fax 66 (0) 2 629-2747

By air, land and sea
1. By air, land and sea (about 4 hours) **Plane** 1 hour and 10 minutes flight on Bangkok Airways (10 daily flights) from Bangkok to Koh Samui. **Car** 20 minutes from airport to the ferry. **Ferry** 2 hours on Lomprayah high speed catamaran (the most reliable and comfortable) to Koh Tao. **Car** 10 minutes to the resort.
2. By air, land and sea via Chumpon (about 5 hours) **Plane** 1 hour and 10 minutes on Air Andaman (4 weekly flights). **Car** 30 minutes to Pak Nam Chumpon pier (Ta Yang) **Ferry** 2 and ½ hours to Koh Tao. **Car** 10 minutes to the resort.

Note: Transfer from airport can be arranged by the resort.

As the Air Andaman flight doesn't catch the ferry, you have to spend the night in Chumpon. Bad weather conditions occasionally alter ferry schedules. There are others options by train or bus from Bangkok to Chumpon (about 8 hours).

60 Units
12 Sailor cottages (with private balcony, fan, private bathroom— shower, cold water) • 26 Superior Sailor cottages • 4 Deluxe Pirate cottages • 3 Captain suites
All rooms have small private balcony, private bathroom (shower, hot water), air-conditioning, satellite TV, telephone, minibar, tea and coffee maker. Captain suites have living room, 2 bedrooms, 2 bathrooms (with bathtub).
15 rooms with fan and cold water in a new building.

Food and Beverage Outlets
1 Restaurant and 1 beach bar
Cuisine Offered: Thai • International
Quality: Average

Other services: Babysitting (on request) • Tour desk • Motorbike and boat rental

Water sports and Activities
Swimming pool • Beach (no swimming at low tide) • Snorkeling (in other places) • Dive center • Kayaking • Fishing • Mountain biking • Hiking

Per room per night

Koh Nang Yuan Dive Resort

Three paradisiacal islets rest in the middle of turquoise and emerald waters harboring a beautiful coral reef, not far from the wild coast. You have a breathtaking view of this spectacular site from the lookout on top of one of the islets. At low tide, the sea lays bare strips of golden powdery sand in the form of a three-pointed starfish that link the islets. At high tide, depending on the water level, it is possible to go from one islet to the other by kayak or by using the rope that serves as an access ramp. Going that way to the restaurant on the main islet for dinner at moonlight is a rather funny experience!

A coral reef encircles the islets and in the sheltered lagoon so formed in front of one of them, directly accessible from the beach, snorkeling is possible. Deep-sea diving is practiced near one of the other islets and the site, being quite renowned, attracts numerous boats during the day, which may, in the long run,

damage the coral reef, and jeopardize your tranquility. You have free rein of the islets only in the evenings.

The flat and rocky central islet is composed of granite polished boulders, weather-beaten into phantasmagoric shapes, whereas the other two are wooded hills interspersed by rounded rocks.

The bungalows are distributed on the three islets with those high up on the slopes accessible by rather steep stairs. Built from wood and on stilts, frequently with corrugated roofs, they were designed without any real architectural concept, the lure at Koh Nang Yuan Dive Resort being the location and the nearby marine depths rather than the architectural feats.

The more enjoyable bungalows are those situated on the islet where a viewpoint has been laid out. Here they are generally equipped with air-conditioning. The standard air-conditioned private bungalows on the edge of the shore, concealed in the vegetation, are a good choice (D9 to D14). The comfortable and spacious air-conditioned suites perched on the hill slopes have a magnificent view at low tide of the curved beach linking the islets. They have a certain character and they dispose of large terraces in wood.

The standard bungalows equipped only with ceiling fans are situated on the most sloping islet, in the middle of the low-lying vegetation and rocks, that overhang the lagoon. Those on the flat central islet are near the restaurant and a small jetty, with the presence of boats and divers during the day as well as a generator causing some disturbance.

The restaurant is in a large open-air bamboo pavilion extended by a surprising terrace looking onto granite chaos.

The islets have neither electricity nor water. A modest generator functions only at certain hours of the day and the water stored in large tanks should be used sparingly.

KOH NANG YUAN DIVE RESORT

46 Moo 1, Koh Tao
(Koh Nang Yuan), Surat Thani 84280
Tel/Fax 66 (0) 77 456-089 to 93
Fax 66 (0) 77 456-088
E-mail info@nangyuan.com

Booking Office in Samui
Tel/Fax 66 (0) 77 427-046

Booking Office in Bangkok
54/9 Moo 19 Plinklao-Nakhonchaisri Road, Taweewattana,
Bangkok 10170
Tel/Fax 66 (0) 2 885-9532
Mobile 66 (0) 1 870-7273
            (0) 9 140-3865
Web www.nangyuan.com

1. By air, land and sea (about 4 hours) *Plane* 1 hour and 10 minutes flight on Bangkok Airways (10 flights daily) from Bangkok to Koh Tao. *Car* 20 minutes from airport to the ferry. *Ferry* 2 hours on Lomprayah high speed catamaran (the most reliable and comfortable) to Koh Tao. *Boat* 20 minutes to Nang Yuan.
2. By air, land and sea via Chumpon (about 5 hours) *Plane* 1 hour and 10 minutes flight on Air Andaman (4 weekly flights). *Car* 30 minutes to Pak Nam Chumpon pier (Ta Yang) *Ferry* 2 ½ hours to Koh Tao. *Boat* 20 minutes to Nang Yuan.
Note: *Transfer from airport can be arranged by the resort. As the Air Andaman flight doesn't catch the ferry, you have to spend the night in Chumpon. Bad weather conditions occasionally alter ferry schedules. There are others options by train or bus from Bangkok to Chumpon (about 8 hours).*

55 Units
There are many types of bungalows: Standards bungalows (with fan or with air-conditioning) • Superior and Deluxe bungalows (air-conditioning, some with living room or another bedroom) • Family bungalows (air-conditioning, living room, 2 bedrooms, 1 with TV) • 4 Suites (air-conditioning, 1 with TV).
All rooms have private balcony, private bathroom (cold water), minibar.
Note: *No electricity, generator from 5 p.m. to 10 p.m.; water in big tanks available from 6 p.m. to 8 a.m.*

Food and Beverage Outlets
1 Restaurant and bar
Cuisine Offered: Thai • Western
Quality: Average

Other services: Safety box (front office)

Water sports and Activities
Beach • Snorkeling • Diving (in front) • Diving center with 2 dive masters and 2 dive instructors • Kayaking

Per room per night

Panviman Resort

After the rather hectic journey through the island, partially swathed by jungle, the arrival at the resort is a marvelous surprise. Situated on a peninsula, Panviman enjoys a panoramic view of the two paradisiacal bays of Thong Nai Pan Yai and Thong Nai Pan Noi, enclosed by wild, forested hills. Just down below stretches the long semi-circular golden-sanded beach, hemmed in at its extremities by round weathered rock formations.

In the midst of trees and pink bougainvillea bushes, pristine villas step down the hillside. Their white rough-cast walls, arches, red-tiled rooftops and small window-panes display typically Mediterranean features. Spaciously bright interiors have a large bay-window opening onto terraces facing the sea that you can discern through the foliage. The simple interior is clean and spotlessly white from walls to floor tiles,

and equipped with functional rattan furniture.

Three two-story buildings in a similar Mediterranean style situated near the reception shelter the rooms with bay or garden views. They are also very pleasant with balcony, well maintained, and of a size similar to those of the villas. Only rooms without air-conditioning offer a smaller living space. "Ocean View" rooms are the most appealing ones inside these buildings.

From the reception, stairways link the villas and descend gently to the nearby beach. The hotel is located at one end of the bay where rocks form a sort of private creek. Here, deck chairs invite you to enjoy this quiet and secluded bay. The beach is practically deserted, with the exception of a few bamboo bungalows concealed in the foliage. Nearby is a small terrace restaurant. A wooden footbridge leading from the hotel garden a bit higher up, allows access to the second bay on the right where several little modest resorts are located.

The Panviman restaurant, in a lofty vast circular pavilion perched on the peak of a promontory separating the two bays, is spectacular. The ideal tables for dining are those near the openings, seemingly suspended above the waves lit by a starry sky. A particularly unforgettable vision is for those fortunate enough to be there at the precise moment when the moon's subdued golden sphere is rising above the bay.

Panviman does not organize any activities. It only assists guests with ferry tickets reservation or hiring of a jeep. It is nevertheless easy to rent a long-tail boat at the small fisherman's kiosk situated in the middle of the beach and go off to discover the superb rocky coast.

Panviman is undoubtedly the most comfortable and ideally situated resort on the island but for those prepared for a little adventure, "**The Sanctuary**," a New Age hotel, must be also mentioned. It offers accommodation for all budgets, from dormitories to beautiful private houses built on stilts, exposed to the surrounding nature (cold water, electricity from 6 p.m. to 11 p.m.). The hotel is known for its small spa, meditation, yoga and an herbal treatment center. Its restaurant serves vegetarian food and delicious fruit juices.

The Sanctuary, Had Tien Beach, P.O. Box 3, Koh Phang Nga, 84280 E-mail: *sanctuary@kohphangan.com*; *www.kohphangan.com/sanct_spa.*

PANVIMAN RESORT

P.O. Box 28, Thong Nai Pan Beach, Koh Phang Nga, Surat Thani 84280
Tel/Fax 66 (0) 77 238-544
E-mail *booking@panviman.com*
panviman@kohphangan.com
Web
www.kohphangan.com/panviman

Booking Office in Bangkok
Gammaco Co., Ltd, 769/30 Prachachuen Road, Bangsue, Bangkok 10800
Tel 66 (0) 2 910-8660 to 04
ext. 107 to 109
66 (0) 1 336-2725
Fax 66 (0) 2 587-8493
910-7383
Web *www.panviman.com*
www.kohphangan.com/panviman.html

 1. By air, land and sea (about 3 hours)
Plane 1 hour and 10 minutes flight on Bangkok Airways (10 daily flights) from Bangkok to Koh Samui. ***Car*** 20 minutes from airport to Maenam beach. ***Ferry*** 30 minutes on Lomprayah high speed catamaran (the most reliable and comfortable) to Tong Sala. ***Car*** 45 minutes to the resort with Panviman resort taxi (about 20 kilometers).
2. By air, land and sea via Surat Thani (about 6 hours)
Plane 1 hour and 15 minutes flight on Thai Airways from Bangkok to Surat Thani (2 daily flights). ***Car*** 1 hour to Tha Thong pier (Songserm Travel) or Donsak pier (Raja Ferry). ***Ferry*** 2 ½ hours to Tong Sala. ***Car*** 45 minutes to the resort with Panviman resort taxi.
Note: *Transfer from Tong Sala pier can be arranged by the resort.*

 42 Units
14 Cottages • 28 Rooms in 3 two-story buildings
All rooms have private balcony, private bathroom (shower, hot water), air-conditioning (except in 14 rooms with fan only), minibar.

 Food and Beverage Outlets
2 Restaurants and 1 bar
Cuisine Offered: Thai • International
Quality: Good

Other services: Internet

Water sports and Activities
Beach • Boat trips around the island (ask the fishermen on the beach)
Others sports and Activities
Snooker • Library • Video room • Taxi rental (ask reception in advance)

 Per room per night

PLACES WITH A HEART

THAILAND

APPENDICES

TRANSPORTATION BY AIR

As of October 2003, five airlines have regular domestic flights: Thai Airways and Bangkok Airways which are the two major airlines and three smaller ones: Air Andaman, PBAir and Phuket Airlines.

In most cases, children (under 12 years) and infant (under 2 years) fares are 50% and 10% of the adult fare, respectively.

The airlines have their web sites where you can usually make a reservation on line or even, sometimes, purchase online an electronic ticket.

AIRLINE DIRECTORY

THAI AIRWAYS

Bangkok General Sales (main office)
Thai Larn Lauang Office,
6 Larn Lauang Road, Bangkok, 10100
Tel: 66 (0) 2 280-0100 to 110
Fax: 66 (0) 2 280-1748

Bangkok International Airport Office (Don Muang)
Information and Reservation Counter
3/F, Passenger Terminal 1 (Departure Floor)
Tel: 66 (0) 2 535-2846 to 47

Note: The airport is located 21 kilometers north of Bangkok Metropolitan Area.

Domestic Airport Office
Reservation Counter
2/F (Departure Floor; next to Terminal II, International Passenger Terminal)
Tel: 66 (0) 2 535-2081 to 82 (24 hours)
Reservations: 66 (0) 2 280-0060 • 628-2000
Web: www.thaiairways.com
E-mail: public.info@thaiairways.com

There are also Thai Airways offices on Yaowaraj Road, Vibhavadi Rangsit Road, Phayathai Road, Silom Road, Samsen Nai Post Office in Bangkok.

Chiang Mai International Airport Office
Tel: 66 (0) 53 277-782 • 277 640 • 277-515
General Sales Office
240 Prapokkloa Road, Amper Mueng,
Chiang Mai 50000
Tel: 66 (0) 53 210-042 • 211 541
Fax: 66 (0) 53 210-042
Reservations: 66 (0) 53 210-043 to 45 • 211-044 to 47
Ticketing: 66 (0) 53 210-041

Chiang Rai-General Sales
870 Phaholyothin Road, Chiang Rai 57000
Tel: 66 (0) 53 711-179 • 715-207
Fax: 66 (0) 53 713-663

Phuket International Airport
Tel: 66 (0) 76 327-144 • 327-246
General Sales Office
78/1 Ranong, Ranong Road, Amper Mueng, Phuket 83000
Tel: 66 (0) 76 211-195 • 212-499 • 212-946
Fax: 66 (0) 76 216-779

Note: Thai Airways runs a Royal Orchid Plus program allowing the members to earn qualifying miles when flying Thai and some partner airlines.

BANGKOK AIRWAYS

Bangkok Head Office
99 Moo 14 Vibhavadi Rangsit Road, Lardyao,
Chatuchak, Bangkok 10900
Tel: 66 (0) 2 265-5678
Fax: 66 (0) 2 265-5500

Bangkok International Airport Domestic Terminal
Vibhavadi Rangsit Road, Bangkok
Tel: 66 (0) 2 535-2497 to 98
Fax: 66 (0) 2 504-2762
Reservation: Tel: 66 (0) 2 265-5555
Fax: 66 (0) 2 265-5556

Chiang Mai
2/F Chiang Mai International Airport,
Chiang Mai 50000
Tel: 66 (0) 53 281-519
Fax: 66 (0) 53 281-520

Phuket
158/2-3 Yaowaraj Road, Phuket 83000
Tel: 66 (0) 76 225-033 to 35
Fax: 66 (0) 76 212-341
Web: www.bangkokair.com
E-mail: reservation@bangkokair.co.th
pg@bangkokair.co.th

Samui
Samui Chaweng Office
54/4 Moo 3m Tambon Bophut, Koh Samui,
Surat Thani 84320
Tel: 66 (0) 77 422-234/512 to 19
Fax: 66 (0) 77 422-235

Airport Office
99 Moo 4, Tambon Bophut, Koh Samui,
Surat Thani 84320
Tel: 66 (0) 77 245-601 to 08
Fax: 66 (0) 77 425-010

Sukhothai
Sukhothai Office
10 Moo 1, Jarodvithithong Road, Sukhothai 6400
Tel: 66 (0) 55 633-266 to 67
Fax: 66 (0) 55 610-908

Sukhothai Airport Office
Tel: 66 (0) 55 647-224
Fax: 66 (0) 55 647-222

Note: The Bangkok Airways departure lounge at Bangkok Airport has free internet access and complimentary snacks.

AIR ANDAMAN

Bangkok Office
3388/56 16/F, Sirinrat Building,
Rama 4 Road, Klongton Road

Bangkok Airport Office
Tel/Fax: 66 (0) 2 996-9119
Tel: 66 (0) 2 229-9555
Fax: 66 (0) 2 367-5060

Phuket Airport Office
Tel: 66 (0) 76 351-374 to 75
Fax: 66 (0) 76 351-373
Web: www.airandaman.com
E-mail: booking@airandaman.com

PBAir

Bangkok Head Office
591 UBC 2 Tower, Sukhumvit 33, Sukhumvit Road
Wattana, Bangkok 10110
Tel: 66 (0) 2 261-0220
Fax: 66 (0) 2 261-0227

Bangkok Airport Office
11/F, Domestic Terminal, Bangkok International Airport
Tel: 66 (0) 2 535-4843 to 44
Fax: 66 (0) 2 504-2959

Web: www.pbair.com
E-mail: sales@pbair.com

PHUKET AIRLINES CO., LTD.

Bangkok Head Office
1168/102 34th-B/F Lumpini Tower Bldg., Rama IV Rd.,
Thungmahamek, Sathorn, Bangkok 10120
Tel: 66 (0) 2 679-8999
Fax: 66 (0) 2 679-8235 to 36
Web: www.phuketairlines.com
E-mail: info@phuketairlines.com

FLIGHT DURATION / FREQUENCIES

DESTINATION	THAI AIRWAYS	BANGKOK AIRWAYS	AIR ANDAMAN	PBAIR	PHUKET AIRLINES
From Bangkok to (and return)					
Chiang Mai	1 h 10 min./11d	1 h 10 min./ 1d + 4w			
Chiang Rai	1 h 15 min./4d				
Chumpon	1 h 20 min./3w		1 h 10 min./4w		
Hua Hin		40 min./4w			
Krabi	1 h 20 min./3d	1 h 20 min./2d		1 h 25 min./2w	1 h 20 min./1d
Lampang	1 h 5 min./2d			1 h 5 min./2d	
Mae Hong Son (via Chiang Mai)	2 h 15 min./4d				
Mae Sot	1 h 15 min./5w		1 h 15 min./5w		
Phitsanulok	45 min./3d				
Nakon Ratchasima (Khorat)	50 min./6w		50 min./6w		
Phuket	1 h 20 min./12d	1 h 30 min./3d			1 h 20 min./5w
Ranong	1 h 10 min./1d				1 h 10 min./1d
Trang	1 h 30 min./ 1d + 3w				
Samui		1 h 10 min./ about 10d			
Sukhothai		50 min./1d			
Surat Thani	1 h 15 min./2d				
Trat		50 min./ 1d + 3w			
From Chiang Mai to (and return)					
Chiang Rai			40 min./2d		
Mae Hong Son	35 min./5d				
Phitsanulok			1 h/3w		
Sukhothai		35 min./1d			
From Hua Hin to (and return)					
Samui		1 h/4w			
From Pattaya to (and return)					
Samui		1 h/1d			
From Phuket to (and return)					
Samui		50 min./2d			
From Samui to (and return)					
Krabi		40 min./1d			
Pattaya		1 h/1d			
Phuket		50 min./2d			

h = hour(s) • min. = minute(s) • /d = daily flight • /w = weekly flight

TRANSPORTATION BY BUS

Intercity bus services—air-conditioned or non air-conditioned buses—offer a fast and cheap means of transport to all corners of Thailand. Roads in Thailand are usually in good condition.

Booking can be made through the following bus terminal:

Northern Bus Terminal	Kamphaeng Phet 2 Road, Mo Chit 2 Bus Terminal, Bangkok **Tel:** 66 (0) 2 936-3674 • 936-3667 to 68
Southern Bus Terminal	Boromratchchonnani Road, Bangkok **Tel:** 66 (0) 2 435-1190 • 435-1200 (air-conditioned bus) **Tel.** 66 (0) 2 434-5558 (non air-conditioned bus)
Eastern Bus Terminal	(Ekkamai station) Soi 40, Sukhumvit Road, Bangkok **Tel.** 66 (0) 2 392-9207 • 391-9829 (air-conditioned bus) **Tel.** 66 (0) 2 434-5558 (non air-conditioned bus)
Central Bus Terminal	Kamphaeng phet 2 Road, Bangkok **Tel:** 66 (0) 2 936-3674 • 936-3667 to 68

Note: There are also many private bus companies that you can book through travel agencies.

TRANSPORTATION BY TRAIN

State Railway of Thailand (Hua Lamphong)

	1 Rongmuang Road, Pathumwan District, Bangkok 10330 **Tel:** 66 (0) 2 223-3762 • 224-7788 **Fax:** 66 (0) 2 225-6068 • 226-3656
Web:	www.srt.or.th
E-mail:	info@srt.or.th

For e-mail reservations, contact this travel agency recommended by the TAT: contact@boonvanit.co.th You can check timetables via the web site of the State Railway of Thailand. It even gives a description of types of cars and rates.

Air-conditioned sleepers and/or berths are very comfortable. If you book in the air-conditioned first class night coach going to Chiang Mai, you will have a cabin for two persons only and meals served in your cabin, for half the price of the plane fare.

CAR RENTAL COMPANIES

There are many international and local rent-a-car companies. Chauffeur-driven cars are also available.

BUDGET CAR AND TRUCK RENTAL THAILAND

Bangkok:	19/23 Block A, Royal City Avenue, New Phetchaburi Road Bangkapi, Huay Kwang, Bangkok 10320 **Tel.:** 66 (0) 2 203-0250 **Direct line:** 66 (0) 2 203-9252 **Fax:** 66 (0) 2 203-0249
Web:	www.budget.co.th
E-mail:	rez@budget.co.th

Budget doesn't have an office at the arrival area of Bangkok International Airport but their station is located just opposite the airport terminal.

Upon arrival, look for Budget staff in blue uniform with the "Budget" sign in their hands. You can contact 66 (0) 2 556-5067 for any concerns.

Note: We found that Budget was pretty good value-for-money. It is also convenient as it has many offices (Chiang Mai, Chiang Rai, Hua Hin, Khao Lak, Khorat, Krabi, Pattaya, Phitsanulok, Samui). One-way rental programs are available. It has a 24-hour emergency roadside assistance.

AVIS RENT-A-CAR

Bangkok:	2/12–13, Wireless Road Bangkok
	Tel: 66 (0) 2 255-5300 to 04
	Fax: 66 (0) 2 254-6718 to 19
	Easy phone center: 66 (0) 2 255-5300 to 04
Bangkok International Airport:	Car rental counter, G/F, Meeting Hall
	Tel: 66 (0) 2 535-4052
	Fax: 66 (0) 2 535-4055
Web:	avisthailand.com
E-mail:	res@avisthailand.com

Avis also has offices in Hua Hin, Chiang Mai, Chiang Rai, Krabi, Mae Hong Son, Pattaya, Phitsanulok, Phuket and Samui.

TOURISM AUTHORITY OF THAILAND

Official web site of the Tourism Authority of Thailand: www.tat.or.th

HEAD OFFICE
1600 New Phetburi Road, Makkasan, Rajatevee, Bangkok 10310
Tel: 66 (0) 2 250-5500
Fax: 66 (0) 2 250-5511
E-mail: center@tat.or.th

TAT supplies information and data on tourist areas to the public. There are now 22 local offices throughout Thailand, such as:

TAT NORTHERN OFFICE: REGION 1 (CHIANG MAI, LAMPHUN, LAMPANG AND MAE HONG SON)
105/1 Chiang Mai-Lamphum Road
Amphoe Muang, Chiang Mai 50000
Tel: 66 (0) 53 248-604 • 248-607
Fax: 66 (0) 53 248-605
E-mail: tatchmai@tat.or.th

TAT NORTHERN OFFICE: REGION 2 (CHIANG RAI, PHAYAO, PHARE AND NAN)
448/16 Singhakhlai Road,
Amphoe Muang, Chiang Mai 57000
Tel: 66 (0) 53 717-433 • 744-674 to 75

Fax: 66 (0) 53 717-434
E-mail: tatchrai@tat.or.th

TAT NORTHERN OFFICE: REGION 3 (PHITSANULOK, PHETCHABUN, SUKHOTHAI AND UTTARADIT)
209/7-8 Surasi Trade Center, Boromtrailokkanat Road, Amphoe Muang, Phitsanulok 65000
Tel: 66 (0) 55 252-743
Fax: 66 (0) 55 252-742
E-mail: tatphlok@tat.or.th

TAT NORTHERN OFFICE: REGION 4 (TAK, PHICHIT AND KAMPHAENG PHET)
193 Taksin Road, Tambon Nong Luang, Amphoe Muang, Tak 63000
Tel: 66 (0) 55 514-341 to 43
Fax: 66 (0) 55 514-344
E-mail: tattak@tat.or.th

TAT CENTRAL REGION OFFICE: KANCHANABURI
Sangchuto Road Muang, Kanchanaburi 71000
Tel/Fax: 66 (0) 34 511-200 • 512-500
E-mail: atkan@tat.or.th

TAT CENTRAL REGION OFFICE: RAYONG
E-mail: tatryong@tat.or.th

TAT CENTRAL REGION OFFICE: TRAT
E-mail: tattrat@tat.or.th

TAT NORTHEASTERN OFFICE: NAKHON
RATCHASIMA
E-mail: tatsima@tat.or.th

TAT SOUTHERN OFFICE: PHUKET
73-75 Phuket Road, Muang District, Phuket 83000
Tel: 66 (0) 76 212-213 • 211-036 • 217-138

Fax: 66 (0) 76 213-582
Web: www.phukettourism.org
E-mail: tatphket@tat.or.th

TAT SOUTHERN OFFICE: SURAT THANI
E-mail: tatsurat@tat.or.th

TOURIST POLICE CENTER
4 Ratchadamnoen Nok Avenue, Bangkok
Toll-free: 1155 hotline service

*Tourist Police Center 24-hour assistance to tourists
with any complaint and emergency.*

TRAVEL AGENCIES

Note: To get a better rate, it is advisable to book through a travel agency or through the Internet.

There are many travel agencies, these are only a few suggestions:

DIETHELM TRAVEL THAILAND, LTD - KIAN
Gwan II Building, 140/1 Wireless Road,
Bangkok 10330
Tel: 66 (0) 2 255-9150 to 70
Fax: 66 (0) 2 256-0248 to 49
E-mail: dto@dto.co.th
Web: www.diethelm-travel.com

DTC TRAVEL COMPANY LTD.
22/1 Sukhumvit Road,
Soi 18, Klongtoey, Bangkok 1110
Tel: 66 (0) 2 259-4535 to 36
Fax: 66 (0) 2 260-0448 to 49
E-mail: info@dtctravel.com
Web: www.dtctravel.com

EXOTISSIMO TRAVEL CO, LTD
21/17 Soi 4 Sukhumvit Road,
Bangkok 10110
Tel: 66 2 253-5240 to 1
Fax: 66 2 254-7683
E-mail: exotvlth@linethai.co.th

EAST WEST SIAM LTD.
(ASIA VOYAGES, FRANCE
AND EAST WEST TRAVEL, THAI)
15/F, Regent House,
183 Rajdamri Road, Pathumwan, Bangkok 10330
Tel: 66 (0) 2 651-9768 to 9
Fax: 66 (0) 2 651-9766 to 7
E-mail: jantana@east-west-siam.com
Web: www.east-west-siam.com
www.asian-oasis.com

*They are specialists in tailor-made tours ("Mekhala
Cruise" on the Chao Phraya from Bangkok to Ayutthaya,
"June Bathra" in Phang Nga Bay...)*

SUNRISE TRAVEL
164 Surawong Road
(opposite Anglo Plaza),
Bangrak, Bangkok 10500
Tel: 66 (0) 2 235-6081 to 83
Fax: 66 (0) 2 237-0782 • 266-7578
E-mail: sales@sunrisetravel.co.th

TIPPANY SERVICE CO, LTD
187/1 Soi Thonglor 9,
Tel: 66 (0) 2 712-8590
Sukhumvit 55 Road, Klongton,
Klongtoey, Bangkok 10110
Fax: 66 (0) 2 712-8594
E-mail: tippany@a-net.net.th

THAI OVERLANDER TRAVEL
407 Sukhumvit Road
(between Soi 21-23), Bangkok 10110
Tel: 66 (0) 2 258-4778 to 80
258-9246 to 47 • 259-6555
Fax: 66 (0) 2 259-6558 • 260-4882
E-mail: todbul@a-net.net.th
Web: www.thaioverlander.com

This agency is particularly good for train tickets.

TICKET PLANNER
31 Sukhumvit Soi 4, Nanatai Klongtoey,
Bangkok 10110
Tel: 66 (0) 2 656-7087 to 88
Fax: 66 (0) 2 253-0087
E-mail: ticketpl@loxinfo.co.th

*Note: These are travel agencies having offices in
Bangkok.*

WEB SITES

For hotel listings, prices and booking with good discount, these web sites may be useful:

www.asiatravel.com
www.hotelthailand.com
www.thailandhotels.net
www.sawadee.com

PHOTO CREDITS

All photographs are by **Marcel Jouve** except for the following:

pp. 11, 158, 159, 160, 161, 321, 325, 327 – **Jean-Claude Moiriat**

p. 30 – **Courtesy of The Regent Bangkok**

pp. 36–41, 77–82, 84, 86, 129–133, 137, 142–145, 158–159, 163–166, 170, 175, 208 – **Anne-Marie Zicavo-Detay**

p. 54 – **Courtesy of Chiva-Som Luxury Health Spa**

pp. 88, 89 – **Michael Schulz**

p. 162 – **Courtesy of Thaton River View Resort**

pp. 168–169 – **Courtesy of Baan Boran Resort**

p. 184 – **Courtesy of Andaman White Beach**

p. 191 – **Courtesy of Mom Tri's Boathouse**

pp. 198–199 – **Courtesy of Amanpuri**

pp. 200–201 – **Courtesy of The Chedi Phuket**

p. 202 – **Courtesy of Cape Panwa Hotel, Phuket**

p. 204 – **Courtesy of The Panwaburi**

p. 264 – **Courtesy of Pimalai Resort and Spa**

pp. 284–286 – **Courtesy of Tamarind Retreat**

p. 301 – **Courtesy of Zazen Bungalows Boutique Hotel**

pp. 302–303 – **Courtesy of The Tongsai Bay**

p. 304 – **Courtesy of Santiburi Dusit Resort and Spa**

pp. 306, 308 – **Courtesy of Le Royal Méridien Baan Taling Ngam**

ACKNOWLEDGMENTS

TRANSLATORS
Marina Demarquis
Catherine Mac Claren

CONTRIBUTOR
Leslie Walsh (Bantak House)

INDIVIDUALS
Nathalie Pham-Macshane
Neil Barnes
Nick James
Michèle Didron

PROJECT MANAGEMENT
Philippe Saurel

EDITOR
Marito N. Antolin

PROJECT COORDINATOR
Wyne G. Paras

MAPS
Paul F. Refuerzo
Mhanny V. Sula
Francis M. Funa
Erwin E. Pujante
Ariel P. de los Reyes

LAYOUT
Rowena L. Lim
Fatima C. Ramirez

MAPS

Nancy Chandler's Map of Bangkok and *Map of Chiang Mai*. "The Market Map and much More." Nancy Chandler, 2002. Nancy's colorful, hand-lettered maps are very useful to discover the two cities. She mentions the best restaurants, the hotels, shops and sightseeing. There are indexes accompanying the maps (*www.nancychandler.net*).

ARCHITECTURE AND GARDEN

The Thai House: History and Evolution. Ruethai Chaichongrak, Somchai Nil-Athi, Ornsiri Panin, Saowalak Posayananda, Michael Freeman. River Books/Asia Books, October 2002.

Thai Style. William Warren, Gretchen Liu, Luca Invernizzi Tettoni. Asia Books.

Heritage Homes of Thailand. William Warren and Ping Amranand. Monsoon.

Classic Thai: Design Interiors Architecture. Chami Jotisalikorn, Luca Invernizzi Tettoni, Phuthorn Bhumidon, Virginia McKeen Di Crocco. Asia Books. Original publisher: Periplus.

Jim Thomson: The House on the Klong. William Warren, Jean-Michel Beurdeley, Luca Invernizzi Tettoni.

Lanna Style: Art and Design of Northern Thailand. Ping Amranand and William Warren. Amulet Production.

Lanna: Thailand's Northern Kingdom. Michael Freeman. River Books.

Thai Garden Style. William Warren and Luca Invernizzi Tettoni. Periplus.

DIVING

Lonely Planet Diving and Snorkeling Thailand. Mark Strickland, John Williams. Lonely Planet Pisces Book.

The Dive Sites of Thailand. Paul Lees. Asia Books, 1999.

TRAVEL GUIDES

Bangkok Guide. Australian-New Zealand Women's Group.

Insight Guide Bangkok. Clare Griffins and Clare Griffiths. Apa Publications.

Insight Guide Thailand. Scott Rutherford. Apa Publications.

Lonely Planet Thailand, 9th edition. Joe Cummings and Steven Martin. Lonely Planet Publications.

Thailand Blue Guide. John Villiers and Gavin Pattison. A & C Black.

Eyewitness Travel Guides Thailand. Philip Cornwel-Smith. Dorling Kindersley Publishing.

Guide Voir Thaïlande. Collectif. Hachette, 2001 (in French).

The Green Guide Thailand. Michelin.

A Guide to Khmer Temples in Thailand and Laos. Michael Freeman. River Books, 1998.

Exploring Chiang Mai. Oliver Hargreave. Odyssey Guides, 2003.

Guides Bleus Evasion. Christine Le Diraison. Hachette (in French).

Le Guide du Routard Thaïlande. Christine Le Diraison. Hachette (in French).

NATURE

The National Parks and Other Wild Places of Thailand. Stephen Elliott and Gerald Cubitt. New Holland Publishers. Asia Books.